RECASTING THE SOCIAL IN CITIZENSHIP

Edited by Engin F. Isin

Previous notions of what constitutes 'citizenship' within a country have been steadily challenged by processes of globalization. *Recasting the Social in Citizenship* shows how citizenship has increasingly been determined by social behaviours – the everyday habits of citizens and non-citizens – rather than by civic or political affiliations. Broadening the discussion to include everyday struggles as well as rights and privileges, this collection of essays looks at topics ranging from environmental and security issues to transnational migration and military life. The volume not only addresses debates over multiculturalism and integration, but also looks at the ways in which personal activities such as eating, commuting, smoking, and sex are governed by the state.

Tracing developments in political and social endeavours that have bound together citizens and non-citizens, the volume explores the social sites that have become objects of government, and considers how they in turn have become sites of contestation, resistance, differentiation, and identification. In doing so, it provides significant insights into the changing nature of citizenship and social governance. *Recasting the Social in Citizenship* is an original and thought-provoking work that will be of interest to sociologists, political scientists, and anyone concerned with immigration and citizenship.

ENGIN F. ISIN is a professor in the Department of Politics and International Studies and Director of the Centre for Citizenship, Identities, and Governance at the Open University.

EDITED BY
ENGIN F. ISIN

Recasting the Social in Citizenship

UNIVERSITY OF TORONTO PRESS
Toronto Buffalo London

Toronto Buffalo London
www.utorontopress.com

ISBN 978-0-8020-9757-6 (cloth)
ISBN 978-0-8020-9637-1 (paper)

Library and Archives Canada Cataloguing in Publication

Recasting the social in citizenship / edited by Engin F. Isin.

Includes bibliographical references.
ISBN 978-0-8020-9757-6 (bound). ISBN 978-0-8020-9637-1 (pbk.)

1. Citizenship – Social aspects. 2. Globalization – Social aspects. I. Isin, Engin Fahri, 1959–

JF801.R42 2008 323.6 C2008-903634-4

University of Toronto Press acknowledges the financial assistance to its publishing program of the Canada Council for the Arts and the Ontario Arts Council.

University of Toronto Press acknowledges the financial support for its publishing activities of the Government of Canada through the Book Publishing Industry Development Program (BPIDP).

Contents

Preface

This book arises from two Social Sciences and Humanities Research Council (SSHRC) projects that were undertaken between 2004 and 2006. In 2003 SSHRC carried out a national consultation on its future directions (SSHRC 2004a, 2004b, 2005). One of its findings was the need to facilitate greater, and more effective, collaboration – both among researchers, and between researchers and users of research, both within Canada and abroad. As a result, in 2004 SSHRC launched the first strategic research clusters design program. This program funded 'projects to identify key research areas, issues and topics that would benefit from improved networking and communications and to propose viable models for such networks, or strategic research clusters.'

I invited Janine Brodie, Danielle Juteau, and Daiva Stasiulis to work together on establishing a citizenship research program. We became interested in building a collaborative program with both a substantive and innovative focus. Although we had known each other as scholars, the project provided us an opportunity to work together and explore whether we could indeed establish a coherent research program while maintaining our different approaches in investigating citizenship. Each of us has been involved in the field of citizenship studies and published articles in the journal with the same name (see, e.g., Brodie 2004; Isin 1997; Juteau 2002; Stasiulis 2002).

We decided to focus on the question of the social in citizenship. We elaborate this concept in our introduction, but suffice it to say that we think it is a crucial moment in the history of citizenship, especially in Anglo-American democracies, to revisit social citizenship after the tumultuous years of neoliberalization (retrenchment from services, privatization of delivery, responsibilization of new agents, and realigning entitlements), on the one hand, and the politics of identity (the emergence of new subjects of rights, new scales of responsibilities, and the articulation of new demands), on the other. The assemblage of rights and responsibilities that constitute citizenship has been reconfigured in many ways by various struggles over resources, entitlements, regulations, and policies so much so that the very meaning of what it means to be a citizen of a democratic state (or even of a non-democratic state) is undergoing significant transformations. Our aim has been to develop a research program that could bring these important issues of citizenship within a common theoretical framework on *the social in citizenship*, which we proposed to recast.

The proposal was funded through two phases: for developing its original idea and for developing its initial stage. The first phase mostly involved establishing a research infrastructure for collaboration including conceptual development. We were able to initiate a dialogue not only among ourselves but with various other agencies, authorities, and organizations revolving around the concept 'recasting the social in citizenship.' We use *recast* rather than more familiar designations such as rethinking, reconsidering, or rediscovering because we wanted to maintain the emphasis that, although the project involved considerable conceptual development, its primary focus has been to develop an integrated research program with practical and political consequences. Indeed, much of our deliberation, especially in its first phase, was really focused on the question of establishing a collaborative research *infrastructure*. We have outlined some of our thoughts in our first report, available from SSHRC. The second phase was dedicated almost entirely to conceptual development following our own priorities as well as concerns that we have identified through the dialogue that we initiated. This book is a result of both of these two phases. We identified research priorities through which we could explore some core issues of the social in citizenship, especially in Canada, and articulated new domains of research. We invited four promising early career scholars in these domains to join us with their research programs. We held a national workshop and deliberated major theoretical and empirical issues. We identified two further domains and decided to expand the project by inviting another two early career scholars. This book comprises eleven chapters outlining these research domains that will need to be developed for recasting the social in citizenship.

Admittedly, developing an innovative research program with scholars whose careers involve different trajectories is a difficult task. Yet, throughout this project we have immensely *enjoyed* working together. It has been rewarding to create and learn simultaneously. I am grateful to Janine Brodie, Danielle Juteau, and Daiva Stasiulis for their enthusiasm and commitment to this effort in collaboration. Without their encouragement, openness, generosity, and dedication the project would never have proceeded. I am also grateful to Sirma Bilge, Xiaobei Chen, Deborah Cowen, Paul Kershaw, Alex Latta, and Kim Rygiel for their commitment and dedication and for their contribution to the very idea of a collective intellectual and political project. I am grateful to SSHRC for enabling us to have this experience. I acknowledge its financial support for the two projects as well as for the publication of this book. I would like to thank the three anonymous referees for their substantial contribution to the book with their detailed reviews of the entire manuscript as well as of each and every chapter. We all benefited from their insightful and incisive reviews. I hope that we were worthy of their critical interventions in how we responded to them. Virgil Duff was absolutely superb as an editor and I am grateful for his wise guidance and advice. Agnes Czajka and Ian Morrison served as research assistants with great skill and engagement; Ian also served as a masterful editorial assistant for the book. I hope that the book makes a case for a collaborative, interdisciplinary, and integrated approach to investigating, contesting, and politicizing citizenship.

Engin Isin
London, January 2008

Contributors

Sirma Bilge is Assistant Professor at the Department of Sociology of Université de Montréal and Director of Intersectionality Research Unit of the Centre d'études ethniques des universités montréalaises (CEETUM).

Janine Brodie is Professor and Canada Research Chair (Political Economy and Social Governance) at the Department of Political Science, University of Alberta.

Xiaobei Chen is Assistant Professor in the Department of Sociology and Anthropology at Carleton University.

Deborah Cowen is Assistant Professor in the Department of Geography and Program in Planning and Research Associate at the Cities Centre at the University of Toronto.

Engin F. Isin is Professor of Citizenship at Politics and International Studies (POLIS) and Director, Centre for Citizenship, Identities, Governance (CCIG), Faculty of Social Sciences, The Open University.

Danielle Juteau is Professor Emerita, Département de Sociologie, Faculté des arts et sciences, Université de Montréal.

Paul Kershaw is Assistant Professor at the College for Interdisciplinary Studies, University of British Columbia.

Alex Latta is Assistant Professor of Global Studies, at Wilfrid Laurier University.

Kim Rygiel is a Post-Doctoral Fellow at the Institute on Globalization and the Human Condition at McMaster University.

Daiva Stasiulis is Professor of Sociology at Carleton University.

RECASTING THE SOCIAL IN CITIZENSHIP

1 Recasting the Social in Citizenship

ENGIN ISIN, JANINE BRODIE, DANIELLE JUTEAU, AND DAIVA STASIULIS

What do we mean by 'recasting the social in citizenship'? Admittedly, the phrase at first appears rather unfamiliar, if not awkward. Is it about 'rethinking social citizenship'? This would mean revisiting social rights such as social welfare and unemployment insurance that have been quite dramatically curtailed in the closing decades of the twentieth century. Is it about 'rethinking the social'? This would mean entering into debates over the meaning and nature of the social and whether the discovery of the social in the nineteenth century has come to outlive its usefulness by the beginning of the twenty-first century (Latour 2005, Rose 1996b). This book addresses both these theoretical issues from a citizenship perspective. What we aim to accomplish by the phrase that gives the book its title is to bring distinct and seemingly unrelated aspects of debates over various forms citizenship such as social or environmental citizenship into a sharper and shared focus. Briefly, the most important debates that so far remain separated are (1) the traditional debates over social citizenship, including the bundle of rights and responsibilities that have been called into question in the past two decades under the umbrella terms 'retreat' or 'decline' of the welfare state (Kymlicka and Banting 2006); (2) the debates over multiculturalism, cohesion, integration, and diversity (Benhabib 2002, Cairns et al. 1999), and; (3) the debates over the nature of the social (Honneth 1996a, Joyce 2002, Rose 1996b, Schatzki 2002). Although Fraser and Honneth (2003a, 2003b, 2003c) debated the trade-offs between recognition and redistribution, as we shall see, framing social struggles under those terms imposes severe limits on our understanding and fails to bring these debates into sharper and common focus.

We coined the phrase 'recasting the social in citizenship' to indicate that fundamental issues of our time are refracted through struggles over citizenship rather than analytical categories of redistribution or recognition. This chapter outlines our approach to citizenship as an integrated social institution. We begin with a discussion of the debates over interpreting social struggles and movements for redistribution and recognition. We emphasize that the ostensible distinction between redistribution and recognition – whether in aims or methods of struggles that remain essentially social – is a false distinction. Then we discuss the nature of the social and its uses in citizenship debates. We emphasize that, although it is important to keep the notion of 'social citizenship' or 'social rights' distinct from civil and political rights, it is also important to maintain a broader and deeper conception of the social that is not reducible to postwar welfare state regimes of social citizenship. It is this broader and deeper conception of the social that we want to recast in deepening our understanding of how the rights and obligations of citizenship develop as social claims and demands.

The Struggles for Redistribution and for Recognition

This task requires the development of a conceptual framework that reconsiders two distinct although related meanings of the social in citizenship. These two meanings can be introduced by identifying two trends in the development of 'citizenship regimes' in various democratic states during the second half of the twentieth century. The first trend, which has been identified as *redistribution*, aimed at alleviating social inequalities inherent in postwar democratic societies by allocating a series of entitlements including unemployment insurance, welfare, social assistance, social housing, and universal health care that collectively came to constitute an understanding and practice of social citizenship as a bundle of *social rights* and as social security (Barbalet 1988). It was British sociologist T.H. Marshall (1950) who gave a definitive shape to these various rights as social rights by outlining an historical development scheme according to which the birth of civil rights in the eighteenth century was followed by the development of political rights in the nineteenth and social rights in the twentieth. Marshall made two essential points about the development of social rights: first, they were the result of working-class struggles to attain social security; second, their development ameliorated class conflict. Thus, struggles for redistribution and the subsequent attainment of social rights made the continuing survival of capitalism possible. While throughout the twentieth century the development of social citizenship as social rights gained through *struggles for redistribution* progressed with different paces in different jurisdictions, social citizenship came to define the essential identity of social democratic societies (Esping-Andersen 1990). Towards the end of the twentieth century, social citizenship understood as redistribution to alleviate social inequality came under considerable attack, and the bundle of rights that had developed previously began to shrink or change considerably (Brodie 2004). As the role of the welfare state in social life was questioned, social citizenship was increasingly defined away from redistribution and towards an approach that came to be identified as 'neoliberal' (Faulks 1998). As a result, emphasis shifted away from social rights and towards *social obligations*. Many Western democracies increasingly enacted neoliberalism as a demand to demonstrate entrepreneurship, sufficiency, autonomy, and individualism (Harvey 2005). Social security was no longer to be sought from or provided by the state but was to be the responsibility of the autonomous agent, the neoliberal subject (citizen or non-citizen) (Rose 1996a). Again, while the pace of change was neither uniform nor identical across various states, its direction has been relentless.

As social rights were reconsidered and the emphasis of social citizenship shifted from rights to obligations, another label increasingly came to define social struggles: *recognition* (Gutmann 1994). Beginning with civil rights and women's movements and rapidly extending to include environmental, gay and lesbian, disabled, peace, postcolonial, and indigenous peoples, as well as racialized groups and movements, various claims developed into *struggles for recognition*. What characterized these struggles was not only or primarily the demand for alleviation of social inequality as such (redistribution of income and wealth) but the demand for recognition of identity (universalism) and accommodation of difference (particularism) in various public and private spheres. With these struggles, hitherto marginalized claims concerning different kinds of citizenship and equality such as sexual citizenship, disability citizenship, multicultural citizenship, environmental citizenship, and indigenous citizenship were articulated with varying degrees of success (Isin and Turner 2002; Isin and Wood 1999).

As Danielle Juteau (1997, 2000) has argued, in the social sciences, dominant approaches have considered these two struggles (redistribution and recognition), which have defined democratic societies for more than five decades, at best as separate and at worst as mutually exclusive or antagonistic struggles. This has often resulted in articulating the question as either/or – redistribution or recognition (Fraser and Honneth 2003a, 2003b, 2003c). Moreover, there has been an unstated assumption of linear historical sequence. It is as if there were first struggles over redistribution and then struggles over recognition followed: the former representing struggles over the welfare state and the latter, cultural politics. As we shall argue, however, both assumptions – separation and sequence – are flawed. We are convinced that maintaining these assumptions in academic studies or practical domains has resulted in inextricable problems and dangerous trajectories. To consider, for example, the question of new immigrants as 'integration' or 'cohesion' – as if it were a question of adjusting already existing cultural identities to a new environment without considering the social processes responsible for the formation of such identities – produces new inequities and intractable problems, instead of successfully addressing existing ones (Stasiulis 2002a). Similarly, to assume that the question of indigenous inequalities could only be addressed by social or economic development policies, as if the development of indigenous cultures remains frozen in the past, has proven ineffectual, if not disastrous. In other words, *economism* (assuming that questions are merely of economic redistribution) and *culturalism* (assuming that questions are merely of cultural readjustment and accommodation) and the analogous separation of redistribution and recognition have resulted in *essentialist* (assuming that identities are fixed and immutable) and *idealist* (assuming that identities are compliant and floating) approaches and policies.

When people mobilize for legalizing same-sex marriage, rally for social housing, protest welfare rate cuts, debate employment insurance, advocate for the decriminalization of marijuana, wear attire such as turbans or headscarves in public spaces, seek affirmative action programs, or demand better health care access and services, they do not imagine themselves as struggling for the maintenance or expansion of social, cultural, or sexual citizenship rights. Instead, they invest in whatever issues seem most related and closest to their social lives, and dedicate their time and energy accordingly. There are two points to make about such struggles. First, they are irreducibly social struggles that arise from social existence. To classify such struggles either as redistribution (economism) or recognition (culturalism) misses their complexity. Second, although they may not clearly articulate this, it is important to acknowledge that when people engage with such issues, whatever differences may separate them in values, principles, and priorities, they are enacting citizenship, even if they are people who are not passport-carrying members of the state. What 'enacting citizenship' means is that individuals perform their fundamental right to have rights (see Arendt 1958) by asking questions concerning social justice. Thus, citizenship is much more than legal status, although formal legal citizenship remains important for accessing social citizenship rights. Citizenship involves the art of being with others, negotiating different situations and identities, and articulating ourselves as distinct yet similar to others in our everyday lives, and asking questions of justice. Through these social struggles, we develop a sense of our rights as others' obligations and others' rights as our obligations. We may interpret or understand our domains of engagement separately from each other in our social lives, but occasionally someone or something reminds us that we are performing citizenship. It is in this deep and broader sense of enactment that citizenship is social.

It is not only we as citizens who understand these issues as separate, if not disparate, in our thoughts and actions. The way in which knowledge about social life is produced, disseminated, and deployed in our societies maintains this separation. Typically, each of these issues falls within a specific discipline within the social sciences and humanities. Criminologists are called on to study the decriminalization of marijuana, and scholars of jurisprudence study the legalization of same-sex marriages. Few, if any, scholars will study these issues as part of the framework of social citizenship rights (e.g., decriminalization of marijuana as social care). Similarly, government ministries, departments, agencies, and organizations conduct their work through the sectoral separation of issues. Even if same-sex rights are among the most significant contemporary policy and political debates, Citizenship and Immigration Canada or the Ontario Ministry of Citizenship and Immigration do not explicitly enter into these debates, viewing them as outside their definition of citizenship policy jurisdiction. Yet, as its policy on civil marriages between same-sex persons illustrates, Citizenship and Immigration Canada does, indeed, become tacitly implicated in debates over sexual citizenship. Similarly, there is a preponderant tendency in public debates towards seeing only matters concerning immigrants and immigration as citizenship matters. Although as citizens we may be inclined to understand and enact these issues separately, for those responsible for addressing them, such isolation and separation inhibits a fuller, horizontal, and creative formulation of policy and enactment of politics for social justice.

In part because these barriers to effective understanding of social issues and formulation of policies are acknowledged, researchers, policy makers, and government agencies increasingly are recognizing the value, and indeed, the necessity of multisectoral and interdisciplinary research and network development. Contemporary policy problems cut across and transcend familiar conceptual and institutional boundaries, and invite different and competing interpretations of the issues and appropriate responses to them. This being said, the ways in which research objects are formed still follow disciplinary practices. Too often research objects are simply assumed to exist, and yet the manner in which they are established means that existing relations remain isolated from one another. Consequently, researchers, policy makers, activists, and publics who would benefit from engaging in dialogue and collaboration are simply brought together only to reinforce *misrecognition* of each other. If we cannot make decisive theoretical breakthroughs and conceptual innovations such collaborative efforts simply bring parallel universes together only to ensconce their separateness. Clearly, the formation of research objects, the production and dissemination of knowledge, and the formation of fields of government are related developments – and approaching social struggles with an already formed conception of whether they are about redistribution or recognition not only misses their complexity, as we have argued earlier, but also has regressive consequences for policy development and implementation.

The Social in Citizenship and Social Citizenship

We have suggested that we need to reconsider two distinct yet related meanings of the social in citizenship. The first involves different dimensions of the social in the formation of citizenship rights, obligations, and identities. The second involves specifically 'social citizenship,' which has been central in defining the post-Second World War identities of liberal states such as Australia, Canada, the United States, and the countries of Western Europe. We shall now elaborate these two distinct meanings.

We introduced these two meanings by discussing two dominant trends in the development of citizenship regimes in various democratic states during the second half of the twentieth century. The first trend aimed to reduce social inequality by redistributing wealth and instituted social rights such as unemployment and welfare benefits (Esping-Andersen 1990). In this way, social citizenship came to define the essence of liberal democracies (Roche 1992). As is well known, towards the end of the twentieth century, social citizenship as redistribution to alleviate social inequality came under considerable attack, and the bundle of rights that had been developed previously began to shrink or change considerably. As the role of the welfare state in social life came into question, social citizenship increasingly came to be defined away from redistribution and towards a 'neoliberal' approach (Faulks 1998, 2000). Emphasis was shifted away from social rights and towards *social obligations*. Again, while the pace of change was neither uniform nor identical across various states, its direction has been relentless (Dean and Melrose 1999). An amalgam of events influenced this change. Among them, globalization, neoliberalism, postindustrialism, and postmodernism first eroded dominant interpretations of social citizenship rights as entitlements to publicly provided social programs and then precipitated ongoing debates and conflicting visions about the very meaning of the social in social citizenship (Dean 1996). Yet, contrary to predictions that neoliberalism would necessarily set all welfare states in an inevitable decline, it is now increasingly apparent that the prolonged retrenchment from the social policies of the welfare state represents a period of transition and not an end point (Esping-Andersen 2002). The critical question of the contemporary period increasingly concerns the nature of this transition. Recasting the social in citizenship can be witnessed in numerous new deployments of the social as an adjective, as expressed by the terms social cohesion, social capital, social exclusion and inclusion, and social economy, which have informed various policy models and programs in the past decade.

The importance of struggles of recognition has been widely debated, crystallizing in various concepts such as 'multicultural citizenship,' 'sexual citizenship,' 'diasporic citizenship,' and so forth (Isin and Turner 2002; Isin and Wood 1999). The recognition that legal, formal status was only one aspect of the experience of citizenship – providing an avenue for exercising rights as well as bearing obligations – has been embraced in many analyses of the partial or 'second-class' citizenship status of collectivities such as women, children, racialized, ethnic, linguistic and sexual minorities, indigenous peoples, and people with disabilities (Brodie 2004, Stasiulis 2002b). A great deal of literature – including that predating the 'return to citizenship' of the past two decades – by feminist, anti-racist, indigenous, and other scholars (e.g., those researching the poor, working class, and people with disabilities) has revealed the relations of power, discourses, institutions, policies, and mechanisms that produced hierarchies of citizenship.

We cannot consider the struggles revolving around social rights in welfare states as struggles for redistribution and those struggles revolving around cultural and sexual rights as struggles for recognition; clearly, the two intersect and overlap so that an effective approach to citizenship cannot ignore their complexity and simultaneity. We must uncover the relations and processes that constitute categories such as 'women,' 'ethnic,' 'racial,' or 'national,' instead of considering them as given. Rather than starting with differences and asking how to label and classify them, we must explain how they are constructed and by whom, and when and why they become salient. We must examine how processes of inclusion and exclusion affect membership in the bounded and unbounded collectivities, and the definition of the polity. We must also focus on the rights component of citizenship, and identify, for each type of right, the measures conducive to realizing equal *and* different citizenship rights.

John Clarke (2004) has described these developments with twin concepts 'denaturalizing difference' and 'desocializing difference.' He argues that during the postwar era – far from being solely focused on 'redistribution' – various social movements struggled to call into question the social differences that were constituted as biological, economic, cultural, and so forth. These movements demonstrated that the universal figure of the citizen was none other than an able-bodied, adult, heterosexual, white, and male figure (55–6). These, what Clarke calls, *socializing* movements had significant effects in policy and politics: 'They revealed conditions of oppression, subordination and exclusion as socially constructed (rather than natural and universal). Such denaturalization also began to make the "normal" visible and contestable' (60). Furthermore, Clarke argues, 'the struggles over women's subordination allowed glimpses of how male power was organized and normalized. Disability activism brought the normative assumptions of able-bodiedness into sight. Contesting racialized subordination made it possible to identify whiteness as a racialized position and identity whose power rested in part on its claimed position as the norm above and beyond its "racial" or "ethnic" character' (60). It is therefore problematic to think that struggles for recognition arrived after the struggles over redistribution were waged. Clarke further argues that indeed if socializing movements called into question the economism of interpretations that reduced struggles over social welfare merely to redistribution, the very developments that now interpret them being merely about recognition reduce such struggles to culturalism. Clarke calls these projects that 'desocialize difference' (62): 'These anti-social projects seek to locate differences somewhere other than the "social" – expelling them from the possibility of social and political mobilization and redress. They attempt to locate difference and inequality in discursive realms where they will once again become safe and manageable' (62). This is akin to what above we called 'economism matched by culturalism.'

Recasting the social in citizenship requires sociological and political perspectives centred on an analysis of social relations at various scales and sites through various analytical perspectives that question the empiricist and normative as well as the essentialist and idealist perspectives. It entails focusing on social processes and social relations that underlie the formation and definition of social groups (majorities or minorities), of those granted fuller or lesser citizenship, and on the social struggles over differentiated rights that help attain equality. The social in citizenship means: (1) these groups are socially constructed; (2) social processes of inclusion and exclusion are at work for each type of right; (3) unequal social relations are centrally located; (4) we cannot start from the premise that equality requires sameness; and (5) differentiated rights can ameliorate historical inequalities and injustices. A focus on the social in citizenship challenges the notion that citizenship comprises a static and universalistic legal status of abstract individuals in nation-states. To interrogate what is social in citizenship means drawing attention to the process-oriented and contested character of citizenship, in terms of both the criteria regarding who are defined as 'fit' candidates for citizenship and the particular historical and place-bound set of rights, entitlements, obligations, performative dimensions, and identities to which it refers.

Citizenship connects three social domains: how the boundaries of membership within a polity and between polities should be defined (*content*); how the rights and obligations of membership should be allocated (*extent*); and how the identities of members should be recognized and understood (*depth*). Although the state has been the primary focus of negotiation across these domains, the continuing rise of new sites and scales of politics has challenged modern understandings of belonging and the meanings of national citizenship. These challenges are compounded for nations that have imagined themselves as ethnically or racially homogeneous. Moreover, the increasing importance of cities as sites for organizing and shaping cultural, social, symbolic, and economic flows has also prompted a recognition of their significance in cultivating or blocking citizenship. Thus, while the state remains the fundamental institution through which all these rights and obligations are negotiated, contested, and allocated, citizenship's correspondence with a single nation (however imagined) is increasingly being called into question by various reimaginings of identity, belonging, and community.

All these challenges have forced upon academics, practitioners, and activists alike an urgent need to rethink the rights and obligations of citizenship. Major social issues such as the status of immigrants, social care, indigenous peoples, refugees, diasporic groups, environmental injustices, and homelessness have increasingly come to be expressed through the language of rights and obligations and, hence, of citizenship. Moreover, not only are the rights and obligations of citizens being redefined, but so, too, are what it means to be a citizen and which individuals and groups are enabled to possess such rights and obligations. In short, the three fundamental domains of citizenship, extent (rules and norms of inclusion and exclusion), content (rights and responsibilities), and depth (thickness or thinness of loyalty) of citizenship are being redefined and reconfigured.

Subjects, Scales, and Sites of Citizenship

We have invited six innovative and cutting-edge scholars to contribute a chapter to the research program: Bilge, Chen, Cowen, Kershaw, Latta, and Rygiel. We contribute to these six chapters with a chapter written by each of us, as well as the present introductory chapter. Each of our chapters also constitutes a synthesis of years of critical engagement with an aspect of citizenship on which each of us has focused: Brodie (social citizenship), Isin (urban citizenship), Juteau (multicultural citizenship), and Stasiulis (transnational citizenship). We aim to elaborate significant concepts (subjects, scales) and sites (immigrant women, children, military, care, security, and ecology) of recasting the social in citizenship and to develop appropriate research concepts at the *intersections* of these subjects, sites, and scales.

Thanks to T.H. Marshall social citizenship has been among the most recognized forms of citizenship throughout the second half of the twentieth century and to the present day. Yet, it has also become one of the most contested. Janine Brodie (chapter 2) traces the development of social citizenship, focusing specifically on shifting regimes of social governance in Canada. Social citizenship rights are most commonly associated with the postwar welfare state, but Brodie argues that postwar social citizenship rights are only one manifestation of a broader political terrain, that is, 'social governance.' Defined as an instrument of liberal governance, social governance attempts to manage the tensions that arise from the shifting demands of production and social reproduction. In so doing, strategies of social governance help to form and re-form both citizen identities and ways of claims making on the state. Brodie focuses on public policy, and specifically social policy regimes, that are periodically recast to correspond to changing philosophies of governance, varieties of capitalism, and the demands of social reproduction. Although Brodie provides examples from nineteenth and early twentieth century Canada, she is most concerned with the contemporary shift in social governance from a regime of social citizenship rights and redistributive politics to a more ambiguous regime currently being constructed around the concepts of social inclusion, social capital, and social economy. She suggests that these new shifts envision and attempt to embed a radically different model of social governance – one that is congruent with the requisites of neoliberalism and that envisions a recasting of social policy, as well as the identities, rights, and responsibilities of Canadian citizenship.

Paul Kershaw (chapter 3) addresses the redistribution of caregiving responsibilities and draws our attention to one of the most important rights that constitute the backbone of modern social citizenship: the right to social care. Yet, so far, we have only thought about health care as medical care and its resource needs. Recasting the social in citizenship entails re-envisioning the terms of belonging in society to answer the question: What are the entitlements and obligations that accompany social care? Kershaw argues that adequate answers demand analysis from a perspective attuned to issues of caregiving that occur outside of medical systems and infrastructure. This perspective is necessary to fully appreciate the meaning of the social in terms of both its *redistributive* and *recognition* imperatives. Kershaw focuses on redistribution of caregiving responsibilities between families, the sexes, and caregivers from developed and developing economies. Kershaw then explores the relationship between caregiving, identity, and social inclusion to illuminate the significance of care for struggles of recognition.

Brodie and Kershaw untangle two conceptions of the social in citizenship, while Danielle Juteau (chapter 4) examines the debates over multicultural citizenship and argues that they have recurrently focused on the opposition between difference and equality, now reformulated in terms of a dichotomy between recognition and redistribution. Bemoaning a choice that stifles equality, and the essentialism that often plagues these debates, critics of multiculturalism advocate its demise. This is a wrong move, Juteau contends, who replaces the philosophical slant that has come to dominate the debate by a more sociologically oriented perspective that returns unequal social relations to centre stage. Juteau demonstrates how this approach helps to overcome static perspectives of a mosaic-like multiculturalism, the reification of difference, the false dichotomization between recognition and redistribution, and the reduction of equality to class relations. Thus Juteau reinterprets recent debates over the proposed establishment of Islamic arbitration tribunals in Ontario in terms of unequal power relations, the intersection between analytically distinct social relations, and the formation of differentiated groups with conflicting interests. Juteau illustrates the centrality of a social relations approach that broadens our understanding of equality and the specific dynamics of ethnic and gendered groups, without falling prey to economism or culturalism.

Taking the critique of multiculturalism in a slightly different direction, Sirma Bilge (chapter 5) engages with it specifically on the grounds of gender equality. Calling into question a common assumption that feminism (or feminist citizenship) and multiculturalism (or multicultural citizenship) constitute mutually exclusive political projects, she argues that such a framing is an ideological construct, playing a key role in delegitimating pluralistic perspectives in citizenship and justifying the return of assimilationism. After portraying the context of the current withdrawal from multiculturalist policies and practices on the grounds of their presumed clash with gender equality, her analysis demonstrates, via the discussion of recent public controversies over the legitimacy of Muslim claims for accommodation, how the peril of multiculturalism for women's rights discourse, has colonized the debates on citizenship and difference, and locked up a necessary deliberation over the limits of group rights and minority accommodation in a flawed dilemma between gender equality and cultural recognition. Challenging the ideological underpinnings of the dominant framing of multiculturalism as a threat for minority women's citizenship, Bilge traces, as well, the colonial roots of the political instrumentalizing of the 'woman issue,' and skilfully reveals the importance of addressing the complexity of subject positions and divides within the category of 'minority women' – or other essentialized categories such as 'immigrant women,' 'Muslim women.' Bilge calls into question the noble feminist impulse to represent subaltern or oppressed women and urges a reconsideration of the workings of much-acclaimed minority women qua model citizens, who enjoy the legitimacy of 'indigenous informants,' while producing hegemonic knowledge tinted with internal Orientalism. Taken together, Juteau and Bilge demonstrate how their sociological multiculturalism would recast the social in citizenship.

Brodie, Kershaw, Juteau, and Bilge provide nuanced analyses of the ways in which social production and reproduction undergird debates over redistribution and recognition.

Daiva Stasiulis (chapter 6) shifts scales and engages with the effects of international migration on citizenship. The transnationalization of social citizenship is manifest in such phenomena as the globalization of care work through the global North's importation of migrant care work from the global South, the novel efforts to harness and manage the wealth and resources of diasporas for the 'development' of the source countries, and medical tourism from the North in the South. Stasiulis submits two significant insights from her analyses: First, the increased recognition given to the international mobility of peoples has challenged the assumption that nation-states where people hold formal citizenship are necessarily the stewards for distributing the most valued provisions for people. There are now many people who do not live in their country of citizenship, many non-members access partial citizenship rights in states where they sojourn, and increasing numbers hold multiple citizenships or a range of forms of rights-bearing and obligations-imposing memberships in more than one country. These transnational actors are making use of their multiterritorialized, multistate locations to better position themselves to accumulate and convert various forms of capital (e.g., economic into social and political) to their own best advantage. Second, the redistribution of public and private resources entailed by these forms of respatialization serves, partly, to undermine national citizenship but also results in deepening the gap between rich and poor citizens, within as well as across countries. More generally, Stasiulis examines how, especially in view of the weakness of the legal infrastructure for a postnational regime of citizenship, the purposive but not necessarily organized practices of transborder migrants are reconfiguring, reshaping, and respatializing citizenship.

Like Stasiulis, Xiaobei Chen (chapter 7) argues that the problematization of the aging of the population and interventions aimed at securing a younger, neurologically optimal, and economically entrepreneurial population lie at the heart of a biopolitics of population. Chen first discusses citizenship through the Foucauldian perspective of biopolitics and the associated notions of population and state racism. By drawing on several sites of contestation over specific immigration and citizenship processes, she explores regimes of truth, strategies and techniques of intervention in the name of population vitality, and modes of subjectification in which subjects are generated through truth discourses and practices of the self. She then examines some new policy developments through which children are increasingly constituted as citizens in their own right and as independent bearers of rights. She illustrates how child-citizens are implicated in biopolitics and racisms in current Canadian projects of restructuring citizenship.

If Chen shows how the birth of the child-citizen is increasingly at the centre of a new biopolitics, Deborah Cowen (chapter 8) shifts our attention to another subject and its constitution: the soldier-citizen. She asks whether the soldier-citizen is emerging both as an exceptional figure within the nation-state and an important model for the assemblage of social citizenship rights. Cowen notes that, despite the increasing attention paid to war in recent social and political thought, the military has remained marginal in academic and public conceptions of citizenship. The soldier-citizen is still understood to be a peripheral and exceptional player. Cowen takes the citizen-soldier seriously. She considers how many norms of social citizenship have been constituted around the figure of the soldier, even while he or she is largely expelled from legal rights and common conceptions of the citizen. She skilfully examines the long legacy of military 'welfare' and the genesis of key social policies in the context of war work. She then highlights the paradoxical implications of the rise of (civilian) social citizenship for military belonging. By paying attention to the emergence of workfare, the contemporary securitization of the state, and the shifting scales and geographies of citizenship, she investigates the military to raise questions about the changing nature of social obligation and entitlement.

Kim Rygiel (chapter 9) illustrates how securitization processes have challenged the modern articulation of citizenship as a bundle of rights, responsibilities, and legal status based on bounded membership in a territorial state. Like Stasiulis and Chen, Rygiel begins by noting that citizenship has become as much about governing populations *between* and *across* states as it is about governing *within* the state. Where Stasiulis draws attention to migrants as actors, Rygiel investigates states as actors in these processes and notes that citizenship now functions through an increased cooperation between state authorities and a harmonization and standardization between states around policies governing mobility. This can be thought of as an increased *internationalization* of citizenship. Yet, more than this, citizenship also increasingly depends on the displacement of power traditionally located in agents of the state to other actors such as international organizations but also private companies and even individuals themselves. Citizenship has become a *globalizing regime* by depending not just on its internationalization but also its privatization as well as individualization. Such shifts have far-reaching implications for the social in citizenship. For if citizenship is being rearticulated in ways that extend beyond, below, and across the state, then this suggests that governing may also be taking place outside of the traditional notions of the state as the container of the social and beyond the social contract on which modern citizenship was configured. But if governing is increasingly occurring beyond the social contract, what are the implications for citizenship and the struggle for citizenship rights? If citizenship is becoming a globalizing regime of government via bilateral and multilateral arrangements and extended social actors, how does this challenge the ontology of the state and with it the notion of the social on which modern citizenship was based? Rygiel draws our attention to these questions by drawing on recent North American and European border control and detention practices.

For Alex Latta (chapter 10) the emergence over the past two decades of environmental movements under the concept of environmental justice illustrates how the social and ecological worlds are inextricably bound up. In these movements, resistance against the unjust distribution of ecological goods and ills becomes combined with demands for recognition and democratization. Latta argues that this combination can be conceived in terms of citizenship, where conflicts over the shape of the social are actively articulated with parallel struggles over the character of human–nature relationships. Ironically, the literature on *environmental* citizenship has largely failed to observe these connections, embracing citizenship instead as a tool for cultivating 'green' political subjects or as a space for normative theorizing about environmental rights and obligations. Scholars of environmental justice have widely identified the relationships between questions of social justice and environmental protection, and have more recently brought the politics of recognition into the mix, but few of them have sought to read these interconnected dimensions in terms of citizenship. Latta contributes an ecological perspective to the project of recasting the social in citizenship, and in so doing adds key questions to the research agenda. If environmental justice constitutes a politics of citizenship, how is the social problematized, amplified, supplemented, or reconfigured by this politics? To put this another way, if citizens are seen to inhabit not only social but also *ecological* spaces and identities, how does this change our understanding of the way that citizenship regimes are constituted and performed, consolidated, and contested?

If Stasiulis, Cowen, Chen, Rygiel, and Latta shift up the scale of analysis, Engin Isin (chapter 11) shifts it down only to question it. Isin insists that the city is the site of the social precisely because the city is a stake in the struggles over the social. He argues that it is impossible to talk about social citizenship without some reflection on city-based citizenship in ancient Greek cities and the subsequent Roman, medieval, and early modern states, but submits that we need to get over our Greco-Roman romance of the city and distill insights from its more recent legal history. In much of that history, urban citizenship has been understood as belonging to the city and social and political rights that derived from that belonging. In other words, rights of citizens who belonged to the city derived from the rights *of* the city itself. The exact nature and extent of the rights of the city were matters of contest throughout that history up to and including the nineteenth and twentieth centuries. While the rights of the city continued as contested matters in the twentieth century, various social, economic, and political transformations engendered new kinds of rights where by claiming rights *to* the city became dominant modes of inclusion, belonging, and democratic engagement. By drawing on some historical examples from Canada, Europe, and America, Isin highlights this difference between rights of the city (focusing on themes of loyalty, virtue, civism, discipline, and subsidiarity) versus rights to the city (focusing on themes of autonomy, appropriation, difference, and security) and illustrate the importance of this difference for struggles over social citizenship in contemporary societies. He then proposes 'translocal citizenship' as a provocative conception of citizenship that flows inherently across borders.

Isin (chapter 12) concludes the book by drawing out the connections among these research sites and highlights significant consequences that follow from them. He lays these consequences out and outlines them as principles that should guide future research on recasting the social in citizenship. He reverses Marshall's conception of civil, political, and social citizenship as a sequential development by arguing that citizenship is social before it is civil or political. He suggests that perhaps recasting the social in citizenship may ultimately mean making this interpretive move.

Conclusion

As it originates from a broader program, the contributions made in this book articulate a research program. Over the past decade the debate over citizenship has expanded and splintered into various strands such as indigenous citizenship, transgendered citizenship, multicultural citizenship, intimate citizenship, cosmopolitan citizenship, and so on. While all this has been consequential in demonstrating that the relationship between citizenship and identity should not be conceived as mutually exclusive zero-sum games, the fact that the formation of identities and their articulation into citizenship are social processes that produce subjects with rights to have rights has been overlooked. Instead, such *social* identities as religious, environmental, sexual, ethnic, and national have been hypostasized, essentialized, and immortalized to appear as though social struggles over citizenship are either about redistribution or recognition as fixed struggles or that these *social* identities undercut and inhibit an ostensibly universal identity of citizenship. We have attempted in this book to illustrate that these are false choices: wearing the veil in public spaces is as social as is being a welfare claimant; recycling and reducing waste is as social as demanding social care is. That may sound rather simplistic but the consequences are, we think, quite significant.

2 The Social in Social Citizenship

JANINE BRODIE

As discussed in chapter 1, the phrase 'the social in citizenship' evokes many different and sometimes conflicting visions of the foundations of modern citizenship regimes. In recent years, the field of citizenship studies has focused on the challenges, both conceptual and political, arising from two different and seemingly conflicting understandings: One examines the social in citizenship from the perspective of cultural politics, while the other often equates the social in citizenship with the strategies of collective provision that were implemented by Western welfare states over the course of the twentieth century. These strategies are generally referred to as social citizenship or social citizenship rights. This chapter navigates through several different accounts of the development of the idea of the social and the enactment of social citizenship in liberal democracies. The aim is not to establish a definitive account of these processes, but, instead, to contextualize post-Second World War social citizenship rights and to open new conceptual spaces for thinking about the fate of social citizenship in the contemporary era of neoliberal globalism.

The task of rethinking the *social* in social citizenship is fraught with difficult conceptual and empirical challenges, beginning with ongoing philosophical debates about the very meaning and ontological status of 'the social' itself. Some theorists understand the social as being an essential part of the human condition, which exists separately from the political, and perhaps even threatens modern political life (Arendt 1958). Others have pronounced the 'death of the social' in these postmodern times. Baudrillard, for example, argues that, regardless of whether the social existed before or exists now, it is 'already abolished in its very simulation' (1983: 86), while Bauman (2000) submits that the social is turning to liquid. Still others contend that the social is a decidedly historical construct, a product of modernity, and more specifically, one way in which Western societies 'thought about and acted upon their collective experience' during the twentieth century (Rose 1999a, 101). This particular enactment of the social, they argue, has dissolved in recent years under the combined pressures of cultural/identity politics and the rampant individualism advanced by neoliberal governance.

More concretely, the social in citizenship is often equated with social citizenship, and the amalgam of social welfare and social security programs that were variously implemented by postwar welfare states. Yet, even this narrower definition, which largely bypasses broader ontological questions, challenges our thinking about the meaning and status of social citizenship in the contemporary era. Social scientists have provided a number of different but complementary accounts for why social policies came to occupy a central place in the political agendas of liberal democracies during this period. Many explanations rest on what has been called 'the logic of industrialization' (Wilensky 1975). According to this account, the social policy agendas of Western welfare states were a necessary response to both the pervasive risks generated by industrialization and urbanization and widespread working class mobilization that threatened to significantly alter, if not overthrow capitalism. This hard-fought but definitive political settlement between capitalists and workers institutionalized the democratic negotiation of class struggle, if not the 'end of ideology.'

For many years, social scientists also have rehearsed, indeed celebrated, an evolutionary and rights-based story about social citizenship. Using the influential work of T.H. Marshall as a template, this story describes how liberal democratic citizenship rights evolved in three distinct stages, becoming an ever more inclusive and substantial institution of liberal governance in the process. As Marshall describes it, liberal citizenship rights thickened over the past four centuries from state recognition and protection of *civil rights* (relating to property, equal treatment under the law, and individual freedoms of thought and association) to political rights (the right to vote, participate in politics, and hold governments accountable) to *social rights* (the right to the collective provision of a minimum level of social security as a right of citizenship). In Marshall's oft-quoted definition, social citizenship ensures all citizens 'the right to a modicum of economic welfare and security, to the right to share to the full in the social heritage and to live the life of a civilized being according to the standards prevailing in the society' (1950: 10). According to this universal rights-based story, modern states granted their citizens fundamental civil rights in the eighteenth century, political rights in the nineteenth century, and social rights in the twentieth century.

Marshall's account was both evolutionary and celebratory. He attributes the achievement of social citizenship rights, in part, to the extension of democratic rights to the working classes, which they used to force governments to redistribute societal resources. At the same time, social citizenship rights enhanced the practical worth of political and civil rights for all citizens. To Marshall, individual freedoms and the legal right to participate in public life mean little if citizens are hobbled by the indignities and insecurities of poverty. Social rights provide substance to political rights and, in turn, underwrite the legitimacy and stability of liberal government and liberal social formations, he submits. The extension and protection of the full range of citizenship rights, Marshall argues, nourish 'a direct sense of community membership based on loyalty to a civilization which is a common possession. It is the loyalty of free men endowed with rights and protected by law' (1950: 40–1). Social citizenship, in other words, is represented by Marshall as an apex in the evolution of liberal citizenship rights, and as irrefutable evidence of the legitimacy of liberal government.

Marshall's work is firmly situated in a broader movement, which, in the immediate postwar years, sought to codify rights and discipline national states to enact and respect them. The 1948 United Nations Universal Declaration of Human Rights, emerging from the atrocities of the Second World War, has been the penultimate expression of this attempt to give substance to citizenship across national settings. Although not legally binding, the signatories to the Universal Declaration agree to protect and advance the civil, political, and social rights of their citizens, including rights to life, liberty, and security of the person; equality guarantees; and participation in government. Importantly, Article 22 asserts: 'Everyone, as a member of society, has the right to social security,' as well as economic, social, and cultural rights 'indispensable for his dignity' (U.N. 1948). This international articulation of the social obviously resonates with Marshall's conception of social citizenship rights.

Yet, if, in the postwar years, social citizenship achieved the status of a citizenship right to be realized and respected, it soon proved to be far more fragile, ambiguous, and fleeting than legally embedded civil and political rights. The ascendancy of neoliberal rationalities of government at the end of the twentieth century systematically attempted to dismantle universal social programs, erode other forms of collective provision, and dismiss citizen claims-making on the state in the name of the social. As a result, it is widely argued that liberal government and liberal citizenship are no longer practised from 'the social point of view' (Rose 1996b: 340). In a sense, the disappearance or reconfiguration of postwar social programs also fuels another kind of speculation about the death of the social. Such speculation, however, is misplaced. It reflects the all too common tendency to conflate the social in citizenship with the spatially and temporally specific forms of collective state provision most commonly associated with the postwar welfare state (Clarke 2007). In the process, such speculation forecloses critical examination of the ways in which the social in citizenship may be differently enacted and intertwined with citizenship identities and practices at different historical junctures and in different political contexts.

This chapter argues that the ways in which the social in social citizenship have been imagined and practised are variable, not the least because various enactments of the social embody, more or less successfully, prevailing governing discourses or political rationalities. Political rationalities, as governmentality theorists contend, are shifting and always contested 'procedures for representing and intervening' (Miller and Rose 1990: 7). They promote particular ways of seeing, and privilege specific vocabularies, styles of truth-telling, and truth tellers. In so doing, they help shape particular kinds of subject positions, not the least the citizen-subject of liberal democracy (Foucault 2003, Rose 1999a, Dean 1999). This approach necessarily focuses on social policy regimes, less with respect to the evaluation of specific policy outcomes than as discursive forms that reflect particular political rationalities, which prescribe commensurate cultural representations of social and political life and citizenship subjectivities. Yet, political rationalities rarely find their exact mirror image in citizenship practices or politics. Their imprint on both the subject and the collective is always mediated by institutional constraints, different forms of resistance and, indeed, the accidents of history.

This chapter is divided into two parts. The first traces the evolution of the social way of thinking, from its 'invention' or 'discovery' in the industrializing societies of Europe, and its subsequent incorporation into the rationalities of liberal governance, to its eventual attachment to citizenship as a right in the twentieth century. I term this process of incorporating the social way of thinking into modern liberal political rationalities as *social governance*. Social governance is only one, albeit a critical variant of the social broadly defined. It provides a way of describing an evolving and reflexive terrain of liberal government, which both represents and intervenes to manage the shifting, and often-contradictory demands of, and tensions between processes of production and social reproduction. Social reproduction is understood here as embracing a broad range of norms, imaginaries, knowledges, policies, and resources, which are required to maintain and reproduce subjects, families, and communities on a daily and generational basis (Bakker and Gill 2003, Cameron 2006). There are endless variations in the ways that different societies have organized to ensure their survival, and continuity. I argue, however, that liberal government, by its very design, is especially challenged to intervene in daily 'private' life in the name of the social. The second part of this chapter examines the ways in which the social in citizenship have been configured in the past two centuries, drawing explicitly on the Canadian experience. This brief historical survey demonstrates that paradigmatic shifts in rationalities of governance are premised on recasting social imaginaries and citizen-subject positions in ways that are congruent with their logics or 'ways of seeing.'

The Social Way of Thinking

The *social*, with etymological roots in the Latin term *socius*, meaning companionship, first emerged in the vocabularies and thinking of the Western Enlightenment. This is perhaps because, as Lefort (1982) has argued, earlier societies had not yet disentangled the social order from the 'order of the world' (187). Social historians tell us that, in early modernity, 'the social' conveyed the ideas of sociability and fashionable living. Later, with the consolidation of capitalism and modernist thought, the social was progressively attached to emerging normative constructions of the essential human condition. Enlightenment thinkers came to identify man as a social animal and the social as a 'vital descriptor' of human uniqueness, community, and agency. By the mid-nineteenth century, the social was frequently used interchangeably with society, evoking such distinct fields of human endeavour as social philosophy, social ethics, and social economy (Schwartz 1997: 277). The social marked off 'man' from fate, nature, and the transcendental, and was increasingly embedded in the distinctly modernist projects of scientific rationality, progress, and the perfection of the human condition.

Importantly, the social was shaped into a powerful emancipatory impulse when, in the 1830s, Young Germany, an influential collection of radical thinkers, fused the adjective 'social' with the 'noun' problem (ibid.: 278). This fusion opened spaces for new ways of representing and intervening in the politics of industrialization. In early nineteenth-century Europe, the social problem was unequivocally cast in the singular and attributed to the unconstrained and unequal distribution of wealth and power of early industrial capitalism (279). Indeed, the idea of *le problème social* quickly spread across Europe, animating the 1848 Revolution in France, the policy platforms of continental social democratic parties, and the essays of such leading thinkers as British liberal John Stuart Mill (Rose 1999a: 117; Schwartz 1997). Also deeply invested in the political struggles of the time, Karl Marx was adamant that *le problème social* was and should remain exclusively understood as the exploitative relationship between capital and labour. Marx worried that the phrase would be pluralized as a raft of social problems and coopted by the middle class, indeed, by 'any man who has a sympathetic heart for the misery of his brothers' (quoted in Schwartz 1997: 279). For Marx, the political mutation of *the* social problem into social problems promised only to conceal the fundamental realities of capitalism and class exploitation and, thus, erode its revolutionary potential.

Despite Marx's anxieties, the social problem was soon redefined and pluralized, both as competing interpretations of *the* social and as a proliferating field of social problems. Social historians have provided rich descriptions of the tapestry of utopian, radical, and charitable pursuits that emerged in the capitalist societies of the second half of the nineteenth century. The social problem was redefined in the singular by, among others, social Darwinists and eugenicists, who offered competing master plans for the perfection of modern societies (ibid.: 281). These also were years when, as conservative social historian Gertrude Himmelfarb explains, society developed its 'moral imagination' (1984). A plethora of voluntary organizations sprung up in civil society, offering hope and help to those deemed to have a problem – and worthy of help – among them, the addicted, poor, abandoned, prostituted, insane, delinquent, and morally and spiritually impaired. Quite independently from the state or the rule of law, this movement for social reform created its own discourses, apparatuses of knowledge, modes of intervention, and fields of expertise. The social understood as a science of society, and as a field of professionalization soon grew up alongside and informed the social reform movement, especially its secular wings. In the latter half of the nineteenth century, social problems were discovered, and solutions devised by the expanding ranks of social science professionals, including social workers, sociologists, and criminologists (Dean 1999: 54).

These ways of intervening in the name of the social were not simply about helping the marginalized and displaced. As studies of this period repeatedly underline, these activities were framed by specific ways of representing both the reformable and the reformers, as well as intervening in processes of social reproduction. Social reformers volunteered their time and resources to rehabilitate those at the margins who were represented as having moral deficiencies and antisocial behaviours. The target of social reform, in other words, was most often the singular aberrant body. But the goal of the social reform movement was not simply, or even primarily, the salvation of wayward or broken people. Instead, these social volunteers targeted moral problems as a way of strengthening the collective, underwriting social order, and creating better citizens, workers, and parents (Rose 1999a: 102). Moreover, these activities demonstrated and confirmed to the reformers their own moral superiority and that of their culture (Chen 2003a). Social reform was understood as the mark of a civilized society because, as was often repeated, only modern societies were sufficiently morally and technologically advanced – the only ones 'modern enough' – to care about the marginalized and to develop and implement strategies for intervention to change their condition. Modern man had a social conscience and 'each isolation of a social problem [was] applauded as another triumph of the modern spirit of reform' (Schwartz 1997: 282, 288).

These historical accounts point to a particular historical moment in the nineteenth century when early modern societies became animated by a social way of thinking, representing, and intervening, when, as Rose puts it, the social emerged as a 'distinctive idiom' (1999a, 26–7). At the same time, these accounts provide few clues as to why this way of thinking was progressively embraced by modern states, or how it came to be attached to citizenship identities and practices. The next section of this chapter discusses two influential accounts of this period of transformation, which draw us closer to what I term as *social governance,* and the perspective on the social in citizenship that I want to develop here. Although very different formulations, both Michel Foucault's (2003) account of disciplinary power and biopolitics, and Karl Polanyi's (1957 [1944]) tracking of the double movement telegraph the expansion of the scope, domains, and institutions of the nascent liberal state as well as claims-making on the state in the name of social citizenship and social rights.

Social Governance

Although Foucault did not frame his work in the language of the social or social reproduction, his influential account of paradigmatic shifts in the deployment of state power in eighteenth- and nineteenth-century Europe intersects in significant ways with the above tracking of the emergence of the idea of the social. At risk of oversimplifying his rich analysis, Foucault argued that, during this period, sovereign power (the power of the king to take life and let live) gradually gave way to two new non-sovereign forms of modern governance – disciplinary power and bio-power, which progressively guided the actions of the state. Described by Foucault as 'one of bourgeois society's greatest inventions' (2003: 36), disciplinary power applied multiple discourses, actors, and fields of expertise to the individual body in order to normalize it. Disciplinary power, Foucault explains, 'centres on the body, produces individualizing effects, and manipulates the body as a source of forces that have to be rendered both useful and docile' (249). The social reform movement, described above, embodied and deployed this kind of power in its various interventions to shape particular kinds of modern citizen-subjects.

According to Foucault, disciplinary power is variously deployed to normalize individuals, while biopower acts to regularize 'man-as-species.' With industrialization and the demographic explosions from the end of the eighteenth century onward, Foucault argues, the modern state increasingly focused on improving the health, efficiencies, and productivity of populations that had been disrupted and diminished by accidental and structural forces. The population, itself a new discursive construct, was understood as being vulnerable to a series of internally generated dangers that 'sapped' its strength, among them illness, epidemics, and industrial accidents (ibid.: 244). Biopolitics was a response to this way of seeing. As Foucault explains, biopolitics was an entirely new technology of power that used new discourses and new forms of knowledge and expertise, such as forecasts and statistical measures, to both constitute and shape a new object of modern governance – the population. 'It is a new body, a multiple body, a body with so many heads that, while it may not be infinite in number, cannot necessarily be counted.' 'Biopolitics deals with the population ... as a political problem, as a problem that is at once scientific and political, as a biological problem and *as power's problem*' (245, emphasis mine).

Biopolitics, Foucault emphasizes, was not exclusively attached to modern states. It established 'not only charitable institutions (which had been in existence for a very long time), but also much more subtle mechanisms that were much more economically rational than an indiscriminate charity ... We see the introduction of more subtle, more rational mechanisms: insurance, individual and collective savings, safety measures, and so on' (ibid.: 244). Foucault also notes that biopolitics did not displace disciplinary power. Each form of non-sovereign power operated at different a scale – the individual body and man-as-species – but they were articulated with one another through discourses and norms (250, 253).

Disciplinary power and biopolitics are critical threads running through Foucault's account of modern governmentality – the 'conduct of conduct' – and the governmentalization of the state. These processes fused the 'hard' artefacts of the sovereign state (e.g., constitutional, juridical, and institutional powers) with the productive powers of knowledges, rationalities, and technologies, which constituted subject positions, managed populations, and orchestrated *'a new organization of the social'* (Brown 2005: 37, emphasis mine; Rose 1999). Yet, as Wendy Brown rightly reminds us, 'Foucault's formulation of governmentality is notably thin' (2006: 79). Brown is particularly concerned with the somewhat ambiguous and secondary role that Foucault assigns to the modern state, especially with respect to legitimizing biopower. Foucault, however, provides few clues explaining why European social formations embraced biopower in the late eighteenth and nineteenth centuries. Clearly, earlier societies were similarly plagued by internally generated threats to the survival and productivity of its members. The appearance and construction of diseases, unemployment, and poverty as 'power's problem' is itself something that needs to be explained (Miller and Rose 1990: 3). What was it about this juncture that brought about this particular way of representing and intervening?

Although Foucault attributes the rise of biopower, in part, to the invention of new technologies such as statistics, which helped to construct the very idea of a population, I want to turn our attention to political rationalities informing the development of the liberal (capitalist) state of nineteenth-century Europe. The liberal social imaginary and its doctrine of societal/institutional pluralism were based on an 'art of separation.' It replaced the old feudal order of natural hierarchies, interdependence, and organicism with a 'world of walls' that marked off different realms – the public, the market, the private (Walzer 1984: 315). Each sphere was to be governed by different rules, hierarchies, and distributive practices, and each was to contribute differently to the vitality and continuity (i.e., social reproduction) of liberal societies (Bowles and Gintis 1986: 98-101). Moreover, the legitimacy and authority, indeed, the very identity of the nascent liberal state, revolved around its capacity to enact this imaginary, specifically, to ensure the autonomy and freedom of the private sector of the market and the private sphere of individuality and freedom.

Of course, this imaginary of separate spheres was (and is) largely performative. The invisible hand of capitalism, as Marx had predicted, stretched over liberalism's walls, producing and reproducing inequalities that threatened the survival of individuals and communities, while the costs of social reproduction often exceeded the capacities of individuals, families, and civil society. The inherent tension at the heart of liberal government thus was that, to maintain its own legitimacy, the state had to fashion the economy, civil society, and the family as autonomous and self-generating and, at the same time, continuously and selectively intervene in these spaces to ensure their 'freedom' to function properly (Dean 1999: 50–1; Hindess 1993). The task of liberal government, then, was to construct and enforce a particular model of societal and institutional pluralism and, at the same time, develop reflexive strategies of intervention to sustain this model. Social governance, I would argue, can be viewed as one such strategy. Since the 'discovery of the social' at the outset of modernity, strategies of social governance have been formed and re-formed to mediate the shifting tensions that lay at the heart of liberal government. These strategies also inform how we understand the social in citizenship.

Karl Polanyi, in *The Great Transformation,* was one of the first to explore the idea of social governance as an emergent property of liberal government and, as a response to its 'barest' form, laissez-faire. Originally published in 1944, Polanyi's book charts the social and political underside of Western capitalism from the onset of industrialization and the implementation of the first era of laissez-faire in the nineteenth century to the Great Depression of the 1930s, the fascist counter-revolutions, and the world wars of the twentieth century. Polanyi proposes that modern capitalist societies are characterized by an inherent and ongoing tension between the principles of economic liberalism and societal protection (1957: 136). He argues that the ascendancy of laissez-faire and of market-driven governance was a unique political construct, never before encountered in the productive or reproductive organization of human societies (69), and implemented only through the deliberate and sometimes violent interventions of early capitalist states. This untried experiment, he suggests, was predictably followed by a breakdown in the social fabric, erratic manifestations of all kinds of political pathologies, oppositional thinking by 'enlightened reactionaries,' the rise of a mix of civil society counter-movements, many offering 'social' solutions to social problems, and, ultimately, a double-movement back to the prioritization of social protection in public policy.

Although Polanyi's work is often cited as a case against liberalized markets per se, it is more accurately read as a critique of market-driven governance, notably, unmediated 'bare' liberalism and its inherent incapacity to comprehend, let alone manage, the complex interplay between forces of economic production and social reproduction. According to Polanyi, any governing strategy that enables 'the market mechanism to be the sole director of the fate of human beings and their natural environment' invites 'the demolition of society' (ibid.: 73). Similar to contemporary critics of neoliberal governance, Polanyi rejects laissez-faire's 'uncritical reliance on the alleged self-healing virtues of unconscious growth' (33). Instead, he argues that the art of liberal governance is to mediate the demands of market creation and unfettered capitalist accumulation by inventing 'protective countermoves' that blunt the market's destructive impact on individuals and social institutions (76). Both Polanyi and subsequent historians remind us that opposition to market-driven governance was fragmented and diverse, as were the early governmental interventions in the economy and in the household in the name of the social. Counter-movements were 'spontaneous' and 'actuated by a purely pragmatic spirit' (141). As Polanyi is often quoted as stating, 'while laissez-faire was a product of deliberate state action … subsequent restrictions on laissez-faire started in a spontaneous way. Laissez-faire was planned, planning was not' (ibid.).

Polanyi links the cultural and discursive designation of the very ideas of society and societal protection, as objects of governance, to the formation of liberal political economies. The 'social problems' named by early capitalist societies were not self-evident, but rather the product of a specific historical configuration of economic, political, and social forces. For Polanyi, the 'discovery of society' was 'an emergent reality' that occurred 'behind the veil' of the market economy. More specifically, he argues that, 'it was in relation to the problem of poverty that people began to explore the meaning of life in a complex society' (ibid.: 85). The naming of the pauper especially intrigues him. 'Pauperism,' he explains, 'fixed attention on the incomprehensible fact that poverty seemed to go with plenty' – a revelation 'as powerful as that of the most spectacular events of history' (84–5). Contrary to conventional accounts, Polanyi concludes, 'social not technical invention was the intellectual mainspring of the Industrial Revolution' (119). His enduring insight, however, is that modern capitalist markets are sustainable only insofar as they are embedded in social and political institutions that regulate, moderate, and legitimate market outcomes (Rodrik 1998: 17).

This last observation draws us back to our focus on social governance and the social in citizenship. As we know, across the twentieth century, the scope and terrain of social governance grew both in scope and complexity, especially under the rubric of the postwar welfare state. Social legislation was designed to improve the living conditions of the poor and labouring classes, to underwrite the health and education of children, to support mothers and families, and to provide a measure of security to those threatened by sickness, old age, unemployment, and injury (Dean 1999: 129). However, contrary to the rights-based story of social citizenship, the development of these social ways of representing and intervening was tentative and uneven both within and across post-Second World War welfare regimes. These programs rarely took the form of a universal right to citizen well-being, but, instead, concentrated on two classes of problems – those generated by the spheres of the private authority of the factory owner and the father/head of household (Donzelot 1988: 405). As Jacques Donzelot argues, public power was increasingly deployed across the twentieth century in the name of social right and the solidarity principle of government, 'wherever the head of the family or a business [seemed] inadequate … to the smooth running of society' (395).

Reflecting on the welfare state, Donzelot contends that, while social policies did indeed 'compensate for the effects of poverty and reduce the effects of oppression,' the primary role of social governance was to 'mitigate society, not reorganize it' (397). The ethical demands for social justice, which had been tied to early articulations of the social problem, were substituted by a range of concrete solutions and various forms of social compensation, while leaving the fundamentals of liberal political economy in place (423). 'Social rights,' Donzelot insists, were 'not absolute but relative and circumstantial. They [did] not require the state to embark in a partisan transformation of society but engage[d] the collectivity in compensating for its own shortcomings and excesses' (23). Mitchell Dean (1999) endorses a similar perspective. The social, he argues, did 'not arise from the implementation of a theoretical model of society:' in other words, it 'cannot be derived from liberal political philosophy'; instead, the social 'is a *condition* of such a model' (53, 54, emphasis mine). Put differently, the ways of representing and intervening generally associated with social citizenship were not anticipated by liberalism's world of walls, but, instead, emerged as a particular historical response to the tensions and contradictions generated by this model.

Before moving on to briefly examine the ways in which the Canadian state has enacted the social in citizenship, we should take stock of the ideas advanced to this point. First, we have navigated through a series of different accounts of the emergence of the social, which challenge thinking about the social either as an essential property of being human or as the evolutionary (teleological) apex in the development of liberal rights. The perspective developed here suggests that the social developed as 'a particular sector in which quite diverse problems and special cases can be grouped together, a sector comprising specific institutions, and an entire body of qualified personnel' (Deleuze 1979: ix). This perspective also locates the emergence of the social within the context of both a specific historical configuration of states and markets and of the multiple roles of the liberal state to underwrite material production, social reproduction, political legitimacy, and social cohesion. Similarly, the social does not represent the simple transfer of charitable activities from an overburdened civil society to the state. The terrain of what I have termed here as social governance is inscribed with particular political discourses, and strategic interventions, which attempt to construct, discipline, regulate, and reproduce citizens and national populations in a particular form. From this perspective, then, the social policies that are identified as giving substance to social citizenship are similarly implicated in this process of representing, disciplining, and configuring. Social policies, as Brown reminds us, 'have cultural, social, and political effects that exceed their surface operations' (2006: 8). They address conditions that, at some time or place, are identified as a 'social problem,' and they may be more or less successful in ameliorating that problem, as it is identified. As discussed below, these same policies also construct and embed particular representations of what citizenship means and what it means to be a good citizen.

The Social in Canadian Citizenship

According to Gøsta Esping-Anderson, the history of welfare states can be viewed as the combination of brief episodes of pivotal change and long periods of politics as usual, which embed and reproduce a broad consensus about the role of government, the substance of citizenship, and the goals of social policy. Three such periods of pivotal change are generally identified – the late nineteenth century, the years surrounding the Second World War, and the current era in which advanced liberal democracies have variously institutionalized neoliberal political rationalities (2002: 1). Although differing from the European experience in important ways, the Canadian case provides an illustrative example of the ways in which the social in citizenship has been differently configured through historically shifting political rationalities. Unlike the European experience discussed in the first part of this chapter, the nineteenth-century liberal state in Canada was not challenged to intervene in the social conditions or social relations of industrializing capitalism, or at least not to the same degree. In fact, it was not until the end of the First World War that industrial production was ranked as the largest sector contributing to Canada's gross national product (GNP), and it was not until the Second World War that industrial workers constituted the largest component of the Canadian workforce. For its first four decades and more, the primary focus of the Canadian state was nation-building, territorial expansion, and the consolidation of liberal government.

Moreover, it is difficult to speak about Canadian citizenship in any meaningful way in these early years. As a former British colony and white-settler Dominion, Canada did not enact its own citizenship legislation until 1947, some eighty years after Confederation. Until then, the Canadian citizen did not exist as a legal entity in either national or international law but, instead, held the ambiguous status of British subject: oaths of allegiance were to Queen/King and Empire. Nonetheless, most Canadians were able to claim a civil rights heritage that had evolved through the British common law tradition (the Napoleonic tradition in Quebec), and political rights were achieved in waves with near universal male suffrage granted in the 1880s and federal female suffrage after the First World War. This said, indigenous Canadians and targeted ethnic minorities, such as the Chinese and East Asians, were denied many of these basic claims to citizenship. Thus, unlike other liberal democracies of the period, there is a decided absence of citizenship discourse in the Canadian public debates until after the Second World War (Brodie 2002a).

The terrain of social governance also was underdeveloped in Canada's early decades. The country's founding document, the British North

America Act (BNA 1867) was penned when the rationalities of laissez-faire liberalism dominated the thinking of both the imperial centre and its Dominions. Social policy development, to the extent that it was anticipated or sanctioned by the founding fathers, was considered a relatively inconsequential local matter and, thus, jurisdiction over emerging social problems was assigned to subnational levels of government. In these early years, the costs of charities, welfare, and education constituted less than 10 per cent of total public expenditure (Wallace 1950: 384). This is despite the fact that the new country endured a series of debilitating economic depressions in 1873–79, 1884–47, and 1893–96.

Although this succession of economic crises obviously threatened national well-being and productivity, the impacts were cushioned somewhat because the overwhelming majority of Canadians were engaged in subsistence agriculture. Consistent with laissez-faire doctrine, material survival and reproduction were constructed as the primary responsibility of individuals, families, local communities, and faith-based institutions (Cameron 2006: 48). Municipal workhouses for the indigent could be found in some larger localities, and women who were widowed or deserted by their spouses were sometimes provided with public financial assistance, but only if they were deemed morally worthy, and often on the condition that they take in laundry or perform some other gender-appropriate work. In most provincial jurisdictions, never-married women and women who left their husbands, regardless of cause, were deemed ineligible for state assistance (Finkel 2006: 75). The socially marginalized were represented as being the authors of their own misfortune, who might benefit from public benevolence, but clearly, they had no right to claim it. As was explained in Toronto's *Daily Globe* in 1877: 'a very large proportion of both men and women who are the recipients of public bounty are notoriously dissipated. Though they are so, we do not advocate a system which would leave them to starve, but we do say that if they are ever to be taught economical and saving habits they must understand that the public have no idea of making them entirely comfortable in the midst of their improvidence and dissipation' (quoted in Finkel 2006: 67).

The public, however, did increasingly call on the state to provide public education, which became the first significant collective intervention in the social field. The case for public education was built on a particular representation of children – as being a reservoir of future citizens – who could contribute both to the nation-building project and to the health of democracy. The future of the nation required educated citizens, so the argument went, and thus, it was incumbent on the state to provide this public infrastructure so that no Canadian child would grow up in absolute ignorance (Wallace 1950: 384). In the late nineteenth and early twentieth centuries, this discourse also was advanced and elaborated by the Child Saving movement, which sought to intervene in families to save abused or neglected children before they fell into a life of corruption and criminality and to teach them how to be useful Christian adults and stalwart citizens (Chen 2005: 37, 127). There was a strong thread of biopolitics informing this early concern with children, as the following quote from an Ontario spokeswoman for a 1910 study on infant mortality suggests: 'We are only now discovering that Empires and States are built of babies. Cities are dependent for their continuance on babies. Armies are recruited only if and when we have cared for our babies' (quoted in Finkel 2006: 72).

The late nineteenth century witnessed sweeping social change across Canada. With almost 40 per cent of Canada's population now living in an urban setting and immigration at its zenith, activism and claims-making on the state became progressively informed by a social way of thinking. Counter-movements, to use Polanyi's term, sprung up in a variety of corners. 'Enlightened reactionaries' pointed to the examples provided by German Chancellor Otto von Bismarck's social policy regime and the writings of the British Fabian socialists as a way of responding to these new challenges (Wallace 1950: 390). Moreover, the growing realities of urban squalor, contagious disease, and high infant mortality propelled a public health movement to demand state provision of public infrastructure often in the name of citizen equality. Clean water supplies, sewage systems, and sanitary waste disposal, it was argued, should be available to all citizens, rather than to only the wealthy few (Finkel 2006: 76–7). As Finkel contends, business leaders similarly demanded public infrastructure, reasoning that it would attract business, increase fire protection, and lower insurance premiums (ibid.). These years also saw the emergence of the social gospel movement, which focused on reforming the poor and infusing the marginalized and new immigrants with middle class Protestant values. The social gospel movement was animated by a complex mixture of diverse thought, including radical Protestantism, strains of socialism, eugenics, and xenophobia (85).

These social undercurrents had some influence on provincial policy agendas in the early twentieth century, counting among their successes the establishment of public utilities, child welfare agencies, prohibition, and perhaps even women's suffrage provincially and federally. The federal government, for example, justified extending the franchise to women because it would 'exercise an important and wholesome influence upon many vital social problems confronting the nation' (Canada 1918: 2559). The early twentieth century saw other tentative steps on the terrain of social governance, with meagre public benefits extended to veterans and their dependents, poor single mothers, and the aged. But all of these measures were means-tested and scrutinized on a case-by-case basis: they were not exemplars of social citizenship as it is commonly understood.

The laissez-faire doctrine of minimal government, however, would soon buckle under the weight of the Great Depression of the 1930s. In these desperate years, the federal government provided financial aid to the provinces to help them deal with their mushrooming welfare obligations, established work camps to take unemployed young men off the streets of Canada's cities, and tried unsuccessfully to implement national unemployment and social insurance schemes. Although the federal division of powers prevented this 'social turn' in the 1930s, what is important for our purposes was the palpable shift in thinking about bare liberalism's prescriptions for social reproduction and the gradual attachment of the idea of the social to Canadian citizenship. The rich history of this period cannot be retraced here: suffice it to say that the myth of capitalism's invisible hand was discredited, even among the ranks of the ruling elite. The 1935 Speech from the Throne, prepared by an otherwise very business-oriented government, described the capitalist system in language rarely heard in the corridors of political power in Canada, before or since: 'in these anxious years through which you have passed, you have been the witnesses of grave defects and abuses in the capitalist system. Unemployment and want are the proof of these … These require modifications in the capitalist system to enable that system more effectively to serve the people' (Canada 1935: 3).

The Depression years also saw a critical re-evaluation of ways of representing and intervening with respect to the poor and marginalized. Communists and socialist diagnoses of 'the social problem' gained an important footing in industrial trade unions, leading to labour militancy as well as violent state coercion. Similarly, an influential circle of engaged intellectuals and social activists embraced many of the key pillars of Fabian socialism and launched a new political party, the Co-operative Commonwealth Federation (CCF), to advance a new vision of a socialist Canada. Meanwhile, mainstream debate increasingly focused on the ideas of collective intervention and social citizenship. An excerpt from a CBC publication, which summarized a 1938 nation-wide consultation on the constitution, gives a taste of this shift in thinking. John Mackay, a Manitoba college principal explained that:

> The aim and structure of social work was further in the past determined by the principle that distress was considered the result of individual deficiencies. A contrary idea is rapidly gaining ground; I mean the concept that *society* is responsible for distress, and a recognition that not only is the welfare of the individual the concern of society, but his well-being is a direct contributing factor to the well-being of others. With economic conditions having entered a most acute phase, widespread distress and mass poverty demonstrated the inadequacy of welfare resources based on private benevolence; governments in consequence are forced to organize social welfare programmes. (CBC 1938: 70, emphasis in original)

This shift in political rationality from private responsibility and provision to collective risk and public intervention was similarly embedded in the 1943 Marsh Report, which is often identified as the founding blueprint for the Canadian welfare state. This influential public transcript reflected the building consensus about both the 'basic lessons to be learned from the thirties' and appropriate parameters of social governance. 'The only rational way to cope with the large and complicated problem of the insecurities of working and family life,' the report explained, 'is by recognizing and legislating for particular categories or areas of risk or need' (Marsh 1943: 9). The report took aim at former 'hit and miss' private and public responses to illness and unemployment, arguing that, even though such risks may never strike particular individuals or families, 'we know from experience that, collectively speaking, these problems or needs are always present at some place in the community or in the population' (10). The Marsh Report provided the federal government with a resounding endorsement of the principle of social security as a template for structuring Canada's postwar welfare state, and as a 'form of investment in physical health, morale, educational opportunities for children, and family stability' (16). The report was equally insistent that social insurance was premised on a new way of thinking about the social, and social governance. Popular perceptions of social insurance, the report explained, were often confused because 'too much emphasis is placed on the second word and too little on the first word of the phrase. Social insurance brings in the resources of the state ... The basic soundness of social insurance is that it is underwritten by the community as a whole' (11).

The federal government began to construct Canada's postwar social architecture, piece by piece, in the years immediately following the release of the Marsh Report. A universal mothers' allowance was implemented in 1944, and a national unemployment insurance plan was set in place in 1945. These planks were soon followed by limited hospital insurance, support for postsecondary education, and an ever more inclusive package of social legislation for families, the blind and disabled, the elderly, and the poor. In 1966 three central threads of postwar social citizenship were set in place – the Medicare Act, which promised universal health care to all Canadians, the Canada Pension Plan (CPP), a payroll deduction scheme that enhanced the universal old age pension; and, finally, the Canada Assistance Plan (CAP), a federal-provincial cost-sharing package that provided social assistance to anyone demonstrating need. These developments paralleled the experience of other liberal welfare states, but paled in comparison with the social architectures of some northern European states.

As I have argued elsewhere, what was particularly unique to the Canadian case was the extent to which the postwar regime of social governance was fused and interwoven with a flurry of federal initiatives designed to build up the cultural and symbolic infrastructure of a new pan-Canadian nationalism, including the enactment of Canada's first citizenship act in 1947 (Brodie 2002b). During the 1950s and 1960s, these national and social projects were built up side by side, and constantly sutured together through state citizenship discourses. In the process, social citizenship was progressively written onto Canadians' sense of themselves and their country. The introduction of social legislation was invariably accompanied by federal pronouncement about the social substance of Canadian citizenship, the equality and well-being of *all* Canadians, and the dignity and security of *all* Canadians. Social policies, in other words, were woven into the nationalist story of who Canadians were and, regardless of their diverse backgrounds, how they constituted a single national community of fate (386). Social citizenship was not simply a citizenship right: it was the glue that held Canadians together and distinguished them, at least according to the nationalist myth, from their American neighbours to the south. Indeed, over a half century since the inception of the welfare state, Canadians continue to define themselves through the lens of postwar social programs, and, especially universal health care.

This draws us to the present conjuncture and the status of the social in social citizenship in the contemporary era of neoliberal globalism. For almost a generation now, the welfare states of most advanced capitalist countries (and the politics that inspired and sustained them) have been progressively transformed by retrenchment and restructuring. Moreover, the assault on the logics and institutions of the postwar welfare state has been most intense in Anglo-American democracies, such as Canada, where governments have enthusiastically embraced the political rationalities of neoliberalism. Beginning in the late 1980s, one Canadian federal government after another has abandoned the concepts of universality and social security, reduced social program spending to levels not seen since right after the Second World War, and shifted emphasis from so-called passive to active welfare interventions, that is, policies offering a 'hand-up rather than a hand-out.' As noted in the beginning of this chapter, these current transformations in social governance betray representations of social citizenship as an apex in the development of liberal rights. At the same time, it is also clear that neoliberal governments have not abandoned the terrain of social governance.

The contemporary fate of the social in citizenship is perhaps too frequently read off the formal logics of neoliberal political rationalities. Accordingly, neoliberal governance is represented as an attempt to revive both the laissez-faire social imaginary of societal and institutional pluralism and the fiction that markets are natural, self-governing, and the primary source of individual well-being, choice, and freedoms. This rationality, moreover, prioritizes market logics over all other goals and instruments of public policy. As Brown argues, 'neoliberal rationality, while foregrounding the market, is not only or even primarily focused on the economy' – it extends and disseminates market values to all institutions and social action and rewards institutions for enacting this vision (2005: 39–40). Read in this way, the ascendancy of neoliberalism relegates the very ideas of the social and social citizenship, as we have come to understand them, to history's dustbin. Social programs are progressively abandoned as all national states are forced to engage in a competitive race to the bottom, while citizens are released from social entitlements and obligations as they maximize their choice and capacities for self-sufficiency (Brodie 2003).

The imprint of neoliberal political rationalities on postwar configurations of the social, however, has been far more varied, complex, and partial than predicted (Swank 2002). While the terrain of social governance in advanced liberal democracies has and continues to be reshaped, it has not disappeared. To the contrary, beginning in the mid-1990s, many Western governments began to talk of the necessity of reinvesting in social programs, although not necessarily in those areas most commonly associated with the postwar welfare state. The United Kingdom, for example, shifted from Thatcherism's punitive social retrenchment and privatization agenda to a New Third Way of active welfarism and social investment, especially in children. By the late 1990s New Zealand, the former poster-child of neoliberal 'rollbacks,' began to 'rollout' a new social ethos, grounded in the discourses and strategies of social partnerships, social inclusion, and social investment (Larner and Craig 2005). In these same years, the Canadian federal government, celebrating the beginning of a post-deficit era, introduced a series of initiatives to reinvest in children, communities, and the future. Most of these initiatives, however, were targeted and delivered through the taxation system.

These and similar developments elsewhere have led John Clarke (2007) to argue that contemporary neoliberalism, while deploying several strategies to subordinate the social to the economic, has not erased it, either from public policy or citizen subjectivities. Clarke enumerates several neoliberal strategies of subordination, which, he argues, embody quite distinct conceptions of the economic and the social and how these may be rearticulated within a neoliberal paradigm. Among them, *erasing* involves the simple elimination of many postwar social programs while *privatizing* and *subjugating* consists of assigning formerly public goods and services to private market providers and imposing the market logics of private profit and supply and demand on previously decommodified public goods. Other strategies of subordination include: *narrowing* or downsizing and targeting social programs to specific groups that are identified as being at risk; *functionalizing* or redesigning social programs so that they primarily address the needs of neoliberal labour markets rather than personal well-being; and *fiscalizing* or transforming social policies that require program planning and service providers into tax credits and deductions, which purportedly allow citizens 'choice' in meeting their social needs. The latter strategy of subordinating the social is closely linked to both *reinventing* the ethos of public management to better reflect the alleged efficiencies of markets, and *economizing,* or encouraging citizens to identify as consumers of public services and to deploy market logics in their everyday calculations with the goal of becoming self-sufficient.

Contemporary advanced liberal states have differently deployed these strategies with varying degrees of commensurability with neoliberal fundamentalism. In Canada, for example, both the federal and provincial governments have relied on erasing, privatizing, narrowing, fiscalizing, and economizing. Increasingly, citizens are expected to shape themselves into self-sufficient market actors who provide for their needs and those of their families (Brodie 2007; Brown 2005: 42). Social policy reform in Canada represents a fundamental shift in thinking that subordinates, if not explicitly rejects, two critical assumptions that informed social governance for much of the twentieth century: first, social structures systematically advantage some groups of citizens and disadvantage others; second, social policy appropriately corrects for systemic barriers and inequalities. Postwar discourses that framed Canadian citizenship in the language of the social and national social solidarities have been supplanted with those that attempt to disarticulate the historical and cultural interface between citizenship and social provision (Ong 2006: 161).

Contemporary social policy reform has both material and cultural impacts on citizen subjectivity and practice. The infiltration of the postwar terrain of social governance with neoliberal political rationalities, as Brown argues, 'reaches individual conduct, or more precisely, prescribes the citizen-subject of a neoliberal order' (2005: 42). This prescription is largely enforced through discourses and strategies of individualization. While commensurate with the methodological and ontological individualism of mainstream economics and classical liberalism, individualization is a distinctly different process that is quite unique in the practice of modern governance. Beck and Beck-Gernsheim characterize individualization as part of a broader contemporary compulsion 'to live a life of one's own' (2002: 22–6). As they explain, individualization has a different meaning than individualism, which is generally understood to be either self-actualizing or self-seeking behaviour. Individualization, in contrast, places steeply rising demands on people to find personal causes and responses to what are, in effect, collective social problems: We are all now compelled to find a 'biographic solution' to systemic contradictions (ibid., xxii). This new rationality demands that citizens imagine themselves separately from group identities and claims-making and conduct their own lives 'at the pain of economic sanction.' Responsibility for social crises that find their genesis in such macro processes as structural unemployment, racism, or unequal gender orders is shifted onto the shoulders of individuals. Living your own life thus includes taking personal responsibility for 'your own failures,' especially dependency on public provision. As a result of this governing strategy, structurally disadvantaged groups are 'collectively individualized' in popular cultural representations, in citizenship discourses, and in public policy (23, 27).

Contemporary social policy regimes have turned from rights-based and collective models of social governance to so-called active models that prioritize the development of human and social capital, individual entrepreneurialism, labour force attachment, and fiscalized redistributive strategies, such as tax deductions and credits, which purportedly enhance individual choice and efficiencies in meeting their social reproductive needs. Although appeals to entrepreneurial citizenship are pervasive and incessant in contemporary political discourse and practice, the ideals of collective provision and social citizenship remain deeply embedded in popular political values. Public opinion polling, for example, consistently reports that Canadians reject privatized health care and prefer their governments to reinvest in social programs as an alternative to tax cuts. At the same time, Canadians continue to make claims on the state to address new social risks associated with economic globalization and postindustrialism, among them, child care, elder care, changing family forms, and intergenerational inequalities. As Clarke (2007) rightly emphasizes, neoliberal tactics to subordinate the social to the economic encounter residual as well as emergent forms of opposition and contestation: The dominant, the residual, and the emergent coexist in a dynamic interrelationship, generating different political accommodations and policy responses across cultural and national terrains.

Conclusion

This chapter has explored many of the conceptual and empirical challenges to recasting the social in social citizenship in an era of neoliberal globalism. The chapter locates the 'discovery' or 'invention' of the social in the material conditions of early industrial capitalism and in the central challenge of liberal government both to legitimize its foundational myth of societal/institutional pluralism and to underwrite ongoing processes of production and social reproduction. During the past two centuries, the terrain of social governance has been figured and reconfigured and variously written onto citizenship subjectivities in response to shifting discursive, cultural, and material contexts. As the Canadian case demonstrates, the way in which the social is interwoven with citizenship discourses is sensitive to national and temporal contexts. Cultural traces, institutional constraints, and resistance, all combine to render the fit between the social imaginaries embedded in dominant political rationalities and the formation of the iconic citizen-subject. Miller and Rose make a similar and critical observation about the fit between prescription and practice: 'while governmentality is eternally optimistic, government is a congenitally failing operation ... "Reality" always escapes the theories that inform programs and the ambitions that underpin them' (1990: 10–11). If this historical overview of the historical development of the social way of thinking tells us anything, it is that the social in citizenship has taken many forms. Neoliberalism may aspire to reassert some approximation of bare liberalism, but the logic and experience of liberal government suggests that it can only reconfigure the terrain of social governance – not by-pass it. Whether the social is dissolved into market logics and individualization or recaptured by a new social way of thinking is a critical question for contemporary citizenship studies and for our citizenship politics.

Acknowledgments

This research is supported by the Canada Research Chairs Programme (CRC). I hold a Tier 1 CRC in Political Economy and Social Governance. I also wish to thank Malinda Smith, Engin Isin, and Catherine Kellogg for their critical reading of this chapter as well as Victoria Miernicki for her able research assistance.

3 Social Care

PAUL KERSHAW

Engin Isin et al. (introduction, this volume) 'invented the concept "recasting the social in citizenship" to indicate that fundamental social issues of our time are refracted through the experience of citizenship.' Their observation reminds us that citizenship means far more than nationality or the ownership of a passport, issues with which it is often associated in the vernacular of North Americans. More significantly, citizenship articulates the terms of belonging in society, in part by defining the entitlements and obligations that accompany full membership. To appreciate fully the social in contemporary citizenship, however, it is worth inverting the observation by Isin et al. to acknowledge that the experience of citizenship is in fact refracted through the fundamental social issues of our time. Care is one such issue. It is integrated in distinct aspects of debates over citizenship, which can and should be bridged in order to better understand how the social is now constituted in countries like Canada. I therefore recast the social in citizenship in this chapter by asking, What is social about care?, with a focus on care for children.

There are multiple answers to this question, which, together, invoke discourses about recognition, redistribution, and the nature of the social. I briefly explore six answers below: (1) seemingly 'private' care is often social; (2) care contributes to retaining the 'multi' in Canadian social commitments to multiculturalism; (3) *un*social labour market norms crowd out care time; (4) care is a social obligation of citizenship; (5) the social in affluent anglophone Canadian provinces cares less than the social in many other states; and (6) medical care, a dominant element of social care and citizenship in Canada, risks cannibalizing investment in other aspects of social care.[1] I conclude the chapter by discussing what these six observations about social care teach us about the social in contemporary citizenship.

'Private' Care Is Often Social

Feminist political economists have long deployed the concept of 'social reproduction' to illuminate the processes involved in sustaining and reproducing people, particularly their labour power and tax payments, on a daily and generational basis (e.g., Bezanson and Luxton 2006). Social reproductive work includes the provision and preparation of food, clothing, shelter, basic health, safety, and psychological nurturance for dependent children, the ill, aged, and disabled, as well as other less dependent adults, and oneself. Much social reproduction, or care, thus occurs in what the social sciences have regularly deemed 'private' places, especially the domestic sphere. One implication is the blurring of the public/private divide, since ostensibly personal care activity has enormously important social implications for the economy. This feminist political economy insight is complemented by the more standard discussion of positive externalities in the economics literature, which justifies the need for social investment whenever individual parties risk failing to invest efficiently in certain activities because they fail to reap the full return from the investment when some value spills over to the broader public. Quality child care is regularly presented as an activity that generates such a positive externality (Cleveland and Krashinsky 1998).

Feminist research that places the experience of Aboriginal women and women of colour at the centre of political economy theorizing extends the notion of social reproduction to include the (re)generation of cultural practices, social values, and identity, both for individuals and collectivities. Findings from the Care, Identity and Inclusion (CII) Project suggest that the relationship between what many deem 'private' caregiving and the politics of recognition is especially evident among minority ethnocultural groups, which cannot count on the public sphere to validate and/or preserve their group identities. The CII project is mobilizing researchers at the University of British Columbia and Simon Fraser University to collaborate with women of colour and First Nations women in Vancouver, Toronto, and a series of Aboriginal reserves to place their perspectives at the centre of theorizing about the social. From such viewpoints, it becomes clear that caregiving in family contexts is intimately implicated in identity politics and issues of individual and collective power. In Canada, and elsewhere, many parents must still compensate for the failure of schools, the media, and other public institutions to validate the identities of some racialized ethnic groups and in the process resist oppression by cultivating a meaningful racial identity in children within a society that still too often denigrates people of colour. For instance, one Aboriginal woman, Jenny, reports, that:

> As a mother, one of the most important tasks that I have undertaken is the role of creating identity in my children. When the girls were very young, I began exposing them to every possible element of their culture; the longhouse practices, funeral celebrations, dance groups in the community, and the maintenance of strong ties with family ...
>
> In supporting the development of my children's identity I have chosen to introduce culture first, and allow this to guide all other aspects of their individual identity. For far too long, my extended and immediate family has had our culture taken away, by banning our culture and the use of our language. I guess you could say that I have turned the tables and made 100% certain that my children have seen and heard and tested every aspect of their cultural identity. And then the other elements of their unique identities can be shaped by their decisions.

Danielle affirms Jenny's insight that public resistance occurs through private care, insisting that it is by no means characteristic only of child-rearing patterns among Aboriginal women. Rather, she explains 'in a society where you are looked upon as a "black" or second class, one needs a lot of self-esteem and positiveness in order to live freely as well as to accomplish your goals in life, since it is a daily struggle.' 'My children,' she adds, 'though born in Canada from African parents are faced with occasional biases and struggles ... I try to teach them at their level to accept criticism and use it as a tool to become stronger when faced with discrimination. I constantly teach them about their origin, educate them to appreciate their identity, especially as name-calling is common among young children. I teach them to be smart about themselves and constantly praise them for their efforts and the open communications, thus building their self-esteem and confidence.'

Bibi, also an immigrant originally from Africa, similarly describes the care she provides for her child's identity as a source of resilience:

> For me, building my children's identities is as important as providing them food and water because it will help them develop survival strategies

> ... I know from life experience that a strong ethnic identity can help anyone to develop self-esteem, the ability to cope with discrimination and racism, and succeed in life ...
>
> When they [my children] talk to me about being different, sometimes with strong emotions, I try to tell them that the only way for them to feel good about themselves is to accept themselves as they are and be proud of it. My objective is to help them to control their emotions and behaviour when they are confronted with discrimination because of their race and also when they have a strong ethnic identity the connection will be easier with other ethnic groups ...
>
> My responsibility as a parent is to help them be stronger inside so they can be able to deal with any kind of exclusion or when they face exclusion, the shock will be less or they may not even be in shock because they are prepared and learned from me that they are Congolese because we (parents) are and it's [more] important to stay in connection with us (parents) than being with connection to the Land (Canadian because they are born in Canada).

The link between identity transmission and resilience emphasized by participants in the Care, Identity and Inclusion Project lends credence to Collins' (1994: 49) insight that care is 'a form of resistance' for some minority mothers whose reproductive and care labour on behalf of their own family and ethnic group defies the expectation of servitude to whites or assimilation into Anglo-European practices, norms, and values (Collins 1991: 140). On this view, the web of relations in which citizens provide and receive care becomes a site where members of marginalized social groups 'express and learn the power of self-definition, the importance of valuing and respecting ourselves, the necessity of self-reliance and independence, and a belief in [our] empowerment' (118).

One implication is that the 'subjective experience of ... motherhood is inextricably linked to the sociocultural concern of racial ethnic communities' (Collins 1994: 47). Domestic care has the potential to function as a form of resistance to oppression that stretches well beyond the particular homes in which the work is performed because it contributes to a broader project of community development. Qua cultural workers, mothers contribute significantly to the project of 'group survival' by transmitting an ethnocentric worldview to the next generation (ibid.; Collins 1991: 145-54). Collins (1991: 143) attributes the survival of certain African customs in North America to the conscious effort made by black women to preserve specific traditions. This observation draws attention to the role served by caregivers, especially women, from minority ethnic groups as cultural conduits in polyethnic countries such as Canada and the United States, which have been built on immigration and colonial acquisition of Aboriginal lands. By working to ensure that children cultivate a proud affiliation with their cultural history, ethnic minority caregivers help to preserve the distinctness of the minority collective racial identity.

Jenny confirms this interpretation of mothering as community development work. She explains that:

> Caregiving is the grounding force to identity. It is here that we shape and mould the beginnings of our children, a beginning that allows them to later remould, reshape, and alter their own personal identity. When the caregiving denies the development of identity or when it denies identity it is merely survival, food, and shelter, the bare necessities. This might have been my mother's existence, a survival mode for years [in the residential school] ... When we nurture our children in a positive, strong sense of culture, Aboriginal culture, the community development is inherent, it is one and the same. In my teaching, very rarely do we separate one's self from the family, from the community, it is all so connected. When we build identity in the home [caregiving] we build community and when we build community, we strengthen the power of the whole.

Caring for the 'Multi' in Canadian Social Commitments to Multiculturalism

If 'private' care contributes to the development of community and group empowerment, then care work is not simply a civic or social contribution because it reproduces labour, taxpayers, pension contributors, or health care providers. Just as importantly, care equally underpins the social reproduction of cultural and other group identities. From this perspective, care is enormously important community development work in a country like Canada that constitutionally aspires to maintain the cultural diversity of its residents, because the identity transmission to which caregiving contributes is critical for retaining over time the 'multi' in Canadian commitments to multiculturalism (see also chapters 3 and 6, this volume).

Interestingly, however, the role that caregiving plays in the politics of recognition is bound to become increasingly contested politically as post-9/11 security threats have moved, for example, British government officials to deem multiculturalism a failure (Kelly and Lusis 2006), and similar misgivings are emerging in Australia, the United States, and Canada. In the latter, the debate over multicultural citizenship is transforming most notably in the wake of the June 2006 arrests of more than a dozen citizens in the Toronto area for attempted terrorist attacks on local buildings, and in the light of the 2007 provincial government sponsored commission about reasonable accommodation in Quebec.

Rejuvenation of the 'social' is explicit in the transformation of multicultural debates. As Nikolas Rose (1996b: 353) remarked over a decade ago, 'while our political, professional, moral and cultural authorities still speak happily of "society," the very meaning and ethical salience of this term is under question as "society" is perceived [as a result of global, multicultural, and other pluralist discourses] as dissociated into a variety of ethical and cultural communities with incompatible allegiances and incommensurable obligations.' The emergence of 'communities' as the terrain of group activity, Rose observes, risks imploding any imagination of 'the social' as a single space, territorialized across a nation, with adverse consequences for social solidarity. As Kymlicka and Norman (2000: 35) warn, 'it is surely true that if ethnic, regional or religious identities crowd out a common citizenship identity, there will be difficulty maintaining a healthy democracy.'

Should Jenny's insight that 'caregiving is the grounding force to identity' be interpreted in this way? Does her observation that 'when we build identity in the home ... we build community' further splinter past (Euro-Canadian) hopes for 'the social'? While a conclusive answer is beyond the scope of this argument, immigrant participants in the Care, Identity and Inclusion Project provide reason to resist this interpretation. Recall Bibi, for instance, who is determined to have her children identify themselves as Congolese before Canadian. She nevertheless insists that 'when they have a strong ethnic identity, the connection will be easier with other ethnic groups.' Renata, a mother from South America, echoes this sentiment. She explains at some length that minority cultural continuity actually facilitates bridging with members of other cultural communities. 'I've thought of all the advantages of creating bilingual children with two cultures,' she comments.

Renata: I think that my kids will have an opened mind to the people who don't only know Spanish but that also know Korean, Punjabi, and Chinese ... because my kids had the experience of being bilingual with two cultures. To raise a child with two cultures it helps them to become tolerant because they have gone through that process in the house where only one language is spoken but outside there is another language. [This] helps them to become tolerant people.

Q: Respectful?

Renata: Yes, respectful of other cultures because my kids will ask for respect for their culture, their background, and this will make them respect other backgrounds. They will learn to treasure the family traditions. This will give them lots of self-esteem towards knowledge of their tradition and maybe they'll feel curiosity for other cultures. I hope that my kids will grow up like adults with less stereotype-likeness in their lives because this damages the society ... One has to be opened to a world that is new to them. I hope that my kids will learn this though being bicultural.

The idea that minority identity retention promotes tolerance emerges in narrative after narrative among CII mothers who immigrated to Canada (although it is much less prominent among the Aboriginal participants). The former thus invite scholars of social cohesion to query more carefully the relationship between bonding and bridging social capital. The mothers in the Care, Identity and Inclusion Project consistently insist on the importance of their children assimilating their parents' culture of origin. But they do so out of an appreciation for the role that minority cultural immersion will play in fostering (1) a centrally important setting for social belonging, the family; (2) the self-esteem to which pride in one's identity will contribute; and/or (3) a corresponding familiarity with the importance that this same pride will play in the lives of members of other social groups. Thus, rather than create barriers, *CII* participants suggest that minority cultural continuity provides citizens with the confidence to engage with others on equal terms, to show respect for differences that aren't worth disagreeing about, while also empowering individuals to resist and demand redress for things that are disagreeable, including any injustices that they endure, whether economic, cultural or otherwise. We can thus read their narratives to impart the insight that 'bonding may enhance bridging.' This observation merits heightened attention among scholars of social capital as the debate about multiculturalism and insecurity evolves in Canada and elsewhere.

*Un*social Labour Market Norms Crowd Out Care Time

As such debates transform, it will remain important to acknowledge that the role caring plays in self-definition and group membership has historically been muted in theorizing, in large part because theorists have occupied dominant ethnocultural perspectives or other group viewpoints from which the collective identity is not at risk. But relative silence does not mean that time for care is unimportant for the development of identity among members of the dominant culture. Caregiving is an activity that facilitates individuals, regardless of their privilege, to explore their place in a family and community lineage as well as the values and life pursuits that this social location affirms. Thus, although the Care, Identity and Inclusion Project, along with the literature associated with Collins (1991, 1994), illuminates the importance of domestic care as a form of resistance among some minority sociocultural groups, it also underscores the broader point that informal caregiving is integral to healthy identity formation among *all* citizens irrespective of the security of their ethnocultural background.

Thus, CII participants' observations about work-life conflict should resonate with citizens, regardless of their majority or minority status. Notwithstanding the deleterious consequences for women's economic security and their inclusion in a range of public places that flow from the gender division of care (a point to which I return below), some CII mothers express frustration about financial constraints that limit the time that they have available for private caregiving. Natasha, a mother who emigrated with her family from Vietnam, articulates this frustration most forcibly.

Natasha: Currently, my husband and I are taking turns working on different shifts so when I go to work there isn't much time for my children. For example, when I come back home after evening shift, my children have already went to sleep. In the morning, I have to prepare breakfast, and drive them to school. In that time, I don't have much time to converse, and teach them Vietnamese.

Q: How do you feel about not having enough time to communicate with your children?

Natasha: Very sad. Many times I think that I don't know English, and my children don't know Vietnamese. I don't know how my children will be when they grow up. When I want to speak with them, how I will I do it? So I can't express my thoughts and feelings. In the future, if they want to confide to me, they won't know how to express in Vietnamese language. Therefore, I feel very sad when I don't have enough time for my children.

Q: What kinds of support or changes would make more time available for you and your husband to have more time for this communication with your children?

Natasha: I have three children. I work full-time. If I want more time for my children, then I have to quit my job. If I quit my job, then the family budget is short. Is there any support or any compensation to help my family if I quit my job?

The answer is 'not much,' as Natasha already knows about Canadian social policy. While barriers to sufficient family time are rarely considered in debates about social inclusion, such debates risk deafness towards a growing chorus of work-life conflicts reported by Canadian employees (Duxbury and Higgins 2003). The connection between care, self-definition, and cultural continuity therefore motivates questions about the *un*social time rhythms imposed by market economies, which disproportionately impinge on the 'life' and 'family' halves of the work-life/family balance concept, including compromising non-employment time and fertility decisions (ibid.). This imposition is neither bounded by cultural community membership, nor even class lines, since some struggle to stave off economic deprivation by long hours in the labour market, while ideal worker norms demand extensive hours on the job of even well-remunerated core employees (Kershaw 2005: chapters 7–8). Private time for care is thus an issue of identity politics, time management, and social inclusion that commands attention from us all, although it is one that becomes more salient only after positioning Aboriginal women and women of colour at the centre of our theorizing about the social. The insights of CII participants in effect invite us all to resist one-dimensional understandings of social inclusion, illuminating more about what is at stake when participating in one's sphere of personal relations, and adding legitimacy to individual desires to spend more time there. In response, there remains need, as I have argued elsewhere (ibid.), to revisit employment norms institutionalized in Canadian employment standards, care leave entitlements, supplementary child care services, and pension reform in order to address the barriers that currently obstruct the fulfilment of care aspirations (and obligations) in our private spheres. These and other related policy envelopes are ripe to become the focus of new debates about a social right to time to care (Knijn and Kremer 1997).

Care Is a Social Obligation (That Many Men Neglect)

The obstacles to work-life balance imposed by the structure of the labour market and the demands of employers continue to reflect the historical evolution of employment norms premised on a male breadwinner/female caregiver division of work, norms that have economically empowered many male citizens, especially those privileged by class and race. I have documented elsewhere that the polarization of paid work-time, in conjunction with the characteristics of workers who labour longer hours, signals that employers in many industries rely increasingly on a core of relatively well-paid, educated, and experienced workers for extended work hours, weeks, and/or years (Kershaw 2005: 135–7). The effect of this labour usage reform is to further entrench the norm of the ideal worker as someone unencumbered by responsibilities that limit one's willingness to commit to the job to the degree demanded by an employer. Occupations that pay well and/or grant substantial responsibility give employees less time to spend on non-paid work aspirations than was the case in the mid-1970s, including caregiving.

The polarization of paid work-time is worrisome for a number of reasons, including the fact that it is associated with increased inequality regarding market earnings (Morissette, Myles, and Picot 1995). However, in a context of in which there remains a very strong gender division of (ir)responsibility for caregiving, the polarization is also an anathema to gender equality. Those who bear primary responsibility for caregiving, disproportionately women, are encumbered with responsibilities that militate against their meeting and/or accepting the temporal demands that are associated with ideal worker norms. This observation helps to explain why the share of management positions accounted for by women actually fell slightly in Canada between 1996 and 2004.[2]

One implication is that caregiving remains at the heart of struggles for redistribution. It is now commonplace to observe that caregiving has historically been, and remains, a social option for men in most countries and cultures. The consequences are striking in Canada. Regardless of their employment status and occupation, women typically retain primary responsibility for work in the home, including caregiving. Stay-at-home parents in single-earner couples are almost always women. Part-time employed women are nine times more likely than men to report that child care responsibilities preclude them from pursuing full-time positions (Statistics Canada 2006: 111). Full-time employed women generally remain responsible for organizing replacement care arrangements while they and their partners are in the labour force, as well as for coordinating the performance of domestic household work. Full-time employed women also consistently provide more unpaid caregiving than full-time employed men, and they enjoy less leisure on average than their male counterparts do (Silver 2000).

To date, we know that the encouragement of some, but not all, to cultivate a disposition to attend to care obligations in childhood, infirmity, and old age has historically led to the exploitation of, and disadvantage for, primary familial caregivers, as well as poorly paid child care providers and domestic workers from countries with less industrialized economies (Bakan and Stasiulis 1997). There is no reason to expect this gender socialization pattern, as it intersects other dynamics linked to class and ethnicity, to produce different results in the future. So long as caregiving is an example of civic work that citizens can opt to perform *or not*, a breadwinner/caregiver division of labour at the level of the nuclear family will marginalize those who specialize in care from the primary location of wealth creation in society. The penalties for interrupting paid employment for family reasons multiply over the life cycle. This feminist insight is now well recognized even in the mainstream literature, with scholars such as Gøsta Esping-Andersen (2002: 86) conceding that 'the cumulative wage losses are potentially huge, not simply due to forgone earnings during interruptions, but also to skills erosion, less experience, and lost seniority.'

Even if we imagine a society in which care specialists are well compensated monetarily for their socially valuable labour, Nancy Fraser's critical insight in her article, 'After the Family Wage' (1994), is that specialists will nonetheless be marginalized from other important areas of social life that offer opportunities for personal fulfilment, social inclusion, and the cultivation of power and status. This marginalization should not be dismissed, given the psychological value that often accompanies labour force participation, as well as the social integration and related social capital that may be cultivated through market involvement and which empowers individuals in civic and political venues. The demand for employment opportunities that is common in the literature by and about citizens with different abilities is one line of scholarship that illuminates the psychological well-being that can flow from labour market attachment.

Given the heightened risk of economic insecurity and social marginalization to which care specialization is linked, Annette Baier (1987: 53) has argued, now over two decades ago, that an adequate theory of citizenship cannot regard socially vital care labour 'as an optional charity left for those with a taste for it.' If society aims to sustain itself, it must formally countenance, accommodate, and enforce all to participate in the care work necessary to provide for its own continuers, 'not,' as Baier puts it, '[to] just take out a loan on a carefully encouraged maternal instinct'; nor, I should add, a loan on low wages in child care settings, or the economic insecurity that underpins migration patterns and remittance practices for many foreign domestics. As part of this process, I have argued that it will be necessary to codify the care obligations that continuers owe those who provided adequately for them during their initial period of dependence in childhood, as well as the obligations that citizens who remain childless owe others who perform socially valuable care work when rearing and, ideally, optimizing early development for, the next generation of citizens. Such codification is the motivation for the concept care*fair*.

Care*fair* builds directly on the dominant social citizenship debates of the day in anglophone countries: namely, the alleged demerits of unconditional welfare benefits relative to workfare, which renders benefit eligibility conditional on the discharge of a now fundamental social obligation, employment (or at least job search). Without lending unconditional support for any specific workfare provision, the care*fair* concept questions why the same logic with which many governments now justify enforcing paid work obligations does not apply equally well to enforcing social caregiving responsibilities for men (Kershaw 2005, 2006). The persistent patriarchal division of care represents extensive male free-riding on the care work of diverse groups of women. The policy and cultural norms that permit men to remain dependent on this labour undermines equality of opportunity and places women at risk of economic insecurity and marginalization from important social areas. Given this morally hazardous dynamic, there is reason to believe that the dearth of care activities performed by many men must become the primary target of a new care*fair* policy framework that will redefine the social to institutionalize an equitable distribution of caregiving across sexes, classes, and ethnic groups. The proposed policy shift demands more than the current crack-down on so-called deadbeat dads which is under way to ensure the fulfilment of their financial obligations to children (Hobson 2002), because such a crackdown does not interrogate the cultural norms and practices that distance care provision from the social conventions that define fatherhood and masculinity as paying, rather than caring personally, for children. Policy architects must instead be similarly tenacious in urging fathers to rescind their patriarchal dividend by performing an equitable share of care, including child-rearing and other familial care.

Tenacious policy change will require restructuring on a number of fronts because the current package of policies to support families with the cost of rearing children often provides one-earner couples (almost always organized around a male breadwinner and a female care specialist) with the most generous benefit (Kershaw 2007), and thus works against the redistribution of labour between the sexes. In response I have proposed a variety of reforms, including adaptation of parental leave benefits to reserve some leave time exclusively for fathers, so that if they don't use it, the family loses it. Pension eligibility reform that rewards caregiving leave more generously than employment will be another important change (Kershaw 2006), as will revisions to income taxation of caregiving and dependency (Kershaw 2002). However, since long hours in the paid labour market for economically privileged participants are maintained and perpetuated by male practices at the very same time that the practices are invoked to explain why men cannot assume additional caregiving loads in non-market contexts, I have also urged that shortening what counts as 'full-time' employment will be necessary through changes to employment standards legislation. To this end, the general reduction of full-time paid work hours over the week or year institutionalized in France and Germany point to an important strategy for remedying the functional division between breadwinner and unpaid caregiver, even though the policies do not specifically target the needs of parents of young children (see Kershaw 2005: 146–50).

'The Social' Cares (Less in Canada)

The claim that care is an obligation of citizenship does not entail that all citizens are socially bound to reproduce. Fulfilment of social responsibilities for child care by citizens who choose not, or are unable, to reproduce may simply mean publicly recognizing the social value of others' child-rearing by personally subsidizing this work and accommodating the flexibility that care provision requires in market and other civil society domains. Making employment arrangements more flexible, including redefining cultural and policy expectations about 'full-time' paid work to welcome shorter hours (as discussed above) is one component of the requisite accommodation.

As for subsidizing child-rearing, Canada, like other industrial countries, has a package of tax allowances, cash benefits, and exemptions from charges, subsidies, and services in kind, by which the population as a whole, including citizens who do not reproduce, support parents with the costs of raising their children. In Canadian provinces, the packages include the Canada Child Tax Benefit, the National Child Benefit Supplement, spousal and equivalent-to-spouse tax credits, maternity and parental leave benefits, child care service operating funding and fee subsidies, universal health care, subsidized dental and pharmacare for children from poor families, and welfare. A recent review of the cumulative package value in affluent anglophone provinces reveals that Canadian governments outside of Quebec are international laggards in this policy area (Kershaw 2007). Counting the value of both provincial and national programs in a rich province like British Columbia,[3] the average package in 2004 came to just $165 in Canadian currency (accounting for purchasing power parities), when health care costs and benefits are excluded. This benefit level is not even one-quarter of the benefit package available in Austria in the same year, which stands alone internationally for the generosity of its benefit package for families with young children. It is also less than half the value available to families in Australia and the United Kingdom, countries with whom Canada shares linguistic, political, and cultural heritages.

Since as Canadians we take considerable pride in our universal health care system, and often refer to this policy domain when distinguishing our national identity from that of our U.S. neighbours, many may question the decision to exclude health care benefits in the above calculation of average package values on the grounds that these would likely see British Columbia's ranking improve by international standards. Although the province's position does improve relative to the United States, it generally falls further below European counterparts when we factor not only the cost of visiting a doctor, but also expenses incurred to purchase a standard prescription for each member in the family once a year, and seeing a dentist for general care along with provision for one filling (Bradshaw and Finch 2002: 102). The latter costs are not typically part of the public health care system paid for by taxes, and thus reduce the modal value of the 2005 package in British Columbia by over $100 per month.

The result is that Canada is relatively weak at encouraging redistribution between families of different income levels, with and without children; and it is also weak at redistributing across individual's life courses, neglectful of the demographic pattern that expenses rise with the birth of a child at a point in life when earnings potential is generally lower. This neglect is problematic from the standpoint of child development, because health and well-being in the early years are not merely a reflection of a child's biology, the resources that parents and other family members can invest in their offspring, nor the child-rearing styles and practices that inform adults' caregiving. Development also reflects the broader social dynamics and institutions through which the entire citizenry organizes itself economically, culturally, socially, and so on. These broader community conditions and practices create an environment for social care that influences individual and familial well-being. In short, 'the social' can be more or less nurturing; and such social care practices are important when it comes to raising healthy, happy children who have the potential to thrive as they mature, as is being suggested by a growing literature about the effects of community membership on child development (e.g., Brooks-Gunn, Duncan, and Aber 1997a, 1997b; Kershaw et al. 2007).

In addition to weak policy infrastructure when it comes to challenging male irresponsibility for caregiving, as discussed in the previous section, the poor ranking of British Columbia and other Canadian provinces outside of Quebec reflects two other policy trends. The first is relatively miserly income assistance rates for the poorest families with young children. Among sixteen countries in the Organization for Economic Cooperation and Development (OECD) for which comparable data are available, welfare for B.C. residents in Canada ranks at the bottom – with the United States – in terms of the extremely low level of disposable income that these jurisdictions make available to mothers with toddlers on welfare (see Table 3.1). The income level in British Columbia in 2004 was just one-quarter of that available to lone mothers in Norway.

One reason for the miserly welfare benefits in British Columbia is the concern that overly generous assistance rates risk attracting citizens to elect idleness over employment. There is reason, however, to be sceptical about this policy assumption, at least with respect to poor women with children, because the countries that report the highest labour force participation rate for lone mothers are the same jurisdictions that provide the most generous welfare benefits, far more generous than Canada's (Kershaw 2007: 27–9). In addition, the fear that a deficient work ethic underpins many welfare recipients' recourse to income assistance misdiagnoses the events that precipitate many women's initial reliance on public support. Qualitative research illuminates that labour market attachments are regularly mitigated by the male citizenry dysfunction for which many lone mothers must compensate, including male violence against women and male irresponsibility for child care (Kershaw,

Table 3.1
Disposable Income for Lone Mother Families with Toddler on Welfare, 2004

Country	Income $
Norway	1,578.15
Austria	1,551.72
Denmark	1,278.26
Iceland	1,189.89
UK	963.06
Australia	878.19
Ireland	865.64
Finland	748.65
Sweden	697.55
New Zealand	683.76
Netherlands	681.94
Belgium	669.24
Japan	641.03
France	620.41
Germany	543.11
BC (Canada)	386.32
United States	155.91

Source: For international figures, author; currency conversions based on Bradshaw et al., data available at http://php.york.ac.uk/inst/spru/research/summs/welempfc.php; and http://www.york.ac.uk/inst/spru/research/summs/childben22.htm. Both last visited 25 Feb. 2008.

Pulkingham, and Fuller forthcoming). Thus, rather than redress an allegedly deficient work ethic, a burgeoning literature is showing that the very low welfare rates in North America circumscribe the labour options of poor women, particularly women of colour, such that they are increasingly obliged to work in very low-paid segments of the labour market for the benefit of modern capitalist economies, but at the cost of alternative career development goals and/or personal caregiving aspirations (ibid., Mink 2002, Davis 2006; Neubeck and Cazenave 2001).

The other contributing factor to the poor ranking of Canada's benefit package in British Columbia is the dearth of affordable, quality child care services available in that province (as well the other provinces, particularly outside of Quebec). A recent report by the OECD (2006) underscores the extent to which investment in early learning and child care services is not a priority in Canada by international standards. Among fourteen nations for which it has comparable expenditure data, the OECD reports that Canada ranks last in terms of child care service spending for children under six years of age, allocating just one-quarter of 1 per cent of GDP to this policy domain, compared with Denmark, the international front-runner, which allocates nearly with 2 per cent of GDP. Worse still, Canada is last by a considerable distance, since the thirteenth-place country, Australia, designates nearly one-half a per cent of GDP to regulated early learning services, 60 per cent more than Canada.

The dearth of public investment in programs like child care services reveals that federal and provincial governments outside of Quebec continue to capitalize on the un(der)paid care work of diverse groups of women citizens. This public pattern reinforces the need to develop further the work of Daly and Lewis (2000) who use the term *social care* to capture the significance of caregiving for political economy research. Their deployment of the concept resists the tendency to privatize and depoliticize the non-medical care on which citizens depend for their well-being by alerting theorists and practitioners to its social value irrespective of whether the care is delivered by the state, voluntary sector, as part of a formal market exchange, or informally in one's private domain. In response, Daly and Lewis (285) use the social care concept to develop three themes: (1) the labour involved in caregiving in order to beg comparison with other forms of work and the circumstances in which labour is carried out; (2) the normative framework of obligation and responsibility, and I would add aspiration, within which so much caregiving is provided, especially in networks of familial and friendship relations; and (3) the economic, physical, and emotional costs of care.

Social Care Conflicts

The way that Daly and Lewis define social care creates conceptual space to position health, elder, child, and other dependent care under one conceptual rubric. This grouping provides an important analytical window through which to examine social architecture in Canada. For the country's ongoing underinvestment, by international standards, in the majority of daily child caregiving, performed disproportionately by diverse groups of women for no or little pay, is facilitated in large part because of the supremacy of another care debate in the Canadian psyche – the debate about medical care.

The right to health care is a backbone of modern social citizenship in Canada. Public opinion poll after poll has ranked this issue at the forefront of the minds and hearts of Canadians for decades. Despite its prominent status in the political culture, health care is nonetheless not immune to the tendency, lamented in this book's introduction, for stakeholders, policy makers, and scholars alike to insulate dominant approaches to health from a broader range of care issues. Most significantly, despite being confronted with funding and personnel crises, we continue to think about health care primarily in terms of the medical care needed to treat illness rather than the promotion of preventive health care.

This tendency is especially evident at present on the country's west coast in the Government of British Columbia's 2007 budget consultations (2006). Glossy leaflets and colour pie charts distributed to residents illustrate that medical care spending is currently absorbing nearly 40 per cent of provincial expenditures (in part because tax cuts constrain total expenditures), and some projections anticipate that this budget item will continue to grow substantially in the coming years as baby boomers age. One consequence, the government implies, and the minister of state for child care has identified publicly on a number of occasions, is that spending in other social areas needs to be reconsidered and potentially reduced. To this end, the B.C. government initially cut funding for child care services by about $30 million annually (Government of British Columbia 2007); despite the fact that the social service envelope of which child care is a modest part, along with programs like income assistance and child welfare represents, less than 9 per cent of provincial expenditures (see Table 3.2 for more detail).

Such spending patterns merit careful scrutiny from a developmental perspective, since the human brain is sensitive to environmental stimulation that can optimize development particularly during the early years, and to a degree that diminishes markedly as human beings mature beyond years three through seven (Keating and Hertzman 1999). By contrast, investment in health and well-being occurs disproportionately in the final years of the life course. Bradshaw and Mayhew (2003), for instance, observe that Canada is among a long list of affluent welfare states that are financing their ballooning elderly populations at the expense of

Table 3.2
Government of British Columbia Expenditures (all $ millions unless otherwise noted)[a]

	2006–07			Change: 2001–02 to 2006–07	
	Nominal $	% of Total Expenditure	% of GDP	Nominal $	% of GDP
B.C. Surplus	4,056	11.9	2.30	491	388
Total B.C. Public Expenditure	34,184	100.0	19.00	13	-16
Health	13,250	38.8	7.40	25	-6
Education	9,519	27.8	5.30	24	-9
Social Services	2,892	8.5	1.60	-15	-38
Total Child Care Budget	392	1.1	0.22	73	28
Less Federal Transfer	187	0.5	0.10		
Provincial Child Care Budget	205	0.6	0.11	-10	-33

Sources: Child care funding per HELP June 2007 Financial Fact Sheet, verified by MCFD in the light of internal budget updates. All other figures are actual results reported in the Government of British Columbia 2007 Financial and Economic Review – July 2007: 22, 82, 83, 90.

[a] This table was prepared in collaboration with Lynell Anderson, Senior Researcher in the Early Learning and Child Care Research Unit at the Human Early Learning Partnership, University of British Columbia.

their children. Per capita spending in Canada on cash benefits and services for families with children is less than one-tenth of the value of per capita spending on benefits and services for seniors. When health care spending is added to the equation, the intergenerational disparity grows further. While government expenditures on the public education system narrow the gap for families with school-aged children, there is no such narrowing effect for citizens in their preschool years (see Table 3.2).

Recognition of the disjuncture between investment and developmental opportunity provides reason to be cautious about new discourses of the 'child-citizen' which imply an overarching policy shift in biopolitical logics that favours the young over the aged. Athough Chen (this volume) offers an insightful argument defending the position that such a shift is under way with regards to Canadian immigration policy, broader analyses of actual social expenditures reveal that the immigration case is far from the norm, as Bradshaw and Mayhew's international analysis of benefits for seniors versus children indicates. Moreover, in British Columbia, medical care expenditures, from which seniors benefit the most (given life course morbidity patterns), dwarf child care service expenditures at a rate of 35 to 1. Thus, while the 73 per cent increase in child care service investments over the past five years in British Columbia because of new federal investments might be construed as support for Chen's analysis, the growth is better interpreted when we recognize that nominal spending five years ago was very modest; with the result that small additional investments since have produce marked percentage increases.

The disjuncture between investment and developmental opportunity is also notable because it worries human capital scholars who warn that future prosperity in nations with aging populations will depend in large part on the extent to which societies hone the developmental conditions in the early years that maximize later skill acquisition and avoid poverty traps that shackle young citizens in poverty for extensive periods (Heckman and Lochner 2000, Esping-Andersen and Sarasa 2002). In this regard, a developmental census of kindergarten children in British Columbia sounds alarm bells, despite the province's relative affluence. On average, 25 per cent of B.C. children enter the formal school system vulnerable on at least one domain of development (e.g., physical, social, emotional, language/cognitive, and/or general communication). Compounding this worrisome average is the finding that vulnerability rates vary tremendously by a child's neighbourhood of residence: some B.C. neighbourhoods report rates as low as 2 per cent, while the most challenging neighbourhood reports a rate of 59 per cent. Diverging socioeconomic characteristics in turn account for between a fifth and a half of this neighbourhood variation, revealing a geography of opportunity in British Columbia that risks systematically entrenching inequalities over citizens' life courses (Kershaw et al. 2007).

Lest we accept without debate that it is appropriate for medical care expenditures to cannibalize social investment in the determinants of lifelong health (McIntosh 2000), determinants that include quality, licensed care in the early years (Kohen, Hertzman, and Willms 2002), there is need to bridge common approaches to thinking about health care with care practices that occur outside of medical systems and infrastructure. We must therefore ask ourselves what medical care we owe one another in a just society as our capacity to save increases dramatically with costly technology and drugs? What does it mean for a society when 80 per cent of health care expenditure is absorbed by citizens in their last year of life? And what does it mean for a society when it can and does spend hundreds of thousands, if not millions, of dollars to save a pre-term fetus – one life – but is remarkably hesitant to invest in health promotion for the population through programs like early learning and care, housing, food, etc., as I document above?

Table 3.2 reveals that the time is now to shift debates about social care investments by asking such questions in affluent provinces like British Columbia. Impressive economic growth over the past five years means that the gross domestic product is increasing at a rate that outpaces even the growth in medical care allocations. Current surpluses thus make new investment in other policy envelopes, like child care services, feasible without cutting elsewhere, including medical care, while cost-benefit analyses suggest that investment in child care services will eventually reduce public expenditures in other policy domains (Cleveland and Krashinsky 1998).

Recasting the Social in Citizenship from Care Perspectives

By analysing *together* the above six seemingly distinct aspects of citizenship in which care factors importantly, there emerge an equal number of noteworthy observations about the social in contemporary citizenship. The first is that social participation may well be served, if not represented, by what is often deemed 'private' activity. Domesticity can be a site of refuge and solace not only because family and fictive kin provide material assistance when times are difficult, but also because they may provide important emotional support by affirming the personal values and self-definitions that individuals need in order to flourish. Since this recognition may be lacking in public domains, especially for members of minority ethnic and faith-based groups, as well as gay and lesbian communities, the positive recognition of one's self-definition that can be found in domestic spaces grows in significance. In such cases domesticity assumes the status of an essential sphere of social inclusion where the nurturing of one's identity fosters resilience and psychological health promotion among individuals who must resist externally imposed denigrating images. Nurturing the identities of individuals in turn has the potential to empower the collective identities of the ethnocultural, religious and sexual orientation groups in which citizens belong. Processes of identify formation that unfold in 'private' spaces are thus crucial for understanding the ability of some individuals and the social groups in which they are members to claim and exercise power in welfare states. Recall the insight shared by Jenny, the Aboriginal mother quoted at length above: 'When we build identity in the home [caregiving] we build community and when we build community, we strengthen the power of the whole.'

By challenging us to reconsider what counts as social activity and resistance, such qualitative evidence invites a second observation: we need to investigate further what count as *the sites* of the social from perspectives that are sceptical of the public/private divide that has dominated so much thinking in liberal theory. While I have argued elsewhere that African American feminist scholarship lends support for the thesis that some 'private' time may indeed be necessary for social inclusion (Kershaw 2005: chapter 6), participants in the Care, Identity and Inclusion Project affirm that the thesis also has merit in Canada and other ethnically diverse populations. Access to 'private' venues, such as citizens' self-defined domestic spheres, is therefore a subject of debate that merits attention when thinking about contemporary citizenship because of the social (in addition to personal) value such access yields.

Contrary, then, to dominant presumptions in the social sciences, which Isin et al. (introduction, this volume) report have traditionally defined redistribution and recognition as separate, even antagonistic, domains of justice, care perspectives motivate a third observation: some struggles for recognition cannot be fully appreciated apart from debates about redistribution, at least in terms of the redistribution of care entitlements and obligations. Although barriers to sufficient family time are rarely considered in debates about social inclusion, state practices in a wide range of public policy domains are implicated, including employment standards and norms that define 'full-time' paid work in ways that render it difficult to thrive in this role while also shouldering primary responsibility for child care. But although employment norms risk crowding out time to care for all citizens regardless of their social locations, barriers to family time continue to loom particularly large among minority ethnic groups. Immigration policies, for example, issue only temporary visas to foreign domestics, which forbid their sponsorship of loved ones until they care exclusively for Canadians for at least two years (Bakan and Stasiulis 1997). New landed immigrants face difficulties in sponsoring elderly family members from abroad (Chen, this volume); and child welfare practices disproportionately remove Aboriginal children from their ethnocultural families and communities (Kline 1995). Such policies are reminiscent of immigration practices before the mid-1940s when Asian-born male migrants were prevented from bringing their own family members to Canada, as well as the residential school system, which inflicted tremendous harm on First Nations by separating Aboriginal children from their families (Dua 1999). Just as these historically enforced separations saw 'the demand for a 'family" context of their choosing become 'a central issue' among members of minority ethnic communities (245), so the redistribution of family time deserves renewed attention as we re-examine the social in the current context, in part out of recognition of the importance of such 'private' time for identity politics.

Just as redistribution of care opportunities is an important issue for public debate, so redistribution of care obligations is equally significant because, as I argue above, caregiving is a social obligation of citizenship. Any adequate reconceptualization of the social must engage directly with cross-cultural patterns that witness many men empowered as citizens by their ability to free-ride on the socially valuable caregiving of diverse groups of women. The ongoing unequal distribution of care responsibilities across sex, race, class, citizenship, and other lines of identity generates deleterious consequences for women citizens and foreign domestics that manifest themselves in the feminization of poverty, the gender earnings gap, occupational segregation, higher rates of time-stress among women, and conditional residency permits for non-citizens. Since remedying such harmful outcomes involves obliging men to shoulder a fair share of caregiving, the care debates that I analyse above motivate a fourth observation about the social in contemporary citizenship: there is reason to embrace (albeit cautiously) the shift in discourse about redistribution that is moving away from a relatively singular focus on social rights to one that adds heightened interest in social obligations (Isin et al. introduction, this volume). While critics of neoliberal restructuring often regard the rise of duty discourses to signal a loss, a retreat from the progressive elements of 'Marshallian' social citizenship (e.g., Shaver 2002, King and Wickham-Jones 1999), care debates show that such critiques are too casual in their eagerness to dismiss the potential value of duty discourses for analytical perspectives that are ultimately critical of neoliberal policy change. At the very least, feminist scholars are among the most fervent critics of neoliberalism (Bezanson and Luxton 2006, Kingfisher 2002), and many have long embraced duty discourses of their own in order to problematize male irresponsibility (Kershaw 2006).

The public failure to oblige most men to perform daily child caregiving to the degree that most women are so obliged, along with very meagre public investments in child care services and welfare benefits by international standards, points to a fifth observation: even in affluent Canadian provinces like British Columbia, the social remains nascent and has considerable room to grow in order to genuinely nurture families with young children. This observation stands in stark contrast to descriptions of the social offered by Tom Courchene (1997: 81) and John Richards (1997: 250), influential commentators about social policy reform in Canada. Over a decade ago, they both argued that the major components of social policy architecture in this country had 'matured' or been well 'established,' notwithstanding the need for some modest adjustments. But this claim misrepresents the social policy history in Canada and other affluent capitalist democracies. Although postwar policy in economies expanded the collectivity's role in care provision through, among other things, enhanced medical care coverage and pension entitlement, the legacy of patriarchy and the sexual division of labour positioned the state to obfuscate from the political arena the majority of daily caregiving performed predominantly by diverse groups of women for no or little pay. In the light of such gender inequalities, as well as the social, economic, and demographic shifts that are implicated with postindustrialism, innovative social architecture development remains necessary with regard to issues like child care services, which were less salient during the first decades immediately following the Second World War.

It is imperative to acknowledge, however, that it is not only gendered power dynamics that obstruct the expansion of social care architecture for families with young children, nor related regressive dynamics that track racialized and class hierarchies. Rather, the above discussion of social care conflicts forecasts a final noteworthy observation about the social in contemporary citizenship. At present, the social care advancement in which Canadians take the most pride – publicly provided medical care – now obstructs other social investment. The obstruction rests in large part with the fact that, culturally speaking, publicly funded medical care is so important to our sense of selves as Canadians; it is a common feature of our social fabric to which we point when distinguishing ourselves from the United States. But this status risks positioning the maintenance, if not enhancement, of medical care investment beyond reproach from either the left or right of the political spectrum. The implication is ironic: since medicalized spending absorbs ever growing shares of public expenditure, if we leave unquestioned the place of medical care in our commitments to social care, we risk our health by failing to invest in its social determinants.

Notes

1 These six answers reflect in part a synthesis of several previous publications in which I examine the place of caregiving in citizenship from a variety of perspectives. The synthesis in this chapter is important for alerting readers to the full potential of the social care concept when recasting citizenship scholarship. But this strength also entails the risk of navigating rapidly over a wide terrain. Readers are therefore encouraged to consult the references to other published works for greater detail about the range of social care themes summarized below.

2 See *The Daily.* Tuesday, March 2006. "Women in Canada." Last accessed 25 Feb 2008 http://www.statcan.ca/Daily/English/060307/d060307a.htm.

3 Given that jurisdictional responsibility for family policy diffuses across federal and provincial boundaries, it is necessary to explore benefit packages in Canada within specific provinces. I have shown elsewhere that the B.C. and Alberta packages cluster with one another in terms of their limited generosity relative to other international states (Kershaw 2007) and that residents of other provinces outside of Quebec should expect that their benefit packages for families with young children will resemble those in Western Canada.

4 Multicultural Citizenship beyond Recognition

DANIELLE JUTEAU

The announcement in the spring of 2004 that the recently created Islamic Institute of Civil Justice (IICJ) intended to conduct arbitrations according to Islamic personal law triggered a flurry of reactions that spread beyond national boundaries and lasted well over two years (WLUWL 2005). The president of the IICJ, Syed Mumtaz Ali, declared that Shari'a-based arbitration would be effectuated within the terms of the Arbitration Act of Ontario set up in 1991 to resolve most civil matters – including family law – privately, without recourse to the court system (METRAC 2005: 4).[1]

From the very beginning, multiculturalism framed the debate. Proponents argued that under multiculturalism the governments of Canada and Ontario recognize the rights of communities to live as fully as possible according to their ethnic, cultural, and religious practices, that the principles of multiculturalism entailed acceptance of such tribunals, and that the Ontario government had already set up a precedent in allowwing Aboriginals and Hassidic Jews to use their own laws (CCMW 2004: 6–14). Throughout the process, prominent members of the dominant majority agreed with this interpretation. For Canada's Minister of Justice, Irwin Cotler, there was no need for alarm, since arbitration according to religious guidelines already existed, and recourse was on a voluntary basis. Marion Boyd recommended such arbitration in her report,[2] 'Protecting Choice, Promoting Inclusion,' submitted to the premier of Ontario on 20 December 2004. She argued that the laws of Canada are based on Judeo-Christian values, and since the latter are inappropriate to other faiths, she recommended the tribunals. At a later point in time, English-speaking Canada's national newspaper, the *Globe and Mail*, also came down in favour of these tribunals in its editorial entitled, 'No cause to dread Islamic arbitration.' Multiculturalism is touted as the quintessential Canadian value, a symbol of 'our' leadership on the international scene: 'Canada is the new world, making possible an experiment where Islamic traditions, fairness to women and democracy can be compatible' (Editorial, *Globe and Mail*, 31 Aug. 2005). Worries about sexual equality were deemed unwarranted.

Conversely, many opponents to the Islamic tribunals were against multiculturalism. The conservative Heritage Party strongly objected, insisting that Canadian values are Christian values and that faiths are neither equal nor of equal value. Therefore, they concluded, the scripture should be the basis of Canadian law. Some feminists opposed to Islamic tribunals also rejected multiculturalism. When in August 2005 Ayaan Hirsi Ali came to Canada to support opposition to religious arbitration, she proffered a strong critique of the Western multiculturalism trap, 'which declares that group rights are more important than individual rights, and that all cultures are equal' (Editorial, *Globe and Mail*, 20 Aug. 2005).

Multiculturalism has thus been propelled to centre stage, at a time when many Western democracies are having second thoughts about its desirability, and what has been a contested site from its very inception remains so. This points to the significance and divisiveness of the issues involved, the shifting meaning of the term, and the often-contradictory practices that it embodies, but also, as this chapter contends, to an impasse that plays itself out in the political and theoretical arenas. Should we simply reject multiculturalism once and for all? This, I believe, would be a hasty move, a wrong one perhaps. Instead, I propose a theoretical move, a shift from the now-dominant philosophical perspective on multiculturalism to a sociological one that focuses on social relations, their multiplicity, and their complex articulation. This approach, that the expression 'recasting the social in citizenship' captures well, broadens the notion of equality and expands its analysis. Social relations analysis allows me to transcend the equality versus difference dichotomy, now recycled as redistribution versus recognition, and to reconceptualize debates around multiculturalism.

First, I explore the debates surrounding multiculturalism, their increasingly frequent link to citizenship, and their embeddedness within philosophical discourses (Barry 2001; Kymlicka 1995; Rorty 2000; Taylor 1994; Tully 2000, 2002; Young 1990). Then I revisit the current state of the debate over recognition and redistribution (Benhabib 2002; Butler 1998;

Fraser 1995, 2000; Honneth 2001; Phillips 1997; Smith 2001; Swanson 2005; Young 1997), tying it to the long-standing opposition between equality and difference. I consider the shortcomings of these approaches, which just can't seem to transcend the old Marxist division of base and superstructure. I engage in this well-travelled path with lenses provided by a sociology that draws on Max Weber's[3] and others, critiques of Marxist reductionism, such as Stuart Hall's account (1986) of vertical and horizontal reductionism. Rejecting vertical reductionism, Hall conceptualizes the political and ideological dimensions of social relations and, more importantly, offsets horizontal reductionism by incorporating 'other types of social differentiation such as social divisions and contradictions around race, ethnicity, nationality, or gender' (10).

I propose a relational and transversal analysis that overcomes the static perspectives of a mosaiclike multiculturalism (Gilroy 2004), such as the reification of difference, the homogenization of groups, the erasure of power differentials, and the reduction of economic equality to class and of ethnic equality to culture. This induces a shift, viewed in ideal-typical terms, from a philosophical-legal discourse that emphasizes the culture of homogeneous groups with static boundaries, to a historical-political one (Foucault 2003) that recognizes existing struggles between and within dominant and subordinate ethnic groups with divergent material and ideal interests. The very different conceptions of multiculturalism and multicultural citizenship brought to light by a transversal analysis are then used to make sense of the different positions articulated during the debate over the proposed establishment of Shari'a-inspired tribunals in Ontario.

Recognition versus Redistribution

Difference versus Equality

Most societies are multicultural, that is, they comprise at least two ethnically differentiated groups; therefore, the basic normative issue is not whether we should have a multicultural society, but rather, what kind of multicultural society we wish to live in (Ten 1993: 61). How should ethnic diversity be handled? Societies such as Canada have developed a politics and an ideology of multiculturalism while others, France, for example, strongly reject it (Withol de Wenden 2003).

For many observers, multiculturalism has represented a step towards greater equality, unlike assimilationism, which imposes the world view of dominant majorities onto others. But it was also immediately challenged on the ground that it reinforces social inequalities. For John Porter (1975), recognizing ethnic differences reproduces status hierarchies. For Kogila Moodley (1984) ethnicized categories reinforce racialization and exclusionary practices. Their misgivings bring us back to an older debate grounded in the Enlightenment and the French republican position, which treats difference and equality as an either/or choice: difference implies inequality, equality therefore requires the erasure of difference. Nonetheless, advocates of multiculturalism have pursued their defence of multicultural policies and practices as a route towards greater symbolic equality. A socioeconomic dimension was eventually added to cultural equality (Breton 1984), as proponents of multiculturalism argued that difference-blind policies were tantamount to inequality and should be replaced by differential treatment such as affirmative action and anti-racist programs.

As the debate became associated with citizenship, a distinct strand of thought, closer to philosophy, appeared. Defenders of multiculturalism, the most convincing being Charles Taylor (1994), viewed the recognition of culture and identity as the fundamental right. For these multiculturalists, culture is central because persons cannot be detached from contingent aspects of personality provided by history, society, culture, and family (Kelly 2002: 9–39). They give priority to the significance of identity, especially to the importance of religion and culture in identity formation. The respect for culture entails a duty to recognize the standing and claims of other cultures. Misrecognition entails inequality, and recognition therefore becomes a central component of equality.

This position has been attacked by scholars such as Brian Barry (2001) who claims that the value of culture is not compatible with an equal engagement towards egalitarianism, culture and equality being fundamentally incompatible commitments. Paul Kelly (2002: 13) summarizes this position: 'The multiculturalist preoccupation with culture is a distraction from the real sources of unequal treatment and injustice. The primacy attached to culture obscures the fact that what minority groups really want are the rights and resources enjoyed by those in positions of dominance and power, rather than the protection of cultural hierarchies that benefit those who enjoy the position of cultural entrepreneurs.'

For egalitarians such as Barry, poverty, unemployment, and lack of education are the truly terrible things. Hence, redistribution, conceived as socioeconomic equality, is preferred over recognition and cultural equality. Although one can disagree with Barry's tone, his emphasis on economic and political imbalances deserves attention. Does acknowledging his question take us back to square one? I do not think so, and we need not share his conclusions. Nonetheless, surmounting this divide, this false opposition between difference and equality requires that we address problematic and unproblematized issues from a fresh angle. For this, I first turn to authors who have sought to connect recognition with redistribution, and explain why their efforts fall short of their goal.

Reuniting Recognition and Redistribution

In her lead article, published in 1995,[4] Nancy Fraser portrays redistribution and recognition as two analytically distinct and irreducible paradigms of justice. While redistribution is about socioeconomic injustices (such as exploitation, economic marginalization, and deprivation), the recognition paradigm sees injustices as cultural (rooted, e.g., in patterns of representation, interpretation, and communication). Fraser indicates how (1995: 73) the two intertwine since the economy is shot through with significations and norms, while discursive practices have a constitutive political economy dimension. Likewise, the remedies to maldistribution and to misrecognition, which are analytically distinct, remain 'interimbricated,' since redistributive remedies require an underlying conception of recognition and vice versa. Both paradigms must be used to explain social struggles, the main question being the relation between the two claims.

Fraser identifies four types of collective formations – class, gender, race, and despised minorities – that are located on a continuum from redistribution to recognition. Gender and race, she affirms, have consequences both in the redistributive and recognition schemes. To eliminate gender discrimination, for instance, one must restructure socioeconomic relations and alter the schemata of recognition. Hence, changes in recognition have distributive consequences, and transformations in cultural status can result in socioeconomic improvements. The problem rests with Fraser's treatment of class and despised minorities, which she reduces to one side of the equation: redistribution or recognition. Yet, class is also about cultural capital (Bourdieu), and despised minorities also encounter economic exclusion. All collective formations should be envisaged as including both components. The two intermediate categories, Fraser adds, point to a dilemma: struggles to overcome maldistribution tend towards dedifferentiation (such as abolishing social classes and the gendered division of labour), and struggles to overcome misrecognition promote group specificity. In this bivalent mode of collectivity, the solutions pull in different directions, as redistribution involves dedifferentiation, and recognition involves differentiation. Fraser seems to overlook that some differentiated groups (such as racialized ones) do question the existence of a category that naturalizes and fixes their identity.[5] Also problematic is Fraser's distinction between affirmative struggles and transformative ones. Affirmative struggles (such as income transfers or gay identity politics) do not abolish classes or despised minorities, in other words, they do not alter the underlying structure. Only transformative actions can destabilize existing categories, redefine their underlying cultural-evaluational structure, and change everyone's sense of belonging (Fraser 1995: 83). Because Fraser reduces structure to the cultural-evaluational sphere, she can argue for sustaining a sexual field of multiple, debinarized, fluid, and ever-shifting differences. She seems to forget that symbolic structures are not free-floating, but are linked to material ones that embody differentiated, unequal, and often conflicting, social positions. Taking objective structures into account yields a different perspective: even though the sexual field is made up of shifting differences, the boundaries remain, as people traverse them through gender and sexual changes. But, then, if differentiated social positions were abolished, one could also envisage what Fraser has discarded, namely, the erasure of sexual boundaries and the dissolution of all sexual difference into a single universal human identity.

Fraser's critics allude to the still ambiguous relation between redistribution and recognition, which are treated as ontologically distinct categories, although they are not posited as such. They incriminate the unfortunate Marxian separation between base and superstructure, and articulate solutions to overcome this divide. In examining them, I will indicate why they still fall short of their goal. I begin with Iris Young, because her assessment, one of the earlier ones, remains most pertinent. She is critical of Fraser's dual systems theory that separates the two forms of injustices. In making this separation (1997: 148), Fraser retreats from the New Left's project of theorizing the material effects of culture, since recognition and identity have material consequences and foundations. And because she fails to understand that political economy is cultural and culture is economic (154),[6] Fraser cannot surmount the old infrastructure versus superstructure dichotomy. Although they are seen as connected, that is, changes in the economic sphere affect the cultural one and vice versa, the two paradigms are treated as distinct variables and are not integrated. Unlike Young, Fraser maintains that she treats recognition and redistribution as interpenetrating, and that she proposes a perspectival duality, not dualism (128).

Young puts forward a materialist theory of culture that does not envisage struggles for redistribution and recognition as contradictory. She qualifies as superficial (1997: 152) Fraser's argument that a group cannot affirm its identity *and* eliminate its unequal position in the division of labour. This is an imagined political tension, since recognition constitutes for most social movements a means towards economic and political equality. In a move against reductionism, Young pluralizes social categories (race, gender, and so on) and combines the cultural and economic dimensions of social action. I agree with Young's position. For example, the nationalist movement in Quebec was about economic, political, and cultural equality, which were inseparable.[7] It is noteworthy that the global struggles of minorities are often reduced to their symbolic dimension, which masks the material aspects of their oppression.

Young's acknowledgment of the diversity of groups and forms of equality (1990) significantly advances this debate. She recognizes power relations and the unequal distribution of opportunities and, consequently, advocates a genuinely multicultural theory that accommodates them. This leads Young to defend outcome equality and proportional group representation, quotas, and affirmative action, as means of empowerment and social equality. Furthermore, her distinction between cultural and social groups is useful, for the latter are no longer envisaged as homogeneous and static, founded on shared attributes. Gendered, ethnicized, and racialized minorities are linked to unequal social positions, and they embrace different material and ideal interests.

Nonetheless, two issues remain unclear. When Young writes that equality is the first and foremost issue while cultural rights come second, she reverts to a narrow definition of equality and cultural groups. Moreover, these groups retain an indeterminate character, being little more than census categories (Kelly 2002: 66). In the end, Young too under-theorizes the link between social relations and group formation, detaching groups from the processes that underlie their emergence.

Anne Phillips (1997) offers an interesting commentary on the Fraser/Young controversy. Their main divergence, Phillips rightly contends, is not whether recognition and redistribution are analytically distinct or interwoven, since Fraser also sees them as interconnected. The key point rather is whether the things that we have separated are regarded as having a life of their own (149–50). Fraser stresses the potential conflicts that arise between the two forms of struggles, and Young is struck by their interconnection. Phillips agrees with Fraser on the very real split between class and identity politics. Because the socialist approach imputed the under-representation of racial or gendered minorities to their class position, the latter, and nothing else, was to be tackled.[8] Although this is problematic for Phillips, so is a politics of recognition, as it often engenders an essentialist notion of a unified voice. This obscures internal economic differences and, in some cases, displaces completely the economic. Yet, a politics of recognition that both emphasizes the cultural and refuses the importance of culture per se can support a politics of redistribution (150).[9] Fraser's deconstructive politics, which destabilize binary oppositions and challenge fixed identities, achieves this; however, Fraser's focus on destabilizing differences stops short of social relations, which narrows down the social.

Phillips (1997) confronts the shift from the material to the cultural, from inequality to difference, and from class to identity politics. She identifies the weakness (145) inherent in 'Left politics,' the hierarchy of causation that has separated the economy from the political and cultural superstructure and that has described real interests in terms of class relations. But now, Phillips notes (146), critics question even the primacy of political economy, and what was supposed to be an enlargement of Marxism has turned into excising the economic. Yet, as she justly reminds us, violence against women, for example, must be situated within the broader framework of women's economic subordination. Why, she also asks, (143), would equality depend on losing distinctive features? Is erasure not impossible, as in the case of racial and sexual difference? Either cultural minorities want to celebrate their difference (recognition) or they want to take their difference into the economic sphere, because colour- or gender-blind policies do not redress maldistribution. Although Phillips is not wrong, she seems to imply that already existing differences are brought into other spheres, rather than explaining how difference is constituted through social relations, which here, once again, are erased.[10] But before moving on to the relations that constitute the social, I turn to Judith Butler (1998).

Poststructuralism saddled Marxism with a focus that did not situate culture within a systematic understanding of social and economic modes of production, and new social movements (NSM) were relegated to the sphere of culture and identity (ibid.: 33–4). The charge that NSM are merely cultural and that a unified and progressive Marxism must return to a materialism based on an objective analysis of class is an anachronism that presumes a stable distinction between material and cultural life. Quoting Laclau and Mouffe, Butler argues that new political formations do not stand in an analogical relation to one another but are overlapping, mutually determining, and convergent fields of politicization (37). How political formations interrelate is examined in her section on queer struggles, which are viewed, contrary to Fraser, as central to the political economy (40). Socialist feminists showed how the reproduction of persons and the social regulation of sexuality are part of the process of production and therefore, of the political economy. Butler rightly connects recognition to redistribution, but she does not emphasize, as do materialist feminists, that the sexual division of labour cuts across society and constitutes an analytically distinct mode of production (patriarchy) or system (*sexage*). The issue is not only a reductionist analysis of class but the erasure of other social relations.

Fraser responds that her work challenges the primacy of the economic, bridging the gap between base and superstructure, and between primary and secondary oppression (1998: 141). To better capture the distinction between redistribution and recognition, she introduces the concept of status group. While it does clarify matters,[11] it hardly seems ground-breaking since Weber introduced it about a century ago – precisely to overcome the reductionism of class analysis. Maybe this is why (some) sociologists experience a feeling of déjà vu in face of a narrative that rehashes old stories. Furthermore, Fraser dispenses with (1998, 2000) the relational dimension that Weber uses in his analysis of group formation. For instance, Weber (1978) singles out differences in economic and social articulations, as well as unequal structures of power, to explain why and when common attributes, a common situation, and common feelings towards a common situation engender ethnic communalizations, groups, and boundaries. Moreover, while Weber clearly differentiates status groups from classes, he also views status groups such as ethnic groups as constructed through economically defined social relations of monopolistic closure (Juteau-Lee 1979). Although Fraser (1998: 143) focuses on devaluation as an impediment to participatory parity, she fails to establish the link between the devalued individuals, their minority position, and the attribution of difference.

Finally, some problems remain in Fraser's analysis of differentiated forms of oppression. Gay and lesbian struggles, she argues (1998: 146), will most probably not threaten capitalism in its actual form, but they do have an economic dimension. This brings Fraser to discard (147–9) the functionalist argument that resurrects 'the overtotalized view of capitalist society as a monopolistic "system" of interlocking structures of oppression that seamlessly reinforce one another,' and to reject destabilization in favour of historicization and the contradictory character of specific social relations. While I agree with her on the first point, I will suggest that we recognize and articulate analytically distinct systems of oppression (Hall 1985, 1986).

In *The Claims of Culture: Equiality and Diversity in the Global Era* (2002), Seyla Benhabib deplores the rehashing of the Marxian dichotomy of base and superstructure that now feeds the split between redistribution and recognition. Most important is her critique of the inadequate treatment of group formation (17) in recent analyses of multicultural citizenship. She singles out Taylor and Kymlicka's faulty epistemic premise (4), a reductionist sociology that produces an objectivist, fixed, and holistic definition of culture and groups and engenders a static mosaiclike view of multiculturalism. Although one can applaud Benhabib's emphasis on the constant creation and recreation of culture – an approach that has informed sociological and anthropological theories of ethnicity since Fredrick Barth (1969) – she limits her argument to the symbolic sphere, to identities and negotiations across imaginary cultural boundaries. Boundaries, she submits, are imaginary since the Other is always inside us; this is not false, but it remains an incomplete statement that masks differentiated, unequal, and conflicting positions and interests. Can we say, for example, that an ethnic majority is positioned within the boundaries of the minority and vice versa? Identities are flexible and hybrid, and boundaries permeable and changing, but there also exists an objective sphere, where dominant and subordinate positions shape distinct life chances, as in the case of Aboriginals and 'Whites.' Because Benhabib focuses on the symbolic sphere, and views multiculturalism as concerned with struggles for recognition, the egalitarian she is prefers the vocation of the democratic theorist to that of the multiculturalist. So, in the end, she too fails to rise above the Marxian dichotomy of base and superstructure.

Finally, Anna Marie Smith (2001) explores the culturalist versus economist divide from a slightly different, and promising angle, which opposes the liberal depoliticization of difference to leftist orthodox thinkers. Smith advocates a radical democratic project that situates cultural analyses of identity politics within political economy contexts, with reference to distribution of wealth, employment trends, urban planning, and welfare policies (103). This sheds new light on Butler's and Fraser's discussions of sexuality. First, Smith points to Fraser's eccentric and analytical Weberianism that underplays historical contexts and trajectories (113–16). The ensuing focus on abstract subjects with a voluntaristic political practice overestimates the possibility of convincing existing subjects of their best interests on the basis of rational arguments (114–17). A poststructural approach that remains sceptical of instrumental rational intentions and underscores the embeddedness of subjects in social structures offers a deeper perspectivism.

Consequently, Smith prefers Butler's deeper perspectivism and deconstructivism, which integrates the regulation of sexuality with political economy (ibid.: 105). Smith's disagreement with Fraser is empirical, since there are economic dimensions to homophobia, *and* theoretical, because the two politics cannot be separated, even analytically. Since the economic sphere contains the cultural sphere within itself as its condition of possibility (106), normative heterosexuality is essential to the functioning of the sexual order of the political economy. In this Derridean interpretative strategy (106), the cultural is the condition of possibility for the economic, which is an inversion of Louis Althusser's totalism (107). But here, Smith argues, Butler subsumes the entire field of social policy under the cultural, remaining blind to the conditioning effects of state, and other, institutions. The weakness of Butler's analysis lies in a deconstructivism that does not go far enough, in a quasi-absence of institutional analysis. Moving ahead requires that we leave structuralism behind and concentrate on mutually constitutive relations. It also means that we not only interconnect different forms of injustices but articulate the social relations underlying maldistribution and misrecognition.

Bridging the Divide: A Transversal Approach

Recent debates surrounding recognition and redistribution point to the difficulties encountered by philosophers and political theorists in surmounting the Marxian divide of base and superstructure, despite their critique of economism. This can be remedied by drawing more systematically from the relational perspective of sociology, a discipline that places social relations at centre stage and theorizes their complex articulation. Doing this takes us back to Stuart Hall, when he argued in the 1980s against a reductionism that 'simplifies the structure of social formations, reducing their articulation, vertical and horizontal, to a single line of determination' (1986: 11). But at the time, academia was poised to discard a discourse overly centred, it was felt then, on oppression, domination, binaries, foundationalism, and essentialism.

Against vertical reductionism, Hall puts to use the concepts of overdetermination and hegemony. Society is to be envisaged as a structure comprised of relations where every phenomenon is fundamentally constituted by a complex set of processes. No social practice is purely economic, cultural, or political, and the mediation between these differentiated levels cannot be simple or immediate. This is not to say that everything interacts in a muddled way but that society presents a specific shape, a configuration, a definite structuration (1985: 91). Against horizontal reductionism, Hall points to a multiplicity of social contradictions, with different social origins, which bring about differentiated categories such as class, race, and gender. When we envisage society as structured by analytically distinct social relations and by the intricate mediation between their material and symbolic components, a broader and deeper conceptualization of the social emerges.

Against Vertical and Horizontal Reductionism

A recent article by Jacinda Swanson (2005) presents a similar take on vertical reductionism. Returning to the anti-essentialist critiques of Marxian theory (Laclau and Mouffe 1985, Resnick and Wolff 1996), she too employs the concept of overdetermination to apprehend the complex relations between economic, political, and cultural processes (2005: 95), each of these categories serving as a shorthand for different aspects of social practices and institutions.

This allows Swanson to identify the (ibid.: 90) multiple and distinct forms of oppression within each of Fraser's overly binarized categories (recognition and redistribution), which must be further disaggregated and reconnected to political processes. Swanson accounts for different types of economic struggles and economic practices that occur throughout society, across different sites such as the household and schools. She (104) favours hegemony and hegemonic formation to dispose of a mechanistic and simplistic notion of structure, and to emphasize the sheer volume and complexity of the conditions of existence of capitalism, sexism, racism, and heterosexism. Hegemony is preferable to the concept of groups, because not everybody in a group is positioned similarly, which explains the diversity of analyses and political responses. This diversity, Swanson finds, is ignored by Young, because of the latter's overly broad distinction between culture and structure (88) does not theorize the permanent or evolving aspects of structures, nor the exact connections among differentiated social positions.

Swanson then focuses explicitly on group formation, and how she proceeds is most revealing. She discards overdetermination in favour of Butler's concept of reiteration, namely, the repetition of social practices since 'ending oppression means convincing and enabling individuals to cease reiterating unjust social practices and to engage instead in more just economic, cultural, and political practices' (ibid.: 105). Swanson introduces the notion of translation (108), a difficult labour through which social movements converge against a backdrop of ongoing contestation over strategies and goals. But why resort to reiteration and translation? Why focus primarily on changing practices and convergence, and occlude domination, divergences, unequal access to resources, vested interests, and resistance to change? Is it because Swanson's emphasis on *conditions* of existence moves attention away from their relational aspect? Because reiteration is about individual practices? Because social practices are separated from social positions? Because translation brings out the diversity of goals rather than their divergences? Or still, because it is easier to relate to counter-hegemonic struggles that translate between different universals (110–11) than focus on oppression and exploitation? Not surprisingly, then, the task for the 'Left' is to identify commonalities among these movements rather than to choose between their sometimes irreducible interests. Focusing on translation and reiteration leads Swanson to define sexism and racism as cultural forms of oppression, while she remains, so it seems, oblivious to their economic and political dimensions, and to their multiple lines of determination. Thus, in the end, Swanson too relegates sexism and racism to the superstructure, or more to the point, links them to an infrastructure that is equated with class. A more adequate answer requires an analysis of horizontal reductionism in complex social formations.

In his Gramscian critique of horizontal reductionism, Stuart Hall (1986: 25) makes a case for a non-reductive analysis of the relations between race, class, and gender. Although the law of value has had a tendency to homogenize labour power, one cannot assume that homogenization exists in any concrete society. In fact, the law of value operates through the culturally specific character of labour power, as becomes evident when departing from a Eurocentric model of capitalist development. As Hall argues, (25–6), capital adapts, it harnesses and exploits these particularistic qualities of labour power, leading to the maintenance and development of the ethnic, racial, and gendered structuration of the labour force: 'We would get much further along the road to understanding how the regime of capital can function through differentiation and difference, rather than through similarity and identity, if we took more seriously this question of the cultural, social, national, ethnic, and gendered composition of historically different and specific forms of labour' (26).

Although Hall acknowledges different forms of the division of labour and the heterogeneity of class subjects, he limits his thoughts to labour power within capitalist relations. He does not clearly link social differentiation to other forms of appropriation and exploitation, which remain analytically distinct from class. The ethnic, racial, and gendered structuration of the labour force will now be articulated with multiple and differentiated social relations.

A Transversal Analysis of Social Relations

Many of the discussions around race and class (Solomos 1988) were precisely about overcoming a Marxist approach that reduced race to class (Miles 1988), such as proposed in models of autonomy and relative autonomy. The autonomy model explored the specific relations through which race was constituted, namely, the appropriation of bodies and labour power through slavery, an analytically distinct system comprising the institutions of slavery and the ideology of racism. This line of thought was carried by Omi and Winant (1986) in their analysis of racial social formation in the United States as an autonomous field of inquiry. The latter comprises, they argues, interrelated structures that exploit and exclude, while also fostering resistance and struggles, and although this organizing principle does not function in a vacuum, it must be differentiated from class, so as to bring out the experiences specific to African Americans in relation to 'whites.'

A similar discussion went on in relation to class and sex-gender. Materialist feminists criticized Marxist and socialist feminists for reducing women's oppression to capitalism and paying little attention, so it seemed, to sexual oppression per se, which affects all women, across race, ethnicity, class (Juteau and Laurin 1989). The rejection of this perspective as essentializing and as postulating a universal woman,[12] indicates a profound, and persisting, misunderstanding. Materialist feminists (not to be confused with radical feminists) used the Marxian concept of social relations to explain the formation of sexualized categories. Colette Guillaumin (1978) theorized *sexage* – the specific set of social relations through which women's bodies and labour power are appropriated – as constitutive of sex classes. These relations pre-date capitalism and articulate with different modes of production. Materialist feminists also theorized how *sexage* operates, how it transforms itself historically, and how it varies in relation to other subject positions. Sylvia Walby, for example, views patriarchal social relations as an evolving system of interlocking structures such as domestic work, paid work, the state, male violence, and sexuality (1986: 52–3). This transversal approach envisages multiple and interlocking social relations that cut across society and operate at different sites.

Applying a Marxian framework to the formation of categories other than social classes subverts orthodox Marxism, while an analysis that recognizes the multiplicity of analytically distinct social relations[13] inevitably transcends horizontal and vertical reductionism. Society can no longer be apprehended as a grid comprising two separate and mechanically related categories of infrastructure and superstructure but emerges as a structured totality that contains a multiplicity of interconnected social relations (SRs), where material and symbolic structures intertwine. For each social field, let's say the racial one, there exists a specific form of exploitation and appropriation. Economic dynamics occur within each social field and cannot be reduced to social class, because economic maldistribution must be further disaggregated into different forms, sexualized, racialized, classed. Finally, economic dynamics must also be apprehended in relation to other dimensions, political, legal, cultural, of society.

(In)equality now appears as broad and multifaceted, involving economic, political, and cultural types of misdistribution, which further tie into differentiated subject positions. I now apply this transversal approach to ethnic social relations, groups, and boundaries, and indicate how it provides an alternate perspective on multiculturalism.

Recasting the Social in Multiculturalism

A Transversal Analysis of Ethnic Relations

A transversal approach envisages ethnic, racial, and national groups as constituted through a specific set of social relations that includes 'voluntary' and involuntary migration – slavery, conquest, and annexation (Juteau-Lee 1979, Simon 1983). Transverse analysis to theorizes how these relations underlie the construction of boundaries, their fluctuation, and the choice of marks that identify the newly constituted groups. It indicates that ethnic boundaries are not drawn automatically around unchanging cultural attributes, and they cannot be reduced to the cultural stuff of which they are made (Barth 1969). In other words, boundaries can remain as culture changes. Through a complex process, relations to the Other and to historical trajectories, both individual and collective, construe boundaries that simultaneously possess an internal and an external dimension. Aboriginals in Canada, for example, were constituted through French colonialism and in relation to their collective history. In other words, French colonialism did not create Aboriginals ex nihilo, but it did transform their position, their boundaries, and their identities (Juteau 1999).

These communities of history and culture comprise economic, political, and normative dimensions. Weber examined how these dimensions interweave, as processes of monopolistic closure create an ethnic division of labour that (re)produces ethnic boundaries (Juteau-Lee 1979). Ethnic stratification espouses many forms: ethnic groups are stratified internally and in relation to one another, and each occupational category is also ethnically stratified. Class analysis cannot account for this. The same applies to gendered inequalities, which only make sense when apprehended in terms of the unpaid and unfree labour performed by women in the private and public spheres. The articulation of analytically distinct relations recognizes different forms of economic exploitation and links them to various political and ideological structures, such as sexism and racism.

Thus, the claims of culturally defined groups cannot be reduced to culture. Aboriginals in Canada vie for economic equality, greater political autonomy, control over language and the judiciary, as well as over their normative orientations. Equality can also not be reduced to the economy, and economic (in)equality cannot be reduced to class. The distinct contribution made by a social relations approach in philosophical discourse will now be drawn out.

Differentiation and the Construction of Difference

In spite of their divergent views, liberal and communitarian philosophers usually share a common blind spot. As Benhabib observes, they essentialize difference – treating it as a given founded in nature or in culture. Ethnic groups are reified and substantialized, envisaged as the sum of individuals sharing ethnic attributes. Adding their differences yields a specific configuration, around which boundaries are traced. Not surprisingly, then, ethnic groups are perceived as static and homogeneous, which occludes the often conflicting material and ideal interests of their members.

Instead of beginning with difference and asking whether it should be taken into account, a transversal perspective treats differentiation as the central process, and difference, as its outcome. Transversal analysis begins with social relations, indicates how groups are constituted, how they are unequal (think, e.g., of Aboriginals and non-Aboriginals, blacks and whites, immigrants and non-immigrants), how this hierarchization connects with differentiation and with the construction of difference, and how marks are assigned (Juteau 2002). As Guillaumin points out (1977), the mark follows, it does not precede, the social relation. In this context, majorities,[14] that is, dominant groups, view themselves as universal, while they assign difference to minorities, that is, to subordinate groups. Veit-Michael Bader (1995) calls chauvinistic the universalism of dominant groups who are blind to their own specificity.

This, I am afraid, is Taylor's problem, when he opposes 'those who value remaining true to the culture of their ancestors' to 'those who might want to cut loose in the name of some individual goals of self-development' (1994: 68). In writing this, he overlooks that minorities are not the only ones who cling to their cultural values. He fails to notice that majorities do not voice such claims because their 'neutral' ideological and state institutions protect their particular values. In a social relations perspective, the effort made by minorities to control their boundaries is not interpreted as a desire to maintain past cultural orientations, but as having power over its content and the direction of change. Furthermore, the past decade leads me to believe that majorities too are very concerned with identity and boundary maintenance.

Social (In)equality and the Many Forms of Maldistribution

The dialectic between the right to equality and its actualization first unfolded around the social component of citizenship. It was argued that de facto equality requires a focus on substantive rather than formal rights, on equality of results rather than equality of opportunity. As more philosophers entered the debate around multicultural citizenship, discussions shifted from the social to the cultural and centred on identity and recognition. The notion of equality was reduced to its cultural dimension such as according equal value to different cultures. This culturalization of equality led to its corollary, the denial of culture and a refusal to take difference into account (Kelly 2002: 3). Equality is once again opposed to difference: it is reduced to the economy, and difference is reduced to the cultural. In this vertical reductionism, maldistribution is opposed to misrecognition, and their interconnections are lost.[15]

The transversal perspective presented here transcends horizontal reductionism, because it does not reduce the groups of multiculturalism to their cultural dimension, and consequently, does not limit their claims to recognition. Recognition is viewed as a specific quest for equality that is part and parcel of a broader redistributive process. Multicultural citizenship is not equated with cultural equality, as ethnic dynamics are seen to involve economic and political processes. Multiculturalism is about, or better still against, (mal)distribution, between ethnic, national, and racialized groups. Multiculturalism can focus on economic matters, involving programs such as affirmative action and anti-racism, but it can also focus on ideal interests – as in the case of the *hijab* or Shari'a-inspired arbitration tribunals. This is why, contrary to Barry, I contend that multiculturalism, at least this multiculturalism, is not incompatible with egalitarianism: it is egalitarianism. When the dualist opposition between recognition and redistribution is transcended, recognition can be envisaged as one dimension of redistribution.[16]

Multiculturalism: From a Philosophical-Legal Discourse to a Historical-Political One

The social relations approach presented here induces a shift, to use Foucault's (1997) terms, from a philosophical-legal discourse (and its pretence to universality and neutrality) to a historical-political one, which posits the existence of an asymmetrical legal order embedded in power structures. Philosophical and legal frameworks have sustained a multiculturalism imprisoned in the mould of the legal subject, abstract universalism, and the unity and legitimacy of power. On the other hand, a multiculturalism informed by political historicism[17] recognizes that past and present unequal relations structure world-system dynamics and struggles between, and within, racialized and ethnicized groups, over material resources and ideal interests, boundaries, and identities.

This shift engenders a radically different conceptualization of multiculturalism. In ideal-typical terms, two types of multiculturalism, and visions of equality, can now be contrasted. In the first multiculturalists champion recognition and the respect of cultural differences conceived as given and shared by a collectivity (Multiculturalism 1); they subscribe to either multiculturalism's liberal or communitarian strands. In the second type (Multiculturalism 2), multiculturalists stress the link between power, hierarchization, and differentiation, and emphasize redistribution that spans the economic, political, and cultural spheres. Paul Gilroy, I think, chooses this second option when he argues that the wholesome dream of multiculturalism has been replaced by 'the dry dogma of a ready-mixed multiculturalism' and that political conflicts in multicultural societies should be understood as existing 'firmly in a context supplied by imperial and colonial history' (2004: 2). The groups involved are no longer viewed as homogeneous and equal, but as traversed by other social relations such as sex and class, by struggles that connect their divergent material and ideal interests with global politics. These diverse ways of envisaging multiculturalism and putting it to use circulate in many quarters, as the following foray into the controversy over the proposed instauration of Islamic tribunals in Ontario, Canada, will illustrate.

Multiculturalism and Islamic Tribunals in Ontario

Multiculturalism, I have mentioned, was propelled to centre stage, and at first glance it seemed as though advocates of multiculturalism were for the tribunals, while opponents were against them. Multicultural values, the latter contend, override the spirit of Canadian equality and create false expectations in recent immigrants about their freedom in Canada[18] (Eisenberg 2005: 2). Denouncing the Boyd Report, the founder of the Muslim Canadian Congress, Tarek Fatah, submitted that multiculturalism had run amok (Kymlicka 2005: 1). Multiculturalism framed the debate, but what multiculturalism?

What Multiculturalism?

Closer scrutiny uncovers a more intricate situation. As Kymlicka (2005: 13) puts it, it was not multiculturalism, but private arbitration that had run amok. The latter was not recommended, nor was it funded, by the multiculturalism program. There were no suggestions that Ontario's Arbitration Act comply with the multiculturalism clause of Canada's Constitution Act constitution. There were no community-based deliberative procedures and no extensive processes of consultation within and between ethnic communities (12). The Arbitration Act was demanded and designed for mainstream society, who wanted a cheaper, quicker, and less adversarial form of dispute resolution. There were only a few critiques, and these stemmed mainly from women's groups. The act does not accord special privileges to religious groups: it establishes a legal framework within which anyone – religious or secular – can agree to use private arbitration to resolve disputes. No group is given special exemptions. As Kymlicka points out, 'the creation of a legal opening for faith-based family law tribunals was not the intended result of a process of multicultural reform; it was the accidental result of a legal reform to the system of private arbitration that was not mandated, inspired or guided by the multiculturalism policy,' (13).[19]

If multiculturalism as a program had nothing to do with the Arbitration Act, the ideology was nevertheless very present, and it framed arguments on both sides. Kymlicka (ibid.: 2–3) reports that different conceptions of multiculturalism, liberal or communitarian, surfaced. While a liberal conception of multiculturalism is based on the principle that individuals should be free to make their own choices about how to express ethnic and religious identity, a communitarian one is based on the principle of cultural relativism – groups should be able to practise their own customs whether or not they respect the principles of individual freedom, human rights, and democracy. Avigail Eisenberg also detects two conceptions of multiculturalism that are not always clearly spelled out. She calls them moderate and traditionalist – or radical (5). Syed Mumtaz Ali's traditional view of multiculturalism, notes Eisenberg, is often shared in Canadian and international interpretations – see Hirsi Ali above – within public and scholarly debates (5). Let me reiterate that both conceptions fit in what I have called Multiculturalism 1.

Clearly, multiculturalism has been put to many purposes, and used strategically by groups with opposing interests (ibid.: 5–6). In addition, people with similar interests – such as gender equality – have held different conceptions of multiculturalism, and therefore they have related differently to it and understood differently the relation between cultural equality and sexual equality. Let me begin to disentangle this.

The liberal perspective, linked to Multiculturalism 1, is often present, implicitly at least, in the discourses defending the Islamic tribunals (Boyd's Report, *Globe and Mail*),[20] but some of its defenders are closer to a communitarian view of Multiculturalism 1. The communitarian perspective is both similar to and different from the liberal one. It is similar in that it shares its shortcomings, substantialism, essentialism, and culturalism, and because (in)equality and power differentials are not viewed in relational terms. But the communitarian perspective is also different from the liberal perspective in that it requires collective rights, and this is not necessarily the correct interpretation of multicultural policies in Canada.[21] This communitarian perspective is what leads to deadlock, to the impasse illustrated by the positions of Syed Mumtaz Ali and Ayaan Hirsi Ali, who actually share a conception of multiculturalism, which reifies gendered and cultural groups, who are then differentiated in terms of their specific conception of sexual equality. As proponents of Islamic arbitration tribunals invoked multiculturalism to package their position for mainstream Canadians, opponents – such as women's groups and most newspapers – were put on the defensive (Eisenberg 2005: 5–6). The very reductionism that brought the 'Left' to reject multiculturalism in the name of economic equality now impelled some feminists to do likewise, to oppose multiculturalism in the name of gender equality, as in feminism against multiculturalism (Okin 1999). Here, defenders and opponents of Islamic tribunals share a common perspective, closer to the legal and philosophical conceptions of Multiculturalism 1.

Not all feminists, however, or other interest groups partake in the views linked to Multiculturalism 1. Implicitly at least, some uphold a vision that corresponds more to Multiculturalism 2 and to an overdetermined and complex structuration of society, although of course they do not use this terminology. More mindful of power relations and against Islamic arbitration tribunals, their different relation to multiculturalism offers an interesting portrait. I first look at women's associations, and then groups with a less specific agenda.

Multiculturalism, Feminism, and Intersectionalities

Women's groups, such as the Canadian Council of Muslim Women (CCMW) and the National Organization of Immigrant and Visible Minority Women of Canada (NOIVMW), as well as the internationally based Women Living Under Muslim Law (WLUML), spearheaded the battle against Islamic tribunals.

The CCWM was among the first to express apprehension when Mumtaz Ali announced his proposal to conduct religious arbitration. It met with Marion Boyd to deposit a written submission on 30 July 2004, and later in the fall to transmit the reports it had commissioned. The nuanced position of the CCWM conveys a two-fold concern, the permission of the government, via the Arbitration Act, for private agreements with binding arbitration for family matters, and permission to use a system of law that is vast, controversial, complex, and according to some Muslims, immutably divinely ordained (CCMW 2004: 2). Some criticisms include the following: the act is flawed; no records must be maintained; the process is private; arbitrators need no training. And who, they ask, will challenge the tribunal's decisions and uphold Charter rights? The CCMW suggests that the Ontario government follow Quebec's example and recognize the inappropriateness of all religiously informed arbitration for family matters (4). The CCMW distinguishes Shari'a from Islamic law: The former is a comprehensive religious term that defines how Muslims should live, while *fiqh* (Islamic law) refers to jurisprudence and is limited to the laws promulgated by Muslim scholars. Although no devout Muslims want to be against Shari'a, Muslim laws vary from country to country, because of the heterogeneity of the community of believers as to gendered and other interpretations of Shari'a. The CCMW is not against Shari'a, but current practices in other countries are not women positive and have adverse effects on them. Finally, the CCMW points to the fragmentation and the further marginalization of already vulnerable women.

The opposition of the CCMW is framed in terms of its adherence to Canadian values, including Canada's Charter of Rights and Freedoms. Article 28 of the Charter guarantees women's equality, and that this right should supersede when a woman might be treated unequally according to the practices espoused by a segment of religious practitioners. The CCMW states its unambiguous support of multiculturalism, as the 'CCMW is a strong believer in Canada's multiculturalism policy, for it celebrates our differences and allows groups such as ours to be proud of our multiple identities' (2004: 9). But it adds a word of caution: the celebration of differences should not lead to fragmentation. Ontario's Multiculturalism Act works within the broader framework of Canada's Constitution Act and human rights legislation. The CCMW cites Gila Stopler (2003) on how liberals tolerate cultural and religious practices that discriminate against women. When a conflict arises between women's rights and cultural practices, the focus should not be on choice, but on disadvantage, that is, does the practice in question disadvantage women? Finally, the CCMW reiterates that liberal multiculturalism can be employed as a tool to oppress women and put to political use in a struggle over competing conceptions of the world and women's place in it.

Thus, the Canadian Council of Muslim Women comes out against the tribunals while supporting a liberal version of multiculturalism (celebration of our differences). Yet it immediately critiques this multiculturalism, which puts choice over disadvantage and uses it to oppress women, thus moving in the direction of Multiculturalism 2.

Women Living Under Muslim Law also led a strong, and international, campaign to stop so-called Shari'a courts in Canada, which clearly revealed that power struggles were being played out in a larger international context. WLUML reaffirmes that Muslim women evolve in both majority and minority contexts, refers to their struggles in Muslim countries, states that extreme right forces manipulate religion to gain political power, and points out that not all immigrants from Islamic countries claim a Muslim identity, in view of their political and social diversity (WLUML 2005: 3). The organization's letter of solidarity, sent to the women of Canada on 4 July 2005, evokes an unholy alliance between fundamentalism and multiculturalism and the political manipulation of culture and identity. Fundamentalists are now articulating strategies in non-Islamic countries, and have managed – in the name of freedom of choice, of anti-racism, and the defence of collective rights – to penetrate progressive circles that adopt cultural relativist positions. The group's strong critique of Multiculturalism 1, which in this case is viewed in communitarian terms, is anchored in an analysis of globally operating power relations. We cannot address the prejudice and discrimination against immigrant Muslim communities, the WLUML affirms, by giving power and legitimacy to extreme right political movements (ibid.: 8). Anti-racists must link with progressive forces, and the WLUML suggests some Canadian women's rights and human rights groups either lent support to the demand for Islamic arbitration tribunals or were afraid to oppose them for fear of being labelled racist or islamophobic (7). Women Living Under Muslim Law questions the possibility of 'choice' for women who are embedded in unequal power relations, since family and community pressures severely limit a woman's right to exercise choice (3). Finally, the WLUML submits, the separation between the public and private domains does not mean that family matters should be relegated to private spaces. So, in the case of the WLUML, there is a strong rejection of a communitarian multicultural perspective and an emphasis on power struggles and differentiated interests.

Following the release of the Boyd Report, in December 2004, the Metropolitan Action Committee on Violence against Women and Children (METRAC) also criticized (2005: 2) mediation as inappropriate in cases when a power imbalance, due to abuse and violence, exists in a family. The committee acknowledges that the secular family law and court system falls short in respecting women's equality and ensuring the safety of women when they leave abusive relations. It recognizes that the public family law system is not really secular because it remains informed by Judeo-Christian principles and values. However, the committee expresses strong concern regarding the suitability of all religious laws or codes in resolving family law disputes and reiterates its commitment to work with, and support the position of Muslim organizations dedicated to women's equality, in particular the Canadian Council of Muslim Women, recognizing that these organizations offer the lived experience and expertise needed to lead this discussion (3).

METRAC's analysis (ibid.: 10–12) contributes essential insights. It points out that, to many immigrants, the Canadian legal system does not seem secular but Christian, and that the Arbitration Act allows private resolution according to any rules of law agreed to by the parties. But the committee opposes Boyd's recommendations. It is disappointed by the lack of gender-based analysis in the report and disagrees with Boyd's premise that women in Ontario are equal to men. While women have achieved formal equality, substantive equality remains largely elusive: women's salaries are lower than men's; post-separation, women and children often live in poverty; women are under-represented at senior levels in business and politics; in most families, women perform more child care activities; the primary victims of violence are women; and women from marginalized communities are particularly vulnerable (11) – since often men are considered to be heads of household holding power and physical discipline is seen as acceptable for 'misbehaviour,' while the women and children have little knowledge or access to their rights under Canadian law. Consequently, the members of METRAC ' take the position that, for many women leaving an abusive relationship, exercising free choice is an illusion' (12): After all the efforts made to bring family law and family violence into the public sphere, returning family law to the private realm is mistaken, as it will re-entrench the power imbalance between men and women. What is crucial here is the committee's observation regarding, first and foremost, women's inequality, which is simultaneously construed by ethnic relations. It does not set in opposition a dominant and 'advanced' ethnic majority characterized by sexual equality against ethnic, more specifically Muslim, communities, which lag behind. The committee's analysis apprehends sex-gender relations as operating across society, espousing different forms as they intersect with class, ethnicity, and race. There is little reference to multiculturalism, as METRAC offers a transversal analysis of sex and gender relations, pointing to sexual inequality, and the dangers of private arbitration for vulnerable groups such as women; at the same time, it recognizes, in an analysis that remains intersectional, the diverse positionalities of women.

Other organizations, such as the Humanist Association of Toronto (HAT), the Muslim Canadian Congress (MCC), and the Progressive Muslims Union of North America (PMU) also have reacted negatively to the Islamic tribunals, opposing all religious arbitration, and the possible privatization of Ontario's family law. Although they accept multiculturalism, these organizations criticize the danger of reification linked to the majority's ignorance of minority groups. Introducing the idea of power imbalances between and within groups, they offer, in effect, a transversal analysis of ethnic dynamics that moves them towards Multiculturalism 2.

The Humanist Association of Toronto questions the existence and possibility of true consent. The Muslim community, the PMU reiterates (2005: 2–3), is diversified, and consequently, internal debates over defining 'Muslim principles' abound. These principles are not codified, therefore, which ones – conservative, feminist, liberal, or progressive – would be used? Would the Canadian government take on the responsibility of answering this question, and in doing so, make rigid what is now fluid? Looking at the track record of those proposing Islamic arbitration tribunals, the PMU fears a restrictive reading of the Shari'a and not confident that the full range of interpretations would be presented (3). Instead, a one-sided view would prevail, the debates *within* the community would not be heard, and cleavages around the relation between Muslim and non-Muslim, women's rights, and the role of the state in enforcing Islamic law would not be taken into account. The PMU also points to the vulnerability of some women and children, and brings to the fore existing power struggles within Islam which are being fought out in minority situations.

Finally, the PMU opposes the Boyd Report on the ground that establishing a multitier legal system (ibid.: 1) would be unjust for minorities and detrimental to all Canadians. This argument requires further comment. Democratic institutional pluralism is advocated by the Québécois and Aboriginals as a path towards self-governance. While this claim is usually viewed as legitimate for these groups, generally Canadians feel uneasy when immigrants and 'ethnic' groups demand similar rights, as did Mumtaz Ali. Boyd rejects this comparison, as does METRAC, who acknowledges the unique position of Aboriginal peoples. HAT also questions the equating of Aboriginals with religious minorities. A deeper analysis that unravels different types of ethnic social relations linked to colonialism, slavery, and voluntary migration would shed light on what defines legitimate and illegitimate claims.[22] Whether full equality requires democratic institutional pluralism for all groups, when a society has adopted it for certain groups in certain circumstances remains an open question, but the answer cannot be disassociated from power relations. I have noticed that often minorities, who have defended institutional duplication, oppose it when they become dominant majorities.

This section concludes with the opposition expressed in Quebec to Islamic arbitration tribunals. During the debate, many opponents to the Boyd Report referred to, and agreed with Quebec's decision, made in 1991, to exclude family law from private arbitration. This decision is partly a reaction to the stronghold that the Catholic Church had on societal institutions in French Canada, and a move towards the secularization of the public space, in the name of *laïcité*. It also can be linked to the dominant representation in Quebec of Canadian multiculturalism – seen as negating the specificity of Quebec and reviled as ghettoizing. During the debate over Islamic tribunals in Ontario, the superiority of interculturalism, the Québécois form of pluralism, was reaffirmed. In May 2005 the Quebec National Assembly unanimously supported a motion by Fatima-Houda Pépin and her colleague Jocelyne Caron to block the use of the Shari'a in Quebec courts. This can be interpreted as Quebec reaffirming its distinctiveness vis-à-vis English Canada.[23]

In the end, Ontario followed Quebec's example. On 11 September 2005, Premier Dalton McGuinty put an end to all private arbitration of a religious nature, and amended the Arbitration Act of 1991 as well as the Children's Law Reform Act. Among these amendments: only Canadian law can be used; the right to appeal an arbitrator's decision cannot be waived, and the award can be taken to court; advance agreements cannot be made; arbitrators must be members of a recognized Association of Dispute Resolution (ADR) organization; they must follow training in screening parties for power imbalances and domestic violence; they are required to keep proper records and submit them to the Ministry of the Attorney General.

Multicultural Citizenship beyond Recognition

The social relations perspective that I have articulated here embraces the multidimensionality of social relations, and in doing so, restores breadth and depth to the social: (1) corrects epistemic flaws such as reification; (2) accounts for group formation; (3) elucidates processes of differentiation and the construction of boundaries; (4) extends the definition of equality to the economic, political, and cultural spheres; and thereby, (5) treats recognition as intrinsic to the redistribution paradigm.

By theorizing multiple and complex social relations, the social relations approach overcomes the Marxian divide between infrastructure and superstructure and recognizes the impact of unequal power relations and competing values within and between groups. As it captures more comprehensively the social relations constitutive of ethnic, national, and racialized groups, social relations analysis displaces the dominant discourse on multiculturalism that is couched in philosophical and legal terms – where there are no unequal social relations, no construction of groups, no changing boundaries, no moving identities, no construction of difference, no conflicts within groups, no disagreements, no ugly power relations. Just a tolerant acceptance of the Others, which dissipates when they cross boundaries and ask too much.

The social relations approach to multiculturalism, which recognizes power relations and differentiated social positions, enlightened the debate over Islamic arbitration tribunals in Ontario. Rather than forcing a choice between accepting or rejecting an inherently essentialized multiculturalism, between an acceptable one and a dangerous one, some opponents to the tribunals, often Muslim, pointed to power struggles within groups, to identities as fluid and differently construed, to interpretations of Shari'a as moving. They indicated that multiculturalism can be used politically and strategically and that its interpretations and forms are diverse. Constructed from a gendered and/or ethnicized position, their perception moves us towards what I have called Multiculturalism 2. Furthermore, I suggest, a multiculturalism envisaged as a site of struggle over competing definitions and conditions of equality could maybe succeed where a ready-mix multiculturalism, with its naive and illusory conception of societal dynamics, has failed.

Acknowledgments

I very much thank Engin Isin for his support and valuable comments on earlier drafts of this chapter.

Notes

1 Since 1991 residents of Ontario have been free to use private arbitration, in accordance if they so wish, with religious law. Catholics and Jews have done so.

2 Protests against the possible establishment of Shari'a-inspired arbitration led the premier of Ontario to commission Marion Boyd, a member of the former New Democratic Party government, to examine all issues, meet with different groups and individuals, and submit recommendations.

3 Weber enriches our understanding of the issues at hand in many ways: his crucial distinction between class and status groups; his analysis of the relation between economic development, culture, and world orientations; his apprehension of social relations as simultaneously based on instrumental (sociation) and value rationality (communalization); the interconnection between material and ideal interests; and his non-reductionist approach to group formation; his analysis of ethnic groups as status groups, which are culturally defined groups, constructed through differentiated economic and social articulations and the structure of power.

4 This essay was triggered by a broad discussion, mainly in the realm of philosophy and political theory, that includes, among others, Butler (1998), Young (1997), Honneth (2001), Benhabib (2002), Kelly (2002), Phillips (1997), Parekh (2004), A. Smith (2001), and Swanson (2005).

5 This is not to say that "real" groups do not exist and that race does not matter. The problem is to envisage racial categories as founded in nature, and colour as an already existing marker.

6 Peter Li (1998) describes the connection between the lower social worth of 'visible' minorities in Canada and their lower market value.

7 Furthermore, Quebec nationalism is about boundary maintenance, and not cultural maintenance; boundaries can be maintained while their cultural content, the stuff of which they are made, varies.

8 But Young's point is different: she argues that ethnic and gendered minorities struggle simultaneously against all forms of inequalities, and that their economic inequality cannot be reduced to class analysis.

9 This point is strongly argued in Phillips' recent book (2007).

10 Observe that here she begins with existing categories rather than explaining their constitution.

11 Pointing to institutionalized patterns of evaluation and interpretation, Butler indicates that status groups refer to the symbolic order, and consequently, that class and status groups rest on different criteria.

12 A theory of *sexage* does not posit that all women are the same and that their oppression as women espouses identical forms. Rather than focusing on biologically or culturally defined women who are then shaped by class, race, and sexuality, *sexage* focuses on the specific social relations that constitute them. The theory of *sexage* uncovers the relations of domination that constitute women; it accounts for the construction of a social category that was and remains essentialized. In other words, the social in women cannot be reduced to a gender that is classed, racialized, and/or ethnicized. But, of course, the modes through which women are appropriated vary. To be appropriated within the family does not play itself out in the same way for wives of bourgeois and proletarian men, or for single mothers. Nor does it entail the same mechanisms for those belonging to the colonial power and the colonized. To consider *sexage* as an autonomous field of inquiry and as an organizing principle does not treat difference as ontological, nor does it fall into the trap of adding oppressions. *Sexage* structures are seen as varying in time and in relation to other systems of social relations.

13 To recognize analytically distinct social relations brings to light how racial and sexual categories are constructed, and how markers, including physical ones, are chosen after the fact to identify their boundaries.

14 I use majority and minority in their sociological sense, of dominant and subordinate positions. A minority cannot be reduced to class, but also to the exercise of political power and control over the normative system of a society. Thus some ethnic groups can do well economically, but be deprived of civil rights. Or, in some cases, immigrants are treated as citizens, but their language, for example, will not receive official recognition. That is not to say that it must, but only that some ethnic groups exert more control than do others in defining what is right and wrong within a given society.

15 This brings us back to the dichotomy between difference and equality, often viewed as irreconcilable. Yet, their separation, as the following example illustrates, is confusing and inadequate Wolf (1994) posits that while 'unappreciated' cultures defend their differences and demand recognition of their identities, women no longer want to be treated like women inasmuch as this identity was used to oppress and exploit them; she therefore opts for equality and rejects difference. In the same book, Habermas (1994) reverses the preceding analysis, and states that the political struggle of women deals with the interpretation of achievements and gendered interests, while ethnic and cultural minorities aim at "overcoming an illegitimate division of society"; consequently, he argues that women seek gendered interests while ethnic minorities seek equality. Both of these authors fail to recognize that the struggles of minorities often include material *and* symbolic dimensions,

as was the case for the Québécois during the Quiet Revolution, and blacks in the United States during the civil rights movement. Their aims were, and remain, the overcoming of an illegitimate division of society and the achievement of economic, political, and cultural equality, the latter involving the right to control and redefine their boundaries.

16 Acknowledging social relations and their multiplicity helps to integrate recognition and redistribution from both poles (Fraser and Honneth 2003c). Misrecognition can be seen as a form of maldistribution that applies to a diversity of social groups, classed, gendered, ethicized, and so on. But it also points to the different dynamics constitutive of these groups, and as such, recognizes their specificity and the specific forms of maldistribution that they entail.

17 Political historicism is the deployment of a field that opposes a coded history integrated to the practice of domination, to history as the consciousness of subjects in struggle against this domination. It links power relations to political combats and relations of truth. Truth stems from subjects who, because of their decentred position, can unmask the domination experienced and those who exert it, by telling the truth of domination (Luzi 2004: 1–5).

18 For a more recent and similar position, see Stein (2007).

19 It should be pointed out, however, that so-called neutral policies affect differently gendered, racialized, and classed majorities and minorities (Vosko 2003).

20 This report is to be read in the post-911 context, when some Canadians expressed either their fear of Islam and others or their strong disagreement with U.S. President Bush's responses. There is a desire to show tolerance and openness, marking Canadian boundaries vis-à-vis the United States. The report stresses choice. It states that the Muslim community should have the same rights as Catholics and Jews to arbitration in terms of religious laws in some civil matters and that such arbitration should be maintained. Boyd nonetheless suggests many amendments, so as to protect the rights of Muslim women: that they obtain a certificate proving that they have received independent legal advice before arbitration; that the decision of the judge be made public in written form and sent to the Department of Justice; and that documents be signed before a witness; she does not request that arbitrators be trained (METRAC 2005: 8–10).

21 Communitarianism should not be confounded with collective rights and the processes of collective mobilization that sociologists examine. Some minorities oppose the formal equality of liberalism to achieve substantive equality. Their demands for collective rights do not necessarily entail disrespect for individual rights and freedoms, *au contraire*, the former are considered essential to the exercise of the latter. Was not the collective self-affirmation of blacks

about equality and the real possibility of exercising individual rights? Was it not about abolishing the unequal power relations that hinder their full exercise of democracy? The important point here is recognizing, and theorizing, inequality between social groups.

22 The PMU is contesting in the name of equality what others, including communitarians, are requesting in the name of equality. Indeed, democratic institutional pluralism, the existence of parallel and analogous institutions (Schermerhorn 1970), is a tool used both by dominant groups, as in Apartheid, and by national minorities who want to control their boundaries; clearly, it is a two-edged sword. Both democratic (ten provincial governments) and undemocratic (Indian Reserves) pluralism was to be found in Canada prior to the policy of multiculturalism, and the two should be kept separate.

23 At the time of concluding this chapter (late 2007), it seems that Québécois (of French Canadian ethnicity) are defining their boundaries vis-à-vis ethnic groups and immigrants in terms of a commitment to gender equality and *laïcité* and vis-à-vis English Canada by a rejection of multiculturalism.

5 Between Gender and Cultural Equality

SIRMA BILGE

Until recently we were all multiculturalists (Glazer 1997), confident that multiculturalists had won the day (Kymlicka 1999, quoted in Joppke 2004: 233). Lately, however, multiculturalism is no longer considered a positive feature of national societies and metropolises (Rex and Singh 2003); instead, in many Western states previously committed to some extent to pluralistic policies and practices, one can read the signs of a 'new consensus against multiculturalism' (Modood 2007), an ongoing purge of their real or imagined[1] multiculturalist past. A new conventional wisdom, praised as 'honest and robust' in Britain, and hailed as 'the new realism' in the Netherlands (Prins 2002), is gaining ground and claims to expose straightforwardly the problems of immigrant/Muslim[2] integration, calling up the old adage, 'when in Rome, do as the Romans do,' while portraying multiculturalism as a 'gangrene afflicting democratic societies,'[3] a 'cultural suicide pact' for an overly tolerant liberal West that came to tolerate the intolerable,[4] deprecating it as hypocrisy or political correctness. While the ubiquity of public discourses hailing the 'death of multiculturalism' should not be hastily equated with the total demise of cultural plurality,[5] various government initiatives do suggest a tendency to redirect public policies regulating majority/minority relations from multiculturalism towards assimilation that some would call civic integration (Joppke 2004) or republican-style citizenship (Statham 2003).[6]

In a context marked by anxieties over global terrorism, Islamic fundamentalism, and securitization of immigration (Huysmans 1995, Bigo 1998), discourses calling for a curb on migration and the abandonment of pluralistic options stand out for their reliance on the fiction of an integrated host society that non-Western immigrants, in particular Muslims, spoiled by multiculturalism, threaten.[7] Central to this new rhetoric is an essentialized 'Muslim difference' construed as a menace to public order, social cohesion, and 'core Western values.'[8] Regardless of national variations, the terms of the debate are consistently linked to the supposed threat of multiculturalism to the nation: to its cohesion and core values (in Britain), its standards and values (in the Netherlands), its *laïcité* (in France), or its *Leitkultur* (in Germany) (Fekete 2004: 18).

In Britain, where multiculturalism seems to have been a rather unplanned process of 'multicultural drift' (Hall 1999), it is in the aftermath of the Burnley, Oldham, and Bradford riots of the summer of 2001 that the Labour government declared that 'it was time to move beyond multiculturalism' along with its blueprint Cantle Report, replacing multiculturalism with a new paradigm of 'community cohesion.' At the same time, the then Home Secretary David Blunkett emphasized the need for a new framework of 'core values' that would set limits to 'the laissez-faire pluralism' of the past. The withdrawal from a supposedly unquestioned commitment to pluralism only became stronger in the aftermath of the 9/11 and 7/7 attacks,[9] as may be seen in the August 2006 implementation of a new advisory board, The Commission on Integration and Cohesion. Launching the Commission, Britain's community and local government secretary, Ruth Kelly affirmed: 'We have moved from a period of uniform consensus on the value of multiculturalism, to one where we can encourage that debate by questioning whether it is encouraging separateness.'[10]

The most radical shift is visibly happening in the Netherlands, once seen as a leading country of multiculturalism in Europe.[11] The results of the November 2006 elections indicate a greater support for populist parties with anti-immigration agendas,[12] and the country has put in place a pre-migration integration exam to select newcomers on the basis of their assimilability: as of 15 March, 2006, all prospective immigrants except those from European Union and other Western countries, mostly applicants for family-reunification or family-formation (would-be spouses), must pass a 'civic integration exam' at a cost of 350 euros, at one of the 138 Dutch embassies before being issued a visa. Included in the optional study kit for the exam is a controversial two-hour DVD, entitled *Coming to the Netherlands*, showing gay men kissing and women sunbathing topless, which has been criticized for being expressly designed to dissuade those from non-Western countries who cannot deal with a liberal society from coming to the Netherlands (Fekete 2006: 4). While prospective immigrants have to pass an integration exam to be eligible for visas, immigrants are required to pass a language test within five years of their arrival or risk being deported. Dutch scepticism towards multiculturalism dates back to the early 1990s (Entzinger 1994), but it is the November 2004 assassination of the filmmaker Theo van Gogh by a Dutch-Moroccan, for religiously motivated sentiments,[13] that made the debate over multiculturalism a full-blown *problème de société,* both nationally and internationally. At a rally organized in Amsterdam following the murder, the then Minister of Integration and Immigration, Rita Verdonk, made Van Gogh's murder an integration issue, declaring that 'it has gone this far, and it goes no further,' a line quickly picked up by other politicians and larger segments of the population.[14]

Yet, this resurgence of nation-centred views of immigrant integration engenders divergent interpretations among scholars, particularly with regard to the content of the nationhood involved: for some, the focus on core (national) values is an utterly de-ethnicized process, nothing but 'local versions of a liberal state becoming more serious than in the "multicultural" past about the minimum liberal' (Joppke 2004: 254), while others take more seriously this renewed assertiveness about national culture and anxieties over its predicted dissolution (Stolcke 1995). Although the ethnic component of these nation-centred discourses on integration and assimilative initiatives cannot be denied, it is too early to tell if we are headed for a full reversal of the tide, from multiculturalism to assimilationism, or whether some form of plural citizenship practices will persist despite anti-multiculturalist rhetoric and 'reform.'[15] It is beyond the scope of this chapter to further develop this debate. Rather, the aim here is to focus analysis on the 'woman issue' and to explore how gender equality has become one of the most sure-fire grounds for challenging the legitimacy of multiculturalism. By asserting this I do not intend, by any means, to render the criticism of multiculturalism morally objectionable, but to tackle the ways in which the feminist project has become instrumental for advocating withdrawal from multiculturalism. In an intellectual context where pluralism ('the differentialist turn') is said to have exhausted itself in social thought, as well as in public discourse and policy (Brubaker 2001: 532), my purpose is to disrupt the growing consensus over the culpability of multiculturalism, which the mass media is only too happy to cover, and to unravel the ideological foundations of one of its most efficient and widespread critiques: that multiculturalism is perilous for women.[16]

Two sets of charges against multicultural citizenship have become commonplace: first, it engenders cultural ghettos, a haven for home-grown terrorism;[17] second, it condones community/family violence against minority women. There are of course more sophisticated critiques of multiculturalism, based, for instance, on its presumed opposition to equity politics;[18] nonetheless the focus of my critical inquiry will be exclusively on the gender-based critiques of multiculturalism, in that they strongly inform the paradigmatic debates over the limits of minority accommodation (such as the *hijab* controversy across Europe and in Quebec or the debates over contested practices like arranged marriages) and operate new forms of exclusion from citizenship.

It is my contention that the current focus on women's status within minorities, mainly among Muslims, is being used as a tool to police the boundaries of the imagined community, whether national or supranational (such as the one found in the expression 'European core values'), and as such it must be met with scepticism. Accordingly, I will argue that denunciation of minority patriarchy and idealization of majority gender relations are part and parcel of the discursive practices of 'boundary patrolling' (Lamont and Molnar 2002: 176) that separate the West and the rest, and set the principles and limits for incorporating the difference. I will develop my argument in three stages: after briefly describing the context of the current withdrawal from multicultural policies and practices on the grounds of their presumed clash with gender equality, I will switch my focus to the ideological underpinnings of this dominant representation that portrays multiculturalism as a threat to women, and then examine the workings of this *doxic*[19] representation with regard to an empirical case, the Muslim veil debate in contemporary France, drawing attention to the colonial roots of the political instrumentalization of the 'woman issue.'

Retreat from Multiculturalism on the Ground of Gender Justice

The current focus on the gendered impacts of multiculturalism needs to be situated within the context of an increased recognition among political theorists that such policies are confronted with a critical tension between accommodating minority groups' claims for equality, recognition, and after power-sharing and securing, at the same time, the fundamental rights and freedoms of individuals within these groups, specifically of those identified as belonging to 'vulnerable' segments such as women, children, sexual minorities, and religious and political dissenters (Green

1994, Shachar 2001, Bader 2005). The problematic social location of these individuals, categorized as 'minorities within minorities,' has become, since the late 1990s, the focus of an ever-increasing scrutiny, occupying the forefront of academic and political debates on multicultural accommodation.[20] Since the publication of Leslie Green's article in 1994 entitled, 'Internal Minorities and Their Rights,' philosophers and political scientists have raised in dozens of articles and volumes the issues surrounding the apparent dilemma between the recognition of group rights for ethnocultural minorities and the protection of individual rights and freedoms within their boundaries, which has become one of the most contentious social and political questions in contemporary migrant-receiving Western societies, given the current context of the 'war on terrorism' and of moral panic over securitizing national borders and immigrant integration.

In this debate over the limits of tolerance in liberal democracies, Muslim difference became the main challenge in a context in which the gender issue profoundly shapes perceptions about Islam and the social desirability of Muslims, especially in Europe. For instance, Anna Korteweg (2006) argues that current concerns about the failure of the Dutch model of integration and the increasing call for strong assimilationism merge with the perceived differences between Dutch/Western gender norms and non-Western/Muslim gender norms. In Scandinavia a similar culture clash is allegedly taking place between the 'Nordic mind' and Muslims pertaining to gender relations, within which the issue of forced marriages – often conflated with arranged marriages – has occupied the centre stage and led governments, starting with Denmark, to pass more restrictive immigration, family reunification, and asylum legislation, while the Norwegian parliament has resolved that mandatory criminal charges must be laid on anyone who forces someone into marriage even if the victim does not consent to the prosecution (Razack 2004, Bredal 2005). As it appears, some mainstream feminists and gay activists in many EU countries have joined an overtly right-wing consensus calling for tougher immigration policies and citizenship legislation, specifically targeting Muslims[21]; the rationale behind this stance is the presumption that Muslims are deeply opposed to homosexuality and gender equality and threaten 'European core values' (Fekete 2006: 2). Hence, the growing consensus over the responsibility of multiculturalism for increasing the risk of 'home-grown terrorism' and condoning violence against women within minority communities constitutes the backdrop of recent reforms in immigration policies and citizenship laws across Europe. While in Sweden and Germany, honour-related crimes[22] are construed as proof of the failure of multiculturalism, in Denmark and Norway it is the issue of forced marriages conflated with arranged marriages that has helped to endorse the retreat from pluralistic options and the adoption of stricter immigration and integration policies.[23] Similarly, in Britain, family reunification and marriage rights were limited following the urban riots of 2001; most strikingly, Home Secretary Blunkett declared that the riots were caused by South Asian young males with 'backward' attitudes and oppressive practices, such as forced marriage, against women (7). Linking topics of urban unrest/insecurity and women's oppression, Blunkett's statement epitomizes the intricate ways in which the gender issue is being construed as the main cause of the failure of Muslim integration in Europe, reinforcing the idea of incommensurable differences between Islam and the West.

Gender equality appears to be the central concern of Canadians as well, shaping the degree of public support for multiculturalism. A recent survey of public opinion regarding Muslims in Canada, administered by Environics Research Group on behalf of the Trudeau Foundation, shows that the public endorsement of multiculturalism is closely linked to whether minorities respect gender equality or not. According to the study, which surveyed 2,021 Canadians, public support for multiculturalism seems to vanish when religious and cultural practices are felt to be a threat to gender equality. Of the 37 per cent of respondents who had a negative view of Islam, 21 per cent mentioned the treatment of Muslim women as the ground for their views, followed by violence (19 per cent), association with terrorism (17 per cent), intolerance (11 per cent), and extremism (11 per cent).[24]

The shift from multiculturalism to assimilationism across Europe and the rising concerns over multiculturalism in Canada need to be considered in parallel with the ways in which the gender question has been utilized to justify military operations in Afghanistan. In a well-orchestrated media campaign mobilizing pell-mell influential women, celebrities, and wives of influential men and celebrities, the war on terrorism has been turned into a rescue mission for Afghani women. Taking over her husband's weekly radio addresses to the nation, the then First Lady Laura Bush advocated for the plight of Afghani women, only a few days after the launching of the U.S. war in Afghanistan:[25]

> I'm delivering this week's radio address to kick off a world-wide effort to focus on the brutality against women and children by the al-Qaida terrorist network and the regime it supports in Afghanistan, the Taliban ... Afghan women know, through hard experience, what the rest of the world is discovering: The brutal oppression of women is a central goal of the terrorists. Long before the current war began, the Taliban and its terrorist allies were making the lives of children and women in Afghanistan miserable ... Only the terrorists and the Taliban forbid education to women. Only the terrorists and the Taliban threaten to pull out women's fingernails for wearing nail polish ... Civilized people throughout the world are speaking out in horror – not only because our hearts break for the women and children in Afghanistan, but also because in Afghanistan, we see the world the terrorists would like to impose on the rest of us ... Because of our recent military gains in much of Afghanistan, women are no longer imprisoned in their homes. They can listen to music and teach their daughters without fear of punishment. Yet the terrorists who helped rule that country now plot and plan in many countries. And they must be stopped. *The fight against terrorism is also a fight for the rights and dignity of women.*[26]

Most revealingly, Cherie Blair, the wife of the then British Prime Minister joined the campaign, as well as other influential figures such as U.S. Senator Hillary Clinton, Mavis Leno (wife of Jay Leno),[27] the playwright Eve Ensler (author of *The Vagina Monologues*), and Eleanor Smeal (founder and president of the Feminist Majority Foundation) all were connecting the 9/11 attacks, the Taliban regime, and Afghani women's suffering.[28] It appears that the focus on (other) women's emancipation, which across Europe has united major feminist organizations with anti-immigration forces from the right end of the political spectrum in their call for stringent immigration policies and their denunciation of multiculturalism, has led feminism in the United States to encourage military interventions. It bears reminding that the campaign for military action never invoked international political economy or the geopolitics of the war, nor did it mention the links between yesterday's Mujahiddins, allies of the West against the Soviets, and today's enemy, the Talibans. The erasure of Western support to ultra-conservative Mujahiddins, who had launched in 1978, before the Soviet military invasion of Afghanistan, a holy war against the Marxist government of Nur Mohammed Taraki, which, incidentally, advanced women's rights by making schooling compulsory for girls and outlawing women trade (Delphy 2002), was crucial for recasting the U.S. intervention in Afghanistan as a rescue mission for women. This recasting required a cultural framing: 'knowledge' about the patriarchal culture of the region, its religious beliefs, tribal customs, and gender norms came to replace the economic, political, and historical explanations (Abu-Lughod 2002: 784). Through the focus on women's status within the (implicitly inferior) non-Western minority cultures – especially Muslim – it is the old colonial rationale of cultural/racial hierarchies that has resurfaced, along with the colonial 'rescue paradigm' (Rajan 1993: 6), or as mordantly formulated in Gayatri Spivak's much quoted (and often with a pathos making the term analytically useless) aphorism: 'white men saving brown women from brown men' (1988: 296).

The question to be answered is why rescuing the 'other women' (epitomized as Muslim women) has become so central in legitimating certain types of national and international action, whether harsher immigration and integration policies (such as the banning of the veil or criminalizing arranged marriages, as is currently being discussed in some Scandinavian countries), or the launching of military interventions. In other words, as Razack (2004: 129) puts it, how has gender equality become a tool for 'policing Muslim communities' within and across borders? I will tackle this question in the context of national policies and practices of 'diversity management,' and interrogate how and why gender equality has become one of the *safest* grounds for de-legitimating multiculturalist options. As it appears in recent debates over female genital mutilation (FGM), arranged marriages, honour crimes, *hijab*, and *niqab*, all of which have been the subject of extensive and often sensationalist media coverage across the Western world,[29] the Muslim woman's body has been put at the heart of the controversy over the future of the policies of multiculturalism and the limits of tolerance, a debate strongly marked by the ideology of an irreducible clash of civilizations between the West and Islam. As pointed out by Anne Phillips (2007: 25), 'the rights of women have come to figure as one of the elements delineating a modern liberal society, and gender equality as what distinguishes such a society from so-called traditional, non-Western, illiberal cultures ... Feminists have not been entirely innocent bystanders here ... feminism has also generated strong binaries between liberal and illiberal groups.'

Accordingly, the rest of my discussion intends to fulfil two related objectives: to unpack the ideological underpinnings of the dominant representation of multiculturalism as a threat to women's rights, and to demonstrate, on the basis of critical race and postcolonial theories and via the discussion of recent debates over empirical cases, how the peril of multiculturalism for women discourse qua *doxa* (Bilge 2006a) has colonized the debates on citizenship and difference and has served to discredit multiculturalism and/or diversity accommodation.[30] The next section examines how the debate over multicultural citizenship came to be dominantly framed as an unsolvable dilemma between gender equality and cultural recognition, and unpacks the workings of the 'Feminism vs Multiculturalism' discourse by interrogating its ideological premise, which has the characteristic of becoming naturalized over time, internalized as common sense, *doxa* (Bourdieu 1979, Teo 2000), and the ways in which it contributes to the stigmatization and marginalization of the very groups (minority women) for whom it claims to speak.

Feminism versus Multiculturalism: A Doxa to Dismantle

Contemporary political theorists and philosophers raise critical questions regarding the conciliation between diversity accommodation and individual rights and freedoms: How are national, ethnic, and religious minorities to be accommodated while at the same time ensuring respect of fundamental rights and freedoms within their boundaries? To what extent should the liberal state accommodate minority groups? How are minority groups to be assured a certain degree of autonomy from the state while guaranteeing at the same time to their members the right to individual autonomy from their respective communities? Under what circumstances should the state interfere in their internal affairs? Even though these questions are not all new, the concern with the in-group effects of state-sanctioned collective rights is quite unprecedented. It is towards the end of the twentieth century that the 'vulnerable segments within minorities' (such as women, minors, homosexuals) and how they may be affected by pluralistic policies accommodating their community became a coveted object of inquiry for specialists on multiculturalism and citizenship. Before that, 'intraminority power inequalities' were not an issue, since the first wave of writings on multicultural accommodation addressed the question of intergroup equity and neglected the intragroup dimension (Shachar 2000). Their concern about the impact of group-differentiated rights was limited to the issue of social cohesion, that is, whether the recognition of cultural rights of minorities would compromise social cohesion or not (Bader 2005).

The growing concern about the intraminority impacts of pluralistic policies regulating majority-minority relations relies on the premise that 'recognizing the rights of cultural minorities will strengthen the power of men over women, or the old over the young within the minority culture. The primacy attached to culture may then lend itself to less democratic or more illiberal practice' (Phillips 1997: 62). It is widely acknowledged that multicultural policies may accentuate in-group power imbalances and subordination of 'vulnerable segments' within minority groups, especially women, by supporting the maintenance of patriarchal structures within minority cultures, a situation that Shachar calls the 'paradox of multicultural vulnerability' (2001: 3), in which 'well-meaning accommodation by the state may leave members of minority groups vulnerable to severe injustice within the group, and may, in effect, work to reinforce some of the most hierarchical elements of a culture' (ibid.).

Without denying the existence of tensions stemming from divergent priorities of social movements struggling against a specific form of inequality, I contend that framing these ordinary tensions between constituents of civil society as an irreconcilable dilemma between women's rights and multiculturalism, as an either/or situation, is an ideological construct serving the majority needs and interests. This relates closely to our collective endeavour of recasting the social in citizenship exposed in the introduction: the seemingly discrete and antagonistic framing of struggles for justice, which include both redistribution and recognition, needs to be unpacked to reveal their articulations to illustrate how categories of power (e.g., 'women,' 'non-white,' 'Muslim,' 'homeless,' 'disabled') are co-constructed through the social relations and processes (re)producing inequality, exclusion, domination, and co-optation. Hence, it is necessary to situate existing tensions and competitions between claims for gender justice and cultural justice (recognition) and groups organized around them within a larger picture, in view of the fact that political competition between equality-seeking movements, what Kimberley Crenshaw calls 'political intersectionality' (1991), usually organized around a single axis of inequality (whether class, gender, race, or sexuality), is a well-documented phenomenon, and to reckon that these competitions fuelled by national and supranational politics do not exclude possibilities of strategic alliances.

The 'women and multiculturalism' issue was catapulted into the centre of academic and public debates on citizenship and group rights in the late 1990s with the publication of an essay by an eminent liberal feminist and Harvard professor of ethics and political science, Susan

Moller Okin, who raised a controversial question: 'Is Multiculturalism Bad for Women?' Okin's essay was published in a well-known democratic political forum, *Boston Review*,[31] reaching a larger audience than do academic journals. In the same issue, twelve other specialists of citizenship and diversity[32] contributed to the debate by responding to Okin's essay. These exchanges, with the addition of four new participants, were published in 1999 in an edited volume with the same captivating and provocative title: *Is Multiculturalism Bad for Women?* One cannot help but wonder why this volume initiated by a liberal feminist and described on its back-cover, by another liberal feminist, as 'bring[ing] together varied voices who help to set the terms for discussing the relationship between feminism and multiculturalism,'[33] does not include any voice representing both projects simultaneously (i.e., the standpoint of a group that has most to lose when multiculturalism and feminism are cast as irreconcilable), namely, a critical multicultural feminist perspective. Although Bonnie Honig's and Azizah Y. Al-Hibri's contributions to the volume, respectively 'My Culture Made Me Do It' and 'Is Western Patriarchal Feminism Good for Third World/Minority Women?' raise certain points in that direction,[34] they do not fully engage, in my view, with the issue of interlocking systems of domination as postcolonial/black feminist writings do. As pointed out by Shachar, positing multiculturalism as a peril for women's equality rights fails to recognize that intergroup inequalities and intragroup injustices are related to one another and are part and parcel of interlocking power hierarchies (2000: 389). This erasure is in itself symptomatic of the relations between Western feminists and women from racialized minorities. In her mordant critique of the ascendancy of difference discourses within feminism, Okin (1994) focuses almost exclusively on an influential book by another white feminist, *Inessential Women* (1988) by Elizabeth Spelman, without seriously addressing the voluminous writings of racialized women. According to Jane Flax (1995: 501–2, 508), this selective account reproduces the elision of racism and 'racial differences' within feminism.

In a context of growing interest on the intragroup effects of multiculturalist policies, especially on minority women, the formulaic representation 'multiculturalism versus feminism' became ubiquitous in contemporary academic and political debates on equality and citizenship, and within the discussions on 'minorities within minorities.' Nowadays, it is widely assumed that policies of multiculturalism work generally to the disadvantage of women, although there is no systematic empirical evidence endorsing that premise. Liberal feminists like Okin[35] have been pivotal in this 'mode of explanation' which itself needs to be explained in terms of the biases, motivations, and purposes generating it. Her critique of multiculturalism as hindering gender equality became influential both inside and outside academia. In political circles, the influence of Okin's stance reaches beyond the expected spheres of mainstream feminism. According to Fekete (2006: 13), Okin's misrepresentation of multiculturalism has been incorporated into the repertoire of the mainstream right, where the issue of domestic violence in immigrant communities became exploited by politicians without a prior track record in gender equality to further their agenda to curb immigration. In academic circles, Okin's influence is palpable in current works in political theory dealing with the double/multiple minorities in which the grid 'feminism versus multiculturalism' that she built seems ubiquitous. Even works refuting her arguments tend to stay in and think through that grid, such as the work of the libertarian philosopher Chandran Kukathas (2001), which raised the opposite question: 'Is Feminism Bad for Multiculturalism?' It should be noted that the logic underlying both questions remains the same: cultural rights and gender equality are depicted as antithetical political claims. After this foundational assertion, solutions offered in the case of a clash diverge: for Okin, gender equality should be given precedence; for Kukathas, it is the opposite – cultural rights should be given precedence, as long as minorities with illiberal practices provide exit rights to their members.[36]

Okin may justifiably be considered the founder[37] and foremost defender of this new trend of criticism of multiculturalism on the grounds that it condones in-group subordination of women and works against gender equality. 'Evidence' brought by such scholarship is less than thorough, in that it often has less to do with multiculturalism than with a laissez-faire[38] attitude conveying a (neo)colonial rationale of cultural hierarchies, and fails to recognize that policies of multiculturalism cannot be understood outside their specific historical contexts and purposes. Without empirical inquiry of the ways in which multiculturalist policies interact with gender equality in specific contexts, such scholarship relies on commonsensical formulas with Orientalist undertones, which assume gender domination to be intrinsic to Other/non-Western cultures (Ahmed 1992, Saïd 2003, Volpp 2005). This line of argument is paramount in Okin's work, as when she argues that women belonging to 'more patriarchal minority culture[s] in the context of a less patriarchal majority culture ... *might* be better off if the culture into which they were born were either to become extinct ... or, preferably, to be encouraged to alter itself so as to reinforce the equality of women' (1999: 22–3). In doing so, these works do not take into account empirical findings showing that policies of multiculturalism interact in various and unexpected ways with women's status and do not systematically disadvantage them; although multiculturalism may benefit patriarchal, often religious, male leadership within émigré communities, reinforcing their in-group authority (Yuval-Davis 1992), attention needs also be paid to other outcomes, which are barely mentioned. Drawing on Irene Bloemraad's empirical work, Kymlicka suggests that multiculturalist policies may contribute to 'the progress of gender parity in ethnic leadership by creating new routes to leadership through the allocation of resources and opportunities to the providers of immigrant and settlement services who are mostly women and by helping the creation of non-profit community organizations which provide alternative, accessible avenues to leadership and advocacy for women' (2005: 65). We need therefore to think outside the dichotomous parameters of the debate, since social reality cannot be abridged either to hegemonic *doxa* of irreducible incompatibility between feminism and multiculturalism or to the defensive (counter-hegemonic) claim that they are strongly compatible with each other. Their interactions need to be historicized in a way cognizant of their complex and varying degrees of complementarities, overlapping, and opposition.

Okin's stance – that cultural group rights reinforce existing hierarchies and work to the disadvantage of women – has succeeded in legitimating the pitting of women's rights against immigrants' rights, allowing mainstream Western feminists to proclaim the incompatibility of non-Western cultures with Western liberal societies (Fekete 2006: 13). Although her thesis has provoked diverse reactions and criticism among specialists on multiculturalism, few have proposed to go beyond a content analysis of her argumentation and bring up the need to deconstruct the tool itself, which sets the terms of the debate. Rather than taking issue with whether multiculturalism is bad for women or feminism is bad for multiculturalism, what needs to be understood is why and how this opposition became the legitimate framing of the debate over equality and differentiated citizenship. In arguing so, I join Leti Volpp's assessment of the debate between feminism and multiculturalism as having limited utility and her call to inspect 'why this binary discourse so frequently structures the parameters of the debate' (2005: 40). Another important source of inspiration is Anne Phillips' recent work in which she offers compelling arguments for a critical multiculturalism, a 'multiculturalism without culture' (2007).

The next section illustrates how the 'peril of multiculturalism for women' discourse is efficiently used to discredit public claims of religious minorities and to refuse accommodation, especially towards Muslims. The case examined is the French controversy over the Muslim veil in public schools. In that context, the dominant framing did not take the form of multiculturalism versus feminism, but that of anti-sexism versus anti-racism (see Delphy 2006).

The Veil Controversy and the Colonial Rescue Fantasy

Of the twelve issues listed by Bhikhu Parekh as most frequently leading to value clashes between majority and minorities, eight are related to practices that suggest, from a majority standpoint, that women occupy a subordinate status within these cultures (2000: 264–5). The practice of Islamic veiling, namely, the headscarf (*hijab*), is one of them. Before tackling the *hijab* controversy in France and its banning from public schools, it is worth making a few historical detours to illustrate how the veil has been a critical site of struggle between European colonialism and anti-colonialist nationalism, and the ways in which Western women have contributed, whether consciously or not, to colonial domination.

The dichotomous framing of the Muslim veil either as the symbol of women's submission to men or that of their resistance to assimilation/Western imperialism has its historical roots in the colonial subjugation where the 'woman question,' caught between colonial domination and anti-colonialist resistance, has been instrumental to both.[39] Admittedly, I would need much more space to elaborate on how women entered into colonial history, but the following examples will suffice to demonstrate that it was indeed a selective and strategic entry manoeuvred to a certain extent by men of power in colonial administration.

Pointing the finger at indigenous patriarchy was a powerful tool for colonial administrators, making the 'Other woman' question instrumental to colonial domination. John Stuart Mill denounced the degenerate civilization, the 'abject position of Hindu women' and the 'effeminacy' of Hindu men to prove that these people were unfit to rule themselves (Chakravarti 1990: 35). Most revealingly, the plight of indigenous women was invoked by colonial administrators such as Lord Cromer, who denounced the veil as an emblem of Egyptian women's subordination by their barbaric men and archaic culture, which justified the civilizing presence of British colonizers. The irony is that the same Cromer was a member of society battling against women's suffrage back in England. The same Victorian establishment that resisted the women's *cause* at home co-opted the language of feminism and redirected it in the service of colonialism towards Other men and the cultures of Other men (Ahmed 1992: 6). This was a very selective concern about the plight of Egyptian women that focused on the veil as a symbol of oppression but gave no support to women's education, for example (Abu-Lughod 2002: 784).

This selective concern is also very obvious in recent French debates over the *hijab*. The banning of the veil from public schools illustrates French legislators' preference for excluding veiled students from public schools rather than tolerating the veil to keep the students within the education system, while early directives such as Prime Minister Lionel Jospin's clearly indicated that priority be given to the right to education. Moreover, this ban achieved the collective definition of the veil as a symbol of women's oppression to their men and their patriarchal religion/culture, and in doing so it followed the colonial path of denying the semiotic plurality and ambiguity of the veil.

Gender dynamics involved in the *hijab* debate in contemporary France are reminiscent of the entrenchment of the woman issue in the French colonial enterprise and the Algerian resistance against it, which is remarkably addressed in Frantz Fanon's much quoted work in anglophone research (much less so in its original French language): 'Algeria Unveiled' (1965). According to Fanon, French colonizers manoeuvred in such a way so as to put women at the centre of the colonial conquest, making them a 'theme of action': 'If we want to destroy the structure of Algerian society, its capacity for resistance, we must first of all conquer the woman; we must go and find them behind the veil where they hide themselves and in the houses where the men keep them out of sight' (37–8). French colonizers' resolution to eradicate everything seen as authentically Muslim,[40] given that under the colonial gaze Islam represented the *essence* of Algerians, provoked a resistance-oriented reinvestment in the tradition[41] making Islam the bastion of Algerian resistance to colonialism. As Marnia Lazreg puts (1990: 758–9), prior to their colonial subjugation, Algerians took for granted their Muslim identity the same way that the French did their Christianity. It is the colonial focus and actions towards Islam that made it the most salient aspect of Algerian identity. Lazreg's analysis remarkably exposes how the French invasion of Algeria relied on two interrelated themes of action: religious difference and women's oppression. While Fanon unmasks the colonial subterfuge of the so-called empowering of indigenous women by unveiling them, the aim of which is really to achieve 'a real power over the men' (1965: 39), he fails to take into account the gendered signification of the veil prior to French colonization. As Anne McClintock (1995) rightly points out, 'so eager is Fanon to deny the colonial rescue fantasy that he refuses to grant the veil any prior role at all in the gender dynamics of Algerian society. Having refused the colonial's desire to invest the veil with an essentialist meaning (the sign of women's servitude), he bends over backward to insist on the veil's semiotic innocence in Algerian society' (365). Fanon's somewhat androcentric reading is echoed by Pierre Bourdieu's early work on Kabylia: 'The veil and the *chechia* ... had been in the traditional context *mere vestimentary details endowed with an almost forgotten significance*, simple elements of an unconsciously devised system of symbols. In the colonial situation, however, they take on the function of signs that are being consciously utilized to express resistance to the foreign order and to foreign values as well as to pledge fidelity to their own system of values' (1961: 156, second italics mine).

Formerly one marker of social identity and differentiation among others, Islam hence gained in the context of colonial domination the utmost importance, the *quintessence* of Algerian people, both in the eyes of colonizers and the anti-colonialist resistance. In a context of strong denunciation of the veil by the colonizers, the colonized made it their resistance flag. Vilified by the oppressor and reinvested in by the oppressed, the veil changed both in its form – it became longer – and its signification (Lazreg 1994). Hence, the veil became a signifying boundary marker between Algerians and Europeans, epitomizing Algerianness and Algerians' 'will to affirm their radical and irreducible difference from the Europeans ... and their desire to defend their besieged identity' (Bourdieu 1961: 155).

Although perspicacious, analyses such as Fanon's and Bourdieu's fail to address fully the gendered nature of colonial domination and violence, and the function of the veil, not only as a resistance to but also a refuge from colonial oppression.

> [Under the French colonial rule] the perceived emasculation of Algerian men was not accompanied by a promotion of the status of women. Colonial intervention meant a loss of status for men, now perceiving themselves as

> reduced to the status of women, and an equally important loss of status for women, from decent (that is, Muslim) to immoral (used as prostitutes for Frenchmen's gain) ... The veil became women's refuge from the French denuding gaze. However, its form changed, becoming longer, and it acquired a new significance as a symbol of not only cultural difference but also a protection from and resistance to colonial-*qua*-Christian domination. (Lazreg 1994: 53)

Speaking for Subaltern Sisters

Central to my analysis is the relationship between Western feminists and indigenous women within the colonial context, since this relationship continues to inform the ongoing debates on the legitimacy of Muslim claims described as oppressive for women, specifically the veil controversy in France. Postcolonial critics of mainstream Western feminism argue that the relationship with 'Other women' has always been part and parcel of the production of the Euro-American feminist subject. In her book, *Home and Harem,* Inderpal Grewal convincingly argues that universalistic feminist discourses, which have seen themselves only in relation to men, have been, in fact, articulated in relation to other women (1996: 11). Studies on different colonial contexts show that Western feminists constructed their historical and political agency by making themselves the voice of oppressed indigenous women. It is in the 'process of campaigning for women whom they considered to be more badly treated than themselves ... [that] Western women could achieve a subject position for themselves, often at the expense of indigenous women's subject position and sense of agency' (Mills 1998: 105). White women's activism to rescue their indigenous sisters served also to advance their citizenship claims back home, a fact supporting my premise that relations and processes that constitute different categories of Otherness ('women', 'non-white,' 'third world') are related to one another. Hence, British women advocating for the rights of their Indian and African sisters were able to construct, in the process, a political subject position for themselves 'which led ultimately to suffrage for British women and women in the "white" settled colonies' (Burton 1992 and Jayawardena 1995, cited in Lewis and Mills 2003: 8).

White women – 'Imperial Ladies' – were hence part and parcel of the colonial enterprise and instrumental to the elaboration and maintenance of gendered racial hierarchies. White women's complicity with colonialism and imperialism has been critically assessed in several historical contexts, and their role in legitimating the civilizing mission of colonialism and its rescue paradigm, that is, saving indigenous women from their barbaric males, has been examined.[42] For instance, in Australia, white women of various classes were agents of colonial oppression and assimilation, by their implications in state and church interventions to Aboriginal family life through child removals (Wilson 1996, cited in Razack 2000: 45–6). In British-ruled India, the relations between British and Indian women were characterized by what Barbara Ramusack called 'maternal imperialism' (1990: 319), wherein denouncing barbaric Indian men played an important hegemonic role. Popular texts, such as Katherine Mayo's book, *Mother India* (published in 1927), disseminated sensationalist portrayals of Indian customs (Bulbeck 1998: 24), provoking an anti-colonialist traditionalism that often led to the deterioration of the status of indigenous women. While using what may be seen as the language of an early global sisterhood, European feminists did consider colonized women rather like their little sisters or daughters than as their equals, referring to them, as Josephine Butler did, as helpless, voiceless, and hopeless. This assignation of a passive victim status to indigenous women erased their activism, which dated back to the early nineteenth century in some cases such as in India (ibid.). Very few feminists addressed the negative effects of colonialism on indigenous women's status.[43] In French colonies, women activists, such as the well-known feminist and suffragette Hubertine Auclert, could further their political agenda for the advancement of women's rights in France through their advocating for the improvement of the living conditions of indigenous women (Lazreg 1994). The ambiguities of their positions and the complex and contradictory social circumstances under which these white feminists struggled must be recalled, as well as their (conscious or unconscious) contribution to colonial domination.

There is an interesting similarity between the ambivalence of white feminists towards 'Other/indigenous women' and the ways in which their struggle might have contributed to colonial domination and the current use of feminist politics for anti-immigration agendas. Yet, a major difference in contemporary feminist politics is the enrolment of some 'Other/immigrant women' in Western hegemonic feminism and their contribution to the current reproduction of Orientalist discourses targeting Muslim communities in particular. Indeed, dialectics involved in the Orientalism qua system of thought and representations shaped by political forces of colonialism and 'based upon an ontological and epistemological distinction between "the Orient" and ... "the

Occident"' (Saïd 1978: 2) – infused with the idea of Western superiority over Eastern backwardness – continue to be activated through the current debates over immigrant integration and women's status within minority communities. In this context, us/them social relations and representations have become ever more complex and symbolic and material boundaries do not overlap; in particular relations between feminism and racialized/minoritized women are multifarious: divisions between white/Western women and 'coloured'/Third World women do not replicate divisions between Western universalist feminism and postcolonial/anti-racist feminism. Boundaries are equally blurred, since there are both Western feminists endorsing anti-racist postcolonial currents critical of liberal/universalist feminism for its Eurocentrism, and non-Western feminists defending a gender-first approach to discrimination and adhering to a universalist Euro-American feminist thought critical of multiculturalism as being harmful to women's human rights. While there is no ontological objection that may be addressed to these complex ideological and political affiliations that transgress dominant cultural expectations on both sides, critical attention needs to be paid to a recent trend in contemporary feminist politics that I have called elsewhere 'internal Orientalism' (Bilge 2006b). I use 'internal Orientalists' to refer to much-acclaimed public figures such as Ayan Hirsi Ali (the Netherlands), Necla Kelek (Germany), Fadela Amara (France) and Irshad Mandji (Canada), who enjoy the legitimacy of their 'indigenous informant'[44] or cultural insider status to produce hegemonic knowledge about their own cultural or religious group. The trouble with these virulent denunciations is their essentialism, the ways in which they contribute to demonizing Islam and are exploited by populist politicians. Their denunciations are hailed (the list of awards they have received is too long to include here). Their stereotypical accounts and clichés strengthen negative representations of Muslims (whether North Africans, Turks, or Kurds), and portray women within these communities as helpless victims, thereby erasing the possibility of other meaningful lives, de-legitimizing forms of agency other than the one that they personally have achieved. Just as with Orientalist dialectics, where the construction of the 'Other woman' (Third World, immigrant, Muslim) as a helpless and voiceless victim of her culture waiting to be empowered and emancipated by the (Western) feminist project enables the construction of the emancipated Western sovereign subject, the dialectics involved in internal Orientalism use a similar mirror image, this time with the internal

Other, here the traditionalist, not-yet-emancipated woman. Such a portrayal not only fails to address the complexity of subject positions and divisions within the falsely stabilized category of 'Third World/Muslim women,' consistently depicted as victims of their culture, but also represents the personal trajectories of the authors as exceptions to the rule and not as evidence that these communities are far less homogeneous than they are believed to be. For instance, the Turkish-German sociologist and author of the much-acclaimed and controversial book, *The Alien Bride* (*Die fremde Braut*), Necla Kelek is seen and depicts herself as an individual success story, an exception confirming the rule, leaving thereby unchallenged the stereotype of the Turkish woman oppressed by her patriarchal culture (Berghahn and Rostock 2006). Criticized for her oversimplistic clichés and negative stereotypes about Islam and Turks, Kelek's book was at the centre of an open letter written by immigration specialists, Professor Yasemin Karakasoglu and Mark Terkessidis, and published 2 February 2006 in the German weekly *Die Zeit*. Signed by fifty-eight other specialists on migration, the letter denounced the increasing use of inflammatory pamphlets and sensationalist essays based on personal experiences by women authors such as Necla Kelek, Ayaan Hirsi Ali, Seyran Ates,[45] among others, to inform public opinion and policy makers on thorny issues such as arranged and forced marriages and honour-related crimes (Berghahn and Rostock 2006). According to the signers, these materials made unscientific generalizations on the basis of individual cases, obliterating the complexity of the empirical findings of scientific studies that are hardly covered by the media (Fekete 2006: 22). Concerns were also raised about the exploitation of these stereotypes to prove that Muslims simply do not fit into liberal Western democracies. Similar critiques have been addressed in France to Fadela Amara, president of the association NPNS (Ni putes ni soumises)[46] for producing anti-Muslim stereotypes while pretending to speak in the name of minority women, *les femmes des quartiers*.

It is worth noting that the feminist co-optation of the voices of 'other' women, which has been analysed at length in the works of postcolonial feminists, prevails in the current context where the 'woman question' is admitted to be the Achille's heel of Muslims' integration in Western states.[47] This benevolent Western(ized) feminist impulse to represent the subaltern/oppressed women furthers the co-optation of their voices, and most significantly serves against their best interests, by joining forces with populist and conservative advocates of harsher immigration policies. As Spivak points out, the benevolent Western intellectual, or her present-day representative, the cultural insider intellectual, can paradoxically silence the subalterns by claiming to represent and speak for their experience, the same way that the colonizers did. The pretension of speaking in the name of the voiceless brown/Muslim sisters, well intentioned as it may be, relies on cultural stereotypes of minority/Third World women that mainstream Euro-American feminist thought continues to produce; the irony is that this co-optation and these negative stereotypes are now reproduced by some minority women themselves, such as Hirsi Ali, Kelek, Mandji, and Amara, who have joined Eurocentric feminism. These stereotypes include 'the image ... of the passive Asian woman subject to oppressive practices within the Asian family, with an emphasis on wanting to "help" Asian Women to liberate themselves from their role ... the strong, dominant Afro-Caribbean woman, who despite her "strength" is exploited by the 'sexism' which is seen as being a strong feature in relationships between Afro-Caribbean men and women' (Amos and Parmar 1984: 9). This negative stereotyping needs to be understood as an implicit by-product of a benevolent universalist/Eurocentrist feminism, which has a tendency to represent the histories and lives of Third World women in the terms of Western female subject constitution (Spivak 1988). This is particularly relevant in the analysis of the dominant framing of the *foulard islamique* issue in France, which has repeatedly emphasized how the veil was an unequivocal signifier of women's subjugation. As we shall see in the next section, veiled women were consistently constructed as victims of their culture, which was depicted by prominent intellectual figures of the French republic as 'the harshest patriarchy of the world.'[48] Central to the construction of this consensual meaning system is the denial of veiled women's agency.

The French Veil Controversy

On 15 March 2004 the French National Assembly adopted a law banning students from wearing 'conspicuous religious symbols' in public primary and secondary schools;[49] the law came into effect on 2 September 2004, on the eve of the new school year. Prohibiting all too-visible religious objects such as the veil, the kippa, and large crosses, the law permits the wearing of discreet objects such as a small cross, Star of David, Fatima's hand, or miniature korans. Although there is no explicit mention of any particular religion, the law is justifiably considered as specifically targeting the Muslim veil,[50] which has caused much controversy in France since the late 1980s and has been referred to as 'national drama' (Gaspard and Khosrokhavar 1995: 11). Dounia Bouzar (2004) rightly reminds us that the prohibition targets only students; veiled cleaning women working in public spaces, including schools, have never been considered an issue or a threat to the French principle of *laïcité*. According to Benhabib, this philosophical principle is not fully translated by separation between church and state or secularization: 'at best, it can be understood as the public and manifest neutrality of the state toward all kinds of religious practices, institutionalized through vigilant removal of sectarian religious symbols, signs, icons and items of clothing from official public spheres' (2002: 95–6). So, it took a handful of veiled teenagers to challenge the principles governing the French public sphere and to generate a decade-long controversy[51] over the legitimacy of the veil in public schools in a country with a Muslim population estimated at between 3.7 and 5.5 million, the largest in Europe.

The banning of the Muslim veil from French public schools implies the closure of a signification process in which the dominant framing had the last say. The ban illustrates that the veil has been successfully and collectively defined as an *unequivocal signifier* of women's submission to men, and as such incompatible with the principles of the republic. It was perceived to transgress specifically two tenets of French republicanism: equality (in this case gender equality) and the principle of *laïcité* (Blank 1999). Numerous empirical studies show the fluidity and semiotic plurality of the veil as a social practice (Gaspard and Khosrokhavar 1995, Venel 1999, Dwyer 1999, Bouzar and Kada 2003, Tersigni 2005), which also includes an aesthetic dimension (Moors 2004, Sandikci and Ger 2005), and much empirical evidence suggests its use as an enabling rather than disabling garment in particular contexts (El Guindi 1999, Hoodfar 2003, Mahmood 2005) and its political reappropriation in order to contest the social exclusion and anti-Muslim racism, in particular by second and third generations of émigré youth (Keaton 2006; Afshar, Aitken, and Franks 2005) – which make wearing the veil, in these specific cases, a process similar to the reversal of the stigma, conveyed in political mottos such as 'Black Is Beautiful,' 'Gay Is Good,' Nevertheless, in French political and media discourses the Muslim veil has been cast without any ambiguity as the sign of Muslim women's submission to Muslim men. Thus, accommodating the veil became morally objectionable, since it came to signify endorsing this submission. Collective definition of the veil as unequivocally oppressive, hence condemnable, prevailed across the political spectrum and resulted in its banning, which was endorsed by up to 70 per cent of the French according to various polls.[52] The following quotations from feminists and mainstream politicians are intended to illustrate the representational consensus reigning with regard to the Muslim veil.[53]

For the reputed French feminist and philosopher Elisabeth Badinter, allowing women to wear headscarves in state schools means that French democracy and the republic display religious tolerance, but in doing so they give up on gender equality.[54] Opposing the veil from the beginning of the controversy, Badinter equates the veil with 'sex oppression' and asserts that wearing the veil cannot involve a choice since it signifies renouncing one's personal autonomy.[55] Revealingly, her understanding of personal autonomy and agency does not refer to the ability to make one's own choices in one's best interests, but includes a value judgment of the *content* of these choices.[56] This 'content-dependent' understanding of agency is a truly humanistic one, reminiscent of the Millian premise (1874) that 'one cannot freely submit to slavery, nor prefer a slothful life to one of Socratic questioning' (Mookherjee 2005: 3), which has been challenged successfully both by poststructuralist and anti-racist feminism. For Badinter, 'even if Muslim girls might appear to choose this practice autonomously, this does not mean that they are autonomous. This is because the content of their cultural norms – namely, the Muslim values of female restraint, modesty and seclusion – are opposed to personal autonomy' (ibid.). What is striking about this account is its exclusive focus on one aspect of intragroup power relations (gender), which totally ignores intergroup (majority/minority) power relations based on (gendered) ethnicity, culture, and religion. Indeed, the subtext of such a definition of agency, involving the choice of liberal values, perpetuates the power relations within which the agency is always already embedded.

For the proponents of the law, massively supported by the French, women do not choose to wear the veil: it is worn either under duress or as a result of alienation. Fadela Amara, the then president of NPNS, declared before the audits of the Stasi Commission: 'I consider the veil to be first and foremost a tool of oppression.'[57] An important feminist organization, *Les Chiennes de garde*, likewise argued: 'What is the veil? First, it is a religious and political symbol. It is the symbol of women's oppression, of the demonizing of their body and sexuality, which makes women indecent by nature, [asserts that they] should be camouflaged, put in chains. For us, the reality and interpretation of this symbol bear no contest.'[58] The pro-law lobby mixed every controversial issue identified as Islamic – Shari'a law, forced marriage, the veil, FGM, honour killings – to depict the veil as oppressive to women and to de-legitimate the anti-law lobbies. For instance, Safia Lebdi, from the NPNS, condemned the anti-law groups for spreading an 'anti-white and anti-French racism' and claimed that '60,000 forced marriages have been contracted in 2004 in France,'[59] while former Primer Minister Alain Juppé warned: 'We must defend secularism – the next step may be separate train compartments for men and women, beaches reserved for one sex.'[60] Paradoxically, being against a law expelling veiled students from public schools came to signify being against the integration of Muslims in French society. At the reception of his Légion d'honneur (the nation's highest decoration), Bernard Stasi, the state ombudsman who headed the commission on the application of the principle of *laïcité,* declared: 'Those who are against the law are against the integration of Muslims.'[61]

The French veil controversy conveys a collective representation of the veil as symbol of women's subordination. The achievement of the collective definition of the Muslim veil as unequivocally oppressive for women, even though anthropological studies show the fluidity and the semiotic plurality of veiling qua social practice, has been realized with the crucial contribution of mainstream feminists, although it would be far-fetched to attribute to French feminists alone the political responsibility of this restrictive dress legislation. Central to the making of the veil into a symbol of women's submission was the cognitive and perceptual distortion, conceptualized by Adrienne Rich (1979) as 'white solipsism,' that is, a tunnel vision resulting from the tendency of Euro-American mainstream feminists to forget the particularities of their (white, middle-class, heterosexual, able bodied) standpoint and to universalize their experience with their claim to represent and speak for all women. This type of distortion is manifest in liberal feminist writings, for instance, in Okin's assertion that 'the situation of poor women in poor countries is not qualitatively *different* from that of most women in rich countries but, rather, "similar but worse"' (1994: 11). This reasoning is motivated by keeping the subject of feminist struggle, 'women,' unified, and the premise of 'common oppression' unchallenged. Okin's claim that 'one can argue that sexism is an identifiable form of oppression, many of whose effects are felt by women regardless of race or class, without at all subscribing to the view that race and class oppression are insignificant' (7) likewise needs to be unpacked, since the 'regardless of race or class' discourse is tenable only for women whose lives are relatively privileged in terms of racial and class hierarchies.

While it is necessary to deconstruct the Eurocentric and imperialist framing of the veil as unequivocally oppressive to women, it is equally necessary to be wary of some anti-imperialist accounts, which invariably see veiling as an act of empowerment and an expression of *resistance* agency, making it the emblem of women's liberation from Western imperialism.[62] The veil cannot be seen as a practice either uniformly oppressive or uniformly empowering. While Lewis and Mills rightly remind us that 'look[ing] for a singular meaning to the veil would be an error of Orientalist proportions' (2003: 18), the scope of their critique needs to be extended to equally reified meanings assigned in resistance and retaliation to ambiguous signifiers such as the practice of veiling. Moreover, discussions of the empowering impacts of veiling need to go beyond the resistance dimension to consider the possibility of *submissive* agencies – an evident oxymoron for an Enlightenment-informed understanding of human agency – that are constituted within the act of 'taking the veil' (here, the submission involved is to God and not to men), such as the ones found in the compelling work of Saba Mahmood (2005), which reveals that the taking of the veil for pious motives is also, in certain cases, a transformative technique of the self.

Conclusion

The 'peril of multiculturalism for women' discourse is premised on a particular subject: the immigrant woman victim of her culture, and as such it constructs women's subordination to men as integral to non-Western cultures (Volpp 2005: 40–1). Although the universalist claims of Western feminism to speak for all women and represent their interests, experiences, and standpoints have successfully been challenged since the late 1970s, what has emerged from this challenge – that is, taking into account women's differences – has often ended up boxing Other women into what Mohanty calls 'tightly packaged discrete cultural units' (1988). Hence, cultural reductionism and essentialism embedded in gender/culture antagonism interpret almost every significant aspect of the lives of minority women – and men – as determined by their culture. Such determinism relies on both an essentialist view of culture, seen as immutable and ahistorical sets of values, beliefs, and practices, often coupled with the idea of the superiority of the Western civilization, and a construction of minorities as devoid of any social agency. Hence, the interrelated processes of cultural reductionism, essentialism, and negative stereotyping, along with the denial of minority agency constitute the building blocks of the dominant discourse on minority women's victimization by their culture, which is itself part and parcel of the current de-legitimization of multicultural citizenship as a viable component of the project of achieving equality and social justice.

The alleged clash between feminism and multiculturalism stems from an impaired liberal dichotomy: equality versus difference. One may hold this line of argument if one defines feminism as promoting gender equality and multiculturalism as promoting recognition of cultural differences. In this light, while the first is understood as equality politics, the second is seen as politics of recognition, void of any social justice aspiration. This dissociation has been criticized by proponents of differentiated citizenship for whom the conditions of equal citizenship include both recognition and redistribution and for whom there is nothing antithetical between the recognition of difference and the pursuit of equality. As Phillips puts it, 'we cannot hope to achieve equality by ignoring differences, for all attempts to pretend difference away – not noticing whether someone is male or female, not noticing whether she is white or black – will end up reinforcing the dominance of already dominant groups' (1997: 143). When justice and equality issues are erased from the horizon of multiculturalism, reducing it to its identity, difference, and diversity components, the injustice of denying minorities the right to a meaningful social existence, which includes the recognition of their culture and the creation of the conditions of a cultural life, disappears.

The current focus on women's status among minorities and the denunciation of their 'much worse' patriarchy must be met with scepticism. What is needed is not a withdrawal from multiculturalism but a new conception of differentiated citizenship cognizant not only of intragroup and intergroup inequalities, but also of the complex ways in which they are connected to one another. It is only then that we may avoid enhancing intergroup inequalities and injustices for the sake of combating intragroup injustices.

Notes

1 By imagined multicultural past, I refer to countries where political and media discourses celebrate the end of multicultural wanderings, although there has never been an official policy of multiculturalism.

2 The integration debate increasingly conflates immigrants with Muslims, which is symptomatic of the 'culturalization' of the issue and the concealment of its social, political, and economic dimensions. When 'the failure of integration' is set in cultural terms, focusing on value differences between the 'host society and its Muslim immigrants,' the blame is easily put both on immigrants – their 'intolerant culture' (Denmark), their 'cultural barriers to inclusion' (Norway) (Fekete 2006: 18) – and on the multiculturalism of the host society that has come to tolerate intolerance/able. This slippage, among others, conveys that 'Muslims have become central to the merits and demerits of multiculturalism as a public policy in western Europe' (Modood 2007: 4).

3 According to the government-appointed chair of the forum for social integration of immigrants in Spain, as reported in *El País* (23 March 2002) and quoted by Fekete (2006: 21).

4 See, e.g., 'The Veiled Conceit of Multiculturalism.' *The Australian*, Editorial, 24 October 2006.

5 At least market-driven multiculturalism or 'soft versions of multiculturalism' as labelled by Rex and Singh (2003: 3) seem to persist. Big cities continue to cultivate their multicultural or cosmopolitan image, although this is far from indicating any concrete multicultural commitment. Yet, according to Dustin and Phillips, policy makers in Britain still seem committed to an *image* of their country as culturally plural; and affirm that the selection of London as the site for the 2012 Olympics was widely attributed to its successful *marketing* as a vibrant multicultural city (ibid., my emphasis).

6 For the revival of assimilationism in Britain, see Back et al. (2002).

7 Sometimes, such accusations are also held by members of minorities. For instance, Tarek Fatah, the founder of the Muslim Canadian Congress and a particularly vocal opponent of religious accommodations, claimed that '[Canada] is being eaten by termites that are being fed by multiculturalism' and lamented the political 'catering to the Muslim far-right by the politically correct.' Quoted in Philippe Gohier, 'Multiculturalism's Last Gap?, *Maclean's*, 24 Sept. 2007.

8 Cultural essentialism refers to commonsensical understanding that 'each culture has a unique, fixed essence that can be understood independently

of context or intercultural relations, and which makes an ethnic group act the way it does' (Modood 1997: 10).

9 The perpetrators of the 7 July attacks in London were born and raised in Britain.

10 'Ruth Kelly's Speech on Integration and Cohesion.' *The Guardian*. 24 Aug. 2006. http://www.guardian.co.uk/britain/article/0,,1857369,00.html.

11 The Dutch model of multiculturalism dates back to the 1979 'minority policy' shaped after the national *Verzuiling* (pillarization) that historically structures the basis of the Dutch nation-state. For the return of assimilationism in the Netherlands, see Entzinger (1994, 2003).

12 The Freedom Party, a far-right fringe group became the fifth-largest party in the parliament. Its leader, Geert Wilders, thinks that the Netherlands is engulfed by an 'Islamic tsunami.' Calling for an end to immigration and a ban on building religious schools and mosques, he declared on television: 'We need more decency in this country, more education and less Islam … We have had enough Islam in the Netherlands. I believe Islam is a violent religion and the Koran is a violent book. There is no such thing as moderate Islam.'(Peter Goodspeed, 'Europe's Tolerance Finds Its Limit,' *National Post*. 25 Nov. 2006.) The extreme right is also gaining ground in countries such as Austria, Belgium, and Norway.

13 Van Gogh was killed by a radical fundamentalist Muslim, after he made a controversial film with Somali-born Dutch politician Ayaan Hirsi Ali, *Submission*, in which quotes from the Koran are projected over the semi-naked bodies of women to denounce the violence against women in Muslim societies. A lengthy letter quoting religious texts and threatening Hirsi Ali was pinned by the killer to van Gogh's body. Analysts note that prior to Hirsi Ali's intervention, Muslim women's status was not a part of criticisms of multiculturalism or Islam in the Netherlands (Prins and Saharso 2006). It is the murder of van Gogh that has put her under the spotlight of the international media. Celebrated by *Time* magazine as one of the 100 most influential people of 2005, she has since received dozens of awards. The popular Dutch historian Geert Mak compared *Submission* to Goebbels's infamous Nazi propaganda film *The Eternal Jew*. For a critical assessment of *Submission*, see Moors (2005).

14 Johanne van Selm, 'The Death of a Filmmaker Shakes a Nation,' *Migration Information Source, Country profile*. Oct. 2005. http://www.migrationinformation.org/Profiles/display.cfm?ID=341.

15 It is worth separating the liberalization of citizenship regimes such as in Germany and Sweden, where dual citizenship is now available, from multiculturalism. As the French example demonstrates, a state can favour an

assimilative model of immigrant integration within a *jus solis* citizenship framework allowing multiple citizenships.

16 In doing so, I do not deny that certain institutional practices, rather informally inspired than formally required by multiculturalism, are prejudicial to women. In prior research, I have brought forth empirical evidence of such situations, in which certain Canadian judges, zealous to show sensitivity to (reified) 'cultural difference' – a principle they *felt* to be dictated by multiculturalism – pronounced inadmissibly lenient sentences in cases of violence against racialized women (Bilge 2005). Yet, it needs to be recalled that while slippages become the object of extensive media coverage, sensible decisions are hardly covered, such as the recent decision of the Supreme Court of Canada to decline to receive as justification Muslim cultural and religious beliefs in 'family honour' in a wife murder case committed by a Canadian from United Arab Emirates. (Janice Tibbetts, 'Top Court Refuses to Hear Whether Religion Can Be a Murder Defence,' *CanWest News Service.* 10 Nov. 2006.)

17 In a documentary, CBS commented on the murder of Theo van Gogh as: 'For the Dutch who have prided themselves for centuries on a tradition of tolerance, it was a painful awakening, the prospect of a *homegrown jihad* in the world's most liberal state' (CBS, 'Slaughter and Submission,' *60 Minutes*, 13 March 2005, my emphasis).

18 For instance, according to Entzinger (1994), multiculturalism is repudiated in the Netherlands on the grounds that 'multiculturalism and equal opportunity are two concepts that, in essence, exclude each other.'

19 Adjectival form of doxa. Bourdieu uses the term in his *Outline of a Theory of Practice* (1977) while theorizing *habitus*, and defines it as the universe of undisputed truths, serving the dominant ideology. Dominant classes have an interest in defending the integrity of the doxa, whereas subordinate classes have an interest in pushing back its limits (169).

20 This refers to a wide range of state policies and measures designed to enable ethnocultural minorities to maintain certain practices and norms of their way of life (Shachar 2000: 385).

21 For instance, in Germany the federal state of Baden-Württemberg introduced a test on values only for Muslim applicants for German citizenship, an initiative relying on the assumption that most Muslims are less fit to integrate into the German *Leitkultur*. Muslims are asked questions on matters of conscience and sensitive issues such as how they would react if they learned that their adult son is gay and will live with a man, or if they think that it is OK to beat one's wife if she is deemed disobedient (Fekete 2006: 3–5).

22 For Jonathan Kay, from Canada's right-wing newspaper, *National Post*, Fadime Sahindal, a young Kurdish-Swedish woman killed in January 2002 by her father for living with her Swedish boyfriend, was 'multiculturalism's latest victim' (1 Aug. 2002). Hatun Sürücü's murder in 2005 in Berlin has been treated in similar terms. (Jeffrey Fleishman, "Honor Killings' Show Culture Clash in Berlin,' *LA Times*, 20 March 2005.)

23 Denmark adopted the most restrictive measures in family reunification across Europe: the Danish Aliens Act of 2002 removed the statutory right to family reunification to 'encourage' integration. The Government's Action Plan for 2003–2005 on 'forced, quasi-forced and arranged marriages,' the title of which illustrates the tendency to amalgamate arranged and forced marriages and to presume coercion in each and every case, states that arranged marriages hinder integration and result in increased immigration, since they are mostly contracted transnationally (Fekete 2006: 6). In Norway, methodologically challenged but much-publicized feminist 'research,' *Human Visas* (by Hege Storhaug, 2003) claimed that marriage was a pretext for immigration and called for stricter immigration controls and shaking off multiculturalism (see Razack 2004 and Bredal 2005 for an in-depth discussion of Danish and Norwegian cases).

24 Marina Jimenez, 'Women's Rights Trump Cultural Habits, Poll Finds,' *Globe and Mail*. 14 Nov. 2006.

25 On 7 Oct. 2001 the United States, with the help of the United Kingdom and the support of an international coalition including the NATO alliance, launched military action against the Taliban.

26 Laura Bush, 'The Taliban's War against Women,' Radio Address to the Nation, Crawford, Texas. 17 Nov. 2001. http://www.state.gov/g/drl/rls/rm/2001/6206.htm (italics mine).

27 Mavis Leno is the Chair of the Feminist Majority Foundation's Campaign to Stop Gender Apartheid in Afghanistan launched in 1997.

28 A special message issued by the Feminist Majority Foundation a few days after 9/11 asserts: 'While law enforcement continues to collect evidence about Osama bin Laden's involvement in the horrific acts of terrorism on September 11, the relationship between the Taliban, Osama bin Laden, and the suffering of Afghan women is very clear. We know that the Taliban militia has been harboring bin Ladin and that, together, they have been leading campaigns of terror against women, women's rights, ethnic and religious minorities, and the western world for many years.' Feminist Majority Foundation, 'Special Message from the Feminist Majority on The Taliban, Osama bin Laden, and Afghan Women.' Retrieved 23 Oct. 2006 from http://feminist.org/news/newsbyte/uswirestory.asp?id=5804.

29 For a relevant synthesis of controversies across Europe which put women, in particular Muslim women, at the centre of the debates, see Dustin (2007).
30 I distinguish official multiculturalist policies from diversity accommodation practices that are also observed locally in settings like France where there are no official multiculturalist policies, where, on the contrary, the national model of identity and integration is formulated as an antithesis to multiculturalism.
31 Oct./Nov. 1997 issue.
32 Such as Will Kymlicka, Bhikhu Parekh, Homi Bhabha, among others. See their respective contributions in Cohen, Howard, and Nussbaum, eds. (1999).
33 As put by Amy Gutmann on the back cover of the volume *Is Multiculturalism Bad for Women?*.
34 For instance, commenting on Okin's perspective, Al-Hibri aptly warns: 'If Western feminists are now vying for control of the lives of immigrant women by justifying coercive state action, then these women have not learned the lessons of history, be it colonialism, imperialism, or even fascism' (1999: 45).
35 See also Coleman (1996), and Nussbaum (1999), esp. ch. 1, 'Women and Cultural Universals,' and ch. 3, 'Religion and Women's Human Rights.'
36 These hypothetical exit rights are highly problematic in practice. As Gutmann (2001: xxi) aptly puts it: 'Oppressed women typically want their rights as individuals to be secured within their own culture, not at the expense of exile from their culture, or the destruction of what and they take to be valuable about their culture.'
37 According to Rebecca Hall (2006), she is 'the one who set up the camp.'
38 One of the examples utilized pell-mell by Okin to prove how multiculturalism wanes women's rights is the French government's toleration of immigrant polygamy. She argues that 'the French accommodation of polygamy illustrates a deep and growing tension between feminism and multiculturalist concern for protecting cultural diversity' (1999: 10). This deduction displays less than thorough scholarship, which is one of the key flaws of her essay (see M. Nussbaum's critique in the same volume). The French polygamy case cannot be attributed to multiculturalism, since the French model of integration strongly opposes multiculturalism, which is seen as incompatible with the ideals of the republic. The French state's attitude towards polygamy may be better explained as indifference or a colonialist-like laissez-faire attitude towards 'less civilized' customs (Fekete 2006: 12).
39 See Lazreg (1994) for struggles between French colonizers and Algerian resistance over the veiling/unveiling of women; see also Hélie-Lucas (1999). See Ahmed (1992) for a discussion of the topic under British colonial rule in Egypt.

40 Mosques were occupied by colonial troops and turned into stables and arms depots; lands entrusted to mosques were declared property of the French state (Lazreg 1994: 51–2).

41 Bourdieu calls this resistance-oriented reinvention and reappropriation of traditions 'colonial traditionalism' (1961).

42 See, among others, Chaudhuri and Strobel, eds. (1992), Jayawardena (1995), Ware (1992).

43 Hubertine Auclert, a well-known French suffragette, is one of the exceptions. Despite her imperial and racially hierarchical feminism, she identified French colonialism's responsibility in disrupting Algerian society, culture, and family life, and its complicity in women's subordination. In a period when dominant colonial discourse was against the extension of French citizenship to Algerian Muslims – justifying their exclusion by the abject position of their women, which made them unfit to become citizens – she defended assimilation via education and argued that France had a moral responsibility to transform secluded women into voters. Ironically, her work, especially her plea against child marriage, had been hijacked by exclusionary political forces, for which it brought additional proof of indigenous sexual perversions. In a context linking sexuality tightly to citizenship, her work was instrumental to constructing Algerian Muslims as fundamentally different and inferior (Clancy-Smith 1998).

44 See Kirin Narayan's compelling article on the ambivalence and complexity of the native/indigenous informant in anthropological work (1997). From an anthropological perspective the native/indigenous informant is an intercultural mediator, a person translating her culture for the researcher who is an outsider. It is ironic that, under the majority eyes, the virulent denunciation of minority culture by an insider is seen as an achievement of intercultural dialogue, as one may see in the dozens of awards given to Ayaan Hirsi Ali, such as the Tolerance Price of the Comunidad de Madrid.

45 A German-Turkish lawyer and SPD member, she holds multiculturalism accountable for immigrant women's sufferings in Germany. She argues the 'wrong' implementation of the multicultural society is responsible for 'insular and hardly accessible parallel societies' where 'forced marriages, honour killings and human rights violations are endemic' (Fekete 2006: 15). It is worth noting that in Germany there is no state strategy of immigrant integration, neither is there any official policy of multiculturalism, but local (municipal) initiatives of moderate diversity accommodation.

46 Neither Whores, Nor Submissive.

47 According to Ronald Inglehart and Pippa Norris (2003), the value clash between Islam and the West is not about democracy but about gender equality.

48 Elisabeth Badinter, Régis Debray, Alain Finkielkraut, Elisabeth de Fontenay, Catherine Kintzler, 'Profs, ne capitulons pas!' *Le Nouvel Observateur*. 2–8 Nov. 1989. http://www.laicite-laligue.org/laligue/laicite-laligue/pdf/badinter.pdf.

49 Its full title is: *Loi n° 2004-228 du 15 mars 2004 encadrant, en application du principe de laïcité, le port de signes ou de tenues manifestant une appartenance religieuse dans les écoles, collèges et lycées publics.*

50 The opuscule written by one of the two senators defending before the Senate the bill banning religious signs from public schools states clearly what the target is. See Lizin (2004).

51 *L'affaire du foulard* started in October 1989 at a Middle School in Creil (Oise) with the suspension of three students for refusing to remove their veils in class, which soon became a *fait de société* under extensive media coverage. In November 1989, a ruling of the Conseil d'État declared the veil compatible with the *laïcité* of public schools. A month later, Lionel Jospin, then the prime minister, issued a statement bestowing to educators the responsibility of accepting or refusing veiled students on a case-by-case basis.

52 A February 2004 survey by CSA for the newspaper *Le Parisien* shows 69% of the population for the ban and 29% against, the support for the ban being more important among Rightists (75%) than Leftists (66%). Among the French Muslims surveyed, the results are 42% for the ban and 53% against. Among Muslim women, the support for the ban is 49%, while 43% oppose it. ('The War of the Headscarves,' *Economist*. 5 Feb. 2004. http://www.economist.com/displaystory.cfm?story_id=2404691). Another survey conducted the same year by CSA for *Le Monde* and *La Vie* shows that 76% of 504 surveyed teachers are in favour of the ban, while 91% of them declare not having veiled students in their classes. ('Voile: les enseignants pour la loi,' *Le Monde*. 5 Feb. 2004: 1.)

53 I exclude countless declarations made by right-wing politicians such as Jean-Marie Le Pen and Philippe de Villiers, whose fervent opposition to the accommodation of Muslim claims is an already well-known fact.

54 Quoted in Clare Murphy, 'Headscarves: Contentious Cloths,' *BBC News Online*. 11 Dec. 2003, http://news.bbc.co.uk/2/hi/europe/3135600.stm.

55 Elisabeth Badinter (1989), Interview with L. Joffin, *Le Nouvel Observateur*. 9–15 Nov.: 7–11.

56 This is far from the black feminist definition of agency that may be found, for instance, in bell hooks as 'the ability to act in one's own best interests' (1990: 206).

57 Reports from *laic.info*, Fadela Amara's audition before the Stasi Commission. http://www.laic.info/Members/webmestre2/La_laicite_en_France.2003-11-16.1123/view.

58 Chiennes de garde, 'Voile: le symbole et l'acte,' Communiqué. 7 March 2005. http://chiennesdegarde.org/article.php3?id_article=383.

59 Quoted in A. Menusier, 'Les pro-voile rejouent "Les Damnés de la terre."' *Courrier International*. 28 April, to 3 May, 2005.

60 Murphy, 'Headscarves: Contentious Cloths.'

61 Alex Duval Smith, 'France Divided as Headscarf Ban Is Set to Become Law,' *Observer*, 1 Feb. 2004.

62 For a critique of 'extravagant affirmations of Muslim women's agency,' see Moghissi (1999).

6 The Migration-Citizenship Nexus

DAIVA STASIULIS

The global mobility of people has increased in velocity, extent, and intensity, and so too has the complexity of its patterns. At the beginning of the twenty-first century, migration trends pose a major challenge to the conventional Westphalian notion of national citizenship, whereby citizen-residents hold exclusive loyalty to and enjoy entitlements within one territorially based nation-state. 'Nation-states' – both senders and receivers of migrants – are in a continuous process of inventing and reproducing the largely fictitious idea that the 'nation' as a cultural, linguistic, and/or ethnic entity maps onto the sovereign territory of the political and geographical entity recognized as the 'state.'[1] Migration, especially of the intense and complex types that characterize contemporary population movements, is a major force calling into question the authenticity of the nation-state itself and the integrity of a bounded nation-state citizenship. International migration introduces a level of racial and ethnic heterogeneity that undermines the myth of coincidence of (ethnic) nation and state. However, and as importantly, insofar as migrants increasingly hold multiple memberships, ties, loyalties, and material and cultural embeddedness in more than one sovereign territory, migration is a force that splinters, spatially disperses, and complicates citizenship.

As Luin Goldring has suggested, the transnational social fields constructed by transmigrants point 'to a need to broaden existing conceptions of citizenship, so that practices that express social, cultural, political, and civil claims/rights are examined in a transnational context' (1998: 168). The significance of migration in building border-spanning links, networks, institutions, and subjectivities, and sustaining various flows globally, far exceeds its actual incidence compared with the planet's population – with migrants estimated to comprise 3 per cent of the global population (International Organization of Migration 2006).[2] This chapter explores the social dimension of how migrations and the social fields that they construct[3] are transconfiguring citizenship into new geospatial and social formations, loosening, pluralizing, but by no means abandoning, the ties between bounded nation-states and citizenship. Here I employ the 'social' aspect of citizenship in a double sense. First, citizenship is fruitfully regarded to be constructed in *relational* terms – as unstable, yet patterned sets of social interactions and arrangements. These are actively negotiated, contested, and reordered by and among individuals, households, states, multinational corporate interests, a range of institutions, transnational communities, and territories, and between the realms of the private and public. As argued in the introduction, 'to interrogate what is social in citizenship means drawing attention to the process-oriented and contested character of citizenship.' Exploring the social in citizenship through the lens of the transnational mobilities of people reveals how hierarchical and uneven the forms of inherited entitlements and obligations are in an unequal world (Shachar 2007). Different agents employ multisited, multidirectional, and transnational strategies to redistribute (or resist the redistribution of) the rights and burdens of birthright and acquired memberships in different states to their best advantage.

Second, I refer specifically to 'social citizenship,' the third category of T.H. Marshall's (1950) trinity of citizenship rights that he identified as integral to the construction and normalization of citizenship in the twentieth century. Social citizenship is most commonly associated with post-Second World War redistributive policies, and the 'amalgam of social welfare and social security programs variously implemented by postwar welfare states' (Brodie, this volume). Nonetheless, disagreement over what is meant by this concept centres on whether its 'essence' is defined in terms of decommodification – that is, entitlement based on non-market principles and universality of accessibility (see Siltanen 2002: 400) or, more conservatively, on civic solidarity, civic equality, and the absence of stigma among the poorest of rights-bearing citizens (Powell 2002). A great deal of ink has been spilled in efforts to understand how neoliberal forms of governance that have swept the Anglo-American democracies and many other polities with formerly robust or at least more developed welfare states worldwide have come to undermine, 'desocialize' (subordinate the social to the economic), and marketize much of the postwar social citizenship regime (Brodie

2002b: 388). Far less attention has been paid to the role of international migration in both facilitating and contesting these processes.

The restructuring and greater economic integration of peripheral regions and countries into the capitalist world economy has acted as a major catalyst for initiating and intensifying international migration. Especially notable have been the consequences for the well-being of individuals, transnational households, and communities of the global accumulation and the redistribution of various forms of economic, social, and cultural capital stemming from novel migration circuits – no longer unidirectional such as South to North, but increasingly circular, recurrent, and multiple. States – both migrant sending and migrant receiving – are major players in enabling social citizenship to 'go global' in forms that reflect neoliberal ideologies and political rationalities that emphasize individual self-reliance, entrepreneurialism, familialism, and the superiority of market mechanisms in securing human well-being. In other words, certain 'inefficiencies' in the provision of social welfare entitlements in well-resourced states such as Canada – for example, lengthening wait times for surgeries, lack of adequate and affordable child and elder care – have provided encouragement for such 'care gaps' to be furnished by individuals (migrant caregivers) and institutions (private hospitals) from the global South, most often with the blessing and endorsement of both the provisioning and the recipient states, as well as a variety of 'middleman' institutions and interests.

This chapter explores some selected social dimensions of emergent transnational citizenship practices – such as the everyday transnationalism of subjects, embedded in border-transgressing familial and other social networks. Also of interest are the forms of transnationalism constructed through the practices of an array of state, market-based, and civil society institutions. The focus is on the redistributive dimensions of social citizenship, as citizenship among transmigrants becomes pluralized across territories and nation-states. I examine the impact of these practices in unbundling the tight articulation of the citizen with the formal state and the concomitant recasting, privatizing, respatializing, and partial denationalizing of state-based citizenship (Sassen 2006: 283, 285, 314, 321). As Saskia Sassen (283) has illuminated, transformations in citizenship resulting from globalization combine partial *denationalizing* moves, whereby the growing articulation of globalization with national economies hastens the withdrawal of the state from various spheres of citizenship entitlement, with moments of *renationalizing*, as states securitize and harden their borders to the entry of illicit and poor migrants. Moreover, human mobility also entails processes of *multinationalizing* citizenship, as transmigrants, who experience a dilution of loyalty to any given state, employ cross-border practices to accumulate partial and contingent rights and entitlements, including forms of social citizenship, and avoid certain membership burdens such as taxes and military service (Faist 2007: 3; Ong 1999).

Migration scholars document how migrants are active agents in not merely *responding* to shifts in citizenship regimes, but also in *facilitating* these shifts and in devising creative strategies to survive them. The migration literature repeatedly reveals how individuals and families design their opportunity structures through movement across nation-state borders and their ability to function and even prosper in at least two, but often more than two cultures, localities, and nation-states. While the immediacy and intensity of contemporary transnational connections have been made possible by the rise of new communications and transportation technologies (Itzighsohn 2000: 1130), 'within the historical context, slower communication (letters) and transportation (multiple crossings) networks had never prevented migrants from living transnational lives' (Harzig and Hoerder 2006: 39). Even populations that have endured forced migration during political tumult (e.g., the expulsion of Asians from Uganda in 1972) have managed to accumulate 'substantial migratory cultural capital' and to develop forms of 'transnational insurance' (Van Hear 1998). Capturing the ability to create a transnational habitus[4] through multiple allegiances, a Gujarati proverb reflects on 'the paradoxical situation whereby many a Ugandan Asian kept his *man* (heart) in India and his *dhan* (wealth) in Britain while still managing to retain his *tan* (body) in East Africa' (Twaddle in Van Hear 1998: 199).

At the individual level, mobile subjects have responded to the citizenship divide between countries in the global North and South, as well as the hollowing out of the social welfare state in liberal and social democratic states that have embraced neoliberal governance. They have maximized their wage-earning capacities and other opportunity structures, in part by suturing together public and private resources across states (Stasiulis and Bakan 2003). As Kelly and Lusis (2006: 836) observe, the idea that the various forms of capital are accumulated and exchanged across borders is now widespread in immigration studies. At the collective level, diasporas[5] have had a major involvement in the economies of their countries of origin through what Orozco (2003) calls the 'Five Ts': 'tourism, transportation, telecommunications, trade and transmission of monetary remittances.' But, in addition, diasporic or transmigration associations are increasingly seen as providing an important partner or bridge between home and host societies in 'co-development policies' whose goal is to benefit home country development and possibly diasporas as well (Ionescu 2006: 25). Conventional models of immigrant incorporation have taken scant notice of such border-bridging practices, assuming that immigrants leave 'sending societies' and seek to become exclusively integrated into 'receiving societies,' in the process transferring their allegiance from their place of birth to their adopted country (Castles and Davidson 2000: 157–8).

A comprehensive mapping of the consequences of the contemporary patterns of global mobility of peoples on the recasting and respatializing of the social in citizenship across societies is beyond the scope of this chapter. Rather, I take as a more modest aim the effort to bring attention to some seemingly neglected elements of the global remapping of 'the social' in emergent transnational forms of citizenship. As taken up in the conclusion, the globalization of key policies and practices that have constituted central dimensions of social citizenship, as manifested in Canada's and other advanced industrialized countries' import of care workers and the outsourcing of health care, are more properly read in terms of partially denationalizing, transnationalizing, and multinationalizing dynamics rather than in terms of *postnationalism*, in the sense that they 'remain embedded in thick, localized environments' (Sassen 2006: 288, 300). Migration and diasporic communities are key to such moves to de-border, respatialize, and re-border social citizenship in that migrants (and their families and descendants) perform critical roles in reproducing social citizenship. Thus, migrants deliver care work in a multitude of migrant-receiving societies, initiate transnational business links with capital accumulated in several regional sites, themselves embody the circulation of capital across borders, provide the initial clientele for relocated social services, and very importantly – build bridges to constructing new social fields whose inhabitants extend beyond particular ethnic or diasporic communities. All of these practices, occurring in border-spanning fashion, have radical ramifications for traditional social citizenship policies and their assumed boundedness within nation-states.

The respatialization of social citizenship is occurring in a global context where the governments of most advanced capitalist countries have embraced some form of neoliberal political rationality, whereas countries in the global South have been compelled to do the same through the International Monetary Fund (IMF) and the World Bank structural adjustment policies. This has meant that the spatial restructuring of citizenship has interacted with processes of privatization and marketization, thus widening the citizenship gap between those with financial means and those who are deprived of the basic means for economic and human security, both in poorer countries and in so-called advanced liberal democracies. The 'mobile social' in contemporary citizenship practices thus contributes to undermining the notion of communal membership in a 'single civilization,' a keystone to T.H. Marshall's (1950) conception of citizenship. These dynamics will be investigated here by briefly examining three transnational phenomena: (1) the provision of social (citizenship) policies in wealthier countries through the importation of migrant care workers to provide child care, elder care, familial care, and health care; (2) the recent intense interest within the international realm and among source countries to engage diasporas as central actors in development; and (3) the burgeoning of medical tourism in countries of the global South, with a focus on India.

I begin by with some fairly general observations about the pluralization and respatialization of citizenship through the lens of transnationalism. In a geospatial matrix where individuals' relationships may exist with two or more states, and where states now rely heavily on market or mixed (public/private) forms of delivery of key social services, citizenship is inevitably partially denationalized, splintered, and respatialized. Thus, it is important to distinguish what is transnational and multinational about emergent forms of social citizenship and to avoid equating them with an unbounded conception of postnational, cosmopolitan, or global citizenship that catapults citizenship onto an ethereal plane above and beyond nation-states and territories.

Transmigration and the Respatialization of Citizenship

Contemporary international migration is iconic of contemporary globalization, which geographer David Harvey (1989) famously described in terms of time–space compression, owing to transportation and communication technologies that have permitted the shrinking of space and the overcoming of distances. Rather than moving from sending to receiving country, during their lifetime an increasing number of migrants experience migration and long-term residence in more than just two countries. Even after they acquire permanent resident status or citizenship in the new country of destination, many continue to migrate to a third or indeed, fourth country. This increasingly common pattern of migration can be called 'multiple' or 'step-wise.'[6] With current migration patterns representing 'fluid but structured movement, with multidirectional and reversible trajectories' (Papastergiadis 2000:7), a keen interest has developed among citizenship scholars in understanding the consequences of such multiple migration for denationalizing, deterritorializing, and respatializing citizenship, and in imagining and constructing contemporary forms of transnational belonging (Basch, Schiller, and Blanc et al. 1994; Faist 2000; Goldring 1998: Mahler 1998, 75–6; Sassen 2006; Satzewich and Wong 2006a).

Like citizenship, transnationalism is a multidimensional and elastic concept, referring broadly to 'multiple ties and interactions linking people and institutions across borders of nation-states' (Vertovec 1999: 447). The study of migrant transnationalism has primarily focused on the construction and maintenance of a plethora of familial, social, commercial, financial, political and cultural networks, institutions, and practices that span national borders and involve subjects whose recurrent mobility defines them no longer as mere migrants but as 'transmigrants' (Glick Schiller, Basch, and Blanc, 1992: 1–2; Ehrkamp and Leitner 2006: 1591). A key insight of the burgeoning literature on transnationalism is that, for a growing number of subjects, their lives are transnational and multisited. In a meaningful sense, transmigrants live simultaneously (or seasonally) in more than one society – the societies of transmigrants' origin and what are usually referred to as the societies of settlement but, with step-wise migration, might additionally involve societies of intermediary or multiple settlement.

Participants in and shapers of transnational social fields include mobile individuals and others – who do not move but have strong ties and a sense of identification with countries of origin, or those in the country of origin who are profoundly affected by the reorganization of wealth and status hierarchies resulting from transmigration.[7] Actors within the transnational realm who are involved in a recasting and respatialization of the social in citizenship may be communities – constituted through common origins in homelands, as well as shared (ethnocultural or religious) values, or shared (occupational or political) interests, hometown associations, commercial interests, global girdling social networks, family or kin-related groupings – and individual migrants, who traverse certain 'ethnoscapes' (Appadurai 1996).[8]

The extent to which transnationalism informs the habitus of migrant lives varies immensely both across and within immigrant communities. Luis Aguiar (2006) observes that when whole kin networks and indeed villages have moved to other countries through chain migration, as has occurred for many southern Europeans resettled in Canada, there is little left of the transnational family or indeed transnational life worlds for these communities. For many other communities, however, transnational consciousness extends beyond first-generation migrants, and a strong sense of sentimental attachment to countries of origin exists among second and later generations. The absence of identification with their country of residence and even, among the second generation, with their country of birth, is striking among minorities constructed and discriminated against as eternal outsiders through processes of racialization.[9]

The border-transgressing lifeworlds of transmigrants have significantly transformed the set of social relations associated with the ideal if not the reality of nation-state citizenship, the chief one being the assumed exclusivity of the relationship between the citizen and one national state. The dramatic rise in the numbers of states that now tolerate if not embrace some form of dual or plural nationality or citizenship, and the increasing prevalence of subjects with multiple (partial or full) memberships in two or more states, are significant signs of how citizenship policies and practices are adjusting to, or in some cases embracing a novel multinational spatiality of citizenship.

By granting citizenship to persons living abroad, including second and third generation, origin or sending states may encourage transnational loyalties and practices that might be particularly attractive to those experiencing alienation and disaffiliation in the country of primary residence (Satzewich and Wong 2006a: 26). In 1983 Egypt granted dual citizenship to permanent migrants with a view to encouraging diasporic contributions to Egypt's development. In 2002 Ghana enacted dual citizenship to facilitate the return and investments of Ghanaians living abroad. In 2005 Armenia adopted dual citizenship to strengthen the ties between the Armenian diaspora and the 'historical Motherland' and to facilitate investment flows from the five million Armenians abroad (Ionescu 2006: 38).

Some home governments have introduced special schemes to ease visa-free movement for non-citizens of later generations. For example, the Persons of Indian Origin (PIO) card scheme is a visa-free regime for persons of Indian origin up to the fourth generation to simplify their return to India and access to various Indian institutions (India, Ministry of Home Affairs, n.d.). Similarly, Ethiopia issues a special identification card to foreigners of Ethiopian origin that entitles them to move freely without visa requirement and to take advantage of national employment opportunities (Ionescu 2006: 39).

Transmigration is seen to be a significant force contributing to the erosion of 'national identities and forms of citizenship in favour of those that are complex, overlapping, and which transcend the borders of nations and states' (Murphy and Harty 2003: 185). As Thomas Faist (2007: 3) argues, when 'citizens combine memberships in and of several states ... we are dealing neither with exclusive citizenship in tightly bounded political communities nor with denationalized citizenship, but rather with a sort of multi-nationalized citizenship.' The continued sentimental attachment and commitment to their country (or locality) of origin existing among people in many diasporas and transnational communities has given rise to what Dina Ionescu (2006:50) calls 'affective capital,' the existence of emotional engagement and a sense of responsibility, 'even pangs of conscience for having left the country or a commitment to make things change, even from abroad' (ibid.). As will be discussed below, such affective attachments are actively cultivated by international (e.g., the World Bank), national, and business elites – who exploit nationalist sentiment to promote and control the flow of economic remittances, 'social remittances,' and diasporic investment in and 'development' of home countries.

The road to increasing tolerance of dual citizenship has been far from smooth, as contradictory policies and pressures within and across states have led to an increasingly complex terrain of intersecting and ambivalent forms of state memberships and accompanying sets of obligation, rights, and entitlements. This complexity undermines any facile suggestion that dual or multiple citizenship is a harbinger of the dawn of a postnational age or global citizenship regime. But what sort of 'multinationalized citizenship' results from dual or multiple citizenship, since we know that nation-states exist in varying degrees of friendship, conflict, dependence, and inequality with each other? Moreover, how do we conceive of the multiple, variable, and interactive loyalties that now inform much citizenship literature, when the multiple states to which individuals have attachments are so uneven in their exercise of sovereignty and thus so diverse in the type and quality of citizenship on offer?

Plural nationality may not be as enhancing of individual and familial rights and privileges as some of the pioneering work on hypermobile flexible citizens (Ong 1999) suggests. Some countries impose a 'lingering nationality' on their native-born, a nationality that comes with certain burdens (such as military service) and even perils (such as a vacuum in diplomatic protection for the dual citizen in the country of origin) that emigration and subsequent naturalization in another country cannot shake (Stasiulis and Ross 2006). Such illiberal citizenship laws reveal how in many postcolonial and newly independent states, citizenship is not necessarily linked to freedom or rights, but rather privileges 'patriotic duty' as a supreme value (Hansen and Stepputat 2005: 26). As Hansen and Stepputat (2005: 20, 27) aver, despite great differences among forms of colonial rule, colonial sovereignties are generally '(1) partial and provisional; (2) spectacular and yet ineffective in their exercise of territorial and social control; and (3) marked by excessive and random violence … Sovereignty in the *post*-colonial world has in many ways remained provisional and partial, despotic and excessively violent.'

The growing body of empirical research that documents transmigrants' multiple attachments, most often in countries of origin and settlement, and the emergence of transnational communities, has fostered heated debate about the effects of multiplying geographical fields of transmigrant participation and identity in undermining state sovereignty and the traditional system of nation-states and national citizenship. Given that the lived experience of transnationalism among transmigrants creates a complex, multisited, and multilayered set of multiple, often hybrid allegiances to states, villages, cities, regions, and communities, this dispersed sense of identity and multiplication in arenas for claims-making clashes with the normative project of nation-state citizenship.

Transnational actors are making use of their multiterritorialized, multistate lifeworlds to better position themselves to accumulate, exchange, and convert various forms of capital – for example, economic into social and political – to their own best advantage (Ong 1999), although the experience of international migration may also involve devaluation of different forms of capital within the transnational habitus (Kelly and Lusis 2006). The ways in which resources resulting from international migration have been globally redistributed is receiving unprecedented attention from international institutions, not only in the historic September 2006 U.N. High Level Dialogue on International Migration and Development, but in the recent extensive collaborations among the World Bank with other institutions active in the area of migration and remittances, including the U.N.-created Global Commission on Migration, the International Organization of Migration in Geneva, and other regional banks and bilateral donors.

I now turn to three specific instances whereby the social in citizenship and social citizenship have become mobile and are being respatialized, pluralized, and multinationalized. The first instance – the provision of in-home care in advanced capitalist countries by female migrant workers – is a classic case of the transnationalization and respatialization of social citizenship. Since it has received far more scholarly attention than the second and third exemplars, which are historically more recent phenomena, however, I will provide only a very abridged examination of this first case.

Provision of Care in the Global North by Migrant Care Workers

One significant area where the nexus between migration and citizenship has assisted in affecting the shift in citizenship regime from liberal to neoliberal in states in the global North is in the provision of various forms of care – child care, elder care, home care of the ill and disabled, familial care/domestic work, and health care. A significant body of feminist work has documented how the growth associated with neoliberal globalization and free trade has been underwritten by the often invisible labour of migrant women from the global South who toil in private family households in the global North (Anderson 2000; Arat-Koc 1989; Bakan and Stasiulis 1995, 1996; Calliste 1991; Enloe 1989; Parreñas 2001; Romero 1992; Stasiulis and Bakan 2003).

The governance of the migration of women workers to provide care for citizens in the global North involves a wide range of public and private 'gatekeepers,' including state policy makers and legislators in both the sending and the destination countries, immigration personnel, emigration bureaucracies, professional accreditation bodies, and recruitment and placement agencies. A number of structural forces, mechanisms, and ideologies have assisted in normalizing the situation whereby migrant women from the South leave their countries, homes, and families to provide care for strangers in more affluent countries. These have included international debt politics and subsequent structural adjustment policies in the South and the restructuring, deinstitutionalization, and de-funding of social welfare programs in the North. The increased presence of married women with children in the labour force, and the rise of new forms of neoliberal political rationality (see Brodie, this volume) valorizing ideologies of privatization, familialism, voluntarism, and the entrepreneurial flexible citizen have also created a demand for this form of in-home care.

A keystone in the ideological bedrock of this transition in both privatized and institutional (e.g., nursing home and hospital) care is the genealogy of racism in receiving societies that has accompanied histories of subordination and exclusion of racialized and ethnicized others. Feminist scholars have shown a particular fascination with the racialized collisions with femininity in constructions of menial and caring labour since the intersections of race and class with gender have served so effectively to undermine gender or feminist bonds among women. Citizenship has been fundamental to driving this process, in the sense that globally migrant women who perform domestic labour and household care work are in highly precarious citizenship positions. They are either non-citizens or with 'partial' status (Parreñas 2001), often undocumented, and usually highly prone to deportation and thus vulnerable to extreme yet 'normalized' forms of labour violations and physical, psychological, and sexual abuse. Moreover, it is not merely differences in class and race that define and reinforce the subordination of migrant care workers but the inequality in citizenship status between citizen-employers and non-citizen employees that fixes this hierarchical relation. Social citizenship rights take on a zero-sum character, whereby female employers are able to access child care and other forms of household care from migrant employees whose own needs for child and familial care are not visibly part of the contract, and whose neglect is poorly compensated for by the provision of material goods. In Canada, to entice workers to accept these jobs, a period of virtually indentured labour under the federally administered Live-in Caregiver Program is sweetened by the promise of eligibility of permanent resident, or landed immigrant, status in Canada. That financial remittances to the sending country from migrant labour have led primarily to time-limited familial consumption, rather than meaningful, long-term development and structural poverty alleviation is one of the reasons that migration organizations are increasingly rethinking the link between remittances and source country development (see below).

In countries such as Canada, with long histories of importing household and child care workers, the demographic bulge of baby boomer elders has created a new avenue for the recruitment and in-home employment of migrant care workers. Even Japan, with a history of hostility to immigration, is in the process of changing its highly restrictive immigration policies to assist in the importation of migrant care workers to assuage its own crisis in elder care. The creation of some of the most transnationalized populations in the world, such as Filipina caregivers, thus both responds to and provides the labour to assist in accomplishing the restructuring of social citizenship in the global North. This primarily female migrant labour is part of what Aihwa Ong (2005: 269) has termed the 'demimonde of immigrant labour,' 'poor or illegal workers who are employed in a multiplicity of low-paid jobs – as electronics factory labor, garment workers, office-cleaners, hotel maids and janitors, restaurant and supermarket workers, farm hands and nannies – all critical to sustaining the 'quality of life in' [affluent neighborhoods].'

This is not, however, the end point in the transnational transformation of citizenship affected by these most flexible of global workers. The political agency of non-citizen workers in many countries has itself adopted a transnational form, whereby migrant rights organizations become affiliated as part of transnational networks linked to grassroots organizations in migrant-sending countries in the global South. The involvement of migrant workers in 'dissident transnational citizenship' practices has contributed to reshaping the performance and prerogatives of citizenship in both host and home countries (Stasiulis and Bakan 2003: 157–68). Thus, the struggles of these marginalized subjects have embraced a double focus – (1) their inclusion within citizenship benefits and full legal status in the countries that employ them and (2) through affiliation with grassroots movements back home, the meaningful and sustained development of their homelands and the right of migrants to return home to a decent and secure life.

Engaging Diasporas as Development Partners

Social citizenship is above all about redistributive policies. The recent interest shown by international non-governmental organizations and sending states of engaging diasporas as development partners represents an innovative form of conceptualizing a global redistribution of citizenship *obligations* (e.g., from the more privileged to the less fortunate). In this instance, it is not primarily wealthier states that are targeted in these development initiatives but rather migrants and their descendants from the South who have materially benefited from migration to the North. Until recently, analysis of the relationship between migration and development most often dealt with the impact of economic development on migration, whereas since the beginning of the new millennium, the focus on causal relationships has been reversed: migration is now viewed as a potential engine of development. Increasingly, migration experts are examining how 'migration affects development, in the sense that the 3 R's of recruitment, remittances, and returns shape who goes abroad, how much money they send home and how its spending affects development, and whether and when migrants return home' (Kuptsch and Martin 2004). Institutions such as the World Bank, the International Organization of Migration (IOM), and the United Nations, have all shown interest in diasporas as vehicles of development.

Two stark economic facts have catapulted diasporas to the centre of attention in the international development agenda as potential motors of source country development. The first is that, since the mid-1990s, the amounts of financial remittances, the portion of migrant incomes abroad that are sent home, have risen dramatically and are now approximately twice the amounts of official development assistance in developing countries (World Bank 2006). A World Bank study estimates that, in 2005, close to 200 million people living abroad sent about U.S. $225 billion in remittances, with migrant remittances to developing countries estimated at U.S. $167 billion (ibid.: 9). This study suggests that an additional U.S. $300 billion in unrecorded transfers could reasonably be added to that figure. Moreover, migrant workers' remittances do not coincide with diaspora remittances, as diasporas include more settled populations than migrant workers (Ionescu 2006: 45).

The second economic trend is the decline in foreign direct investment (FDI) and capital market flows to many developing countries in recent years, such that some analysts view remittances as the only financial flow to developing countries still on an upward path. Yet, although remittances 'are the most visible, stable and tangible link between migration and development,' there is no consensus about whether remittances provide a permanent ladder out of poverty (Hamilton 2003). Those who support remittances argue that they raise the level of national savings and provide a steady source of foreign exchange, which finances large trade deficits and services external debts: remittances not only provide a crucial social safety net for poor families, they also have multiplier effects within an economy (Barry 2006: 30; African Foundation for Development 2000: 10; World Bank 2006). Detractors point out that remittances support unsustainable and often conspicuous consumption and stopgap poverty alleviation among migrants' families, that they often decline with family reunification, and that they may foster dependency on external resources, rather than constitute long-term investment (Hamilton 2003). As Kimberly Hamilton (2003) suggests, the enduring challenge 'is to link individual and family decision-making related to remittance expenditures and investments to broader development goals.'

Rethinking among economists of the potential of diasporas for the development of source countries has also meant scrutinizing the unabated emigration of skilled people from developing to developed countries whose inception can be traced to the 1960s and 1970s (Balasubramanyan and Wei n.d.: 2). According to a World Bank study (Docquier and Marfoulk 2004), between 1990 and 2000 more than 80 per cent of the skilled workers in Surinam, Guyana, Jamaica, and Haiti emigrated. Among Asian countries, the Philippines, India, and China have the largest stocks of skilled emigrants abroad, numbering around a million persons from each of these countries. In central and Eastern Europe, it is the young and most dynamic who go abroad to work, leaving important gaps in the more advanced sectors of the labour market and causing shortages in sectors most important to the country's socioeconomic advancement and broader social fields, most notably health care and education (Ionescu 2006: 40). The migration of health care professionals from developing countries has been driven by the below-subsistence level of wages and poor, often exploitative, working conditions in home countries. In addition to losing the investment associated with educating their nationals who choose to go and work abroad, the loss of skilled workers causes an 'innovation and creativity deficit' (ibid.)

Previous discussions of such South to North skilled worker migration would have focused exclusively on human capital loss or 'brain drain.' More recent analyses, however, are examining the potential of these highly-skilled labour exports for 'brain gain,' 'brain circulation,' and 'brain banks,' whereby emigrants lend their expertise and capital to business ventures and development efforts in home countries (O'Neill 2003). Sending countries are attempting to capitalize on the preference of many migrants for circularity over permanent migration and are enacting policies to facilitate the circulation of *social* remittances, defined by Peggy Levitt (n.d.) as the ideas, practices, identities, and social capital that migrants remit home. There are numerous examples of sending countries' government programs with the objective to match the needs of human capital in the home country with the supply of diaspora skills abroad. Skills-matching programs and human resources banks or databases include general professional databases such as the African Experts and Diasporas database launched in 2002 in collaboration with the International Organization on Migration; the Philippines' Brain Gain Network, developed by a government body overseeing information and technology development in the Philippines; and the South African Network of Skills Abroad. In addition, some sending countries have inaugurated sector-based programs that focus on specific needs in the home country associated with social citizenship – notably in the health and education sectors – and target the respective professional groups in the diaspora (Ionescu 2006: 42). Home countries, intent on facilitating 'brain circulation,' have focused on students. Thus, the Chinese government successfully enacted policies in the mid-1990s to provide strong incentives for the return of students educated abroad. Between 1995 and 1998, the number of such returnees increased by 13 per cent annually, and more than 4,000 high tech companies have already been set up by returning students (ibid.: 43).

Home countries are intent on attracting not only the skills and knowledge of diasporic subjects but their financial investment in the home country. The economic potential of diasporas is manifest in the income of educated and successful professionals and entrepreneurs working in developed countries. For example, *Fortune* magazine places the wealth generated by Indian information technology (IT) experts in the Silicon Valley at U.S. $250 billion, or more than one-half of India's GNP (Balasubramanyan and Wei n.d.: 3). Beyond remittances, financial transfers between host and home countries can take a variety of forms, including foreign direct investment (FDI), trade, savings, start-up or business investments, purchases of real estate, and humanitarian support. The effect of each of these financial transfers on long-term development is extremely varied and difficult to generalize. For the most part, however, diaspora investments through FDI, enterprise creation, and trade are 'generated by self-interest and driven by profit motives, even though an altruistic element and investments in social projects might also be present' (Ionescu 2006: 44). This means that their contribution to long-term poverty reduction, community development, and to building an infrastructure of social security for poorer and more marginalized groups is likely to be minor at best.

There are also huge variations in the propensity of the diaspora to invest in the country of origin. Thus, while in 2002, about half of the U.S. $48 billion FDI in China originated from the Chinese diaspora, only about 10 per cent of India's U.S. $4.43 billion FDI was generated by Indian diasporas (ibid.) The 2001 Indian government's High-Level Committee on the Indian Diaspora accounted for the relatively low level of investment in India by Indian expatriates in terms of India's unfavourable FDI environment and major administrative burdens (47). National variations in diaspora investments and trade can be explained by differences among home countries – such as FDI and taxation policies, macroeconomic conditions, and in the conditions under which diaspora groups exist (45). Thus, 'diaspora with access to jobs that reflect their educational attainment, skills and experience, the ability to travel freely, and an overall degree of integration within the host society will be able to play more effective roles as development players than those marginalized and stigmatized by laws, policies and hostile public opinion' (African Foundation for Development 2000: 19).

Source states are increasingly courting their emigrant communities to attract investments from them by introducing a number of measures and programs that provide members of the diaspora with preferential treatment under the investment and banking laws of the country of origin. Carrots – such as investment incentives, tax exemptions and breaks, special issue bonds for diasporic subjects, dual citizenship laws, and the portability of social security benefits – have proved far more effective than sticks, which include efforts of sending countries to tax their overseas citizens.[10] Key to the many institutional, legal, and symbolic efforts to leverage the economic power of diasporas by home countries has been the building of social capital (networks and shared norms, values and understanding to facilitate cooperation within and among groups) and 'affective capital' – the sentimental attachments, sense of belonging, responsibility, and commitment of diasporas to become involved in change in the home country. Many of the targets of diaspora-induced development involve investments in regions and localities of origin, where diasporic subjects have family ties and property and, thus, a more rooted and often nostalgic sense of belonging and identity.

Considerable ideological work is being undertaken to cultivate and cement a sense of loyalty in wealthy diasporic subjects to their homelands and to encourage them to invest their resources in the 'development' of these countries. The Indian government's invitation to ethnic Indians with non-Indian citizenship (people of Indian origin) and its citizens living abroad (non-resident Indians) to 'invest in a new India not just financially, but intellectually, socially, culturally and, above all, emotionally,' through annual events such as the Pravasi Bharatiya Divas (billed as the 'global Indian family's annual get together') is based on a twinned appeal to overseas Indians' profit motives and to their patriotism and emotional attachment. As steel titan, British-based Lakshmi Mittal, purportedly the world's richest person of Indian origin stated: 'I love my country – but I must get returns as well' (quoted in Barry 2006: n112).

The fifth Pravasi Bharatiya Divas, held in New Delhi in January 2007, co-organized by the Ministry of Overseas Indians and the Confederation of Indian Industries (CII), took as its theme, 'Rooting for the Roots – Meeting India's Development Challenges.' This theme manifested a realization among Indian political leaders and captains of industry that India's efforts to become a global economic power, reflected in the tremendous growth to its economy of 8 per cent annually since 2003, has enriched the elites and middle classes but failed miserably to benefit three-quarters of India's 1.1 billion people who live in poverty. Thus, while the sponsoring organization's goals were clearly focused on global business networking initiatives, the purpose of the conferences was also to stimulate non-resident Indians and persons of Indian origin to 'contribute their bit' to India's socioeconomic development (Bhushan 2006).

As will be argued below with respect to one of the fastest-developing corporate sectors in India – private hospitals for medical tourists – the impact of investment by diasporas on the welfare of the local population is intimately tied to the attendant redistribution of public and private resources, and thus to the quality of social citizenship on offer in high-growth developing countries. Absent from much of the recent international high-level focus on migration and development is a more nuanced exploration of what is meant by 'development,' and specifically an analysis of the relationship between 'economic growth' and 'development.' The prominence of business interests organizing and attending events such as India's Pravasi Bharatiya Divas, means that discussions about development and poverty reduction occur in the same spaces where the opportunities for investment in a booming real estate market and joint business ventures are eagerly discussed. The diaspora and thus extraterritorial nation that are being imagined through such events and the new overseas citizenship policies are not the descendants of nineteenth-century indentured labour migration, the 'brain drain' professionals of the 1960s and 1970s, or the lower-class migrant labourers to the Gulf of India region. Rather, the diaspora that is being courted for its contribution to the development of the 'new India' is represented almost entirely by the wealthy who reside mainly in the advanced industrial states. As Peter Van der Veer (2005) argues, there are also political motivations in the custom-fitting of the Indian diaspora. The Hindu nationalist Bharatiya Janata Party (BJP) spearheaded reforms embracing overseas Indians – such as the introduction of the Person of Indian Origin card and the convening of the government-level diaspora committee in 2001 that resulted in the creation of 'overseas citizenship,' all moves targeting the 'new Hindu middle-class professional and entrepreneurial migrant especially from the United States' (Van den Veer 2005: 285).[11] This illustrates how nationalist and state ideologies have been central in constructing particularistic transnational social fields and selectively extending citizenship benefits extraterritorially. This is a far cry from the postnationalism envisioned in terms of rights flowing from the principles of universal personhood (Soysal 1994).

Medical Tourism in the Global South: The Case of India

My interest in this third and final example of respatialization and transnationalization of social citizenship, where the mobility of persons in this case is from North to South, was sparked by two observations, one personal and the other research-based. During a holiday in Kerala, south India, in 2005, acute eye pain prompted me to visit an eye clinic, recommended by a waiter, in a neighbourhood of Thiruvananthapuram, where the landscape is covered with medical facilities of many sorts. In addition to a plethora of eye clinics, there are clinics for cosmetic surgery, labs for medical imaging, dental centres, and so on. In conversing in my yoga class with other visitors, who were staying at Kovalam Beach in inexpensive rooms for months at a time, their cotton clothes stained brown from the ayurvedic massages they received daily, it was clear that these Westerners were also medical tourists seeking Western diagnostic services and medical procedures for a fraction of the cost back home.

Indo-Canadians, even those of modest means, make trips regularly to India, to visit family and friends and participate in important social events, including births, marriages, deaths, and religious activities (Patel 2006: 155). From my interviews conducted in 2005 with transnational Indians in Canada, it emerged that rather than put up with long waits for specialist appointments, many would regularly attend to many of their personal medical requirements during their frequent visits to India, finding these services faster, cheaper, and more thorough.

If judged on the basis of the country's poverty and standard of living,[12] India would seem an unlikely destination for health tourism. Approximately three-quarters of the population live at or below subsistence levels, especially in rural areas where residents have little or no access to basic health care, adequate nourishment, or clean water. Yet, India is currently considered the leading country promoting medical tourism and medical outsourcing, where subcontractors provide services to the overburdened medical care system in Western countries. For most patients flocking to India from the United States, Canada, and Great Britain, the considerations are cost, with medical procedures often costing one-tenth to one-quarter what they would at home. In Canada lengthening waiting times for pain-alleviating surgeries such as hip and knee replacements and lifesaving (e.g., cardiac) operations are significant manifestations of the deterioration of the public health care system. Yet, for others, the draw to become a medical tourist is the chance to combine a tropical vacation with elective surgery. Online health travel agencies such as Med Journey provide beguiling descriptions of health tourist destinations such as Kerala, which is said to offer 'an equable climate, a long shoreline with serene beaches, tranquil stretches of emerald backwaters, lush hill stations and exotic wildlife, waterfalls, sprawling plantations and paddy fields, Ayurvedic health holidays, enchanting art forms, magical festivals, historic cultural monuments, and exotic cuisine' (Med Journeys n.d.) India is not the only country to actively promote medical tourism, with Thailand, for example, having built a reputation for its cosmetic surgery as early as the 1970s, but with 'uninsured and underinsured Americans [now] boarding planes [to Bangkok] not for the typical face-lift or tummy tuck but for discount hip replacements and sophisticated heart surgeries' (Kher 2006). South Africa specializes in 'medical safaris – visit the country for a safari, with a stopover for plastic surgery, a nose job and a chance to see lions and elephants' (CBC News online, 18 June 2004).

In India the field of medical tourism has such lucrative potential (forecast by government and private interests to reach up to U.S. $2 billion by 2012), that Indian Finance Minister Jaswant Singh in 2003 called for India to become a 'global health destination' (Marcelo 2003). Yet, it is too facile to see the medical tourism boom in India only in terms of comparative costs and waiting times. Its emergence is also born out of a transnational migration circuit and social field constructed by transnational Indian subjects, with the active participation of many other state and market actors, in an international political economy where India based its initial high growth in the field of information technology. India's top-rated education system is producing not only computer programmers and engineers, but also, according to a 2004 estimate, between 20,000 and 30,000 physicians and nurses each year. Given that such health care workers have long histories of migration to Britain and its colonies, many Britons, Canadians, and Americans are accustomed to being treated by expatriate Indian doctors. It is estimated that there are more than 35,000 specialist doctors of Indian origin in the United States alone. While previously these physicians might have been reluctant to return to India where medical colleges until recently lacked high-end diagnostic equipment, the development of private Indian hospitals with technological levels on par with or surpassing hospitals in Europe and North America are drawing Indian doctors back to India. To deal with backlogs in diagnostic imaging, which the Canadian Medical Association estimated account for a large part of the delay for nearly 50 per cent of patients waiting for surgery, 'teleradiology' – the electronic transmission of test results to cheaper and faster venues (involving timely access to time zones during daylight hours) – has the potential to substantially relieve the backlog. Foreign and domestic-trained Indian physicians who have returned to India are at the forefront of establishing medical businesses to provide outsourcing of services such as teleradiology: radiological tests such as X-rays, MRIs, and CT scans sent to India to be read (Mackay 2006).

Two of the largest medical corporations in India are Apollo, which has forty-six hospitals in three countries, and Wockhardt Hospitals Group, which has eight hospitals in India. Dr Pratap Reddy, the founder of the Apollo hospitals network, is credited with corporatizing India's health care, having returned to India after completing a residency in the United States, and setting up the first Apollo private hospital in Madras in 1982. Each of these corporations have struck deals with private health insurers such as the U.S.-based Blue Cross and Blue Shield and the British health insurer Bupa, and their hospitals receive 'gold standard' accreditation through organizations such as the Joint Commission International. In Canada, some provincial health care providers have reimbursed the full costs of surgery in India, undoubtedly a cost-saving measure (CBC News Online, 18 June 2004).

Canada has thus far moved more slowly than the United States in establishing the legislative framework to transmit medical data across national borders. Apollo already provides overnight computer services for U.S. insurance companies and hospitals, as well as working with large pharmaceutical companies with drug trials. For instance, multinational drug firms in the United States and Europe, including Novo Nordisk, Aventis, Novartis, GlaxoSmithKline, Eli Lilly, and Pfizer, have all evinced increasing interest in outsourcing drug research and clinical trials to India, attracted by its well-educated English-speaking workforce, favourable domestic tax regime for foreign investment, and what has chillingly been referred to as its 'treatment naïve' population, simplifying patient enrollment and trial management (Venter 2005). The spurt in growth to Apollo's business was provided by the Indian government's deregulation of the Indian economy in the 1990s, which drastically cut bureaucratic barriers to expansion and made it easier for medical corporations to import the most modern medical equipment. In addition, the Indian government supports such expansion through its National Health Policy that legally considers treatment of foreign patients as an 'export' and thus 'eligible for all fiscal incentives extended to export earnings' (CBC News online, 18 June 2004).

The first patients for treatment in Apollo hospitals were Indian expatriates who returned home for treatment. Medical corporations in India have hungrily eyed the estimated 20 to 25 million strong Indian diaspora, particularly wealthy first- and second-generation expatriate Indians who are aware of the high quality and low costs of India's private hospitals. Their hope is that these expatriates will combine regular visits to India with non-emergency procedures such as eye operations, dental work, cosmetic surgery, and knee replacements. Medical tourism has spawned a cottage industry of travel agencies and tourist companies, such as the Vancouver-based Surgical Tourism Canada Inc. that offer foreign medical tourists package deals including flights, transfers, hotels, treatment, and postoperative vacations.

Some Indian health care critics, such as CEHAT, a health think tank in Mumbai, have mounted criticisms that the medical resources and personnel are being drawn to profit-making private sector medical tourism at the expense of the local population's primary health care needs. Apollo has notably responded to this attack on its questionable ethical stance as a corporate citizen by setting aside free beds for the poor, setting up a trust fund, and pioneering remote, satellite-linked telemedicine across India, rather than only to profitable overseas hospitals. However beneficial such corporate gestures and policies may be, they cannot efface the fact that health tourism, at its most gruesome, has left entire villages in India populated by men with one kidney, financially indebted by their post-surgical care. The fast-expanding international trafficking and trade in human organs for transplant have left these villagers more destitute than ever, thus reinforcing the global citizenship divide between the rich and poor (Cohen 2003).

Despite India's recent economic gains, foreign exchange reserves, human resources, and relatively stable political environment, its public health care regime has been collapsing since the 1990s, while its unregulated private health care sector has been flourishing. Health care policy in India has shifted from being conceived in the postcolonial period as a comprehensive universal health care system, as defined by the Bhore Committee in 1946, to a selective and targeted program-based health care policy, with the public domain being confined to family planning, immunization, selective disease surveillance, and medical education and resources. Outpatient care is almost a private health care sector monopoly, and the hospital sector has also increasingly surrendered to the market. The decline of public investments and expenditures by the central government in the public health care sector since the introduction of the World Bank's structural adjustment policies in India in the early 1990s have so adversely weakened the health of the poor that India now has higher rates of malnourished children than does sub-Saharan Africa (46% compared with 35% for sub-Saharan Africa and only 8% in China) (Bhalla 2007; Gangolli, Duggal, and Shukla, 2005). The flight of resources, physicians, and technology to the private hospital sector to service foreign patients is merely an intensification of the type of marketization and commodification of health care delivery in the context of the global integration of India's economy that has led to severe class inequities in health and a shocking incidence of infant and maternal mortality, rapid spread of HIV/AIDS, and resurgence of various communicable diseases (Gangolli et al. 2005: iii, 19).

Medical tourism is exemplary of what Sassen (2006: 314) refers to as the 'partial and specialized unbundling of national state territoriality,' whereby the shift to a neoliberal citizenship regime has catalyzed a variety of subjects to seek new means of accessing services associated with social citizenship (healthcare, education, elder care, etc.) across two or more nation-states. As neoliberalism has privatized and eliminated many citizenship entitlements, it has loosened the number of relationships and interdependencies between states and citizens, prompting better resourced citizens to seek services from private providers in other overseas markets. The growth in medical tourism, which involves wealthy citizens of the North travelling for surgical procedures to other countries, can also be read as an instance of this privatization, commodification, and globalization of social citizenship, responding to realities such as the longer life spans in advanced states and the declining commitments of these states to organize and financially support key social services such as adequate health care.

Conclusion

In this chapter I have argued that one dimension of the transnational reorganization and respatialization of citizenship that has received insufficient scholarly attention pertains to its social dimensions – both the social relations that underlie particular geopolitical constellations of citizenship policy and practice, and social citizenship, understood as the right of citizens to a minimum level of social security. I have illustrated processes of transnationalization and multinationalization of citizenship through the global North's importation of migrant care labour from the global South, the intensified efforts to harness and manage the wealth and resources of successful migrants and diasporas for the 'development' of source countries, and medical tourism from the North in the South. These forms of transnationalized citizenship practices should not be conflated with postnationalism – which locates the imperatives of rights, obligations, and identities above states, territories, and localized environments. Just as importantly, far from being premised on universal human rights, the transnationalization of social citizenship has intensified the hierarchical and exclusionary character of citizenship itself insofar as it is premised on neoliberal principles of commodification and marketization of key social services. It is also actualized through the responsibilization of individual citizens to look after their own needs, often by supplementing eroding public services with those made more readily available though costly private alternatives. The innovation exists in the novel geospatial, binational or multinational patterns of accessing such services across nation-state borders. Source and destination national states are not in control of the transnational social fields constructed by transmigrants and diasporas, but they do play an increasingly interventionist role in facilitating recurrent and institutionalized exchanges between transmigrants/transnational communities and their countries of origin.

The question is: who benefits from the respatialization of citizenship resulting from transmigration? Wealthier transmigrants, with regular and sustained contacts across borders and knowledge of opportunities in their source country and country of residence, are well-positioned to weigh the benefits and costs of accessing opportunities and avoiding risks in different sites where they have sustained ties and membership.

Thus, while migrants from India may have moved to North America and the United Kingdom to enhance their job and business opportunities and gain more robust social citizenship benefits, the erosion of social welfare in these regions may mean that the more affluent among them return to India to better access – as entrepreneurs, professional workers, and consumers – more affordable and accessible high-quality private sector medical services. The transnational social field that they have laid down, however, provides a bridge for the development of institutions and practices that respatialize health care for a broader transnational clientele, defined not by ethnicity or nationality but by social class. As observed by Ravi Duggal, a health care researcher in Mumbai, 'for years we have been providing doctors to the western world. Now they are coming back and serving foreign patients at home' (Ramesh 2005).

Immigration and integration policies of destination countries shape the ability of transnational individuals and communities to contribute to the development of their countries of origin. It is notable that supranational institutions such as the World Bank, whose structural adjustment policies were important catalysts for stimulating migration from developing countries, as a means for these countries to pay back their foreign debt, are now looking to wealthier migrants from these countries to ameliorate some of the extreme failures of such World Bank policies through financial and social remittances. For their part, source countries, intent on attracting the economic and social remittances of not only migrants but larger diasporas, have reformed their foreign investment, banking, taxation, and citizenship policies, in some instances treating their extraterritorial citizens and persons of ethnic origin as preferred citizens. The 'mobile social' in citizenship is rooted in the inequalities that exist between the global North and South and between social classes – but it is also the 'mobile social' that responds to, challenges, and above all, reproduces these global and class-based inequities.

Acknowledgments

Research for this chapter was supported by a Social Sciences and Humanities Research Council of Canada Standard Research Grant on 'Border Crossings and Multiple Citizenship' (410-2005-1395). Preliminary ideas for it were discussed at a September 2006 meeting with members of the Socius network, and an earlier draft was presented to the Social Science division, University of British Columbia–Okanagan, 25 January 2007. The chapter has benefited from the feedback received in these gatherings, the astute comments and sound editorial advice of Engin Isin, the careful reading provided by Christine Hughes, and lively conversations with the ever-transnational George de Witte.

Notes

1 Despite the mythical status of the concept of 'nation-state' and the divergence of virtually all current states from the ideal model of nation-state, I will conform to the conventional political science conventions regarding the terms *nation-state* and *national state* to refer to existing sovereign states, cognizant also of how powerfully the myth of sovereign nation-states is legitimized and upheld legally and in the international order of states (e.g., in the United Nations system). 'Nation-state' is also here deployed to distinguish it from other 'sub-national' (e.g., local) forms of state and supra-state forms of governance.

2 According to the International Organization on Migration, there are an estimated 191 million migrants worldwide in 2005, up from 176 million in 2000 (IOM 2006). As one indication of the disproportionate impact of international migration, the remittances migrants send back to their source countries are estimated to be double the size of official development assistance, and some states' economies are so dependent on migrant remittances that economists have predicted their collapse should the remittances be stopped (World Bank 2006). An increasing number of migrant sending states thus have strong economic incentives to strengthen their ties with their emigrant citizens.

3 My understanding of the term *field* is derived from Pierre Bourdieu (1986) – a vertically and horizontally organized social arena in which people manoeuvre and struggle over the appropriation of certain (social, economic, cultural) forms of capital.

4 Habitus is another key concept developed in Bourdieu's (1977, 1986) writings, defined as a system of durable and transposable 'dispositions' (lasting, acquired schemes of perception, thought, and action). Individual agents develop these dispositions in response to the determining structures (such as class, family, and education) and external conditions (fields) that they encounter. They are therefore neither completely determined by 'objective' structures nor entirely the result of the individual 'subjective' behaviour of actors. Kelly and Lusis (2006) suggest that while Bourdieu was

often unclear about the social or spatial boundaries of habitus formation, for many transmigrants, habitus has become 'transnationalized.'

5 Some theorists, insist that the term *diaspora* should be confined to populations whose dispersal from an original region to two or more regions occurred through forced migration originating in some catastrophic event, as occurred for the paradigmatic Jewish diaspora (Challiand and Rageau 1995), while others (e.g., Cohen 1995) regard diasporas as formed from multiple processes including forced and free migration, trade, conquest, settlement, and the cultural flowering of 'exile' communities. Others (including Khachig Tölölyan, the editor of *Diaspora: A Journal of Transnational Studies*), employ an inclusive and extensive catch-all definition of diaspora, synonymous with 'transnational community' (see Van Hear 1998: 5–6, for a discussion of these conceptual debates). In this chapter, I employ the terms *transnational community* and *diaspora* loosely and synonymously to underscore the fact that diasporas, while incorporating 'settled,' multigenerational populations in regions outside the originating region, nonetheless are not static entities and are reproduced through networks, movement, and exchange between 'home' and 'destination' countries (Ionescu, 2006: 10).

6 I gratefully acknowledge Nana Oishi for her contributions in the conceptualization of these multiple patterns of migration.

7 As Levitt and Nyberg-Sörenson (2004: 3) point out, those who do not move are connected to migrants through the networks of social relations that they sustain across borders and are exposed to constant and often regular flows of economic and social remittances.

8 By *ethnoscape*, Appadurai (1996: 33) means 'the landscape of persons who constitute the shifting world in which we live: tourists, immigrants, refugees, exiles, guestworkers, and other moving groups... [who] appear to affect the politics of and between nations to a hitherto unprecedented degree.'

9 Thus, in a recent study by Reitz and Banerjee, using 2002 Statistics Canada data, visible minority immigrants in Canada, not surprisingly, were considerably more apt than white immigrants to report having been victimized by discrimination. However, second-generation visible minorities were strikingly more likely to report having experienced discrimination than first-generation visible minority Canadians (42% vs 36%), and a large minority (43%) of this racialized second generation failed to identify as Canadian, at twice the rate of second-generation whites (Jiménez 2007: A5).

10 Barry (2006: 39) discusses the case of Eritrea, which successfully persuaded its overseas citizens, approximately one-quarter of its total population, to pay the Eritrean government 2% of their income annually as a 'healing tax.' However, about 15 years following the second Eritrean Civil War (1980–81),

the relationship of these non-resident citizens to the government of the Eritrean People's Liberation Front soured, as the government 'cast doubt on the "authenticity" and commitment of those citizens who failed to come home and criticize the government from abroad' (39–40).

11 Van der Veer persuasively argues that if these reforms to citizenship policies and symbolic events were primarily economically motivated, the Indian government would more likely have targeted the migrant labourers in the Gulf region, who are 'by far the most important economic actors in terms of remittances and other effects on the Indian economy' (2005: 285).

12 The official definitions of the poverty line in India are hotly disputed and intensely political. Based on intake of calories and a benchmark of 650 grams of food grains daily, some critics argue that these poverty definitions (Rs. 368 and Rs. 559 per person respectively for rural and urban areas as of October 2005) are in reality 'starvation lines,' make little provision for other essentials of life, and only serve to make the government's development efforts – or lack of them, look good. Mohan Guruswamy and Ronald Joseph Abrahama, authors of a recent study at the Centre for Policy Alternatives in New Delhi, suggest that a true definition of poverty should include all the basic needs of human life with a modest modicum of quality. By their calculations, a person should be deemed poor in India if he or she has a monthly per capita expenditure less than Rs 840 (about Can $22) or does not have access to drinking water, proper shelter, sanitation, quality secondary education, or an all-weather road with public transport. At the suggested expenditure level, nearly 79 % of India's current total population would be below the poverty line, which is three times the current official poverty rate of 26.1%. Indicative of the current poverty levels are the following social facts: '37.7 per cent of Indian households do not have access to a nearby water source; 49 per cent do not have a proper shelter; 69.5 per cent do not have access to suitable toilets; 85.2 per cent of Indian villages do not have a secondary school; and 43 percent of the villages do not have an all-weather road connecting them' (Indo-Asian News Service 2006).

7 The Child-Citizen

XIAOBEI CHEN

Holding their newly adopted daughters from China in their arms, a group of parents got off the trans-Pacific plane that had just landed at Vancouver International Airport, stretching their legs with a sigh of relief. Moving along with others comprising a mixture of immigration statuses, nationalities, languages, and ages, they navigated through the airport corridors and made their way to the Canada Immigration counters. There, an immigration officer beamed at the parents and proclaimed, 'Oh, these are our favourites!'[1]

In an article published in 2004, Tom Kent, a prominent Canadian economist and one of the chief architects of Canada's social programs of the 1960s echoed that immigration officer's favouritism. He boldly put forward a proposal for child- and youth-oriented immigration and refugee policies, with priorities to be given to 'children who are orphaned or in young families.' Kent's article, especially the part that called for 'switching the emphasis of immigration policy to youth, to children especially' (2004: 28), quickly caught the attention of the media (e.g., Goar 2004; *The Province*, 24 August 2004) – and alarmed immigrant and refugee organizations.

Since the mid-1990s Canada has restricted the entry of elderly parents and grandparents by administrative delays and has drastically reduced the proportion of parents and grandparents in relation to other family class categories of immigrants such as spouses, partners, and children (McLaren and Black 2005). In May 2006 a lawsuit was filed against Citizenship and Immigration Canada (CIC) for illegally discriminating against people who applied to bring their parents and grandparents to Canada and causing waits to escalate to as long as a decade in 110,000 family reunification cases (Jiménez 2006).

These and many other sites of individuals, groups, and the state enacting, negotiating, and contesting entry and rejection, belonging and non-belonging need to be taken seriously in both citizenship theory and studies of 'vital politics' (Rabinow and Rose 2003: 24). They raise questions about the management, or 'regularization' in Foucault's words (1989: 247), of the ethnic, economic, and biological composition of the population, the logic of today's 'state racism' (Foucault 1997), and its complex entanglement and tension with ordinary racism on the basis of skin colour and ethnicity. This chapter explores these questions with a focus on one aspect of the recasting of the social in citizenship, namely, the ascendance of children as rights-bearing citizens and as citizens with seemingly unassailable political and ethical claims. I suggest that Foucauldian concepts of biopower and biopolitics are useful in analysing the recasting of the social in citizenship, with social citizenship and the recasting of the social conceptualized as a mode of governance and subjectification.

The chapter consists of four sections. In the first I consider citizenship through the Foucauldian lens of biopolitics and the associated notions of population and state racism. Then, I examine empirical developments that suggest that children are increasingly constituted as citizens in their own right and as independent bearers of rights. The third section examines the sites of contestation over specific immigration and citizenship processes, and following Rabinow and Rose's analytical schema, I explore regimes of truth, strategies and techniques of intervention in the name of population vitality, and modes of subjectification in which subjects are generated through truth discourses and practices of the self. The final section concludes with remarks about biopolitics and racisms in current Canadian projects of recasting the social in citizenship.

Through these discussions, I advance the argument that biopolitics – specifically the problematization of the aging of the population and interventions aimed at securing a younger, neurologically optimal, and economically entrepreneurial population – is central to the processes of recasting the social in citizenship in Canada in the twenty-first century. Biological capital, in the forms of younger ages, minimal neurological risks, and good health, is nowadays considered essential for optimizing a state of life and achieving an overall state of equilibrium and regularity. The Others that pose a threat to the population lack biological capital because of their health risks and, simply, their older ages. State racism, focusing on the vitality of the population that is not necessarily culturally and ethnically defined, seems to destabilize ordinary racism with its desires and even demands for non-white and non-European immigrants who bear precious biological capital; but at the same time the ideology of whiteness, more specifically that of Western superiority (Dyer 1997, López 2005) underlies the appraisal of the relative value of biological capital.

Citizenship as a Biopolitical Project

Dominant approaches to citizenship studies have considered citizenship struggles for redistribution and recognition as two separate, and even antagonistic domains. This conceptual orientation presumes a fundamental divide between equality and difference, both analytically and politically, and fails to capture the reality of citizenship struggles, as noted in chapter 1 and other chapters in this volume (see also Fraser and Honneth 2003a, 2003b, 2003c; James 2006). My approach is to conceptualize citizenship politics to be about situational, discursive, and dialectic negotiations of the terms of entitlement to redistribution through recognition politics, and vice versa, rather than about any abstract notions of equality or essentialist notions of difference.

Thus, the social in citizenship entails two meanings: (1) a way of defining certain problems as worthy of collective responsibility and (2) social relations of class, gender, 'race,' ethnicity, and so on. That these two aspects are co-constitutive has been well illustrated by critical studies of social policy. Despite its assumptions of social citizenship, social policy has always been characterized by differential treatment of social groups and such differential treatment has been politically contentious. As shown by the vast body of literature examining the gendered and racialized features of social policy, social relations of difference have structured the organization of welfare states in various ways.

Feminist scholars have critiqued the encoding of the ideology of women's roles within the rules of social policy and the regulation of women's lives accordingly (see, e.g., Gordon 1994, Abramovitz 1996, Brodie 1996, Little 1998, Tillotson 2000). In a similar vein, the colour line has marked the policy and administrative boundaries of redistributive programs. Historians have documented that racism has been at the root of opposition to social welfare programs and the exclusion of racialized minorities from certain social programs (see, e.g., Quadagno 1994). Welfare racism is also a defining feature of the more recent neoliberal and neoconservative restructuring. Social welfare and its recipients have been racialized by the belief that those receiving welfare payments are primarily members of certain minority groups, that they are welfare prone because of personal and cultural deficiencies, and that they constitute a collective internal enemy that is threatening the very foundation of society (see, e.g., Neubeck and Cazenave 2001). Given that constructed differences matter in how social groups are positioned vis-à-vis social programs, it only makes sense that the struggle for equality takes into account social relations of difference.

At the same time, if differential treatments are politically contentious, undifferentiated treatments can be equally so, as is evident in criticisms of social policy such as Canadian child welfare and social assistance programs for First Nations people. These social programs, based on the tenet that there be no distinction between Indians and other Canadians, are seen as an assimilationist policy in disguise that has been used to undermine First Nations cultures (Monture 1989, Davies 1992, Kline 1992, Canada Royal Commission on Aboriginal Peoples 1996, Crichlow 2002, Shewell 2004).

Whether the contested injustice derives from differentiated or from undifferentiated treatment in social policy, the decisive factor is power, that is, the dominant group's power to define when and how Others should be treated differently or the same in their access to social citizenship, and with what objectives. This points to the need to analyse how social relations of difference are constructed, transformed, or suppressed within and through social policy. Studies that centralize social relations in their analyses of social citizenship tend to focus on the effects of ideologies of gender, racial, ethnic, and class differences – as independent variables – on social programs. My interest in this chapter is to examine how the problematization of social policy can operate in valorizing or suppressing social relations of differences. The conceptual tools that I draw on are Foucauldian notions of governmentality and, specifically, the governmentality of biopolitics.

In the literature, citizenship is generally conceptualized in three conventional ways: (1) as legal status or membership in a nation-state; (2) as political, civil, social and other rights and obligations; and (3) as civic virtues. Foucault and those who have been influenced by or elaborated on his work have used notions such as the regime of truth, mode and technology of power, and subjectivity to pose different questions about citizenship. For example, Aihwa Ong (1996, 1999, 2003, 2006) in her analysis of cultural citizenship considers citizenship to be a Foucauldian process of 'subjectification,' by which she means 'the self-making and being-made within the webs of power linked to the nation-state and civil society' (1996: 264). White and Hunt (2000), responding to what they consider to be a romantic impulse underlying much scholarship since 'the return of the citizen' (Kymlicka and Norman 1994), assert that citizenship operates as a technology of government and that particular kinds of citizens are produced through various relations of government, including the care of the self. Applying similar conceptions, Veronica Schild explores social citizenship as 'one paradigmatic form of governing through which subjects and needs are produced' (2000: 277) through social programs in Chile; Triantafillou and Moreita (2002) examine how techniques of citizenship are linked to the production of 'delinquents' in colonial Malaya.

Biopower and biopolitics, provocative concepts proposed by Foucault, have received increasing scholarly interest recently. In his 1976–77 lectures published under the title *Society Must Be Defended* (1997), Foucault describes biopower as a new rationality and technology of power that emerged in the second half of the eighteenth century and grew in strength and prevalence in the nineteenth century. His last lecture in the series contains an explication of the concept of biopower in contrast to, first, the old conceptualization of sovereign power and then disciplinary power. Perceiving the emergence of biopower as 'one of the greatest transformations of political right,' Foucault characterized biopower as 'precisely the opposite right' to sovereignty's old right as theorized in the field of political thought (241). While one of the sovereignty's old rights is the right to take life or let live, biopower is to make live and to let die.

Quickly turning to 'the level of the mechanisms, techniques and technologies of power' that interest him (ibid.: 241), Foucault further differentiates biopower from disciplinary power in respect to their objects of knowledge, the targets they seek to control, and the different instruments they use. Directed at the individual body, disciplinary power is an 'anatomo-politics of the human body' that was established at the end of the seventeenth century and in the course of the eighteenth century; biopower is described as a '"biopolitics" of the human race,' addressed to 'man-as-species.' In contrast to the individualizing mode of disciplinary power, biopower is 'massifying' (243). In other words, 'biopolitics deals with the population, with the population as political problem, as a problem that is at once scientific and political, as a biological problem and as power's problem' (245).

Foucault argues that it was precisely the emergence of biopower that inscribed racism in the mechanisms of the state (ibid.: 254). In other words, it was racism that articulated sovereignty with biopolitics (Valverde 2005), more specifically sovereignty's old right to kill and the new right of biopower to make live. Foucault emphatically characterises the 'vital importance' of racism to states functioning in the mode of biopower: '[racism] is the precondition for exercising the right to kill. If the power of normalization wished to exercise the old sovereign right to kill, it must become racist. And if, conversely, a power of sovereignty … wishes to work with the instruments, mechanisms, and technology of normalization, it too must become racist,' (1997: 256). Racism articulates the state's role with regard to death and life in two ways: (1) racism fragments a population into those who must die and those who must live, and (2) racism furnishes the state with a bio-logic that death, removal, rejection, and the absence of elements that pose a threat to the population will improve life in general, make it healthier and happier (255). Thus killing, defined broadly, is justified in the name of the vitality of the population, not the safety of the sovereign and territory.

For Foucault, state racism (occasionally also described as modern racism; 1997: 258) is key to understanding why dominating modern societies have the most elaborate theory on the sanctity of human life and are at the same time among the most murderous in the nineteenth and twentieth centuries, and remain so today. State racism is distinct from traditional and ordinary racism, which involves mutual contempt and hatred between races, and from racism as an ideology used by states or a class to mask social conflicts and deflect hostility. The specificity of state racism lies in the fact that it is internal to the operation of sovereign power and biopower in modern states. It refers to a conscious delineation of a population as a political question for the state and the necessary definitions of both external and internal enemies to the well-being of the population. The definition of a population, or race as in state racism, may or may not overlap with the boundary of a race in the sense of scientific racism.

Using the example of the Nazi regime, Foucault offers a brief but insightful analysis of the correlation between racism, murder, and disciplinary and regulatory biopower exerted through control over reproduction and heredity as well as insurance against illness and accidents. He observes that genealogically Nazism was the heir of the new disciplinary power and biopower mechanisms established since the eighteenth century (1997: 259). Indeed, it is worth remembering that well before T.H. Marshall's (1950) theory of social citizenship and the common impression of social citizenship rights taking root after the Second

World War, it was Bismarck's Germany that was the first to enact a variety of social reforms including health insurance (1883), accident insurance (1884), and old age pensions and disability insurance (1889).

These social reforms and later ones in other lands are often understood as the result of hard struggles of progressive politics and the attempts by states to reduce the appeal of socialism for the working class. This is not incompatible with understanding social reforms and their outcomes as biopolitical projects. Indeed, as Foucault points out, socialism has made no critique of the theme of biopower (1997: 259). In socialist states such as the former Soviet Union, China, and others, redistribution provisions in the name of social citizenship rights were/are imbued with state racisms and biopolitical logics.

Public policies that mark out the boundary of citizenry and institutionalize citizenship rights can be seen as state racist biopolitical projects in so far as they entail the following (Foucault 1997, Rabinow and Rose 2003): (1) a consciousness of a population of living beings whose biological existence and well-being is a political problem that concerns the state, and a consciousness of external and internal enemies to the well-being of that population; (2) a host of authorities producing a regime of scientific truth concerning a population, its vital characteristics such as birth rate, mortality rate, the ratio of births to deaths, the rate of reproduction, longevity, incidence of disabilities, incidence of accidents, and epidemics, which are also defined as biopower's fields of intervention; (3) aims of intervention such as lowering the mortality rate, reducing the incidence of accidents, increasing the reproduction rate, maintaining an optimal average, equilibrium, or regularities of a population's vital characteristics; (4) regulatory mechanisms or strategies for intervention at the general level such as 'health-insurance systems, old-age pensions; rules on hygiene that guarantee the optimal longevity of the population; the pressures ... on sexuality and therefore procreation; child care, education, et cetera' (Foucault 1997: 251); and (5) modes of subjectification in which individuals are made and self-made into adopting certain ideas and practices in the name of the vitality of individual and collective life.

The Birth of the Child-Citizen

In the late nineteenth century and most of the twentieth century, health, character, and morality were considered crucial to the vitality of a population. Social reform discourse that emerged at the turn of the twentieth century was saturated with references to the strength of the nation, the well-being of the population, which at the time was overtly defined as white in scientific racism's terms. How is the population defined today? In other words, what is the population that is considered to be a political problem for the state? How is its vitality defined, especially in relation to citizenship politics? What are the current objects of biopolitical knowledge? What are the fields of intervention and thus justified political and ethical claims? What are the modes of subjectification within the current set of truth discourses and mechanisms of biopower?

In this section I argue that the young are now considered to be a crucial element of the vitality of the population. Indeed, the position of children in citizenship projects is worthy of serious consideration in citizenship theory and studies of vital politics. In processes of reimagining the terms of social interventions, rhetoric about children usually generates effective justification for claims on collective resources in a neoliberal atmosphere. Justification is characteristically constructed on the basis of defining features of children and childhood: innocence, helplessness, vulnerability, victimization, and developmental uniqueness, especially early neural development. Elsewhere, I have argued that these indicate a reconfiguration of a citizenship regime vis-à-vis the child and childhood. Such reconfiguration can be described as the 'birth of the child-citizen,' that is, the emergence of a child-citizen discourse in cultural, legal, and political settings (Chen 2003a).

Historically, substantive aspects of citizenship, particularly the rights connected with being a citizen, were defined from the standpoint of adults, to the exclusion of children. Much historical work has documented campaigns for citizenship waged by various groups of adult non-citizens, among them slaves, women, and resident aliens, and the consequent expansion in the twentieth century of citizenship rights to virtually all natural-born adults and naturalized residents. During those processes, children remained non-citizens; the closest connection to a citizenship regime that children had been accorded was the recognition of children as future citizens, or citizens in the making.

When social policies around children emerged in the last few decades of the nineteenth century, as my research on the history of child protection shows, the policies were those recognizing children's future status, their future significance as adults. John Joseph Kelso, considered the architect of Canadian child welfare, pronounced in 1891 that 'in the child we see the future citizen, and carrying the same principle farther we see typified in his expanding intellect the future state and nation' (quoted in Chen 2005: 53).

It should be noted here that while citizenship was a central concern to child welfare pioneers, that concern emerged in the context of nation-building and social and moral reform. Thus, unlike the Marshallian understanding of citizenship in terms of rights, which was typical of the second half of the twentieth century, the discourse of citizenship several decades before that had been about the virtues of citizens. At the same time, since this earlier discourse about citizenship virtues was situated in the context of overarching concern with the collective moral tone of Canadian society, it also differs from today's New Right discourse on citizenship virtues, which downplays the collective and emphasizes individual economic liberty and responsibility (Chen 2001, 2003a).

In the postwar welfare state era, the central citizen identities that justified social, political, and moral claims – that is, the worker-citizen, and the parent- (more accurately, mother-) citizen – were adult-centred. Where social welfare policies were explicitly designed around children, the financial benefits were, as Jenson points out, (1) those recognizing the extra costs of raising children by transferring income to parents (Family Allowance), and (2) those recognizing the extra burdens of balancing work and family responsibilities (maternity leave within the Unemployment Insurance system and tax credits) (Jenson 2001). In other words, needs and claims were perceived from the standpoint of adults.

How are things different today? What do I and other scholars mean by the term *the child-citizen*? This term is not without contradictions because children are not in fact full citizens. They are not accepted as full citizens (see, e.g., Stasiulis 2002b). Adults can and must participate in the aims and activities of the society, but children cannot, at least not to the same extent even in countries where mechanisms have been developed to facilitate children's participation. Furthermore, it is not as if all claims in the name of children have been satisfied. There is a point to be made, however, about being analytically and politically alert to the increasing currency of child-focused discourses, because child-citizenship is not merely a redistributive child welfare issue, it is also about a rearticulation of social relations through citizenship practices and reformulation of citizen subjectivities. Although we should be careful not to downplay the seriousness of the actual sufferings of victimized children and be mindful of how much needs to be done to improve children's well-being, I believe it is worthwhile to explore why and how discourses on victimized children have exploded since the 1970s and have dominated the public policy agenda at the turn of the twenty-first century.

I use the term *child-citizen*, with its inherent contradictions, to describe a host of empirical developments that suggest that children are increasingly constituted as citizens in their own right and as independent bearers of rights. These include: (1) A model of active citizenry for children has been advanced by children's activism movements and the United Nations Convention on the Rights of the Child (e.g., Minow 1986, O'Neill 1992, Stasiulis 2002b). (2) Children are taking a central position in people's awareness and imagination of the nation and citizenship. Today children provide images of national vulnerability, victimization, hope, or degeneracy as in the case of school shootings by teenagers (Best 1990, Ivy 1993, Berlant 1997, Scobey 2001, Chen 2003c). (3) In public policy processes, the rhetoric about children generates justification for claims on collective resources in a neoliberal ideological framework, one example being the child poverty campaign (Chen 2001, Jenson 2001, Wiegers 2002, Nadesan 2002).

These developments indicate a reconfiguration of the citizenship regime vis-à-vis the child and childhood: the 'birth of the child-citizen.' While growing acceptance of the idea of children as independent individuals entitled to rights is in keeping with the global expansion of human rights discourse since the Second World War (Stasiulis 2002b), the notion of the entitled child-citizen and its effects need to be examined as part of the larger project of reimagining the social and restructuring citizenship, with reference to the ascendance of neoliberalism and new biopolitical problematizations (Chen 2003a).

In the past few years in public policy redesigning processes in Canada there have appeared critical commentaries about the child-citizen as a key claimant bearing social rights. These have brought to attention the intersection of scientific knowledge, especially developmental psychology and neurology, social policy and service practices for children, and the broader transformation of the citizenship regime. My previous work on the recent restructuring of child protection policy and practice (Chen 2001, 2003a, 2005), especially Ontario's Child Welfare Reform (1996–99), shows that current child protection aimed at 'keeping kids safe' is predicated on the rationality of 'children's rights to safety.' On this discursive site, while in the past children were constituted as merely representing the future of the nation and the state, today their rights have acquired independent existence. The restructuring of child protection systems is characterized by a child-centred approach. In British Columbia as well as in Ontario, the reforms have been overwhelmingly supported by the public, political parties of all stripes, the media, and many child welfare professionals, united by the outrage engendered by sensational images and stories of children murdered by parents[2] and the seemingly unassailable mission of guaranteeing children's safety. Highlights of the reforms include a standardized risk assessment system, emphasis on the child's best interests over those of the family as a whole, stricter regulation of professionals' duty to report suspicions of child abuse and neglect, and a shorter time-frame for permanent placements of children.

The reforms are sustained by a discourse of the threatened, endangered child who deserves protection from her or his own parents, mostly bad mothers. In the discourse of children's rights, the child-citizen is constituted through references to her or his innocence, unique developmental vulnerabilities such as dependency needs, sexual maturation and psychological and neurological risks (e.g., impairment of attachment or understimulation resulting in inadequate synaptic connections), which are elaborated in the new field of developmental victimology (see, e.g., Finkelhor 1995).

Jane Jenson (2001) has developed analyses of the child-citizen as independently bearing social citizenship rights. Her work draws on federal social policies and political discourses. She observes that children, particularly the youngest, have become the new 'model citizen' with social rights in recent 'post-deficit' years. The state concentrates its attention on children, as shown in a range of programs under the National Child Benefit and the National Child Agenda. These programs emphasize the 'early years' and aim at promoting healthy child development and giving all children an 'equal start' (108). The state defines such social spending on children as good investment, rather than service provisions for parents as in the pre-restructuring years (112–13). The emphasis on the 'early years' and the investment logic are obviously attributable to the growing influence of recent neurological discoveries, especially those about the formation of neural connections (synapses). As Majia Holmer Nadesan (2002) has argued persuasively, preoccupations with entrepreneurship and competitiveness in the global market are embedded within the concerns with early childhood development, stimulation, and formation of neural connections.

Shifts in areas of domestic social policy reveal that children have come to occupy a crucial position in citizenship and vital politics. Scientific discourses about children's developmental uniqueness, especially their distinctive neurological promise and at the same time fragility, have become cornerstone rationales for social policy. The redrawn fields of intervention have been marked by phrases such as 'child-centred,' 'early years,' and 'head start,' whereby the child, especially the young child, is made into the model citizen with the most legitimate claims. What are the effects of these truth claims, strategies for intervention, and modes of subjectification on how we as a society care for/govern children, and what are their effects on the redefinition of social rights and social relations of difference?

First, the conception of the child as an entitled citizen has clear benefits for some children and even some parents such as working poor parents. This is obvious with child-centred social welfare policy providing income assistance and funding for supportive, community-based services such as Better Beginnings Programs in a time of widespread cuts to social spending. In child protection, however, the results are more ambiguous. In British Columbia and Ontario, we see a steadily increasing number of children being taken from their parents and placed in substitute care, which is expensive but also often a most unsatisfactory way to look after children.

Second, the discourse of the child-citizen, operating in an ideological context of responsibilizing, seems to privilege aims that are fundamentally of personal significance, excluding questions of addressing structural problems and social justice. As such it shapes and limits possible claims. Currently the objective of child protection is to guarantee the personal safety of the individual child. Other social programs aim at creating equal opportunities for early development and education. Here we see the connection between the discourse of the child-citizen and the discourse of the active, entrepreneurial, self-reliant, neoliberal worker-citizen. To be sure, as before, children are seen as national resources, but today we invest in children so that they grow up to be independent entrepreneurial 'knowledge workers,' valued for their problem-solving abilities, creativity, talent, and intelligence suitable for working relatively autonomously on projects that are complex and non-repetitive (Nadesan 2002).

Third, the discourse of the child-citizen validates age as a key social difference to be recognized in social policy (and immigration policy as discussed in the following section) and redraws the boundary of the entitled citizen category. The criteria of entitlement seem to be innocence, victimization, good potential return for the investment in social spending as related to children's unique neural development features. It results in positioning the child's interests independently of and, even, in opposition of those of parents. It operates to push adults and even older children's needs into the background. For example, in the case of child protection, the child-citizen discourse construes parents, many of whom are poor single mothers, as potential perpetrators of harm to be risk-managed or punished, as opposed to being helped and supported through social entitlements.

Finally, the notion of the child-citizen has problematic implications for democracy. Children may appear to be model citizens entitled to social spending and intervention. Rarely, however, are children accepted as full citizens when it comes to participation, notwithstanding the U.N. Convention's stipulation about children's participation rights (Stasiulis 2002b). In child protection, adult professionals act on behalf of children and define what counts as victimization, risks of harm, and children's best interests, and adult professionals draw up protection plans. The acquisition of rights for children to social spending and social caring has been dependent on the modern, Western concept of childhood that stresses the innocence and frailty of children. The other side of this concept is the separation of children from reason, wisdom, sexuality, competence, and autonomy. Thus, the model child-citizen – infantile, innocent, passive, and helpless – is entitled to social citizenship rights as deemed fit by adult experts, but denied the political and civil rights to be an active participating member of society. A child-centred citizenship model is inherently paternalistic. It recognizes social rights, but downplays and even excludes, the democratic requirement of collective actions by citizens mobilized to make claims.

The Biopolitics of Immigration

Similar to the ascendance of the child-citizen discourse in domestic social policy, on the site of immigration, age – specifically the differentiation between the child and the adult, especially the elderly – has emerged as an important determinant of desirability and worthiness. The favouritism shown to young children by the immigration officer and by Kent's policy proposal mentioned at the beginning of this chapter needs to be understood in the ideological context discussed above in which children are increasingly constituted as citizens in their own right and as independent bearers of rights. When an immigration officer at the Vancouver airport announced to parents with a baby adopted from Asia that 'these are our favourites!' what visions of the ideal immigrant and citizen underlie that statement? What are the effects of a child-centred ideology?

Against the backdrop of concerns about low birth rate and an aging population, vitality is nowadays defined as an optimal ratio between the elderly and the young, meaning a younger population, for the objective of maintaining a state of life, which is commonly understood in terms of continuing economic growth and the sustainability of social policies such as pension, health care, and other social programs. I argue that, at least partly as a result of this, in deliberations on immigration the Canadian population, in the biopolitical sense, is defined, not on the basis of scientific racism's conception of race or even ethnicity, but as a 'pure biological entity' with its ethnic and linguistic variations, much like the former Soviet Union and China's state racist perceptions of their populations (see Kelly's comments on Australia's bionationalism, 2004). This of course is not to suggest that we have entered a post-race, post-ethnicity era. What it does suggest is that the relative and shifting signification of race and ethnicity is increasingly established through the prism of biological capital considerations. This is best illustrated by two categories of family class immigration programs: intercountry adoption and the sponsoring of parents and grandparents.

To parents intercountry adoption is a matter of family formation; to the Canadian state it is part of the family class immigration. Since the early 1990s, more than 25,000 foreign children, about 70 per cent of whom are female, have been adopted to Canada, at a steady rate of between 1,800 to 2,200 per year. Children from Asian countries (mainly China, the Republic of Korea, the Philippines, and India) account for 70 to 80 per cent of the total number of adopted children; China alone is the source of 60 per cent of intercountry adoptions to Canada (Adoption Council of Canada 2007, Chen 2003c). The vast majority of adoptive parents are middle-class white Canadians in professional occupations such as public service, journalism, academia, and high-tech industry.

In comparison, Canadians who apply to sponsor the immigration of their parents (the majority of whom are elderly women) are first-generation immigrants, who usually came to Canada from Asian countries. According to statistics compiled by the advocacy organization Sponsor Your Parents (SYP), the inventory of family class cases for parents at all overseas visa offices on 26 November 2004 indicates that about 70 per cent of all applications were submitted to visa offices in Asian countries (mainly China, the Philippines, Pakistan, India, and Singapore), followed by Syria, and then some Caribbean, African, and East European countries (SYP 2007).

For several years now, Citizenship and Immigration Canada has arbitrarily separated family class cases into two groups: a priority category that includes spouses, partners, and children from a secondary category of parents and grandparents.[3] The contrast between the treatment of adopted children and that of parent applicants is flagrant. Family class applications go through two processes: application to sponsor a family member that is processed in Canada and application to immigrate that is processed overseas. Applications to sponsor adopted children are reviewed daily on a priority basis and are usually completed within ten days of their receipt at a Case Processing Centre in Canada; in contrast, the processing time for applications to sponsor parents takes twenty-eight months or more. Assessment of applications for adopted children's immigration is usually completed within a matter of days.[4] It mainly depends on the time required to complete the medical examination or whether there are complications in the adoption process (CIC 2007). In contrast, processing of applications for sponsored parents takes anywhere from three to even possibly ten years depending on the country ofresidence (SYP 2007). Such lengthy waits are caused directly by intentional administrative delaying tactics. For example, for an eighteen-month period from 2003 to 2005 the Case Processing Centre at Mississauga froze the processing of this category of cases. During that period, Citizenship and Immigration Canada continued to receive new applications, and its website still indicated that it would take twenty-one months to process, when not a single application was being processed (Canadian Bar Association [CBA] 2005). Moreover, since the mid-1990s, the number of parents admitted have dropped significantly (McLaren and Black 2005); over the two years of 2003 and 2004, there was a 75 per cent reduction in quotas ('targets') for this category. As the Canadian Bar Association put bluntly it, 'if CIC continues to set a quota of processing only 5,500 applications per year, it will be close to 20 years before currently filed applications are processed. By then, most applicants will either be dead or medically inadmissible' (CBA 2005: 4). In 2005, the then Minister of Citizenship and Immigration Joe Volpe raised the number of parents who can immigrate to Canada from 6,000 to 18,000 a year for 2005 and 2006 (CIC 2005a, 2005b). However, as Sponsor Your Parents points out, even with the 'increase,' the new quotas will be substantially lower than historical levels and 'it will take 6 years to clear the current backlog [of 110,000 parental sponsorship cases]' (SYP 2007).

The sharply differentiated approaches to the immigration of adopted babies and to sponsored parents raise questions about who benefits from the family reunification program. In the history of Canadian immigration, until the 1960s, family reunification provisions primarily benefited Europeans. The vast majority of immigrants originating from Asian, Caribbean, and African countries had to endure long-term family separation or forced bachelor life because of the prohibition on the entry of family members (Li 1998, Agnew 1996, Kérisit, and Côté 2001, McLaren and Black 2005). Comparing the two groups, adopted babies and sponsored parents, it is obvious that adoptive parents, mostly of European descent, are accorded preferential treatment and support in forming families and their adopted babies are welcomed to Canada with open arms; at the same time, elderly parents from mostly non-European countries are seen as undesirable elements, and these families' entitlement to being reunited are seriously frustrated, if not practically quashed. McLaren and Black (2005) make the further observation that the current practice adversely and perversely targets elderly women. While it is plain that elderly women from non-European countries are especially affected by the restriction, questions remain: what rationales govern these practices? Are the assumptions and aims behind such discriminatory practice articulated with racial, gendered logics and/or something else, and how?

What follows examines biopolitical rationales that largely frame deliberations on immigration, specifically the human capital discourse. Before getting into that discussion, it should be briefly noted that critics have argued that cultural preference in favour of North American nuclear families is also at work. For example, Citizenship and Immigration Canada justifies the restriction of parental immigration as necessary because of the importance of economic immigrants and Canada's commitment to 'reuniting close family members,' which means 'process[ing] spouses, partners and dependent children on a priority basis' (CIC 2004). It is obvious that the priority given to spouses and children is based on the ideology of the Canadian nuclear family, not the extended Asian or African family, which, as Li (2004) points out, is associated with foreign cultures in a demeaning way and seen as contrary to Canadian family values. McLaren and Black argue that 'in excluding parents and grandparents from the "immediate" family, immigration policy has targeted them as not only less important, but also possibly threatening' (2005: 14). However, it is my view that the cultural preference of the nuclear family is of secondary importance in comparison with human capital reasonings for the following reasons: (1) Historically, sponsored parents were not singled out for restrictive measures until the 1990s. (2) It is evident that

Citizenship and Immigration Canada's primary concern is to 'leave enough room for skilled workers' (internal CIC communications 2002, quoted in SYP 2007) and that when political pressure was exerted to have economic immigrants and fewer family class immigrants sponsored parents were assigned secondary status through administrative measures. (3) As the following discussion will show, opposition to the entry of sponsored parents and advocacy for an immigration policy favouring child immigrants are anchored in concerns with human capital, not with the preservation of the norm of the nuclear family.

Directly related to biopolitical logics, human capital discourse forms an important part of the ideological context for the differentiated treatment of adopted children and sponsored parents: Human capital discourse, in combination with the ascending conception of the child as the ideal immigrant and citizen, in effect, valorizes the biopolitical difference between young age and old age on the site of immigration. Immigration policy is a central component of biopolitical governance. The very notion of immigration entails a consciousness of a population and a definition of its characteristics – racial, ethnic, cultural, linguistic, reproduction rate, sex ratio, participation in the labour market, and so on. To make immigration policy is to devise interventions to bring in 'the right people' to preserve, improve, or even to transform certain characteristics of the Canadian population and to keep out enemies that would perceivably menace the well-being of the population (for a similar argument, see Walters' study of deportation, 2002). Admission of immigrants to Canada has always been fundamentally imagined as a solution to challenges identified in Canadian society. As such, varieties of human capital discourse have always affected immigration policy (Li 2003 2004, Ley 2003, Abu-Laban and Gabriel 2003, McLaren and Black 2005). Immigration policy has traditionally been concerned with addressing existing economic problems, with the objective of meeting the perceived immediate needs for labour, skills in particular occupations, or capital. Typically, problems such as a shortage of doctors in rural areas, a shortage of truck drivers in New Brunswick (*Toronto Star*, 25 September 2005), a need for trades people (Clark 2005) and even unskilled labour to fill job vacancies (Saunders 2006), which create economic burdens in major cities (Bauder 2005), and a dwindling population and diminishing economic base in small, non-urban communities (ibid.) have been identified as valid grounds upon which to formulate effective immigration policy.

Concerns for Canada's 'changing demographic and labour market context' (Solberg/CIC 2006), 'future economic and demographic troubles,' 'threats to our security' (Saunders 2006), 'global competitiveness,' and maintaining the level of social services such as health care and education (Campion-Smith 2005; *Star Phoenix*, 27 September 2005) have made regular appearances in public debates and government papers. In comparison with the 'present needs' thinking, these concerns tend to reflect anxiety about problems that may confront the Canadian population at some point in the future. Statistics showing trends and projections are produced to indicate the likelihood of such happenings. An aging population, together with an ever-deepening shortage of skilled workers (see, e.g., *Toronto Star*, 25 September 2005; CIC 2006) and the prediction that the number of births to Canadian parents will come to equal the number of deaths between 2025 and 2030 (Solberg/CIC 2006) signal worrisome demographic trends and future economic troubles. The forecast of Canada's median age hitting 42.5 years in 2020, in contrast to Europe's 52 years, suggests the inevitable heating up of the emerging global competition for immigrants (*Toronto Star*, 30 September 2005). As I will illustrate in the following discussion, it is precisely this future orientation that makes it possible for age, or more accurately, younger ages because of their greater distance from the mean age of the population, to be considered valuable biological capital.

One of the conspicuous future troubles identified is the looming disappearance of a way of life that the Canadian population have become accustomed to. In addition to a desire for continuing economic prosperity, the continuity and regularity of the existing level of social security has increasingly been named to be an equally important dimension of the Canadian way of life. Anxiety about the welfare state being drained by immigrants has been a long-standing theme. The cautions are that immigrants lower the Canadian standard of living because of their 'low earnings capacity' and failure to pay their fair share of income tax, on the one hand, while drawing on social services such as health care and education, on the other, according to a report released by the Fraser Institute, a right-wing think tank (Grubel 2005, Campion-Smith 2005). One commentator associated with the Fraser Institute, Martin Collacott (2002, 2005), points the finger directly at elderly parents and warns that their arrival in large numbers will deplete the Canadian health care system. In these discourses, elderly parents are singled out as an undesirable burden on society and even as a threat to the Canadian way of life. Parallel to the neoliberal bashing of the racialized 'welfare queen,' elderly parents are constructed and attacked as burdens on the welfare state – to be kept out of Canada because of their age.

In addition to the anxiety about the drain, reflections on immigration in relation to social citizenship have been characterized by an intensifying preoccupation with recruiting future contributors to social programs to offset the consequences of the greying of the population. A new discourse articulates immigration with social policy centred around the issue of the aging of the Canadian population, whereby immigration of the young is seen to be a means to slow down if not reverse the aging trend of the population and to mitigate the risk of the collapse of the social security system. The right immigrants – those who are youthful, healthy, with high earning potential and thus taxation potential – are imagined as contributors, who are needed to keep contributions to and withdrawals from social programs in balance (*Star-Phoenix*, 27 September 2005; Campion-Smith 2005). For example, it has been argued that more immigrants are needed to offset the health care burden in Canada because data from the province of Saskatchewan show that a 'disproportionately high rate of seniors means more people demanding pharmaceuticals, and fewer taxpayers to cover the cost of a publicly subsidized drug plan, leaving it to individuals to struggle with a greater share of the burden'(*Star-Phoenix*, 27 September 2005).

Although human capital theory foregrounds the need to attract economic immigrants who are educated, skilled, and prepared for the labour market – the so-called plug-in-and-play immigrants (Jiménez 2005) – arguably children and youth have come to be seen as precious human capital in the context of the aging population. This is made apparent in Tom Kent's (2004) policy proposal advocating for a youth, and especially, a child-centred immigration policy. Kent's proposal rests on three formulations of children's unique human capital value to the Canadian population. The first is what I term *children's demographic value* to Canada. Canada needs children and youth immigrants – their young ages – to counter problems associated with the country's diminished fertility and aging society. Kent claims that 'in the early 20th century the immigrants most needed were farmers. Later they were skilled industrial and professional workers. In this century, the need is different again. Youth is prime. In a market economy, reduced supply enhances value. Our diminished fertility, making fewer young Canadians among the old, calls for switching the emphasis of immigration policy to youth, to children especially' (28).

Kent makes it clear that immigration without discriminating about age simply will not solve the problems confronting Canada's aging society.

Only an influx of immigrant children, not immigrants of the same average age as Canadians now at work, would effectively replenish Canada's aging population. He provides an example of ranking the relative merits of potential immigrants: 'as scarcity moves up the scale, an adaptable 20-year-old may have more to give to Canada than a 40-year-old professional' (ibid.). What this calculation suggests is that merit is not simply attached to present ability to participate in the labour force; rather, it is attached to the relative distance between individual ages and the mean age of the population. Children's biological and economic value lies precisely with the greater distance from the mean age. While right-wing commentators are fixated on seeing elderly parents as a drain on the Canadian welfare state, Kent's pro-immigration stance nevertheless shares their unabashedly utilitarian human capital discourse, with the exception that his definition of capital with good return potential is in terms of the biological property of young age and its value relative to Canada's aging society.

Second, according to Kent, young age also means optimal adaptation capacity: child and youth immigrants 'are the most adaptable of immigrants. They have less changes to make' (ibid.). This is advantageous to Canada because popular settlement cities such as Toronto and Vancouver have already experienced 'too much tension.' Kent does not explain what this tension is, as if it were self-evident; but from the context, it would be safe to infer that he is alluding to cultural and linguistic heterogeneity brought in by adult immigrants that threatens to tear apart the traditional social and cultural fibre of major Canadian cities. The focus on the adaptation of immigrants to the majority assumes the legitimacy of Eurocentric norms in Canadian society; it also entails ethnocentric and even racist judgment about the inferiority of foreign values, languages, and patterns of behaviour. The biological capital in children's young ages apparently derives from their cultural 'innocence' and mouldability that render them more amenable to 'normalization.' In this regard, adults, especially elderly ones, compare unfavourably with children because they are more of a non-assimilation problem, and are seen to be cultural, linguistic, and financial (settlement services) burdens to Canada.

Third, the value of child-immigrants also lies with the fact that they allow Canada to build a national humanitarian identity. As Kent puts it, another advantage of an immigration policy that accords priorities to 'children who are orphaned or in young families' is that the humanitarian cause of rescuing children from deprivation and despair is one of the most appealing causes. Oblivious to the contradiction between the utilitarian logic and the claim of moral high ground, Kent argues that such a cause, once institutionalized by official action, will bind the nation together and provide a constitutive piece of positive national identity.

In the previous section, I argued that the child-citizen discourse circulating in social policy domains rests on a number of defining features of children and childhood: innocence, helplessness, vulnerability, and developmental uniqueness. If the child is discursively constructed as the ideal citizen in social policy making, it seems that the construction of the child as the ideal immigrant similarly assumes these features. Here, young children's cultural innocence, flexibility, lack of agency, and thus amenability to assimilation are viewed to be advantageous to Canada, especially in the case of orphaned children. The unnamed Others of the 'easy,' unburdened, and unburdening child immigrants are 'difficult' adult immigrants who are seen to be set in their ways and to be bringing cultural tensions to Canada.

Biopolitics, Racisms, and Recasting Citizenship

This chapter has focused on the emergence of the category of children and youth as the ideal immigrant and citizen in the transformation of citizenship. Drawing on Foucauldian concepts of biopolitics and state racism, it provides an analysis of two cases whereby considerations of the worthiness of immigrants are articulated with the recasting of the social in citizenship. Biopolitical logics are premised on a conception of a population as a mass of living beings whose existence and well-being are of fundamental concern to the state. State racism furnishes the state with the capacity to pose questions of biopower and sovereign power at the same time – determining who is to be included and let to thrive and who is to be excluded, rejected, or removed – so as to improve the happiness and health of the population. As a concept, the notion of 'state racism' poses questions about who is included in the population and who are considered to be the external and internal enemies of the population, and it provides an avenue for analysing how biopolitical objectives, knowledge, and interventions aimed at the thriving of the population are articulated with sovereign power's right to kill, reject, and exclude. In this chapter, the two concepts of biopolitics and state racism have facilitated analysis of, first, the human capital rationale that governs the juxtaposition and differential treatment of two categories of primarily non-European immigrant applicants – adopted children and sponsored elderly parents; and second, the increasing salience of the factor of age in the definition of vital properties of a population, the categorization of human beings, and the devising of inclusive and exclusive interventions.

Under the rubric of human capital discourse, children and youth's developmental potential, demographic value, cultural 'innocence,' and linguistic flexibility are deemed to be essential biological capital constructive to the vitality of the Canadian population. One of the enemies is represented by the figure of elderly parents whose entry to Canada would purportedly aggravate the aging trend of the population, pose a threat to the sustainability of social programs such as health care, pension, and social assistance, and add to societal tensions because of linguistic and cultural maladaptation.

Commenting on Australia's immigration policy, Mark Kelly remarked that there is a move away from a White Australian policy towards 'a nationalism which is premised simply on the interests of the nation as an economic, demographic entity' (2004: 58). A similar observation can be made about current Canadian immigration policy that is centred around cost-effective accumulation and maximization of human capital regardless of skin colour. Increasingly, biopolitics in Canada is being marked not by the problematization of the racial genetics of the population, but by the age profile of the population. In other words, one current mode of articulating biopower and sovereign power is framed by demographic concerns, which spotlight age, defined in terms of relative demographic value.[5] Biopolitical interventions through immigration are a site of recasting the social in citizenship as they valorize a social relation between child immigrants and elderly immigrants. Child immigrants and sponsored parents are both reduced to their age and are granted differential access to immigration and social citizenship on that basis. Consequently, emerging contentions over citizenship have been shaped by the biopolitical language of age and the associated subjectivities. Scholars critical of the exclusion of sponsored parents emphasize the term *elderly* 'to signify age as a differentiating social category that shapes migration identity, experience, and power' (McLaren and Black 2005: 3). Counter-discourses recognize elderly parents as contributors to their working children, young grandchildren, and community. Advocates for sponsored parents draw on human capital discourse by articulating parents' essential but often unpaid caring labour at home and contribution to community that are overlooked and demeaned (McLaren and Black 2005). In a petition to the House of Commons organized by Sponsor Your Parents, petitioners sought to communicate to the House that 'parents provide much needed social benefits of child and home care to their working children and help in preservation and passing of traditional and cultural values from one generation to another' (SYP 2007). At protest rallies, young children stood in the front and held up placards marked with statements such as 'I miss my grandparents' or 'I love grandpa, grandma' (ibid.), emphasizing elderly applicants' emotional value to their grandchildren. A field of recognition politics on the basis of age is emerging in dialectic with negotiations for equality.

In the midst of the intensifying political significance of age, what can be said about citizenship politics on the basis of race or ethnicity? What the preceding analysis suggests is that race or ethnicity has been decentred in biopolitics and state racism in two ways: first, the population, as a political question to the state, has been defined to be an economic and demographic entity, not on racialized or ethnic terms; and second, the problematization of age, not race or ethnicity, has become central to linking biopower and sovereign power. Arguably, this decentring has happened since Citizenship and Immigration Canada's introduction of the point system emphasizing education, language skills, and work experience in the assessment of immigration applicants; the increasing relevance of age is but a more recent modification of the same process. This argument may be challenged by the observation of the uneven effects of the human capital logic along the colour line, as many critics of the language requirement have pointed out since the introduction of the point system. Indeed, in the two cases examined in this chapter, such discrepant effects are also quite manifest in the preferential treatment of adopted children whose entry to Canada results in the formation of families for adoptive parents who are mostly white, and in the discriminatory treatment of sponsored parents wishing to be reunited with their children living in Canada, the bulk of whom are of non-European backgrounds. As well, one can argue that the colour-blind importation of human capital, on the one hand, and the rejection of potential menacing 'burdens,' on the other, serves the entrenched interests of the white majority (Kelly 2004). While politically these are important observations, in analysis distinctions need to be made between rationales and their actual effects. The history of the colour-coding of immigration and citizenship clearly reveals a racist biopolitical logic that drew on scientific racism's presupposition of the existence of racial groups on a hierarchy of superiority and inferiority. In contrast, the biopolitical logic that governs current thinking about immigration and citizenship is characterized by a human capital reasoning that categorizes human beings on the basis of their economic potential as knowledge workers, entrepreneurs, and biological capital in terms of their demographic values, not on the basis of racial categories. Biopolitical logic is concerned with the sustainability of social welfare provisions that depend on an optimal ratio of those drawing benefits from social programs and those contributing to social programs, rather than with the interests of the whites. That is why not all people of colour are thought of as undesirable immigrants and treated unfavourably. The reasoning behind the opposition to sponsored parents' entry to Canada is formulated in terms of age and identity as non-contributors, not on the basis of race. In this regard, it is worth noting that while the bulk of sponsored parents subjected to unjustified delays in the immigration process are from Asian, African, and Caribbean countries, some are from East European countries. The advocacy organization Sponsor Your Parents consists of people with Asian as well as East European backgrounds.

To argue that race or ethnicity have been decentred in biopolitical logics, however, is not to suggest that race or ethnicity have been rendered irrelevant or simply replaced by another set of social relations – age. Age does appear as a focal concern in biopolitical logics involved in the cases examined in this chapter; however, as my analysis of Kent's argument about children's value as superior adapters has shown, the validity of age-centred reasonings is partially linked to the ideology of Western superiority and dominance. This suggests that how race or ethnicity matters has contingently shifted with the ascendance of human capital rationalities. In other words, signification of race and ethnicity is increasingly established through the prism of human capital rationalities, which at present privilege considerations of age, specifically individuals' demographic value.

To summarize, this chapter argues that biopolitics, specifically the problematization of the aging of the population and interventions aimed at securing a younger, neurologically optimal, and economically entrepreneurial population are central to the processes of recasting the social and restructuring citizenship in Canada in the twenty-first century. Theoretically, the analysis of the discourse of the child-citizen shows that redistributive concerns and struggles for recognition of social identities are not separable in the reality of citizenship struggles. The emergence of the child-citizen is not simply a matter of redistributive child welfare programs. The processes that produce the child-citizen rearticulate social relations between children and others, especially the elderly, by redrawing the cartography of access to citizenship entitlements and by reformulating social identities.

Acknowledgments

I want to acknowledge the Killam Trust, the Social Sciences and Humanities Research Council of Canada, and the Human Early Learning Partnership at the University of British Columbia for providing funds for the research that this chapter draws on. I would like to extend my sincere thanks to members of the Recasting the Social in Citizenship Network, especially Engin Isin, for their useful feedback on earlier drafts of this chapter. I am grateful to Mariana Valverde, Alan Hunt, and Pat O'Malley for their help with making the revisions. Thanks also to Susan Salhany at Carleton University for her excellent research assistance.

Notes

1 Interview with an adoptive parent, 20 Nov. 2002.
2 Child homicide cases, despite their rarity, tend to capture the most publicity in media and coroners' inquests; however, it was accidental deaths and ostensibly their prevention that became the rationale for Ontario's Child Welfare Reform and similar policy changes in other provinces. For a detailed analysis of the Ontario Child Mortality Task Force's problematic handling of child mortality statistics, see Chen 2003b.
3 Since most sponsored family members in this category are parents, rather than grandparents, to the sponsors, in the rest of the chapter I routinely refer to them as parents only.
4 Personal communication with the staff of an intercountry adoption facilitating agency, 8 Jan. 2007.
5 Another obvious mode of articulation is through national security concerns, especially since the 9/11 attacks.

8 The Soldier-Citizen

DEBORAH E. COWEN

Over the past thirty years national militaries across the advanced capitalist Anglophone world have taken a serious interest in the social welfare of soldiers. The United States, the United Kingdom, Canada, and Australia have all enhanced recreation spaces, renovated base housing, restructured pensions, and initiated programs to support the Quality of Life and Work-Life balance of military personnel. Military bases today are designing creative communal child care facilities. Dual *deployed* parents are told to rest assured that their young ones will be well cared for back home through the extensive network of social services and community supports now established on bases. New military family service organizations have been created, for example, Defence Families of Australia was founded in 1986, Britain's Army Families Federation was created in 1982, and Canada's Military Family Support Program in 1991, while Britain's Royal Air Force recently started employing community development workers.[1] This expansion of social support for soldiers is indicative of a broader trajectory in the contemporary recasting of the social in citizenship. Soldiers are subject to new and improved forms of social policy and provision, with militaries offering extraordinarily elaborate, although not necessarily generous, systems of social welfare for personnel. However, at the very same time, *civilian* social welfare has been targeted, downloaded, privatized, and the notion of social rights largely left behind.

Both this expansion of military welfare and the reformulation of civilian social citizenship have been centrally organized around changing notions of entitlement. In a resurgence of classic liberal logics, soldiers are understood to be deserving of social rights as they serve the nation with their lives. Meanwhile, for civilians, entitlement has become a precarious affair, as obligation has come to govern their citizenship. Social entitlement has been reworked such that need has become stigmatized as dependency, and deeply shunned. Social rights have not disappeared, but are more explicitly contingent on contribution, particularly through work. The effects of these shifts are clearly very different for civilian and military citizens; soldiers' social entitlements are enhanced while civilian insecurity intensifies. Nevertheless, a common logic is operative and recasts the social in citizenship for both military and civilian citizens. Workfare – the expectation that citizens work for basic social support or lose their entitlement to collective care – has come to distinguish deserving from undeserving citizens.

In this chapter I suggest that a focus on the military reveals crucial dimensions of the social in citizenship that are otherwise hidden in plain view. Soldiering is an exceptional occupation and form of belonging. It is exceptional in the sense that scholars typically treat it as an anomaly and bracket the norms and logics governing its practice from the study of work and citizenship. This is the case despite the fact that many military social policies have been in existence much longer than their civilian counterparts and served as the model for civilian provision. Key social technologies of the welfare state were initially engineered to support the battlefield, even as they came to transform relations in factories and households.

Military work is also exceptional in the sense that it complicates and even compromises the categories of civilian social welfare. Obligation and entitlement have been key concepts through which scholars periodize citizenship in liberal state societies. In T.H. Marshall's classic work (1950), the development of social rights was the *defining* feature of social citizenship, and more recent accounts confirm that the 'shift in emphasis from charity to entitlement has long been viewed as a central metaphorical turn in the construction of the welfare state' (Struthers 1998: 179). Yet, for military personnel, benefits are *earned* by virtue of their service. A form of entitlement certainly characterizes soldiers' welfare, but it is a right that is contingent on contribution through service.

Likewise, the soldier eludes the distinction between redistributive and recognition-based politics that has come to define so much contemporary political analysis. Any attempt to distinguish the cultural and material dimensions of an institution like the military, which has been vital in defining citizenship, identity, territoriality, and sociality, is destined to fail. The soldier is a paradigmatic case of a politically defined worker – soldiers are 'employees of society' to borrow from

Nikolas Rose (1999: 64)[2] – but they do not easily fit the laws of capitalist economy or democratic politics. Social identity and social location are furthermore impossibly entangled in the military histories of citizenship, and initiating analyses through these categories erases the important political work of warriors.

These exceptional qualities of military welfare – its exclusion from civilian history and status as a model for civilian forms, and its simultaneous incompatibility with common (civilian) categories, make the soldier an important subject for the study of social citizenship. In what follows I suggest that an investigation of the military histories and geographies of work and welfare yields new insights about the role of organized violence and nationalized work in shaping social forms of citizenship, and alerts us to some ominous trajectories in its contemporary recasting.

Genealogies of the Soldier and the Social

Perhaps the oldest form of social policy, military pensions have been traced back to the Roman Empire and likely emerged even earlier. However, as Craig, Wilson, and Clark (2002) argue, pensions acquired newfound importance in the context of the modern European state system where they helped to build nationalisms. Modern forms of social citizenship have been national geographical forms, and the emergence of welfare in the West is inseparable from the nationalization of the state. Following Radhika Viyas Mongia (2003: 197), I use 'nationalized' to signal a 'conjuncture between the "nation" which is held to be a primarily sociocultural category describing forms of community, and the "state," which relates to forms of governance,' although I would also emphasize the crucial role of modern territorial politics. The modern state was *historically nationalized*; a project that was fundamentally geographical and deeply colonial, although never complete. The soldier has been a central agent and subject of this nationalization. On the one hand, soldiers fought the wars that redefined territorial jurisdiction as an object of loyalty worthy of the ultimate sacrifice, while on the other hand, the management of a military labour force provoked experimentation in social policies that gave us the precedent for national and social forms of government, like pensions. This is not to suggest that there was an immediate correspondence between nationalized states and the emergence of social citizenship. Early liberal charity models of poor relief were dominant until the late nineteenth century and are antithetical to our conceptions of social citizenship. These models were organized around the propertied masculine individual, and it was needs-based charity rather than any notion of entitlement that governed the provision of poor relief. Liberal political theorists argued that the poor owed a debt to the nation for their dependency, and this ideology informed the system of workhouses that administered poor relief in eighteenth – and nineteenth – century Britain and Europe.

The military occupied an important place within the classic liberal model of national obligation. In various ways, liberal theorists like Locke and Hobbes rationalized the existence of the state in the name of the defence of the individual and of individual property. National military forces were important because they would protect the collective (though individual) property of the body politic. Conveniently, military service became a means through which the poor could repay the nation for their welfare. After describing the poor as 'the foster children of the country,' Jeremy Bentham (1843: 420), for example, argued that a system of pauper workhouses would have a 'collateral benefit of a most important nature' providing a 'nursery – a supplement – and in part a succedaneum – to the existing system of national defence.' For Bentham 'national force' could be strengthened 'without expense to anybody' by having paupers who live in workhouses serve in national defence on weekends and labour in the workhouse during the week. In fact, military conscription was common among the emerging nationalizing states, but in practice this was a conscription of *unpropertied* men, thus strengthening the historical connections between liberalism, workfare, and military service (cf. Cowen 2006).

By the late nineteenth century a powerful new set of practices and ideas interrupted the individualist thrust of liberalism, salvaging it from the social unrest emerging in response to the massive inequalities of early industrial capitalism. As Jacques Donzelot (1988) has argued, a new school of social economists proposed techniques for managing the class conflicts that were becoming a frequent and serious threat to the social order. In the 1880s German Chancellor Bismarck implemented the first state-run social insurance programs and showed that 'subversion can be combated only by freeing the state from the so-called liberal definition which limits its role to guaranteeing the established order – an easy target for revolutionaries – and by realizing its true vocation as society's cement' (ibid.: 398). Following Bismarck's pioneering experiments with social insurance, the new school succeeded 'in making the discourse of solidarity prevail over rival schools – liberal, traditionalist or socialist' (ibid.: 399). Social insurance gave the state an active role in shaping society. It forged a relationship between the state and the individual, collectivizing the very risks to life that accompanied accidents, injuries, and old age within industrial capitalist society. This appealed to the working classes who were regularly injured in factory work, and for whom the individualism of liberalism couldn't account for the classed nature of bodily injury. Bismarck's insurance technique enlisted the working class in the project of nationalism in a way that classic liberalism had failed to do.

Soldiers and Solidarity

While Donzelot demonstrates the path-breaking nature of Bismarck's experiments, he virtually neglects the military dimensions of these social technologies. Bismarck's insurance technique provided a means for the state to manage, but not eliminate, conflicts between labour and capital largely by extending entitlement to care for injured bodies, but it was developed first to cultivate soldiers' loyalty to the warring state. These techniques were crucial for supporting the wars that defined the territorial borders of the nationalizing states in Europe and their networks of colonies around the world. Bismarck's challenge was to mobilize and unify the support of a population divided by class, religion, and region. His mass army relied on mass loyalty, and social insurance was an integral part of a nation-building strategy. The passage of his social legislation 'provided a unifying catalyst that called for the end to provincialism (and thus the end of localism) and the beginnings of the modern nation state' (Kirwin 1996: 205). In this context, pensions were an effective means of harnessing the loyalty of war workers. If soldiers were 'protected from injury, given pensions, and their families looked after,' Kirwin (205) submits, 'they would be more willing to give totally to the war effort.'

Many other emerging states also instituted military pensions around this time, and some even predate Bismarck's initiatives. For example, France and the United States both extended pensions to soldiers during their revolutionary wars (Dutton 2002, Skocpol 1992). However, unlike Bismarck's initiatives, these policies remained targeted towards soldiers and their dependents. In Canada, militia pensions have existed since 1812, and since 1901 in their modern incarnation. The official rationales for military pensions reveal the crisp logic that called for special services for soldiers. Pensions mitigate the peculiar work conditions of the national soldier, and thus, as Bismarck had already discovered, were an efficient means of managing the human resources for war. A 1938 Canadian military document outlines how, 'if a young man is to be attracted into a profession from which he may have to be retired on pension in middle age through no fault of his own, it is clear that his financial and other conditions of life up to that age, and his prospects thereafter, must receive special consideration.[3] Long before the initiation of civilian pensions in Canada, this simple logic supported pensions for soldiers.

A genealogy of intimate association between war and welfare goes beyond pensions to include the creation of family policy first for soldiers (Christie 2000, Dutton 2002, Guest 1985, Titmuss 1958, Skocpol 1992); wartime innovations in housing design, management, and financing (Bacher 1988, Christie 2000, Hardin 1999, M. Marsh 1990); and health care, including neonatal and child care (Christie 2000, Finkel 1977, Guest 1985, Titmuss 1958). So while Donzelot and others have identified the landmark invention of solidarity and the practice of social insurance as crucial historical shifts in civilian struggles of industrial capitalism, these were initially experiments to manage military forces. To fight national and colonial wars, states had to harness the productive and reproductive labour of the population. To encourage service and ensure loyalty, state strategists worked to engineer support for the nation-state. The welfare of the national population becomes 'recognized by our rulers,' in wartime, argues A.M. Low (1943: 164), when 'it is vitally necessary to make the maximum use of "manpower" and to maintain high morale.'

As strategy on the battlefield became more sophisticated and relied on the 'quality' of men fighting modern wars rather than simply the quantity of their bodies, states became more concerned for the health of the overall population from which soldiers would be drawn. Welfare historian, Richard Titmuss (1958: 22) argues that, at times of war, states develop a keen interest in the biological and psychological characteristics of the population. 'The growing scale and intensity of war,' he writes, 'has stimulated a growing concern about the quantity and quality of the population.' Titmuss outlines how Western states were concerned, first, with the simple quantity of men (to fight as soldiers), then with the quality of minds and bodies of recruits (to fight as skilled soldiers), then with the general civilian population (in the interest of ensuring decent quality *future* recruits), and finally, with the morale of the population (to maintain popular support for national struggle). The challenges of the battlefield provoked experimentation that generated some of the earliest technologies of the emergent social state.

National Geographic

Social citizenship and the welfare state of the twentieth century were nationalizing projects but the bulk of scholarship naturalizes rather than questions this production of geographical space and scale. The problem of national spatiality is one important example of the broad neglect of space in twentieth century thought. As a number of scholars have now argued, we have inherited and reproduced perspectives that emphasize the historical at the expense of a geographical imagination; our traditions neglect the entwined operation of space and time. In contrast to a Cartesian conceptualization of space as a given that sanctions its peripheralization, a rich body of scholarship has emerged that sees space as socially and politically produced (Harvey 1973, Massey 1977, Smith 1984, Mackenzie 1989, Soja 1989, Lefebvre 1991, Gregory 1994, McDowell 1999, Isin 2002b). Geographers have worked to resuscitate a spatialized history, politics, and imaginary, but few have investigated the connections between the project of nation building and the historical nationalization of warfare.[4] Yet, a national imaginary and national political geography emerged alongside the nationalization of the space of war.

Recent attempts to reread foundational texts in military and political thought with geographical questions in mind are helpful in this regard. Clausewitz (1976: 7), the most influential modern military strategist, is best known for his widely cited maxim, 'war is nothing but a continuation of political intercourse with an admixture of other means.' While the maxim brings war and politics into relation, it also defines war through its *contrast* to politics. War occurs when politics-as-usual is surpassed. This theory of war and politics, influential as it has been for modern political thought, cannot account for the role of war and military practice in generating civilian political forms. However, Clausewitz's ideas can be read not simply for what they said but for what they *did.* Hardt and Negri (2004) suggest that Clausewitz's attempt to distinguish war and politics must be understood in relation to the articulation of modern theories of state sovereignty, which had the goal of ending civil wars and investing nation-states with a monopoly on legitimate war (see also Foucault 1997: 48). As Hardt and Negri point out, war was effectively 'expelled from the internal national social field and reserved only for the external conflicts between states' (2004: 6). They argue that by making war something that is always already separate from politics, in a context where war was constituted as an international and not domestic relation, Clausewitz exteriorizes war to the sovereign nation-state: War happens *between* not *within* nationalized states.

Nationalism and National War

The nationalization of war was thus central to the nationalization of modern geographical imaginaries. As an incomplete project this nationalization has by necessity been continually reproduced. The ideological and practical work of the soldier remained crucial throughout this history, simultaneously shaping class, gendered and racialized relations at home while fighting war abroad. National war, particularly as it transformed into mass war with the First World War, was also vital to the construction of nationalisms. As the boundaries between military and civilian worlds crumbled, mass warfare transformed people into national citizens (Moreno and McEwan 2003). Susan Buck-Morss (2000: 26-7) suggests that it is 'within the mass-conscripted, national army that a synthesis between the citizen and the state is subjectively experienced, and the gap between civil society and the state appears to disappear.' In nation-states, she asserts, 'army comradeship is *the* communal act of political solidarity' (ibid.). As a war of mass armies "par excellence," asserts Doorn, the First World War 'taught the political leaders how to mobilize great masses of people and resources' (1975: 55). In Canada, the story was more complex. While a system of selective service was implemented, the military had to rely primarily on voluntary soldiers because of the domestic political crisis provoked by the war. In 1917 riots broke out in Quebec to protest conscription for what was seen as a British war. The army killed four men. The social specificity of Canadian national identity – its anglophone contours – were blatantly clear precisely when the population was being asked to sacrifice and serve. Despite this state violence, French Canadians voluntarily served in the military in large numbers, although persistent racism and Anglo control kept them contained in the lower ranks.

The Second World War brought novel contributions to the development of nationalism, particularly as a result of the practical experience gained during the First World War by labour and the state that could be built on in managing large-scale projects. The complex social machine organized by the state during the Second World War showed off the capacities of government at war and raised questions about the possibilities in times of peace. In one 1942 article celebrating William Beveridge's plan for postwar reconstruction and social security, Britain's

Guardian newspaper explained that one of the most 'attractive features of the plan' was the extension of social security 'to the whole population, which carries forward our war ideas of equality and community.' Indeed, the expansion of welfare during and after the Second World War is also centrally implicated in nation-building. 'The citizenship whose history I wish to trace is, by definition, national,' asserts Marshall (1950: 95), in his classic essay on social citizenship. While scholars of the welfare state have largely presumed a national geography of universal social policy, the space of political collectivity is increasingly becoming the subject of inquiry. Janine Brodie (2002b: 383) argues that 'the idea of social citizenship was conflated with federally inspired discourses of pan-Canadian nationalism' and that the Canadian state 'has played an inordinate role in trying to shape a national identity and to underwrite national unity in order to contain sub-national and ethnic conflicts and to build support for its many nation-building projects.' This universal nationalism, however, was organized around ethno-racial and linguistic norms of whiteness and Anglo identity.

Genesis of the Welfare State through War

The postwar welfare state was just that – post war. Allied countries crafted plans for reconstruction at the height of the Second World War. Reconstruction programs were simultanously plans for reintegrating veterans, for building a national economy (cf. Mitchell 2002), and for reworking the relationship between states and citizens. The British Beveridge Plan radicalized popular visions for the future by introducing universal models of social security and social entitlement. It directly influenced reconstruction in countries like France (Kershen 1995), Australia (Jenkins 1945, Oppenheimer 2005), and Canada (Guest 1985). In the United States, the GI Bill – the largest social welfare program ever assembled in that country – offered a different model of postwar welfare. The GI Bill was not organized around broad notions of entitlement by virtue of citizenship; rather military service remained the central arbiter of entitlement. Nevertheless, the GI Bill had profound and lasting effects on citizenship through the introduction of new forms of entitlement.

Many scholars explain postwar welfare as a product of the complex political relations surrounding the Second World War (Offe 1984, Guest 1985, Mann 1988, Habermas 1990, Harvey 1989, Kirwin 1996). During the war, the strength of organized labour surged, particularly in essential wartime industries, while socialist parties that offered meaningful alternatives to the status quo were on the rise (McInnis 2002). The service and sacrifice of the national population for war furthermore generated a common sense of entitlement to benefits. The recent memory of the Great Depression and the newfound power of national government to coordinate and manage the economy for war also boosted popular support for experiments in national social security (Guest 1985). War dramatically changed government. 'The convergence of social and economic policy was itself a product of war mobilization,' argues Jytte Klausen (1999: 8; see also Kirwin 1996: 206). Rose (1999a) echoes this argument when he explains how the pressures created by the war to coordinate all stages of the production process, while also maintaining morale, led to new forms of social and economic management in central government. 'The techniques deployed in each of these areas were not new,' Rose explains, 'but their interlinking in a coherent programme transformed each, and established the conditions for the emergence of a new conception of work and its regulation in the post-war period' (77).

The experimentation with social policy during and after the war was possible because it responded to demands of citizens *and* states. Citizens had seen the tremendous new capacities of the state in organizing work and life for war, and they expected these to be applied to secure postwar peace. Meanwhile, these new capacities for coordinating policy and managing complex social and economic relations at the national scale had a growing constituency in government. A new cadre of public managers carved out greater roles for themselves through the expansion of state administration. Mass war-work during the Second World War enabled a key shift from the voluntarism of early charity models to the sense of entitlement that accompanied postwar social citizenship. Nevertheless, while entitlement governed social citizenship, a contract persisted at its core. William Beveridge (1942: 9) observed that 'social security must be achieved by co-operation between the State and the individual. The State should offer security for service and contribution.' Feminist welfare state historian Nancy Christie (2000: 91) echoes this observation in the Canadian context, where she suggests a 'broadly conceived and unspecific notion of service to the State undergirded the immediate postwar concept of social citizenship.' In the same way that military welfare benefits are a right but also contingent on contribution, postwar welfare was organized around a paradoxical notion of entitlement. This common logic is not a coincidence. In fact, the model for the postwar welfare state was a military one, and the model citizen at its core was a war worker. Leonard Marsh, a student of William Beveridge, used military policies as the standard for national provision in his blueprint for postwar welfare in Canada. The military model was central; Marsh's plan opens with the claim that 'soldiers, sailors and airmen and their dependents really have a microcosm of social security already' (Marsh 1943: 2).

Feminist scholars have long argued that the model citizen at the centre of the social welfare state was described in universal terms, but was nevertheless a particular masculine subject. Postwar citizenship was organized around a model of the 'national worker-citizen,' but in the context of what has been termed a 'male breadwinner welfare state.' This breadwinner welfare state organized policies and programs around the male wage earner and his dependents. It forcefully elevated a specific model of citizenship, social reproduction, nuclear family, and public and private domains to universal status. This model was simultaneously gendered and racialized and anchored in the central role of the nuclear family and the white male breadwinner as head of household. Despite important differences across states, the U.S.-style GI Bill and the British- and Canadian-style reconstruction plans all distributed benefits in highly gendered and racialized ways[5].

The welfare state was organized around work and class relations were central to this project. Class did not disappear from postwar capitalism, even as strong technologies of social insurance were premised on an ideology of national citizenship that mediated class conflict. Prominent scholars have described the post–Second World War welfare state in this way – as a class compromise that was temporarily mediated through the nationalized state (Habermas 1990, Marshall 1950). The welfare state modified the extremes of class conflict; the equality of one tempered the discord of the other. By offering concessions of social and economic rights, welfare encouraged the working class to feel that it had a stake in the nationalized state (Offe 1984: 194). Rather than see any inherent conflict between class-centred accounts and those that prioritize questions of race or gender difference, it is useful to consider how the implicit norms of the postwar welfare state were constructed around a historically and geographically specific standard of the wage labourer (Habermas 1990: 54-5). The wage labourer is a culturally defined economic subject, and his social contours defy any opposition in the politics of distribution and recognition. Male breadwinner citizenship is simultaneously economic, gendered, and racialized. This national worker-citizen is an economic and social actor fashioned in the image of the war-working citizen.

The Private Social Self and The Breadwinner Family

I have argued that the postwar welfare state was a nationalizing project that transformed the relationship between state and citizen. However, as the brief discussion of the male breadwinner welfare state suggests, the private family was also accorded a new and pronounced role in governing citizenship. In 1943 the U.S. Congress even temporarily suspended the conscription of fathers for fear of irreparable disruption to family life. The family played an important role in managing morale during the Second World War and in organizing social and economic life afterwards. 'Our whole social order,' Captain S.A. Sutton, an officer of the Canadian Wartime Dependents' Allowance Board, argued, 'depends on the willingness of men in the Armed Forces to eventually return to their homes and resume their responsibilities as husbands and parents (cited in Christie 2000: 260).[6] For state planners, building the postwar family measured with an urgency that paralleled efforts to rebuild the postwar economy. National and personal security was calibrated largely through the family.

The family also became a pressing management issue for militaries in countries that established voluntary professional armed forces. Barracks would no longer do for the career soldier – instead he and his family required everyday lives that rivaled civilian comforts. 'At every military, naval or air force base "new married quarters" had to be constructed' at the start of the Cold War, Richard Preston (1972: 78) asserts, to the extent that, by 1956, the Canadian military could assert that 'most operational Royal Canadian Air Force stations are actually small-scale cities' (ibid.). A 1956 article that spanned thirteen pages in the *Canadian Geographic* magazine, written to 'sell' armed forces careers, enumerated the full range of services available to men in the services: 'They comprise a place of work, clean and comfortable living quarters and complete facilities for recreation including bowling alleys, gymnasiums, swimming pools, hockey rinks, playing fields, theatres and libraries. They have their own newspapers, schools and places of worship.'

Military family housing was not a copy of civilian housing, nor was it an attempt to camouflage military lives to pass as normal. Rather, postwar subdivision design and construction techniques were largely engineered during the Second World War through the work of people like Bill Levitt of Levittown fame. Levitt worked as an engineer and architect for the U.S. Navy and his experience building the standardized housing of the military, 'the architectural equivalent of the uniform,' as a recent article in the *New York Times* (2006) put it, was instrumental in defining the iconic postwar suburban form. 'Armed with this ability, he decided after the war to apply the same techniques to creating massive housing divisions at the outskirts of cities,' Brunn and Crosby (1999) explain. Civilian suburbs were largely built for returning veterans and their expanding families, who were subsidized with loans and land grants: as surely as the Homestead Act of 1862 filled the prairies and the Far West, the GI Bill created and filled the suburbs (Michael Bennett, quoted in Katznelson 2005: 116).

The GI Bill and the opportunities it created were highly racialized. Among other measures, Katznelson (2005) reports that less than 100 of 67,000 mortgages insured through the GI Bill went to non-white people. In Canada, too, veterans' land grants were racialized, although differently. Aboriginal veterans were denied the land grants that were accorded to white veterans, and some even had their tribal lands expropriated by the state and distributed to white veterans. Distribution to some was clearly dispossession of others. Suburban reproduction also relied on labour power that women were expected to supply. As, Rosemary Sales (2002), argues in the British context, this gendered labour was also racialized in the sense that white women were expected to return to the home after war, while caring work and pink collar formal employment became the terrain of immigrants: 'Migration helped to sustain the hegemony of this model ... by meeting some of the labour needs of postwar economies, immigrants filled a gap in the labour market that indigenous women might otherwise have been expected to fill' (460).

Class *Post* War

Postwar welfare transformed citizenship and work across advanced capitalist countries. The large-scale extension of education for returning veterans was crucial in this regard. According to Hobsbawm (1994: 295), a revolution in educational attainment and of 'occupations which required secondary and higher education' transpired, which was 'almost as dramatic as the decline and fall of the peasantry, and much more universal.' The growth of industry and the specialization of work during this war required rapid and large-scale extension of training and education for workers. Postwar benefits were also critical – in Canada they sent over 280,000 to university and vocational training programs (Morton 1990: 227), but this training had an uneven geography, for it was the rapidly urbanizing and industrialized regions of the country that were investing in higher education in the decades following the war, and where educational attainment grew most significantly (CFPARU 1975a).

In the United States, education was a crucial element of postwar transformations and here too it was highly uneven. While the GI Bill promised college education for all veterans, in 1947 alone more than 20,000 black veterans could not find institutions willing to accept them (Katznelson 2005: 132). The same exclusion took place in the area of training in trades and agricultural management. For the large number of mostly white veterans who did access postwar benefits, life changed dramatically. So too did the class structure of national society. Perhaps most importantly, through its financing of home ownership, education and training, and business loans, the GI Bill 'created middle class America' (113), or at least the ideology thereof.

The growing middle class was increasingly urban and professional. Ironically, in countries like Canada and the United Kingdom, where armed forces enlistment was voluntary, the growth of the middle class, an indirect byproduct of military models of welfare, created a recruitment crisis for the military. Growing numbers of citizens shunned the military and other static and highly disciplined forms of work. As recruitment rates dropped and attrition rates grew to near crisis levels, the militaries began to study and consult each other on the problem. By 1974 the Canadian military reported 'major socio-demographic shifts in the potential recruit population,' which could be traced through 'change in the behaviour, values, and career expectations of younger servicemen' (CFPARU 1974: 1). They flagged 'unscheduled attrition of well-educated enrollees, an apparent intolerance for aspects of military service and career policies long considered non-negotiable, and pressures for expanded benefits,' and indicated that these same transformations had been observed in other Western nations (ibid.). Through their study of the changing nature of postwar work and society, they identified fundamental shifts in the national recruit-aged population's orientation to work. 'He expects challenging work,' and 'advancement at a rate which may be inconsistent with his skills and experience; a result of his perception of the importance of education per se to career success,' and perhaps most troubling for the military, they found that the new class of young male worker-citizens 'tends to reject traditional inclusive authority patterns and status arrangements' (34).

These broad shifts in orientation to work were also tied to the changing terms of employment contracts and, in particular, the effects of the welfare state on the social wage. A range of benefits had once been the exclusive preserve of military personnel but became more widely available as part of universal social citizenship. This fractured the economy of military employment, and intensified the recruitment crisis such that by the early 1970s, military recruits were increasingly the 'fall-out' of the labour force (CFPARU 1975b: 15). The dramatic overall decline in the quantity and quality of applicants to the armed forces had spatial as well as social contours. A drop in recruitment in urban areas and in regions experiencing economic growth was stark in many countries. Reporting on one study from the early 1970s, Barrie Newman (1976: 202–3) explains that 'higher recruitment was to be found in those areas which suffered from structural unemployment or a limitation of employment possibilities,' namely, 'the three northern regions of England and the Scottish region.'

The late 1960s saw the rise of broad resistance to militarism, colonialism, and nuclear technologies around the world. Doorn (1975: 58) observed 'a declining legitimacy of the armed forces ... there is a feeling in many western countries that the armed forces are facing a crisis as a result of their increasing popularity with the public.' Social movements of the very groups cast as dependents and outside of normative citizenship organized en masse. They worked to 'demilitarize' citizenship, for example, in the area of welfare benefits. The U.S. welfare rights movement, feminist and civil rights activists all helped to transform federal expenditure and notions of entitlement. 'Common opposition to the Vietnam war,' David Segal (1989: 90) explains, united 'previously neglected interests,' which 'became mobilized as social movements seeking access to various citizenship rights and entitlements.' The demands of the civil rights and women's movements for enhanced social rights had some important and very tangible success. Segal traces the shift in spending at the federal level that these efforts provoked and notes that civilian welfare budgets finally outpaced veterans' expenditure in the 1960s (91). War was central to the social movements and widespread radicalism of the 1960s in many ways. African American veterans of the Second World War, for example, played a central role in the civil rights movement in the postwar decades.

After having risked their lives for a highly unequal nation, black veterans asserted their entitlement to civil and social rights. The transformative experiences of warfare, along with massive direct opposition to war, combined with a desperate sense of the precarious nature of life itself in the era of the atomic bomb. This latter point, Hannah Arendt (1970: 19) argues, helped prompt the student activism of the 1960s. Acting boldly, she suggests, was reasonable for a generation that regularly pondered its own potential annihilation.

The demands of social movements provoked new state policies in the area of employment equity and discrimination, which eventually transformed military practice. Distinct groups would be protected from the abuses of the state and citizenry, and even the military would have to change its practice. In Canada this included official languages policy, the Royal Commission on the Status of Women, and multiculturalism legislation, the Charter of Rights and Freedoms, and employment equity statutes. New legislation combined with dire recruiting conditions and pushed the military to look to new groups to fill its ranks. People of colour, women, Aboriginals, and immigrants (as well as non-status migrants more recently in the U.S. case) – the very groups denied equal or any status in the military in the immediate postwar period came to be courted with an expanding list of social and political entitlements. The inclusion of new groups into the military labour force along with rapidly changing norms of work and the family called for new forms of provision for military personnel. The rising numbers of women in the military, of single parents, and of families where two parents were enlisted, changed the military community quite radically. The combined goals of accommodating new target populations and making the military a more attractive employer led to the expansion of military welfare and the creation of new programs to serve pregnant personnel, multilingual and multifaith communities, dual deployed households, and soldiers without citizenship status.

From Universalism to Targeting

Neoliberal ideologies have provided the most powerful critiques of postwar social citizenship. But neoliberalism has also been centrally concerned with the problem of military service. For neoliberal thinkers, the duty to give to the state in the form of one's life was as serious a concern as the obligation to give property to the state in the form of taxes. Friedrich von Hayek once identified the 'military type of society' that he saw emerging in postwar reconstruction plans as adverse to the 'commercial society' for which he was fighting. In his critique of social security, Hayek (1944: 131) argued that the army offers 'the only system in which the individual can be conceded full economic security and through the extension of which to the whole of society it can be achieved for all its members. This security is, however, inseparable from the restrictions on liberty and the hierarchical order of military life – it is the security of the barracks.' Neoliberal notions of citizenship were initially fringe ideas, particularly at the height of the popularity of Keynesianism, but the theories of the Chicago School became increasingly commonsensical to growing numbers in the late 1960s and early 1970s. Postwar economic growth slowed and the recession triggered by the oil crisis of the 1970s compounded economic stagnation, while at the same time, social movements made demands for more just and inclusive forms of citizenship. People whose image and norms had been universal increasingly felt their particularity, as white and male, were exposed as categories of relational identity (cf. Berlant 1997). Together these shifts revealed the limits of the postwar model of white male breadwinner citizenship, both in terms of its social exclusivity and in terms of its inability to guarantee economic security to even the chosen few.

Neoliberal critiques of the universalism of the welfare state cultivated a constituency just as policy became more socialized and less militarized. As women, people of colour, and other minoritized groups were finally able to benefit from state welfare, the neoliberal diagnosis of welfarism as institutionalized dependency cultivated a constituency. Popular support for cutbacks to the welfare state came from groups that had earlier benefited from its generously. 'In times of crisis the upwardly mobile groups of voters who received the greatest direct benefits from the welfare state development can develop a mentality concerned with maintaining their standard of living,' Jürgen Habermas (1990: 57) suggests, 'and [they] may ally themselves with the old middle class, and in general with the strata concerned with "productivity," to form a defensive coalition opposing underprivileged or marginalized groups.' But critiques of state welfare also came from progressive forces; fed up with the bureaucratic and paternalist state they called for choice, local autonomy, and participatory forms of governance. In this way, attacks on state welfare garnered a large and heterogeneous constituency that effectively dissolved any consensus supporting its ideals.

The genealogies of neoliberal government are complex and well beyond the scope of this chapter; however, these political forms continue to unite antiwelfarism and military workfarism. Critics of (civilian) social entitlement have explicitly identified the military as a 'natural' space of social rights, in contrast to the 'monstrous' excess that yielded civilian entitlement (Rose and Miller 1992). In a highly influential statement that migrated through global media and into U.S. Democratic Party policy, military sociologist Charles Moskos asserted that the United States has created a GI Bill without the GI.[7] Moskos' claim was, in fact, central in structuring the Democratic Leadership Council's (DLC 1988) document entitled *Citizenship and National Service*, which asserts that 'the time has come to answer national need with national service.' It proposes 'the Citizens Corps ... essentially a new G.I. Bill,' and asserts, 'a move toward national service is a step away from the prevailing ethos of entitlement.' A central goal of the Citizens Corps is 'putting disadvantaged youths to work in the service of their neighborhoods and communities ... giving deprived youths the experience, discipline and self-confidence they need to overcome formidable barriers to opportunity' (ibid.). In 1993, Bill Clinton created 'AmeriCorps,' perhaps the largest single outcome of the DLC proposals. AmeriCorps funds 75,000 'volunteer' positions annually for American citizens to work with not-for-profit and faith-based agencies in the areas of environmental clean-up, public education, and community development.

Just as recognition and redistribution were entwined historically, they are together central in the current recasting of citizenship. Entitlement-based forms of national service, most centrally the military, target distinct groups for inclusion. Altough the meaning of 'disadvantaged' varies geographically, people of colour, indigenous groups, women, and lesbians and gays are now frequently targeted for recruitment. For the U.S. armed forces Latinos are 'by far the most promising ethnic group for recruitment, because their numbers are growing rapidly in the U.S. and they include a plentiful supply of low-income men of military age with few other job or educational prospects,' Andrew Gumbel reports (quoted in Berkowitz 2003). The Canadian military prioritizes the recruitment of Aboriginal people, who offer the irresistible combination of high birth rates, high unemployment rates, and citizenship status to recruiters. At the same time, the military explicitly instructs recruiters not to discuss its own significant violence against Aboriginal peoples.[8] The Canadian military has also developed recruitment materials and strategies that target South Asians, Afro-Caribbean Canadians, and lesbians.

Meanwhile, the British armed forces have initiated 'dedicated minority-ethnic recruiting teams' (Hobsons 2006). Moreover, for the first time, in 2006, 'sailors in the Royal Navy have been given permission to take part in a gay march in full naval rig: a ruling is understood to have come from Vice-Adml Adrian Johns, the Second Sea Lord and Commander-in-Chief of Naval Home Command, and is part of a plan to encourage more gay people to join up (Rayment 2006).

A military neoliberalism is not unique to the heavily militarized United States, where the armed forces are so central to citizenship, where welfare has been much less rights-based, and where military service has long been explicitly organized as workfare.[9] It is also emerging in countries that are far less militarized and that are more oriented towards rights-based social citizenship. In Canada expansion of military welfare has been under way since the late 1990s, and it received a tremendous boost with the election of Stephen Harper's Conservative government in 2004. Mirroring GI Bill discourse, Prime Minister Harper harkens back to postwar reconstruction in his current bid for expanded military social security. He announced that 'our troops, commitment and service to Canada entitle them to the very best treatment possible' (CTV News 2006), as he launched the new 'Veteran's Charter,' a benefit plan which he touted as the 'most comprehensive since the end of the Second World War.' Indeed, more than a decade earlier, Harper had proudly declared that "universality has been severely reduced: it is virtually dead as a concept in most areas of public policy' and explained that 'these achievements are due in part to the Reform Party' (1994) Harper's party at the time (since merged with the Conservatives).

Paradoxes of Obligation and Entitlement

The high stakes game of life and death at the heart of modern social welfare has been recast. 'Soldiering is the highest calling of citizenship,' Canadian Prime Minister Stephen Harper (2006) explained to a group of military personnel and media, but 'not because you are ready to die for your country, though every soldier is prepared to do that. No, it is the highest calling of citizenship because you are ready to live for your country.' But whether framed as a sacrifice of life or death for the nation, the peculiar case of the soldier and the social begs for close scrutiny. Indeed, this renewed focus on welfare and quality of life for an institution that has tenuous links to 'life' – in both quantitative and qualitative terms – is intriguing and significant. Foucault (1989: 209) sees a 'paradox to this history,' namely, that 'the state began to practice its greatest slaughters' at the 'same time as it began to worry about the physical and mental health of each individual.' But if we consider the soldier as the protagonist of state welfare, this paradox quickly dissolves. Putting the soldier at the centre of social welfare in the way I've tried to do here reassigns the problem to our current perspectives rather than to the history of practice and makes *civilian* social entitlement seem strange and historically novel. When more democratic and less instrumental forms of social support have existed, they have been the achievement of labour and social movements making forceful demands at strategic moments.

Today, the military exploits the growing economic insecurity of citizens with promises of social rights and economic security. As the demand for soldiers grows to fuel perpetual warfare, and the supply of uninsured citizens and 'aliens' swells, military citizenship becomes a crucial social form. Indeed, the military is a literal reserve 'army' of labour. Yet, while the soldier has again become an important model citizen, there is no single model at the centre of the social today. A defining feature of the reconfiguration of social citizenship has been the end of universal policy directed towards the population in general, and the rise of targeted, residual, and means-tested approaches. When social rights are no longer guaranteed by virtue of citizenship and instead are contingent upon active forms of contribution, then some citizens are deemed worthy of support while others are deemed undeserving. It is in this context that the soldier has become so important today – as a model of the 'deserving poor.'

The challenges of military recruitment in the contemporary context are managed in a variety of ways other than through expanding entitlements, but these too have tremendous implications for the social in citizenship. States are relying on entirely different people to do their dirty work than they had been before. On the one hand, states increasingly employ private military companies to do highly skilled 'security' work, while on the other hand, they are intensifying their recruitment of non-citizens into military service.[10] If social citizenship has long been tied to national service, the loosening of those linkages is taking complex forms today. The rupture between citizenship and soldiering suggests epochal changes in familiar social and spatial political forms.

Recasting the social in citizenship remains a daunting prospect so long as we see sociality mobilized through insecurity and neurosis (cf. Isin 2004). An *anti-social* social guides the current reconstruction of our unavoidable material collectivity. But the social can be recast along different lines. Countless movements contest the combined productivism, securitization, nationalism, and racialization of state citizenship today. Rejecting the Clausewitzian externalization of struggle that allowed for the nationalization of the state and warfare, social movements recentre citizenship within and across bordered national space in cities and (other) occupied territories. In contrast to the sovereign spaces and binary logics of inside/outside and entitlement/obligation, a convergence of claims for the *right to the city* mark our present (see Isin, this volume). Movements that claim the right for undocumented people to dwell in place, or that reclaim indigenous land stolen by the state may seem like a long way from the battlefield or barracks, but they aim directly at territorial laws and the cannibalistic economy of 'human resources' that have informed the nationalizing projects of the state. In this way, struggles of the city once again offer an immanent redefinition of the social in citizenship, and so too of the socialized soldier.

Coda

It is impossible to make sense of the socialized soldier as an exceptional citizen of state welfare if analysis proceeds from the distinction between redistribution and recognition. These concepts, abstracted as they are from space, describe what are understood to be fundamentally different kinds of political claims. Where 'redistribution' refers to long-standing demands for access to material goods, claims for 'recognition' are understood to have emerged more recently in the context of identity politics and are oriented towards making space for cultural difference. Premised on the separation of material and symbolic, economic and cultural, and fact and value in political claims and relations, and implicitly if not explicitly centred on the state,[11] this distinction is disabling of the kind of analysis I have offered here. The military models of worker-citizenship that shaped civilian politics of welfare after the Second World War were starkly gendered and deeply racialized. 'Symbolic' particularities organized 'material' relations and helped provoke the political claims of identity politics that emerged in later years. Recognition-based claims, for example, the right to wear a turban or be transgendered and serve in the military, are simultaneously cultural and economic claims for the right to work, earn benefits, partake in the central symbolic act of national defence, and to be different. Struggles for political rights, economic rights, and for cultural change are deeply entwined but not always in predictable ways, as we see in the military's recent practice of celebrating and promoting religious, cultural, gendered, racialized, and sexual difference as a labour market strategy to draw in recruits.

In a regime of citizenship wherein social rights have largely rested on productive contribution to a nationalized state, and where social ordering and cultural distinction are inextricably entwined, distinguishing between recognition- and redistribution-based claims undermines the urgent intellectual and political work ahead. This distinction presumes the epistemological categories of nationalized spaces through which modern statist forms of social citizenship have been ordered. Rather, shifting paradigms might also mean shifting space and scale, so that national territory and the bodies that defend it are no longer the basis for deserving citizenship or solidarity.

Acknowledgments

For stimulating discussion and helpful comments I am grateful to the members of the SO network who participated in the 2006 workshop at York University – Sirma Bilge, Janine Brodie, Xiaobei Chen, Engin Isin, Danielle Juteau, Paul Kershaw, and Daiva Stasiulis. Engin Isin provided dynamic intellectual leadership and extraordinary editorial guidance in the preparation of this collection. Further thanks go to Leah Vosko for thoughtful comments and questions on this research, and to the fellows at the International Center for Advanced Studies at New York University, where I presented this work in the fall of 2006. For particularly helpful engagement I thank Jane Anderson, Ulla Berg, Julia Elyachar, Alan Hunter, Maimuna Huq, Tim Mitchell, Sherene Seikaly, Ella Shohat, Margaret Somers, and Diana Yoon. As ever, Neil Smith provided tremendously productive and challenging comments.

Notes

1 The RAF has employed Community Development Workers since 2003, see http://www.airwavesforfamilies.com/.

2 Rose (1999a: 64) offers us this phrase in his discussion of the transformation of citizenship after the Second World War, but it applies well to national soldiers long before this moment.

3 'Extracts from the Report of the Committee on the Conditions of Service of Officers of the Royal Navy, The Army and the Royal Air Force' (Restructuring of

the Militia Pension Act), July 1938. National Archives of Canada. RG24, vol. 8114, file 1280-232.

4 See, however, the recent work on 'critical geopolitics' for some helpful contributions, including Dalby (1991) and Ó Tuathail (1996).

5 For details on the racialized distribution of GI Bill benefits, see Katznelson (2005). In Canada postwar veterans, benefits prioritized the norms of white Anglo soldiers. For instance, the Marsh Plan was modelled after Canadian military benefits, which favoured smaller families and thus Protestantism over French Catholicism (see Christie 2000: 290). For more details on the Canadian case see (Cowen 2008) and for Britain see Sales (2002), who writes: 'The British welfare state was essentially national, with the benefits of social citizenship expected to be confined to national citizens. The racialized and gendered nature of social citizenship was illustrated in the often quoted phrase from the Beveridge Report, "housewives as Mothers have vital work to do in ensuring the adequate continuance of the British Race and British ideals in the world" (Beveridge 1942, cited in Williams 1987: 9). The assumption of female dependence on the male wage, the "male breadwinner model", was institutionalized as women's access to social rights was largely channelled through men.'

6 From the National Archives of Canada, Dependents Allowance Board.

7 Moskos (2005) recently reiterated this claim. He asserted that 'now is the time to consider linking all federal aid to college students to some form of national service. Through federal grants and loan subsidies for college education we now pay students not to serve their country. We have created a G.I. Bill without the G.I.'

8 The 'Oka crisis' offers a good example of this organized violence. The military was deployed to the scene of an Aboriginal land claim and standoff with local developers in numbers six times greater than their deployment in the first Gulf War, reaching 14,000 soldiers. The military described their 'work' at Oka as a success, but they adopted a policy that instructed recruiters not to mention or discuss the events with prospective aboriginal recruits (Edwards 2002: 3).

9 Segal (1989: 91) provides a brief history of military programs that have aimed to reduce minority youth unemployment, as well as make them eligible for veterans' benefits – 'welfare programs that did not carry the stigma of benefits programs that did not involve service.'

10 Canada is now contemplating following the U.S. in dropping citizenship as a 'requirement for military service.'

11 I thank Engin Isin for making this helpful point.

9 The Securitized Citizen

KIM RYGIEL

Securitization processes have challenged the modern articulation of citizenship as a bundle of rights, responsibilities, and legal statuses based on bounded membership in a territorial state. With the 11 September, 2001 terrorist attacks in the United States and the subsequent U.S.-led 'war on terror,' followed by attacks in Bali (October 2002), Istanbul (November 2003), Madrid (March 2004), and London (July 2005), many countries have seized the moment to implement new border control and detention arrangements. While such policies are about securitizing the social body on which traditional notions of state security depend, the implementation of such measures has not led simply to the re-entrenchment of the modern territorial state. This process of securitizing citizenship, paradoxically, has facilitated the development of citizenship into a globalizing regime of government. Here I refer to citizenship *not* as it is more commonly understood to denote a legal institution, status, and membership within a political community (usually that of the nation-state), which entails rights and obligations that vary according to the nation-state but which, nevertheless, typically include various degrees of political, social (including economic), and cultural rights *within* the state (Marshall 1950). Rather, following Foucault, I refer to citizenship as *government* to encompass the broader political relations involved in shaping the 'conduct of conducts,' that is, in terms of the relationships of power, discourses, practices, technologies, and subjectivities involved in governing others and in self-government (Foucault 1982: 138). This broader definition enables me to loosen the connection between citizenship and the state since these governing relations, while they may be articulated in and through the state (or at least as conventionally understood), may also take place beyond, between, and across states as well as through non-state actors and individual actors, through forms of self-government.

My argument is that by securitizing citizenship, technologies of governing are employed that displace the governing of populations from authorities and sites traditionally located in the state to other sites and actors such as private companies, international organizations, and even individuals and their own self-government. I refer to these changes in their totality as indicative of citizenship becoming a *globalizing regime of government*. Citizenship is now as much about governing populations *between* and *across* states as it is about governing *within* the state. Rarely is citizenship discussed in terms of how it functions as an international regime of governing, with some notable exceptions such as Hannah Arendt (1968), Barry Hindess (2000, 2002, 2003), William Walters (2002), and Peter Nyers (2003). As Hindess (2000) has argued, to fully comprehend the functioning of citizenship we need to understand it not just as 'an aspect of life within a state' (1495), that is, as a 'complex package of rights and responsibilities accruing to individuals by virtue of their membership of an appropriate polity' (1486–7) but also in its international dimension as the 'international management of populations' (1495).[1] Citizenship functions through the increased cooperation between state authorities, and through international organizations, involving a harmonization and standardization around policies governing mobility. This can be thought of as an increased *internationalization* of citizenship. But more than this, citizenship also depends on the displacement of power from traditional agents of the state to private companies and even individuals such that we might also consider the ways in which citizenship as government is not just internationalized but also *privatized* and *individualized,* and so we might speak of citizenship as a globalizing regime of government.

These shifts have far-reaching implications for the social in citizenship. If citizenship is being rearticulated in ways that extend beyond, below, and across states, this suggests that governing may also take place outside traditional notions of the state as the container of the social and beyond the social contract on which modern citizenship is configured. Moreover, if governing increasingly occurs beyond the social contract, what are the implications for citizenship and the struggle for citizenship rights? If citizenship is becoming a globalizing regime of government via bilateral and multilateral arrangements and extended social actors, how does this challenge the ontology of the state and, with it, the notion of the social contract? This chapter investigates these questions by drawing on recent examples of border controls and detention practices implemented across North America, Europe, and Australia in the post-9/11 environment.

The issue of security cannot properly be understood without also looking at it through the lens of citizenship. From this perspective, the post-9/11 period is far from being simply about strong state security and the reaffirmation of belonging in a national polity. Rather, this moment has as much to do with new claims and citizenship struggles for rights (especially mobility rights) and access to resources, for which mobility is a key strategy. Border controls and detention practices are about much more than state security. Securitization processes construct and then marginalize certain groups as threatening and undesirable. They also reveal the contested nature of citizenship, as these same marginalized groups (asylum seekers, non-status or undocumented migrants, immigrants, people of colour, and/or of Arab, Muslim, and Middle Eastern origins) respond to securitization processes by making claims to the right to belong in a polity legally but also, more substantively, in terms of material, political, and cultural well-being. The politics of citizenship that securitization gives rise to extends beyond struggles for redistribution and recognition *within* a polity like the state, for through securitization processes, citizenship is itself transformed as a governing regime. As a globalizing regime of government, citizenship involves restricting the mobility of people who choose to migrate (especially from South to North) as a strategy of accessing the North's greater resources. Thus, citizenship is recasting the meaning of the social in terms of what it means to be a citizen, away from notions of a rights-bearing subject towards technocratic and depoliticized definitions of citizen as an authorized body. This has profound implications for the future of democratic citizenship. Of course, the securitization of citizenship is also being challenged by these groups, involved in their own recasting of the social in citizenship. The No One Is Illegal and No Border movements, for example, are challenging the very grounds that underpin modern citizenship, based on notions of a securitized and legalized subject, on which to legitimize the awarding and withholding of rights and resources. In the process, these movements present alternative visions of what the social in citizenship might entail.

Securitizing Citizenship

In the aftermath of the terrorist attacks and the waging of a 'war on terror,' many countries (and particularly Anglo-American countries such as the United States, United Kingdom, Canada, and Australia) have implemented citizenship policies and practices as a way of securitizing the state. Security studies scholars have noted that securitization involves processes whereby 'an issue is presented as posing an existential threat to a designated referent object (traditionally the state). The special nature of security threats justifies the use of extraordinary measures to handle them. The invocation of security has been key to legitimizing the use of force, but more generally it has opened the way for the state to mobilize, or take special powers, to handle existential threats' (Buzan, Waever, and de Wilds 1998: 21; see also Waever 1995). Securitizing the social body has occurred through a fixation with 'identity management' based on gathering information about populations in order to distinguish between outsiders and the body politic (Muller 2004: 280). By doing so, certain groups are constructed as threatening to the social body of the state, while citizenship is securitized as part of a larger politics of 'securitization of the inside' (ibid.: 283).

Within this context a range of border controls and detention practices have been implemented in countries throughout North America, and Europe and in Australia. These include biometric forms of identification, such as biometric passports and national identity cards, as well as traveller registration programs. They also include border programs that use risk-profiling and data-aggregation technologies, such as Canada-U.S. border inspection programs, NEXUS and NEXUS-Air and Free and Secure Trade or FAST (CBP 2008, CBSA 2007, CBSA 2008) and Canadian Immigration and Customs pre-screening programs, such as CANPASS and CANPASS-Air (CBSA 2007a, 2007b). To this list, can be added programs that facilitate the sharing of information about travellers through Advanced Passenger Information and Passenger Name Record (API/PNR) systems, in full operation in the United States and Canada since 2003 and being integrated with European API/PNR systems (ICAO 2004a, CBSA 2005, White House 2002, Bennett 2005). In addition to these border controls, new detention arrangements have been implemented since 11 September 2001, involving what are often extraterritorial and extralegal forms of detention, including offshore processing camps for asylum seekers in Australia (HRW 2002a, AI 2002, Vanstone 2003), proposals for 'zones of protection' in Europe (U.K. Government 2005), and extraterritorial and extralegal camps for terrorist suspects such as Guantánamo Bay, as well as practices of extraordinary rendition and electronic forms of detention through electronic tagging and monitoring in the United Kingdom (ibid.).

These are just some of the ways that certain individuals and groups become subject to practices of securitizing citizenship in the name of fighting a 'war on terror.' Yet, although many of the policies noted above were seemingly implemented in response to terrorism, they need to be understood within a larger theoretical and historical context as reflective of the ongoing changing nature of citizenship as *government*. Many of these policies were under consideration or development before 2001. This was in response to the governing problematic of how to manage populations within the context of globalization and the demands for more open territorial borders to facilitate the movement of capital, goods, and services (and some people), while at the same time maintaining the logic of state security and its demands for relatively closed territorial borders (Pellerin 2005, Coleman 2005). Thus, although it may be tempting to read responses to 9/11 and subsequent terrorist attacks as a re-entrenchment of national security and territorial borders, I submit that this is to miss much of what the moment reveals about the securitization and changing nature of citizenship as a regime of government that is increasingly becoming more global in scope. The intensified usage of technologies of citizenship to govern reveals that the project of 11 September does not return us to a period of strong state security and state government control as traditionally conceptualized. Rather, it provides a moment in which to reflect on the changing nature of citizenship, the state, border ontologies, and the implications that these have for recasting the social in citizenship.

Globalizing Citizenship

John Torpey (1998) has argued that historically states and the international state system have come to 'monopolize the legitimate means of movement' and that an important part of this process has been the role that identification systems have played. Given this, it is perhaps not surprising that the post-9/11 securitization of citizenship has materialized in large part through border controls based on identification systems such as passports, national identity cards, and registered traveller programs. These are forms of regulating mobility based on the identification and registration of populations using biometric, risk-profiling, and data-mining technologies. The use of such identification systems as border controls may have intensified in the aftermath of 9/11, but their implementation must be understood as part of a larger history of the regulation of mobility by states to which Torpey refers. This is a history, as Nandita Sharma (2006) notes, where migration has come to be problematized as a human activity only fairly recently with the experience of migration across and through *nationalized* spaces. It is within the context of nationalized spaces that border controls play an increasingly significant role, with national regulations being highly gendered, racialized and classed processes associated with nation-building and empire (ibid.). Furthermore, in contrast to the so-called great age of migration of the nineteenth and early twentieth centuries when 'migration was mainly out of Europe,' today 'most cross border migrants ... are from the Global South' where, 'In stark contrast to the experience of people out of Europe a century or more ago, today's international migrants, particularly those from the Global South, face intense restrictions on and increasing criminalization of their mobility to and within the national spaces they try to make home' (ibid.: 125). Border and detention policies implemented in response to terrorism must be situated as part of a longer history of state control over the movement of peoples, first, through nationalized, spaces, and second, in response to the displacement of peoples as a result of imperialism and, most recently, neoliberal forms of globalization. While it is beyond the scope here to review this history in greater detail, much has been written on the variety of reasons for regulating people's mobility and the linkage with reasons of statecraft (e.g., Andreas and Snyder 2000, Bigo 2002, Coleman 2005, and Hollifield 2004); with political economy, including neoliberalism, the crisis of the welfare state, and the growth of the informal economy (e.g., Bommes and Geddes 2000, Hayter 2001, Rudolph 2003, Sharma 2006, and Stalker 2000); and with issues of culture and identity (Ceyhan and Tsoukala 2002, Jacobson 1996, Joppke and Morawska 2003).

Yet, within this longer history of states regulating mobility what is perhaps different in recent years are the strategies and technologies used to do so. These include border controls that rely on a combination of biometrics, risk-profiling, and data-mining technologies, on the one hand, and detention arrangements that are dependent on forms of extraterritoriality and extralegality, on the other. Taken together, these new strategies and technologies of controlling populations and their movement are producing changes to the processes of governing, that is, changes to the types of governing relationships and the actors involved as well as to the sites of governing. I refer to these changes collectively in terms of citizenship becoming a globalizing regime of government.

In making the argument that citizenship is becoming a globalizing regime of government I wish to draw attention to how globalization processes are shifting citizenship practices in ways that displace governing power from government authorities to other actors such as international organizations, private companies, and individuals and through political technologies such as risk profiling, biometrics, and data aggregation. This process of globalizing citizenship involves the dispersion of power and politics from the territorial state to other sites such as extraterritorial detention camps, the body politic, and the individual body. I develop this argument by looking at concrete illustrations of the securitization of citizenship through examples of border controls and detention practices. While border controls divide populations into desirable and undesirable groups and then regulate their movement accordingly, detention practices halt the movement of less desirable groups altogether. Detention practices, in effect, remove from society those groups of non-citizens or abject subjects thought to be undesirable or as not belonging properly within a state.

The point of this discussion is to reflect on how such examples show changing governing relations and actors, which can then be understood as indicative of a shift towards citizenship becoming a globalizing regime of government. My aim is to provide a more complex vision of citizenship that shows how governing practices involve multiple actors, practices, forms of power, and sites of politics that extend beyond, below, between, and across the territorial state rather than simply within it. This, in turn, has implications for how we conceptualize the state. To identify these changes in governing we need to conceptualize the state not as a well-defined territorially bounded political community but as an assemblage of criss-crossing processes involving a range of actors and practices that challenge the way we think about the relationship of governing and space and the location of politics.

Border Controls

As mentioned, the post-9/11 securitization of citizenship has materialized in large part through implementing border controls based on identification systems such as passports, national identity cards, and registered traveller programs that bring together biometrics, risk-profiling, and data-mining technologies. Close examination of these types of border controls reveals not only an increasing internationalization of citizenship through harmonization and standardization of policies, but also an increasing privatization of citizenship with growing dependence on private companies in governing mobility.

Identification documents and registered traveller programs are increasingly harmonized and standardized through bilateral and multilateral agreements between states and facilitated by international organizations such as the U.N. agency, the International Civil Aviation Organization (ICAO 2004a). To take one example, Advanced Passenger Information and Passenger Name Records (API/PNR) systems are now being implemented in the United States, Canada, Australia, the United Kingdom and the European Union (e.g., CBSA 2005, White House 2002). These traveller registration systems require airlines to submit information about their passengers to the governments of the destinations to which they are flying – including citizenship, frequency and destination of travel, and payment details (Bennett 2005, EPIC 2006). This information is then checked against other databases, such as immigration and criminal databases, and the information is pooled to create risk profiles determining whether or not a traveller is 'high risk.' Not only are countries individually implementing such systems, they are also increasingly sharing information on travellers, thereby, creating, in effect, a centralized international database of personal information that can be used in profiling (Privacy International 2004, Statewatch 2003). Moreover, such systems are being harmonized and standardized between and across countries, as called for by the International Civil Aviation Organization (ICAO 2004a).

The effective harmonization of a risk-based classification system could potentially lead to greater standardization of differential mobility rights between countries, making it that much more difficult for those in certain racialized, gendered, and economic groups to travel. Risk profiling enables populations to be subdivided and classified according to the perceived level of risk they pose, their movement then managed according to a regime of differential mobility rights justified on the ground of security. Accordingly, those identified and classified as 'low risk' are fast-tracked across borders while those considered 'high risk' are subjected to greater border security measures, their mobility regulated and subjected to higher levels of surveillance. Constructions of 'high risk' and 'low risk' travellers are, of course, highly gendered, racialized, and class-based (Rygiel 2006, Curry 2004). For example, 'low-risk' travellers are constructed around the identity of economically advantaged professional and business elites, often male and white, whose mobility for work and travel is encouraged (Curry 2004).

Travel policies and regulations such as those used across the Canada-U.S. border (e.g., NEXUS, CANPASS, and FAST) use risk profiling to expedite the travel of 'low-risk' travellers through a pre-approval process while simultaneously making travel more difficult for members of 'high-risk' groups. In contrast to 'low-risk' profiles, the category of 'high risk' targets and restricts the mobility of individuals, who since 2001 are largely of Muslim, Arab, and/or Middle Eastern background, and in particular, young men in the most economically productive age groups, along with immigrants, refugees, and people of colour more generally (see, e.g., Colc 2002, Finn 2005, Sharma 2006).[2]

Registered traveller programs illustrate how citizenship is becoming a globalizing regime of governing; first, by revealing how citizenship policies are being internationalized through the sharing of information about travellers between states (with the possibility of creating a common database in the future). This sharing and even pooling of information is occurring, however, not just through bilateral and multilateral cooperation. If it were, the question might be why not then just speak of the internationalization of citizenship? Rather, such systems illustrate how citizenship is globalizing because the cooperation between state authorities to regulate mobility also, paradoxically, results in a regime of governing that in certain ways circumvents the international state system and its institutionalization of mobility rights through a 'passport culture' (Cohen 2003, noted in Sharma 2006: 125). State agents may facilitate the internationalization of citizenship through the harmonization of risk-classification systems, and in doing so, they are able to circumvent the current international passport regime where one's passport has come to be accepted as recognition of certain mobility rights. This can be seen in cases where risk profiling has resulted in 'high-risk individuals,' like Syrian-born Canadian citizen Maher Arar, being subjected to 'extraordinary rendition,' a practice where U.S. authorities have deported foreign-born citizens, suspected of terrorist-related activities, to countries known for their lax human rights laws for the purposes of interrogation, often involving torture (Brown and Priest 2003, Stasiulis and Ross 2006, and Mutimer 2007).

Risk profiling means that, even with citizenship, individuals of certain birth origins and national and religious backgrounds can no longer be confident of their rights to mobility based on rights they are entitled to as a result of their passport and current citizenship. The internationalization of citizenship through the sharing of risk-profiling systems creates a stronger, in the sense of more regulatory, regime of governing mobility. At the same time, it undermines the ability of state authorities to ensure the mobility rights supposedly guaranteed by virtue of citizenship and passport. Moreover, risk profiling can potentially be used to cast a wide net around individuals, who are treated as suspicious and then subjected to greater surveillance and restrictions on their mobility, and on other rights, as well. Profiling does not simply interrogate criminal actions – it also interrogates who a person is, who she or he associates with, and a range of conduct considered suspect (including, e.g., such activities as reading books on the Middle East).[3] Thus, risk profiling potentially regulates much more than movement, encouraging individuals to self-regulate aspects of their daily living and lifestyle choices.

Such programs also reveal how citizenship as government is increasingly privatized and individualized. As government authorities increasingly turn to data-mining companies to conduct security and identification checks, governing populations is operationalized through privatized forms of governing. Traveller registration programs displace power away from state authorities to private companies when these companies are contracted by governments to take on much of the surveillance and data-gathering work. This can be seen, for example, in the case of the employment of data-aggregator companies such as Acxiom or ChoicePoint, which are in the business of compiling and selling databases of personal and consumer information.

In the United States, the automated pre-screening system, called the Computer Assisted Passenger Pre-Screening System (CAPPS II) was initially introduced by the government's Transportation Security Administration (TSA) to check the personal travel details of airline travellers against a variety of government and private databases such as terrorist watch lists and immigration and credit databases. The program gathered and sent airline passenger information to data aggregators in the business of compiling consumer dossiers. They, in turn, provided governments with an 'authentication score,' indicating a 'confidence level in that passenger's identity' (ACLU 2003: 1; Murphy 2003). The TSA then provided its own 'risk assessment function,' running the personal information through government databases, like criminal and immigration databases, to develop a risk score of 'high,' 'low,' or 'unknown' (ACLU 2003: 2). Once the computerized system issued the risk score, 'an encoded message' was to be 'printed on the boarding pass indicating the appropriate level of screening,' with the idea eventually of transmitting the information 'directly to screeners at security checkpoints' (U.S. DHS 2004). After receiving much public criticism from the U.S. Congress and American privacy and civil liberties groups, the TSA decided to replace CAPPS II with a new 'scaled-back' passenger pre-screening program called Secure Flight, introduced in August 2004 (Singel 2004). Secure Flight requires aircraft operators to submit to the TSA information about travellers when airline reservations are made so as to check passengers against terrorist watch lists and 'no-fly' lists (TSA, 'Secure Flight Program'; EPIC, 'Secure Flight'). If a name appears similar then that person may be asked to undergo additional screening or be deemed ineligible to fly (TSA, 'Secure Flight Program').

The growing dependence of government authorities on private companies like data aggregators provides a good example of the way control over populations and their mobility, traditionally the responsibility of states, increasingly involves sharing these governing practices with private companies. In fact, privacy and civil liberties groups argue that it is private companies that gather consumer information for marketing purposes that have actually given momentum to data-surveillance systems like registered traveller programs: 'a major factor driving the trend toward data surveillance forward is the commodification of personal information by corporations' (Stanley and Steinhardt 2003: 4). Unlike governments, private companies are neither representative of nor responsible to citizens. Thus, their growing involvement in monitoring the movements and habits of individuals raises all sorts of concerns, long voiced by privacy and civil liberties groups, over issues of accountability, access, and ownership of information.

Finally, these identification types of border controls depend on forms of governing that take place at the level of the individual body. Biometric passports, for example, are being standardized through the International Civil Aviation Organization, which adopted in May 2003, 'a global, harmonized blueprint for integrating biometric information into passports' (ICAO 2004b: 1). The goal is to ensure 'global interoperability' by 2010 through the implementation of machine-readable passports with standardized features such as facial recognition biometrics, a contact-less integral circuit chip holding a minimum of 32 kilobytes, and common programming language for data storage (ICAO 2004a: 2).

The shift towards biometric border controls is about more than efficiency through 'global interoperability.' Biometric technology is a more insidious form of border control in that it enables a more invasive level of control aimed at governing the individual body by knowing the detailed bodily make-up ('body data') of every individual encountered. Biometrics reconceptualizes the citizen from a political subject with rights to an authorized body who, in keeping with neoliberal forms of governing, is deserving of citizenship rights only after being authorized and authenticated. As Benjamin Muller has argued, biometrics shifts the discourse of citizenship to one of 'identity management,' the significance being that

> Identity management vis-à-vis biometrics attempts to transform citizenship into a quest for verifying/authentication 'identity' for the purpose of access to rights, bodies, spaces, and so forth, thus (purportedly) stripping away the cultural and ethnic attributes of citizenship. By concealing such matters in the technological and scientific discourses of biometrics, the ethnic/racial characteristics of citizenship practices – insofar as it is obsessed with restricting access to specific spaces (that is, airports) and rights (that is, free movement) – are stripped away. (Muller 2004: 280)

This has implications for how we think about citizenship and citizenship politics. The shift from thinking of citizens as political subjects with rights to authorized bodies evokes a depoliticized and depoliticizing bureaucratic means of legitimizing the distribution of rights and resources. Biometrics invites us to see others and ourselves in terms of our biological characteristics as members of the human species first – Agamben's (1995, 9–10) notion of 'bare life' – and only then as political beings with rights, by virtue of being members of the political community. Biometric technologies are thus ultimately designed to regulate access to space, and through space, access to rights. The exclusionary character of biometrics is hidden, however, by the fact that it presents itself as simply another neutral tool of technology designed simply to acknowledge whether or not an identity is authorized to enter a space.

In terms of governing mobility, biometrics is a more efficient way of governing through citizenship and border controls since it works towards flexibilizing the border and providing possibilities of governing beyond the strictly territorial borders of the state to governing at 'e-borders,' or any place where identification can be verified electronically, which can now potentially become a border. Mark Salter (2004) contends that such new travel arrangements requiring biometric travel identification work to 'delocalize the border' (80). Salter argues that new travel arrangements in which biometric identification is used, such as the 2002 American Enhanced Border Security and Reform Act, relocate the border to U.S. embassies where visa decisions on exit and entry can be made 'up-stream,' that is, prior to travel (ibid.).[4] As Salter explains, this delocalization of the border 'represents an attempt by the American state to defer or extend the border security regime beyond the physical limits of the state' (ibid.: 81). This delocalization, or deterritorialization, works by shifting the border to extraterritorial points like embassies. Salter's argument could be extended here to note that biometrics enables the border to become located in virtual space wherever information stored on databases can be verified. In essence, biometric identification transfers the territorial border of the state onto the individual body. If an individual's body becomes the primary means of identity verification, there is a sense in which borders can be flexibilized and made to exist wherever a body can be checked.

Detention Practices

To the issue of border controls we can add the proliferation of spaces of detention. As former United Nations High Commissioner for Refugees (UNHCR) Ruud Lubbers has noted, there is a 'worrying more general trend towards increased use of detention – often on a discriminatory basis' (2002: 22). Since 2001 individuals identified as 'high risk' have been subjected to intensified detention practices aimed at halting their movement altogether, placing many individuals in limbo for several years, with their rights severely curtailed. This flourishing of detention and other abject spaces across industrialized countries in the global North (Isin and Rygiel 2007) illustrates how citizenship is globalizing as a regime of government. It reveals an increased harmonization around the use and forms of detention centres as governments coordinate policies. It also illustrates the displacement of state power to international organizations and private companies, which are increasingly responsible for managing detention, as well as to individual bodies, through alternative forms of detention like electronic tagging and monitoring. As with border controls, detention reveals not only the internationalization but also the privatization and individualization of citizenship, which taken together suggest that it makes more sense to speak of citizenship as a globalizing (rather than as an international or state-based) regime of government.

Countries such as the United Kingdom, United States, and Australia have taken advantage of the 11 September moment to conceptualize, if not develop, the idea of a global 'managed migration' system. This involves not just the harmonization of asylum policies between countries, but also the development of a new international system to manage population flows across and between countries, to which the creation of new forms of detention spaces that depend on notions of extraterritoriality are integral. Human Rights Watch (2002b: 5–7) notes the similarities between U.K. proposals for 'zones of protection' and excised offshore places and processing centres in Australia and has documented attempts by Australian authorities to encourage other governments (particularly the United Kingdom) to adopt similar approaches to its own. Moreover, the language of the U.K. government's report (2003: 1, 10) speaks directly to the desire to harmonize extraterritorial detention arrangements as part of a 'managed migration system' (20) and a 'global vision' stating that 'to manage global flows we need global solutions' to be·based on the coordinated efforts of 'our fellow English speaking nations' (22).

In the U.K. proposal two types of detention spaces are envisioned: regional protection areas (RPAs) and transit processing areas (TPAs). RPAs would be safe havens, based on the safe third country principle, to be set up near refugee-producing areas or source countries. For example, Iraqis might apply to an RPA in Turkey and Somalis to a centre located in a northern African country such as Morocco (U.K. Government 2003: 26). In contrast, TPAs are proposed as extraterritorial processing areas to be created along the borders of the European Union in countries like Romania, Croatia, Albania, and Ukraine, where asylum seekers would be held while awaiting the review and processing of their claims (AI 2003). The idea behind such spaces is to enable asylum claimants to seek protection without having to migrate to another country like the United Kingdom. Regional zones of protection would operate through the involvement of three players: an international organization – either the UNHCR or the International Organization for Migration (IOM) – a 'funding state' interested in using the camp as a 'form of off-territory protection' for asylum seekers; and a 'host state' (U.K. Government 2003: 22). These zones would not be considered 'international territory,' but nevertheless would be 'controlled by an international organization' (12). Whereas regional areas would be run by the UNHCR, the IOM would run processing centres (AI 2003: 7).

Mirroring the U.K. proposal, the Australian government developed a policy of 'excised offshore places' in 2001, where parts of Australian territory were removed from Australia's 'migration zone' so that anyone arriving without a visa at such a place would be ineligible to apply for a refugee protection visa unless the minister of immigration personally granted it (Vanstone 2003). Excised places include Christmas

Island and the Cocos (Keeling) Islands in the Indian Ocean, Ashmore and Cartier Island in the Timor Sea, and even 'any Australian sea installation or offshore resource (such as an oil rig)' (ibid.). As well, the Australian government created 'offshore processing centres' (the 'Pacific Solution'), enabling the government to 'move an offshore entry person to a declared country where any claims they may have for protection can be considered' (ibid).[5] 'Declared countries' are countries or islands with which the Australian government has negotiated agreements, often in exchange for money, to establish processing centres to review the claims of 'unauthorized people,' such as those arriving by boat and 'intercepted in Australian territorial waters' or those arriving 'at an excised offshore place' (ibid.). Two such 'declared countries,' Nauru and Papua New Guinea (Manus Island), have made arrangements with the Australian government to 'house' refused and unlawfully arrived asylum seekers in makeshift camps in exchange for payment of upwards of 10 million dollars (BBC News 2001).

Finally, there is the example of detention camps built by the U.S. government to hold suspected 'enemy combatants' in the war on terror on Guantánamo Bay, a U.S. naval base in Cuba converted into a detention centre to hold some 650 foreign nationals from over forty different countries, many of whom were arrested in Afghanistan in 2002. The U.S. administration uses the extraterritoriality of the camp to bypass procedures and stipulations under both domestic and international law.[6] By designating individuals with the status of 'enemy combatant,' authorities have been able to hold them unlawfully in isolation outside of the law and subject only to the quasi-legal procedures of military tribunals, which provide them with less rights than should be theirs were they to be tried under international or U.S. law as prisoners of war or even as criminals (terrorists) (Butler 2004, Sands 2005).

Although these proposals are developed and implemented by individual states, they increasingly establish a system that is designed to include a large number of participating states and affect a large number of migrants, refugees, and foreign nationals, particularly from countries in the global South, thus producing a much larger international impact. Moreover, these models of detention are based on governments increasingly handing over state responsibility for dealing with refugees and asylum seekers to, often international, third parties. However, it is not just to international organizations that states may concede responsibility for governing refugee and undocumented migrants. Such proposals also depend on states giving up sovereignty to private companies. Over the years there has been a growing trend towards the privatization of detention, with private companies like the Management and Training Corporation and Wackenhut Corporation increasingly responsible for the running of alternative detention spaces (Tazreiter 2003, Lahav 1998). The increasing privatization and also internationalization of citizenship – through standardization and the involvement of international organizations – indicates that citizenship is globalizing as a regime of government.

These examples represent new developments in creating spaces of detention that depend on extraterritoriality to forge new governing relations. In both the U.K. and Australian cases, extraterritoriality facilitates new governing arrangements that circumvent the international system regarding the treatment of refugees. Under the 1951 Refugee Convention countries have an obligation to offer refuge to those with a well-founded fear of persecution. The Australian example, however, turns away such people to incarcerate them like criminals on islands where they cannot properly access legal rights and Australia's legal system (AI 2002; HRW 2002a, 2002b). As in the U.K.'s vision, Australia has set up a parallel system of dealing with asylum claimants, one that enables the government to be less stringent in its commitments to both Australian and international law. Moreover, as in the U.K. proposal, the Australian model reveals new arrangements in governing. Australia acts as the funding state, providing money to other countries and islands willing to 'host' Australia's detainees in detention camps that are administered by an international organization or managed by private companies (Vanstone 2003).

Finally, in terms of extraterritoriality, territories are reclassified in terms of an ambiguous category as 'excised offshore places,' so that they no longer belong to the zone of Australia's territorial integrity. The idea here is to reclassify territories where asylum seekers most often land such that individuals are not eligible to make asylum claims under the protection of Australian law. Offshore processing centres represent 'creative' arrangements for what amounts to essentially contracting out detention. Refusing to hold individuals on its mainland, Australia now sends any persons arriving on its shores by boat to detention camps for processing, thereby preventing certain individuals and groups from accessing rights on Australian soil, under Australian law, as refugees. The case of Guantánamo shares obvious similarities in that here too the choice of the island has specifically to do with its extraterritoriality and the ambiguity over whether the United States or Cuba has sovereign jurisdiction. As Amy

Kaplan (2005) illustrates, much of the debate about whether, and how, to prosecute 'enemy combatants' and indeed whether they should be granted any rights at all (such as the right to habeas corpus) has turned on the ambiguous nature of the space as falling inside and outside U.S. sovereign jurisdiction.

To these examples illustrating how citizenship is being securitized, yet in the process also globalized, we can add the increasing use of individualized forms of detention such as electronic forms of monitoring, tagging, and tracking (as opposed to holding individuals in detention facilities), as were passed in the United Kingdom's 2005 Prevention of Terrorism Act. These measures give governments the power to detain individuals, like terrorist suspects, in their homes in cases where there is not enough evidence to charge them with a crime before the courts. Similar measures are also proposed for failed asylum seekers, according to the U.K. government's 2004 Asylum and Immigration (Treatment of Claimants, etc.) Act (Section 36). Failed asylum seekers may be required to wear electronic tags (or use voice recognition technology by telephone), with the idea of eventually using global positioning satellite (GPS) technology to enable the government to continuously monitor or track their movements by satellite.

Such proposals reproduce the logic of treating certain individuals, considered to be 'high risk,' as criminals. Of interest is also the way such proposals give rise to the possibility of imagining border controls independent of physical, territorial state borders, border crossing zones, or the walls of a detention centre. As with biometric forms of border controls discussed earlier, these alternative electronic forms of detention work by transferring territorial borders to the site of the body where, by wearing an electronic tag around the ankle or wrist, an electronic signal is transmitted or can be tracked by global satellite, so that an individual's movements can be tracked regardless of whether state borders are crossed. This is the ultimate vision of how citizenship policies can govern the mobility of people, regardless of whether the state's territorial borders are weakened by globalization processes, and at the same time enabling borders to remain relatively open to facilitate the flow of capital, goods, and desirable 'low-risk' populations. E-tagging here provides an example of thinking about how citizenship might be globalizing as a regime governing mobility since, in this example, governing is transferred to the site of the individual body, and thereby mobility can be regulated not just at state borders but at any virtual border where equipment can be set up to read the electronic signals.

The post-9/11 period is replete with examples of the way citizenship is being securitized through a host of border controls and detention practices. What emerges, however, is not a shift towards a resecuritization of the modern territorial state with fixed territorial borders but the globalization of citizenship, where governing depends on a much more complex set of relations that involve state authorities but also, and increasingly, non-state, private and international actors, as well as alternative spatial forms of governing through flexibilizing and localizing the border.

The Ontology of the State

Thus far I have referred to the way citizenship increasingly involves new configurations of power and collaborations of governing. This includes the harmonization of border and detention policies between countries in the global North, the displacement of state power to other actors like international organizations and private companies, and finally, a shift towards governing through border and detention arrangements that control and discipline at the site of the individual body. I have argued that, taken together, these changes in governing suggest that citizenship is becoming a globalizing regime of government.

The first insight that emerges is that the securitization of citizenship has not led to the re-entrenchment of traditional notions of strong states and state-based notions of security. Rather, securitization processes have actually helped transform citizenship into a globalizing regime of government by enabling new relationships, involving a range of actors and locations within, between, and across states. At the same time, this globalization of citizenship does not necessarily imply that the state itself is weaker. State authorities can be less directly involved in governing and yet the state (meaning the entire assemblage of authorities and actors, laws, and processes of the polity) can be stronger as a result. As a whole, this dispersion of power from state to other authorities, and its inscription into the political body, makes for a stronger state and regime of governing through citizenship. Similarly, citizenship becomes a more efficient regime of governing when actors other than state governments, like private companies, international organizations, and individuals, participate in their own governing.

The second insight that emerges is that a globalizing regime of citizenship must be understood not just in terms of state *territories* but through the global *flows* of *state spaces* as an integral part of a globalizing citizenship order. By studying the governing practices around border controls and detention that citizenship enables, a more complex picture of global politics emerges than the one we are more familiar with, which is a vision of global politics based on interactions between contiguous, spatially separate, and territorially bounded states (Agnew 1994, Ruggie 1993, P. Taylor 1994, and Walker 1993). This more complex view suggests that if we want to understand how citizenship is changing, and the new developments in governing and forms of politics that it engenders, we need to think of states in terms of overlapping, penetrating, and intermingling spaces, or in terms of 'space as flows,' as Doreen Massey (1994: 5) puts it, that are created out of, or by, these very governing practices themselves. From this perspective, citizenship is more than the condition and institution of legal rights and membership located within a bounded, separate container of space that we call the state. Citizenship is a regime of *practices* enabling the governing of individuals, groups, and populations that *creates* state spaces, and not as bounded containers but as assemblages of overlapping governing relations involving a range of actors and forms of political relations, knowledge, and powers.

Reflections on the securitization of citizenship reveal not only the ways in which citizenship is shifting and the need, therefore, to reconceptualize our thinking around the ontology of the state, but also the need to critically investigate the border ontologies that are so much a part of our thinking about security and the state and the conceptualization of the state as the container of the social. As the illustrative examples of border and detention arrangements demonstrate, the territorial borders of the state are being transformed but in much more complex ways than either simply being strengthened or weakened or even transgressed. Borders are reimagined in new ways through strategies of 'flexibilizing' the border and notions of virtual borders and common borders, through the harmonization of border controls and detention policies. Borders are also reimagined through practices of 'localizing' the border, where territorial borders are displaced onto the body politic and individual bodies. What is important about this more complex way of understanding the changing nature of borders is that it engenders new governing relations and configurations of power.

For example, the harmonization of border and detention policies reveals that, by creating common policies, states must also give up degrees of sovereignty. But this is a matter of more than just pooling sovereignty, for such governing practices also induce a new way of conceptualizing the border. As countries in the global North (and Anglo-American countries in particular) come to adopt a view of being united in waging a 'war on terror,' they share similar ideas about desirable and undesirable populations and practices of governing 'high risk' and 'low risk' groups. Through the process of sharing rationales and practices of governing, a shift in the geographical imaginings of borders also occurs, whereby the regulation of one's own state borders is connected to a vision of regulating common borders. By engaging in practices of governing their own territorial borders, state governments have the sense of belonging to a much larger shared territory, in this case of belonging to an Anglo-American sense of identity in fighting a 'war on terror.' Border controls may regulate and reaffirm the territorial borders of the state, but as they do so, they also paradoxically transgress these borders both in practice, through the harmonizing of policies and pooling of sovereignty, as well as conceptually through re-envisioning the border as a common one of identification.

Extraterritorial detention centres and zones of protection reveal new ways of conceptualizing borders. Australia's excised offshore places, for example, reveal the way that the government expels territories from its sovereign domain to avoid acknowledging asylum claims. In the process, Australia governs, paradoxically, by deleting or shedding certain territories precisely to be able to preserve its territorial integrity as a whole. Similarly, new detention arrangements like the offshore processing camps in Australia, proposed zones of protection in Europe, or American camps like Guantánamo Bay, use forms of extraterritoriality outside the state's territorial sovereign jurisdiction to avoid the responsibilities that come with governing within the territorial space of the state (Kaplan 2005; Sands 2005: 143–73). Such examples suggest that there are new ways of governing populations that depend on new ways of conceptualizing the border and governing through it. This, in turn, reveals that the regulation of borders and populations are constantly shifting performances of governing. To understand how citizenship is changing, we need to reflect on how this logic of reimagining borders relates to new governing relationships and strategies of shifting responsibility as part of a global politics of governing populations.

It is not just through transnational and international practices that borders are reconceptualized. Border and detention practices operate by localizing the border – transferring the border from the fixed territorial location onto the body politic and the bodies of individuals. I noted how biometric controls and electronic tagging allow for the movement of people across borders while at the same time enabling authorities to maintain their surveillance capabilities. This shift in strategies is one of monitoring the individual as a mobile body, as she or he moves through space rather than trying to fix an individual's movement in space through containment at physical territorial borders.[7] If one of the effects of globalization is the increased mobility of persons, and if one of the problems of governing is the ability to regulate the territorial borders of the state, this issue can be addressed by shifting the practices and logics of governing so that what becomes more important is the state's ability to govern over its *population* rather than over its *territory*.[8] Yet, the use of border controls and the localization of the border also result, paradoxically in undermining the very territorial borders that they are supposed to strengthen. Because border controls shift the focus inward to a concern with the borders of the body politic and with governing bodies rather than geographical borders, the result is a blurring of the inside/outside borders of the state. For instance, the repeated claim on which recent border controls are dependent is that it is because territorial borders are porous that terrorists have been able to 'infiltrate' into the body of the citizenry, thus, requiring citizens to be vigilantly on the lookout for anyone who does not belong. Paradoxically, this logic reveals a shift away from border controls fixed on physical territorial borders to a concern with control over bodies. In turn, this suggests that borders are not as clearly defined as they are often made out to be. It reveals that not only are the territorial borders of the state not fixed in some essentialist kind of way but also that they must be 'performed' and are continually being (re)configured through governing practices (Campbell 1998).[9] The study of citizenship as a globalizing regime of government brings to the forefront that, if we want to understand in a deep way the kinds of changes occurring in global politics today, what is needed is a shift in the way we think about borders, that is, a change in the *ontology* of borders. Reflecting on the way the border is localized reveals that the inside and outside of the state are always in the process of being produced. This has implications for thinking about a politics of resistance, since if borders are produced through certain governing practices, they can also be unmade or remade differently.

Reconfiguring the Social in Globalizing Citizenship

The shifts I have thus far discussed in terms of citizenship as a globalizing regime of government and the new state and border ontologies that this entails have far-reaching implications for the social in citizenship. If citizenship is being rearticulated in ways that extend beyond, below, and across the state, this suggests that governing may also take place outside traditional notions of the state as the container of the social and beyond the social contract on which modern citizenship was configured. If governing is increasingly occurring beyond the social contract, what are the implications for the redistribution of rights and responsibilities that citizenship entails? If citizenship is becoming a globalizing regime of government via bilateral and multilateral arrangements and extended social actors, and if this challenges the ontology of the state, what are the implications for thinking about the notion of the social on which citizenship has been based?

The globalization of citizenship suggests the possibility of the deepening and spreading of inequality through the more exclusionary aspects of citizenship. I have suggested that the globalization of citizenship as government is further entrenching a more hierarchical regime of differential mobility rights, with greater rights awarded to a new transnational class of desirable citizens while restricting the mobility of those perceived as less desirable. After 11 September 2001 this has particularly affected individuals of Muslim, Arab, and/or of Middle Eastern origin, along with other more marginalized people such as refugees, undocumented migrants, and people of colour more generally. Such changes may have serious implications for democratic conceptions of the social, where border controls work to reorient our understanding of the citizen away from a political subject with a 'right to have rights' (Arendt 1968) and towards an increasingly depoliticized construction of the citizen as a 'low-risk individual,' a body authorized and authenticated through identification checks (Muller 2004). As citizenship globalizes, the opposition may no longer be 'one of citizen vs non-citizen, but between those citizens who are deemed essential and necessary and those who are dismissed as accidental and dispensable' (Nyers 2006a: 24). We are witnessing shifts in policies and practices that render the notion of citizenship and the right to have certain rights based on one's membership in the territorial state – one of the most fundamental assumptions of modern citizenship (despite all its problems, as Barry Hindess notes) – as eroding. Yet, rather than being replaced by a more democratic articulation of citizenship, as transnational and postnational scholars of citizenship have suggested (e.g., Soysal 1994), it is possible that we are witnessing the establishment of a more exclusionary regime, one that further globalizes inequality and recasts the social in citizenship in less progressive ways. Furthermore, many of these changes to citizenship are occurring through more technocratic and bureaucratic means, through border and surveillance technologies, and clandestine and extralegal forms of detention. Those shifts in governing are taking place largely outside the realm of public debate and the parameters of deliberative democracy. If this is so, the implications for the articulation of a democratic social polity on which citizenship is to be based are grave.

The shifting governing structures of citizenship also, however, provide a historic moment in which to re-envision the social in citizenship in more democratic ways. As Engin Isin explains, citizenship has often been associated with 'that particular point of view of the dominant, which constitutes itself as a universal point of view – the point of view of those who dominate the city and who have constituted their point of view as natural by representing the city as a unity' (2002b: 275). The globalization of citizenship reveals that there is nothing 'natural' about citizenship and thus about this articulation of citizenship. A great deal of political work is involved in governing through citizenship. As non-citizens, and those marginalized through citizenship, insist on their right to be political (and their 'right to have rights'), they too are recasting the social in citizenship by disrupting the dominant notions invoked in the making of the new global mobility regime and its virtuous 'low-risk' cosmopolitan traveller-citizen. In doing so, they reveal the unnaturalness of this citizen-subject and all of the political work that goes into its making. This then is a political moment, for 'becoming political is that moment when the naturalness of the dominant virtues is called into question and their arbitrariness revealed' (ibid.).

Border controls and detention practices are designed to halt the movement of undesirable individuals and populations. They often do so within more ambiguous spaces of governing that are outside the public eye and the jurisdiction of state sovereignty, national security, and the courts. Yet, by doing so, such practices seem to recognize politically what increasingly greater numbers of abject populations subject to these policing practices also realize, namely, that 'formal citizenship is neither necessary nor a sufficient condition for substantive citizenship. The new claims to citizenship are new, and not only because they force the state to respond to new social conditions. They are also new because they create new kinds of right, based on the exigencies of *lived experience*, outside of the normative and institutional definitions of the state and its codes' (ibid., 265, my emphasis). This means that citizenship need not be tied to the territorially bound notion of the social that often accompanies more institutional and legal understandings of citizenship. The emphasis on citizenship as a practice of claiming rights (and indeed as a social relationship between groups struggling for rights, recognition, and the redistribution of resources) enables us to see citizenship in broader formulations independent of a spatially bounded political community. If throughout history, citizenship has, in one sense, always been about the rights of the dominant group, in another, it has also always been about how other marginalized and non-citizen groups have been able through various political strategies to subvert the dominant claims and assert their rights as political beings (ibid.). Within this context, citizenship can be viewed as necessarily dialogical (and hence the need to focus on the social in citizenship), for citizenship cannot be understood without acknowledging the construction, conditions, and politics of its Others – the non-citizens and the abject subjects. As Isin astutely observes:

> the focus on otherness as a condition of citizenship assumes that in fact citizenship and its alterity always emerged simultaneously in a dialogical manner and constituted each other. Women were not simply excluded from ancient Greek citizenship, but were constituted as its other as an immanent group by citizens. Similarly, slaves were not simply excluded from citizenship, but made citizenship possible by their very formation. The alterity of citizenship, therefore, does not preexist, but is constituted by it. The closure theories that define citizenship as a space of privilege for the few that excludes others neglect a subtle but important aspect of citizenship: that it requires the constitution of these others to become possible. (2002b: 4)

Thus, because citizenship is a dialogical process, focusing on the social in citizenship enables us to understand how citizenship is also in the process of being constituted as much by those marginalized by it as from the perspective of the dominant groups (the citizens) that benefit by it. This opens up space for critically thinking about how we wish to envision the social and its relationship to citizenship. The securitization of the social that comes with citizenship as a globalizing regime of government certainly means the furtherance of inequality, the stripping away of the rights of some, and the shift towards more undemocratic forms of governing. Yet, at the same time, the globalization of citizenship has opened up the opportunity to re-envision border and state ontologies. Understanding the shifting nature of governing through citizenship demands that we reconceptualize states in ways that loosen the spatial imperative. As a growing body of critical scholarship has recently argued, this involves thinking of states as assemblages and flows of spaces, rather than as contiguously bounded territorial spaces and spaces of bounded political community (e.g., Haggerty and Ericson 2000, Hardt and Negri 2000, McNevin 2006, Ong and Collier 2005, Zureik and Salter 2005). This provides an opening for re-envisioning the social on which citizenship depends. Recognizing that citizenship is constituted by the alterity that already exists within it, we might seize the moment in which to rethink the logic of security away from its violent modern forms as the 'struggle to efface, erase, or eradicate alterity' and towards a different configuration of the political, one whose purpose is 'the struggle *for* – or *on behalf of* – alterity' (Campbell 1994: 477).

From this perspective, the securitization of citizenship does not have to lead to a more exclusionary social body. The paradox of this moment is that the securitization of citizenship and the more exclusionary vision of the social that it works to promote is also the same moment that has produced the globalization of citizenship, based on unravelling the fixed, bounded notion of the social on which modern citizenship has depended. The question is whether we can seize this moment as one in which to strengthen the dialogical construction of citizenship by building political movements in support of citizenship's Others. There are, in fact, a range of such types of initiatives already under way through the No Border and No One Is Illegal movements, as well as movements working towards the regularization of the status of undocumented and 'illegal' migrants (Hayter 2001; McNevin 2006, 2007; No Border Network 2002; No One Is Illegal U.K. 2003; Nyers 2003; Sharma 2002; Walters 2002; Wright 2003). Such movements challenge what it means to be a citizen and the exclusionary nature of the social on which the securitization of citizenship is based. They 'place a dint in the logic and legitimacy of the territorial state and in the framework of belonging it represents' (McNevin 2006: 142). Specifically, these movements challenge the notion of fixed and closed territorial borders and the way people are rendered either 'legal' or 'illegal,' citizens or non-citizens as a result of them. Border or immigration controls are viewed as racist and as rendering persons 'illegal', 'non-persons,' and 'outside the law' (No One Is Illegal U.K. 2003). Instead, these groups work from 'the standpoint of those who are displaced and on the move' towards 'justice for (im)migrants' as well as indigenous peoples, who have been similarly negatively affected by experiences of colonialism, 'national borderlines,' and 'border controls' (Sharma 2002). In doing so, these movements are important for the way in which they make visible and audible the presence of non-citizens *as political subjects*, thus challenging the way refugees and other irregular migrants are often understood and rendered 'speechless and agentless' (Nyers 2003: 1087).

Against these alternative visions for change, however, there is also the very real possibility that the securitization and globalization of citizenship offers dimmer prospects. After 11 September 2001 some suggested that the principle aim of border control and detention policy changes was to target non-citizens. David Cole, for example, has argued that 'while there has been much talk about the need to sacrifice liberty for a greater sense of security, in practice we have selectively sacrificed *noncitizens'* liberties while retaining basic protections for citizens' (2002: 955). My arguments here suggest that the situation may be even more alarming than this. Many of the policy changes used to strip away the liberties of non-citizens are also being used as a basis on which to transform the status of some citizens into second-class citizens and into abject subjects – to blur the distinction between non-citizens and citizens altogether, with profound consequences for the ability of some to struggle for redistribution, rights, and recognition of even being a citizen-subject with a right to have rights. Under this new regime, the criterion on which to access rights is no longer even the problematic one of the modern regime of belonging to a polity in a territorial state. Rather, it becomes a case of whether one is (or how much one is) risk-worthy. This has grave implications for the future of deliberative democracy if we believe that 'in the end, the true test of justice in a democratic society is not how it treats those with a political voice, but how it treats those who have no voice in the democratic process' (ibid.). We are at a juncture when abject subjects, those who have been denied political voice, are demanding en masse to be included within the current citizenship regime. Like 11 September, this too provides a historic moment in which to consider how our current regime of citizenship as government might be radically altered. Our collective response to this moment – whether through more oppressive forms of border controls and detention or through strategies of inclusion and recognition – will have important implications for the future of democratic citizenship.

Acknowledgments

I would like to thank Engin Isin for his intellectual mentorship and invaluable feedback throughout various stages of the research and writing of this chapter, and to Haideh Moghissi, Sandra Whitworth, and Daiva Stasiulis for their engagement with earlier versions of the research. The chapter has benefited from feedback received at the Citizenship, Identity and Social Justice Conference at the University of Windsor and the 2007 ISA Convention in Chicago, for which I especially thank Peter Nyers for his input as discussant. Finally, I am grateful to Feyzi Baban for his intellectual insights, discussion, and comments. This research was supported by the Social Sciences and Humanities Research Council of Canada.

Notes

1 As Hindess explains: 'In contrast to this internalist perspective, I suggest that an understanding of the impact of citizenship in the modern world must focus on its role in dividing a global population of thousands of millions into the smaller subpopulations of territorial states... This involves consideration not just of the role of citizenship in bringing together members of particular subpopulations and promoting some of their interests, but also of the effects of rendering the larger population governable by dividing it into subpopulations consisting of the citizens of discrete, politically independent and competing states' (2000: 1488).

2 Evidence of this is in the overwhelming numbers of such groups who have been detained and/or arrested as a result of such policies since 11 September 2001. While these policies are supposed to help identify 'terrorists,' they have been used in the widespread registration and detention of men of Middle Eastern, Muslim, and/or Arab background. For example, the American Civil Liberties Union has noted how U.S. government programs like the Immigration and Naturalization Service's program of fingerprinting and registration of males over the ages of 16 from Middle Eastern countries and/or of Muslim background were used as a 'pretext' for 'mass detentions' (ACLU 2002). In Southern California alone, some 700 men of

Muslim and/or Middle Eastern origin were arrested after voluntarily complying with the registration and fingerprinting program (ibid.).

3 The U.S. government has identified book choice as one such area to be monitored with anyone checking out from libraries or buying books on the Middle East as potentially suspicious. To this effect, Section 215 of the 2001 U.S. Patriot Act expands government (Federal Bureau of Investigation) power to seize and search records held by a third party (including financial records, Internet use, medical history, travel itineraries, and book purchases, or library records). Moreover, third parties like bookstores and libraries are not permitted to disclose the fact that they have been court ordered to pass on their records so that those who are the subjects of the surveillance remain ignorant of this fact. See ACLU (2003), 'Surveillance Under the USA Patriot Act.'

4 In a similar way the Canada-U.S. Smart Border declaration talks of 'clearance away from the border' and 'developing approaches to move customs and immigration inspection activities away from the border' (U.S. White House 2002, point #15). While the specifics remain to be worked out, the idea includes having the border inspection services of one country working out of the other (ibid.).

5 Australia's 'Pacific Solution' was terminated in February 2008, as promised by the newly elected Prime Minister Kevin Rudd and the Australian Labor Party, with the removal of the final twenty-one remaining detainees off the island of Nauru (Bartlett 2008).

6 The U.S. Supreme Court rulings in *Rasul* v. *Bush* and *Hamdan* v. *Rumsfeld* initially seemed to uphold the right of detainees to habeas corpus to challenge their detention before a U.S. court of law. However, the 2006 Military Commissions Act challenges these earlier rulings by attempting to suspend habeas corpus for those who are determined to be 'enemy combatants' and 'unlawful enemy combatants,' giving the president or defence secretary almost unrestricted authority to make such determinations, and granting immunity from prosecution for all officials involved in acts of detention and treatment (abuse) of detainees (as of November 1997). See CCR, 'FAQs: The Military Commissions Act.'

7 Deleuze (1992) alludes to this in his discussion of the shift from disciplinary to control societies.

8 This can be thought of in terms of Foucault's discussion of biopower and the shift from a 'territorial State' to a 'State of population' (Agamben 1995: 3).

9 Campbell writes: 'we can understand the state as having 'no ontological status apart from the various acts which constitute its reality'; that its status as the sovereign presence in world politics is produced by 'a discourse of

primary and stable identity'; and that the identity of any particular state could be understood as 'tenuously constituted in time ... through a stylized repetition of acts,' achieved, '"not [through] a founding act, but rather a regulated process of repetition"' (1998: 9).

10 The Ecological Citizen

ALEX LATTA

Since the mid-1990s there has been a veritable explosion of literature concerning 'environmental justice.' The majority of this work has focussed on a grassroots movement in the United States that has made environmental justice the banner terminology for its activism against discriminatory patterns of environmental health risks (e.g., Bullard 1994, Camacho 1998, Faber 1998b). Comprised of a loose network of communities, non-governmental organizations, and academic resource/research centres, the environmental justice movement arose in the context of individual communities' battles against toxic waste dumps, incinerators, petrochemical plants, and a range of other industrial activities with severe implications for human health. The movement found its immediate origins in protests during the late 1970s against toxic waste, which became rearticulated in terms of environmental racism in the early 1980s. At that time, communities of colour began to awaken to the fact that their homes, schools, and places of work suffered a disproportionate degree of exposure to environmental pollutants. Taking a longer historical perspective, the roots of the environmental justice movement can be traced further back, particularly to the U.S. civil rights movement of the 1960s, but also to antecedents in other sectors, such as the labour movement and First Nations' struggles. Viewed in its broadest scope, environmental justice has also been connected to a cultural politics of ethnicity, gender, and sexuality (Peña 2005, Pulido 1996, Stein 2004).

Although the majority of both activism and research on environmental justice has been conducted in the United States, increasing attention is being given to its utility as an analytical paradigm for understanding similar struggles around the world. There is, for instance, a small but not insignificant literature on environmental justice in Canada (e.g., Debbané and Keil 2004, Draper and Mitchell 2001, Jerrett et al. 2001, Pushchak 2002, Teelucksingh 2002, Westra 1999). Much of this work is directed at identifying cases of apparent environmental *injustice*, but it is also evident that numerous social actors in Canada are engaged in a politics that combines issues of social justice with parallel ecological concerns. Among environmentally related non-governmental organizations (NGOs) in Canada, a number of recent examples suggest that the language of environmental justice is increasingly attractive as a way of naming this interweaving of agendas.[1] In the United Kingdom, the recently formed Coalition for Access to Environmental Justice provides a new space for coordinating campaigns among a range of NGOs,[2] and in Europe an emerging research and advocacy network promoting the cause of environmental justice in central and Eastern Europe provides another regional example of the growing currency of the paradigm.[3] Scholarship applying an environmental justice lens to the global South has also begun to appear (Comfort 2002, Martinez-Alier 2003, McDonald 2005), and more recent edited volumes almost uniformly make a point of addressing the global dimension (Agyeman, Bullard, and Evans 2003; Bullard 2005b; Byrne, Glover, and Martinez 2002; Hofrichter 2002). Moreover, the issues at the centre of environmental justice are fast becoming integrated and recombined within a broader global justice movement, which seeks to mobilize marginalized communities around the world in a common front against the advance of transnational corporate power. Environmental justice activists from the United States have been key participants in network building to advance the cause of global justice (Bullard, Johnson, and Torres 2005), and there is evidence that the notion of linking environment and justice has begun to gain broader currency. Reference to environmental justice appears, for instance, in the Dialogue Paper authored by the NGO participants leading up to the 2002 World Summit on Sustainable Development (Third World Network, Environment Liaison Centre International, and Danish 92 Group 2002). Among international NGOs, Friends of the Earth International,[4] Via Campesina,[5] and EarthRights International[6] are leaders in building a global movement that fuses issues of social justice with those of environmental sustainability. The discourse of environmental justice has also been picked up by smaller regional NGOs, such as South Africa's Environmental Justice Networking Forum[7] and Chile's Latin American Observatory on Environmental Conflicts.[8]

It is probably premature to speak of a concerted global environmental justice movement. Furthermore, it is important to recognize that the specific political interpretation of the concept varies as it is transported to different contexts and taken up by a variety of social actors (Debbané and Keil 2004). Nevertheless, it is the methodological premise of this essay that the paradigm of environmental justice is broadly applicable to a variety of settings around the world, where the intersection between social justice and ecology becomes a nexus for political struggle. Drawing on the literature associated with the paradigm (which remains heavily weighted towards the U.S. context), the aim in this chapter is to demonstrate that environmental justice struggles can fruitfully be read in terms of their import for evolving regimes of citizenship. When social actors articulate demands for justice, there are usually clear implications for the codes and practices that govern collective human life – for the fabric of the political body wherein citizens are constituted and governed. Since the question at hand is the specific valence of the *social* in citizenship, political speech and action that actively connect ecological and social domains in a discourse of justice is of significant import. It has been widely observed that environmental justice departs from classical environmental politics, particularly that of the North American variety, by sweeping away a long-standing dualism pitting nature (as wilderness) in opposition to society (as humanized landscape). Environmental justice has brought humans back into ecological questions, as actors who live, work, and play *in nature*. There has been virtual silence regarding its specific implications for a broader *social* politics. If environmental justice has brought society back into nature, it has no less brought ecology (back) into the politics of social justice.

As a preliminary way of underlining the significance of this development, it is instructive to review the trajectory of the American environmental justice movement in light of the parallel historical trends that provide the context for this collection, namely, (1) a shift from redistributive policies towards a neoliberal emphasis on individual responsibility and (2) a rising politics of recognition. The movement's gestation in the early to mid 1980s corresponded with the period in which the basis for social citizenship within the welfare state began to come under serious attack. Furthermore, the consolidation of the neoliberal political agenda in the mid-1990s coincided with a coming of age for environmental justice as a *self-conscious* movement. Hence, just as neoliberal policy was dismantling redistributive social rights, environmental justice actors were bucking the trend by demanding that distributive rights be *extended* to the environmental sphere. The significance of the movement comes into even sharper relief when we consider its political trajectory beside that of mainstream environmentalism. The latter also enjoyed its upswing during neoliberalism's period of consolidation, but rather than challenging the erosion of regulatory regimes, many environmental organizations focused on an agenda that dovetailed with the neoliberal ideology of individual obligations, emphasizing the importance of personal attitude change and individual commitment to strategies like recycling, green consumerism, and less polluting modes of transportation. Environmental justice has pulled in the other direction, putting the regulation of toxic waste and polluting industries *back* on the agenda of government. Moreover, environmental justice actors have pursued discourses of political rights and agency that emphasize not individuals but communities. Finally, since the distributive injustices they seek to address are so evidently linked to issues of race, class, and cultural survival, the movement has become part of the new wave of social mobilization around issues of recognition. Of course, this schematic account of the trajectory of environmental justice is particular to the United States, but the emergence of ecological dimensions in a global justice movement is indicative of shared experiences and convergent political agendas in other parts of the world.

Given the confluence of issues relating to redistribution and recognition in environmental justice, it is clearly a fertile site to begin mapping the changing terrain of the social. At the same time, however, the socio-ecological politics of environmental justice can be understood as a field of contested relations where the rights, practices, and identities of citizens are contested and reconfigured. Using the language of the introduction to this collection, we can think of environmental justice as comprising 'everyday struggles, [in which] people develop a sense of their rights as others' obligations and others' rights as their obligations.' Reading environmental justice through the lens of citizenship makes the intersection of redistribution and recognition legible not simply as a fortuitous strategic combination of agendas, but rather as an integral knot of emergent political being (Isin 2002b). Within this knot, the enactment of citizenship is a transformative process, where distributive issues become linked to more radical questions of sustainability, and claims to recognition overflow the containers of classical identity politics to include human–nature assemblages. That the language of citizenship has so far been mostly absent in the literature on environmental justice amounts to a significant oversight, indicative of the problematic compartmentalization of knowledge production that this collection seeks to address. The project of 'recasting the social in citizenship' provides an ideal analytical frame for posing questions that address this oversight and in so doing chart the broader political significance of environmental justice. How has casting social justice in environmental terms acted to intensify, supplement, problematize, or reconfigure the social in citizenship? To put this question another way, how have struggles for environmental justice changed the way that the social is embodied, performed, and contested as a dimension of citizenship?

To set the stage for exploring the way the social in citizenship can be fruitfully reimagined at the fertile political nexus of environmental justice, this chapter begins with a significant methodological caveat. It is necessary to explain the approach taken here alongside another possible (and perhaps more obvious) route to addressing questions of the ecological and the social in citizenship. A rapidly growing literature on environmental citizenship also addresses these questions, although from a much different perspective. Via an explanation of the reasons for not pursuing this other avenue of inquiry, it is also possible to offer a more precise articulation of the particular understanding of citizenship that informs the subsequent analysis. The second part of the essay outlines the various dimensions of environmental justice, which span distributional, substantive, and procedural claims for justice. The third section looks more closely at the cultural dimension and issues of recognition. It is here, I argue, that demands for social justice and environmental sustainability have become most forcefully cemented together within a radical or 'insurgent' politics of citizenship. A fourth section briefly examines some of the hurdles that have prevented environmental justice principles from being converted into formal citizenship rights. Finally, the chapter concludes with a more focused consideration of how the social in citizenship has been transformed through its encounter with the ecological in the context of environmental justice.

Environmental Citizenship

The rapidly growing literature on environmental citizenship might have seemed a more fitting location in which to begin investigating the ecological dimension of the social in citizenship (see, e.g., Barry 1999, Curtin 1999, Dobson 2003a, Dobson and Bell 2006, Dobson and Valencia Sáis 2005, Doherty and de Geus 1996). Indeed, existing scholarship on environmental citizenship is not without treatments that engage directly with its potential articulation to social citizenship. Howard

Newby (1996), for instance, draws on the theoretical basis provided by T.H. Marshall's work (1950) to situate an emergent environmental citizenship in clear continuity with earlier expansions of citizenship rights and responsibilities in response to the changing character of social and economic order. Newby is particularly concerned with the sustainable management of the various global commons, and calls for research to explore the challenges of building the collective spaces necessary for the emergence of a global environmental citizenship. More recently, Joaquín Valdivielso (2005) also addresses citizenship in terms of a continuity between evolving questions of social order and those of environmental sustainability. He suggests that aspirations of ecological citizenship towards a more equitable and sustainable world can play an important role in renewing and reconstructing the 'moral cement of social commitment' (252) in the wake of the disarticulation of social citizenship wrought by neoliberal globalization. Finally, Graham Smith (2005) takes quite another tack regarding 'the social,' arguing that the social economy (socially based enterprises such as cooperatives, credit unions, and fair trade organizations) would be an appropriate sphere in which to cultivate the values and practices of a 'green' citizenship.

These and other contributions to the literature on environmental citizenship contain important insights relative to the place of the social in citizenship. Nevertheless, as I have argued elsewhere (Latta 2007) the majority of scholarship on environmental citizenship takes a normative approach, in which the most central element is an ideal 'green' citizen, who takes on a set of responsibilities revolving around individual choices regarding consumption patterns and lifestyle. When this model is scaled up, as in the case of Newby's arguments, the question becomes one of designing the appropriate institutions for effective international cooperation on environmental matters in order to create the institutional infrastructure that could administrate the rights and duties of global environmental citizens. There are two problems here. First, the actors – the green citizens – seem to occupy unproblematized subject positions as (potentially) 'responsible' individuals. Second, the issues to which environmental citizenship is presumed to respond are also constituted in an unproblematic way. Global warming, ozone thinning, biodiversity loss and the like are assumed to be self-evident in terms of their content, their universal relevance, and their susceptibility to resolution through individual vigilance and 'good governance.' Without wanting to diminish the importance of such issues or the value of normative visions, the questions of who environmental actors might be, how environmental problems are experienced in specific places, and what constitutes 'responsible' citizen conduct or 'good governance,' are all highly political. In other words, they are issues that would seem to beg treatment within the democratic practices of an evolving citizenship, rather than as scientific and/or philosophical a priori to citizenship. With respect to the scaled-up context of global issues, there are a number of more recent contributions that have argued for a postinternationalist model of ecological citizenship, drawing significantly on the theoretical context provided by cosmopolitanism (Christoff 1996, Dobson 2003a, Jelin 2000, Valencia Sáis 2005). These treatments go a long way towards addressing the emergence of global environmental citizenship as a process involving numerous social actors. They also tend to foreground issues of democracy and justice. Andrew Dobson's work on the topic (2003a), for instance, seeks to situate a postcosmopolitan environmental citizenship in the direct material relationships of unequal ecological footprints, from which a political imperative for citizen responsibility emerges. Nonetheless, the *negotiation* of more just arrangements remains largely outside the practice of citizenship in such formulations.

I have previously cast my criticisms of the existing literature on environmental citizenship in terms of an effort to broaden the research agenda. My choice here to tackle the problem of the ecological dimension of the social in citizenship through the lens of environmental justice should be viewed in the same light. To the extent that a specifically ecological nexus can be seen to be an emergent element within contemporary citizenships, it must be understood not only in terms of a 'green' set of responsibilities or governance institutions, but also in terms of citizens' capacities to *actively politicize* that which is understood as ecology or environment, as well as the broader social relationships that constitute such understandings. In this conviction, my thinking follows that of a number of other scholars, among them Gilbert and Phillips (2003), MacGregor (2006), M. Smith (2005), and Torgerson (1999). What these theorists share is an appreciation for the way that citizenship is not merely a framework for political practice, but also its object. In this sense, citizens may be understood as actively contributing to the evolution of a public sphere, in which different kinds of ecological questions are construed as political matters, and the terms which define legitimate speech about those questions are negotiated.

Of course, there are many different kinds of social subjects who might be seen as contributing to an emerging environmental public sphere. Moreover, many of these actors (transnational corporations, governing elites) may favour very restricted definitions of citizenship practice vis-à-vis the environment. As Engin Isin (2002b) emphasizes, the construction of citizenship simultaneously involves the construction of alterity – of subject positions and forms of speech that do not fit within the harmonious or unifying spaces of citizenship narrative. In this context, centring the present analysis on the voices and actions of socially marginalized political actors can be seen in part as an answer to Isin's call for research that unearths the voices of those who find themselves outsiders to dominant citizenship regimes. As the environment is brought into citizenship, often within carefully circumscribed institutional parameters delimiting a narrow range of legitimate forms of speech,[9] environmental justice activism reopens spaces in which the dominant socioecological order, and the associated citizenship regime, are both put in question. Adapting terminology from James Holston (1998), we might label such actors as 'insurgent' ecological citizens. Around the world, citizen insurgence focused on environmental issues is a central part of the rising challenge to the expansion of market relations and neoliberal regimes of governance.

Dimensions of Environmental Justice

Demands for environmental justice actually entail a combination of justice claims. Agyeman (2005) identifies three essential components to the concept: distributive, substantive, and participatory (26). With its roots in a critique of environmental racism, environmental justice in the United States has been primarily driven by a distributive framing of the issue. Distributive injustice can also be seen as the spark for similar movements in other polities where race is a decisive factor in determining who suffers the burdens of unhealthy environments. South Africa offers one such example (McDonald 2005). Distributive justice, however, is also the Achilles heel of environmental justice, in the sense that proponents of a broader paradigm of ecological sustainability may see distributive issues as amenable to superficial solutions (more evenly spread environmental ills) in place of real change (an overall reduction in ecological harm). Dobson (2003b) has highlighted this possible reading of environmental justice in the United States, with the polemical argument that 'the objective of the environmental justice movement is to have environmental "bads" more fairly distributed across the country, so that wealthier communities have their fair share of landfill sites' (85).

Although there are definite tensions between distributive and other forms of environmental justice, Dobson's charge is perhaps unfair. There may not be, as he puts it, a *necessary* link between social justice and broader sustainability, but proponents of environmental justice have *actively* sought to make this connection. Hence, the movement in the United States has consistently paired its campaign around distributive injustice with the assertion of environmental rights. One example of this can be found in the Principles of Environmental Justice declaration, which emerged from the 1991 First National People of Color Environmental Leadership Summit. The notion of environmental rights signals a substantive dimension of justice, where the mere distribution of ecological goods and bads is not all that is at stake. The declaration asserts that '*environmental justice* affirms the sacredness of Mother Earth, ecological unity and the interdependence of all species, and the right to be free from ecological destruction' (Bullard 2005b: 299, original emphasis). In South Africa environmental justice advocates were successful in securing the constitutional recognition of environmental rights in the 1996 Bill of Rights. The Bill recognizes citizens' right to an 'environment that is not harmful to their health and well-being' and also to 'ecologically sustainable development' (quoted in McDonald 2005: 258). In a Canadian example, the Conservation Council of New Brunswick (2006) articulates a comprehensive list of environmental rights in its Charter for Environmental Justice, including Aboriginal rights for the First Nations of the province. It is worth further note that the charter lists not only rights, but also obligations, a sign of the way that environmental justice begins to map onto the broader embodiment of citizenship.

The third dimension of environmental justice listed by Agyeman, procedural justice, is more complicated and multifaceted than the first two. In its most basic sense, just procedure is about having equal access to fair decision-making processes. Where such access is lacking, the remedy seems quite obvious: more inclusive procedures that take into account the interests of all stakeholders in any particular environmental decision. Examples of this principle translated into policy include the Aarhus Convention, in Europe, and the Ontario Environmental Bill of Rights, in Canada. What such remedies tend to neglect, however, are broader societal relations of inequality and unsustainable development. For instance, the question of whether to site a waste incinerator in a particular community is an exceptionally narrow one with respect to effective democratic inclusion. It limits a community's capacity for self-determination to a trade-off between economic benefits and clean air, and it also fails to account for the fact that the community in question may find itself in a socioeconomic condition that favours acceptance of a Faustian bargain. Hence, understood only in the limited sense of fair process, the procedural dimension of environmental justice begs the question of the broader character of liberal democratic citizenship. In fact, for many environmental justice scholars, procedural justice is seen to include a wider range of societal measures to create the conditions for socially just and ecologically sustainable communities. In part to signal this forward-looking and more cohesive socioeconomic project, Agyeman (2005) advances the term *just sustainability.* As a paradigm that has grown out of the encounter between environmental justice and sustainable development, just sustainability names an emergent political space where community groups are organizing to pursue concrete objectives in terms of local socioeconomic development and environmental health.

While the implications of environmental justice activism for the social in citizenship could certainly be examined in terms of the emerging practices of community development that Agyeman identifies with the paradigm of just sustainability, my focus here is more on the oppositional, agonistic, and performative aspects of environmental justice struggles, where the spaces and political agents for alternative modes of community development are initially cultivated. To arrive at an appreciation of these aspects, the arena of procedural justice needs to be more closely examined in order to explore the way that environmental justice links socioecological activism to a broad and radical push for meaningful democratization. In significant part, this connection is enacted through a cultural politics of recognition and identity. It is in the context of these links between social, ecological, and cultural politics that environmental justice poses its most radical challenge to existing ideologies and embodiments of citizenship.

Identity, Recognition, Political Voice: From Justice to Citizenship

David Schlosberg (2004) argues that most existing theories of environmental justice are limited by their failure to adequately take account of the way that demands for social and environmental equity become articulated to justice claims revolving around the linked issues of recognition and political participation. Drawing on theoretical frameworks advanced by Nancy Fraser and Iris Young, Schlosberg is highly critical of understandings of environmental justice that primarily highlight its distributional elements. Relative to Agyeman's account, Schlosberg groups the distributive and substantive dimensions together as equity concerns, while prying open the notion of procedural justice to reveal a complex intersection between group identity, the dynamics of intergroup recognition, and the possibilities for meaningful engagement in broader political debates regarding the socioeconomic roots of injustice. For Schlosberg, the concatenation of these elements within environmental justice makes it an important site for the politics of a 'new pluralism' (1999), founded not on the liberal notion of tolerance, but rather on an embrace of multiplicity 'as the precondition of political action' (16). Engagement across difference and practices of solidarity amid diversity are key elements of this new kind of political practice, which Schlosberg perceives as forming the basis not only for the organizing strategies of environmental justice activism in the United States, but also for the emergence of a similar global movement (2004). A new politics of difference is not only vital to the structure of the movement, but also central to the character of the justice claims that its actors make before the larger polities within which their political subjectivities are located.

That difference or identity is central to the politics of environmental justice should come as no surprise, given its roots in mobilizations against racially defined injustices in the United States. As the movement has become integrated with wider discourses of oppositional politics, however, difference has arguably become an even more central element linking the cause of social justice with environmental concerns. In particular, it is crucial to note the importance of ethnicity, gender, sexuality, and class as key sites of identity-based struggle in the evolving politics of environmental justice. Cultural issues have come to centre stage, most notably as the struggles of indigenous peoples have been drawn into the framework of environmental justice. Hence, as Schlosberg argues, calls for greater equity in the face of economic globalization have been accompanied by 'a call for recognition and preservation of diverse cultures, identities, economies, and ways of knowing' (2004: 524). The field of environmental justice has likewise expanded to include issues related to gender and sexuality. It has been widely noted that women form a disproportionately high percentage of grassroots environmental justice activists in the United States, and they are increasingly responsible for the work of articulating such struggles within the context of a broader movement (Bullard and Smith 2005). Giovanna De Chiro (1998) goes so far as to call environmental justice an 'unmarked' women's movement, since its female activists challenge traditional gender roles at various scales (within the household, in the community, and in the broader political sphere), even though changing gender roles is not their primary goal. That environmental activism by women of marginalized communities should present such challenges speaks to the way in which environmental *injustice* arises out of relations of power that depend on the interlinked oppression/exploitation of women and nature. Similarly, Cate Sandilands (2004) notes the 'co-relations between the social organization of *sexuality* and ecology' (110, my emphasis; see also Gaard 2004, and Unger 2004). In response to these co-relations, Sandilands identifies an active cultural politics 'to displace the interstructured power relations of heterosexism and ecological degradation' (2004: 111). Finally, while the rise of the neoliberal agenda has been associated with a general attenuation of the labour movement, environmental justice has provided new spaces for class-based political mobilization (Faber 1998a, Harvey 1996).

It is important to note the way that these various axes of resistance-oriented identity building cross over and hybridize within the environmental justice movement. The connections between race or ethnicity and class are perhaps the most obvious, since many marginalized communities suffer from injustices in which racial and socioeconomic relations of power are mutually reinforcing. There are many other articulations worth highlighting. Celene Krauss (2002), for instance, documents the conjunction of gender and class in the activism of women blue-collar workers, while De Chiro (1998) emphasizes the particular role of women in defending ethnic and local cultures. Such hybridization of identities in the field of resistance comprised by environmental justice is important; it demonstrates the fluidity of identity in response to changing political realities and hence the role of cultural politics in seeking or cultivating political voice.

Indeed, the links between recognition and political voice are key to reading environmental justice as citizenship practice. David Schlosberg (2004) puts the relation between identity/recognition and politics quite simply: 'if you are not recognized, you do not participate' (519). Arguing in a similar vein, Laura Pulido (1996) suggests that, although having an identity of *some* kind is not an option for human subjects, in the case of subaltern peoples – whose identities have been debased or effaced by cultural majorities – developing an *affirmative* identity is a precondition for other kinds of political action. She remarks that 'it is the power of self that is the crucial first step in imagining the possibility of resistance or another reality' (47). Drawing for a moment from outside the environmental justice literature, Curtis (1999) offers a particularly acute articulation of this relationship between recognition, justice, and citizenship. She observes that a persistent non-recognition facilitates the commission of injustice, in that those who are seen to lie outside the normal spaces of citizenship are literally *not seen*. This invisibility means that they are unable to make claims on the broader human collectives in which their lives are embedded. Hence, the ability of social actors to make calls for justice hinges on their simultaneous effort to emerge from this space of oblivion – to take possession of their own public identities and demand recognition as political interlocutors vis-à-vis these collectives.

Something like this emergence from oblivion seems to take place in the context of environmental justice, often described by some as a kind of awakening process, where the dominant ideologies governing social order are shrugged off and radical political subjects are born. Girdner and Smith (2002), for instance, identify the development of a critical consciousness as the first step in environmental justice activism, an insight that 'begins to "unmask" the ideology of popular participation and democracy' (58). They go on to explain that, confronted with an awareness of their expendability in the name of progress or economic development, grassroots activists go through stages of politicization that involve turning to local and popular cultures in order to build a collective project of resistance (see also Krauss 2002). Following Isin (2002b) we might describe this awakening and politicization as a process of 'becoming political,' whereby those who are outsiders to dominant regimes of citizenship challenge the terms by which they have been rendered expendable. As Isin puts it, 'becoming political is that moment when one constitutes oneself as being capable of judgment, and associates oneself with or against others in fulfilling that responsibility' (2002b: 276). While becoming political is not identical to obtaining citizenship in a formal sense, it is the moment in which the rights, practices, and identities of citizenship are put into question and opened to revision.

There is a final link in this series of connections between justice, recognition, political agency, and citizenship, which is particularly crucial with respect to the environmental dimension of injustice. This is the link between identity and place. In many environmental justice mobilizations, but especially in the context of indigenous peoples, the politics of recognition and social justice are often constructed around the defence of particular spaces, such as neighbourhoods or traditional territories. Pulido (1996, 1998) and Devon Peña (2002, 2003, 2005), for instance, highlight the importance of place-based identity projects in the struggles of Chicano communities in the American Southwest. Both authors argue that the ability of Chicano agriculturalists to revalorize their identities as ecological stewards of the lands they inhabit is crucial in their efforts to secure an effective political voice. In this way, insurgent practices of citizenship take on a certain ecological rootedness, through particular communities' or people's connections with the specific landscapes to which their collective identities are articulated. Indeed, the defence of particular places can perhaps be conceived of as the spatial equivalent of the affirmative reconstruction of identity, wherein the uniform spatial projections of citizenship's dominant universal (national territory, private property) are disarticulated and reconfigured according to local topographies of livelihood, collective identity, and social reproduction. Along these same lines, place-based resistances challenge the meta-knowledge of experts – which typically receives official sanction as pre-political truth within the dominant orders of citizenly deliberation – replacing such expertise with the situated knowing of local experience.[10] In this sense, the link between identity politics and place in environmental justice constitutes an important site for the democratization of knowledge, expanding the role of citizens in generating shared understandings of human–nature relationships in the places where they live, work, and play.

By making claims to the capacity for judgment and creating networks of association with others in order to speak out against injustice and defend specific human livelihoods and habitats, environmental justice presents a radical challenge not only to the *material* projects of transnational capital but also to the *cultural* and *ideological* orders of existing regimes of citizenship. As such, it is rapidly becoming one of the key sites of radicalization in the broader politics of 'anti-globalization.' Applying a Gramscian lens to the movement, Alem Seghed Kebede (2005) argues that because of the comprehensive character of the social critique arising out of environmental justice, it should be considered a counter-hegemonic movement. In other words, its political implications reach far beyond specific areas of environmental policy, and the movement becomes a space where a concerted challenge to the dominant order takes root. Others have seen similar radical tendencies in environmental justice, but the difficulties of scaling up from place-based struggle and working towards concrete alternatives should not be underestimated (Girdner and Smith 2002, Harvey 1996). Indeed, even within the local and regional spaces of environmental justice mobilization, there is reason to be cautious in asserting the transformative potential of the movement. In practice, the process of becoming political vis-à-vis the ecosocial dimensions of existing citizenship regimes is invariably marked by numerous diversions and setbacks.

The Limits of Environmental Justice

Thus far I have presented distribution and recognition as mutually reinforcing dimensions of environmental justice, recombining within a radical participatory milieu to ignite the reawakening of a politics of citizenship. In fact, the terrain occupied by environmental justice actors is substantially more complex and equivocal. While ultimately the realization of justice does seem to depend on mutually reinforcing and transformative combinations of these elements, it is important to note that there are also tensions between the various agendas. Such problems are particularly relevant with respect to the encounter between environmental justice as an oppositional movement and the various policy instruments and ideological paradigms that have been deployed in response to it. Not surprisingly, the latter have developed unevenly around the world. In the United States, Executive Order 12898, promulgated in 1994, mandates all federal agencies to address the issues surrounding environmental justice by applying the legal principles found in the 1964 Civil Rights Act and the 1969 National Environmental Policy Act (Bullard 2005a). This has set the stage for an exceptionally litigious field of contest, with challenges to industrial siting decisions made on the basis of racial discrimination and/or failure to follow adequate procedures in environmental impact assessments. In the case of court challenges based on racial discrimination, environmental justice has become mired in the reductionist politics of liberal rights, and certain distributive aspects of justice (such as race) have effaced others (such as class). Moreover, challenges on the procedural front have had to contend with the depoliticizing language and practices of technically based impact assessment. Neither route addresses claims to substantive ecological rights, and neither bodes well for the more complex and radical synthesis of environmental justice as a site of political becoming, where marginalized groups stake a claim to citizenship (for an illustration of these hurdles, see Kurtz 2005).

Policy agendas in other parts of the world have been different, but marked by similar shortcomings. In the European Union, the Aarhus Convention, which entered into force in October 2001, sets the stage for greater access to information, public participation, and 'access to justice' with respect to environmental matters (United Nations Economic Commission for Europe). In this instance the emphasis on procedural elements of justice seems to have left any mention of distributive justice or substantive rights off the agenda. In Canada, the Ontario Environmental Bill of Rights is also nearly exclusive in its focus on procedural rights, and it was perceived at the time of its passage that a trade-off had been made between the substantive and procedural dimensions in order to secure broad support for the legislation (Emond 1994). Moreover, subsequent to its passage the procedural rights it entails provided relatively little protection against neoliberal reforms to environmental regulation during the Conservative provincial government of Mike Harris. In South Africa, as has already been mentioned, substantive rights to a healthy environment are enshrined in the Constitution, and equitable procedural rights are provided for in legislation governing social and environmental impact assessments. Nevertheless, David McDonald (2005) notes that only in a few instances have the substantive rights been translated into concrete legal or policy outcomes. Scott and Oelofse (2005) similarly observe that impact assessments in South Africa still fail to achieve inclusive participation. What is more, McDonald highlights the fact that the limited issue of environmental racism is of decreasing relevance next to the social and environmental pressures generated by the government's embrace of neoliberal economic policies. As in the United States, the South African example shows the way that the radical implications of environmental justice are not easily transferred to the policy sphere, especially when it comes to translating formal recognition into meaningful democratic participation in determining the broader direction of socioeconomic development.

McDonald's observations reveal that the environmental justice agenda faces significant challenges, especially in light of the way neoliberal ideologies and modes of government that have successfully disarticulated previous modes of politicizing the social. The interlinked claims for justice that have become the source of strength for the radical trajectory of environmental justice are susceptible to being undermined or co-opted, particularly when the language of recognition, distributive justice, or inclusive participation is taken up by dominant political actors and woven into policy structures whose real goals and functions are to protect the reigning socioeconomic model. In their study of impact assessment procedures in South Africa, Scott and Oelofse (2005) are hopeful about the possibilities for truly inclusive decision-making processes, guided by the paradigm of social and environmental justice, but note the difficulties that arise as the paradigm is refracted through the dominant ideological framework of ecological modernization (see also Bond 2000, Debbané and Keil 2004). Ecological modernization is based on the assumption that environmental health and economic growth can be win–win outcomes, through the application of market-based policies (such as emissions trading), technological advances, and what we might call good ecological governance. The latter element includes a collaborative, rather than oppositional approach on the part of the environmental movement (Mol, P.J. 2000), and, as Scott and Oelofse highlight, a technocratic orientation to the management of environmental protection. There is plenty of discursive space in the governance paradigm of ecological modernization for the absorption and domestication of popular demands for recognition, participation, and fair process. In this way, significant portions of the environmental justice agenda can effectively be colonized by ecological modernization, while substantive and distributive environmental justice continues to elude marginalized communities.

Conclusion: Environmental Justice and the Social in Citizenship

Activists have faced clear difficulties in transforming environmental justice ideals into robust public policy that enshrines its principles in the more formal dimensions of citizenship. Nevertheless, as an element in the political culture of resistance to neoliberal projects, the paradigm continues to provide an important conceptual fulcrum for various kinds of organizing and solidarity-building. Moreover, it remains attractive as a language with which to address economic and political power and in so doing open new spaces of debate in the public sphere. Indeed, in some jurisdictions, such as Canada, there is reason to believe that environmental justice is only beginning to catch on as a significant discourse for organizing dissent against dominant tendencies in environmental policy.

Putting aside questions of the trajectory of environmental justice as a movement, I return now to the questions posed at the outset of the analysis. While some of the answers to these questions are clearly intimated in my earlier treatment of the links between environmental justice and the politics of citizenship, further refinement will help relate these insights to the project of this volume. As a mode of organizing political mobilization around the related issues of ecological sustainability and social justice, how does the paradigm of environmental justice intensify, supplement, problematize or reconfigure the social in citizenship, and how might the understandings of environmental justice outlined in this chapter lead to new insights about the way that citizenship is embodied, performed and contested?

For a start, it seems most obvious that environmental justice has contributed to the (re)assertion of 'the social,' both in terms of redistribution and recognition, as a key site of the contested virtues, rights, and responsibilities associated with citizenship. To fine-tune our understanding of this *intensification* of the social via the politics of environmental justice, it is useful to return to the thematic schema for this book – that of investigating the relationships between struggles for redistribution and recognition. By now it should be clear that environmental justice is a site at which such relationships abound, but it should also be evident that there is a third crucial element in this mix: participation. Indeed, I have argued that participation, in the robust sense of identity formation around claiming the capacity for public judgment, is pivotal. Participation actively links the dimensions of redistribution and recognition, while drawing both into a broader politics of citizenship. Reading the social in citizenship in terms of a dynamic between redistributive and identity politics is substantially related to the way that material welfare and culture are (or are not) conceived of as *political* matters. Are these issues of public judgment or of private initiative and preference? In this sense, matters of redistribution or recognition are enfolded in questions regarding the character of democratic institutions and practices, as well as the relations of power delimiting the insides and outsides of the polity. Hence, the intensification of the social in citizenship, giving it a new lease on life in the face of neoliberal ideology, is part and parcel of a politics of radical democratization located in environmental justice.

It is important to consider the ways that the discourses and practices of environmental justice have simultaneously created spaces in which the social is supplemented, problematized, and reconfigured. On one level, *supplementation* occurs as environmental and social concerns become linked issues. So, following the aforementioned treatments of environmental citizenship offered by Newby, Valdivielso, and Smith, environment emerges as an element of citizenship either by following the path of the social in becoming another instance of an expanding set of rights and obligations (Newby 1996), or by becoming allied in some way to the defence and advancement of social rights and obligations (G. Smith 2005, Valdivielso 2005). There is certainly something of this kind of supplementation to the environmental justice movement, but what I have been arguing for in this chapter has much more the character of *problematization* or *reconfiguration*. How is citizenship altered when the social and the ecological are seen to be intrinsically and inextricably interwoven fields of justice and politics? Coming from a different angle, how is the social reshaped when issues of redistribution and recognition become embedded in an ecological dimension of citizenship?

With respect to the redistributive aspect of the social, bringing in an environmental dimension makes the traditional scenario of social welfare highly problematic. In the context of the welfare state, social citizenship meant access to a series of entitlements, essentially entailing a more equitable sharing of wealth throughout society. In the era of environmental justice, this economistic version of the social now seems narrow. Rather than simply challenging neoliberalism's erosion of the welfare state, environmental justice has opened a new terrain for social politics, where inequality is embedded in landscapes and neighbourhoods, and more generally, in the ecological metabolisms through which human society reproduces itself. Furthermore, environmental justice increasingly points towards an important scale shift, where the globally inequitable character of these metabolisms becomes increasingly untenable. As already noted, theorists of environmental citizenship, such as Sáiz (2005), Dobson (2003a), and Jelin (2000) have made similar conclusions regarding the role of environmental matters in scaling up the politics of citizenship, but an emerging global justice movement embodies that which their analyses largely fail to identify – the political agents demanding social and ecological justice across 'international' space, and hence occupying the incipient spaces of a global citizenship.

With respect to recognition, environmental justice has engendered or participated in another series of realignments in citizenship. Because it links up the social and the ecological in articulating citizen identity, environmental justice has given birth to a new kind of political space, or to a new way of embodying and performing citizenship. We might read this newness in terms of nature's presence/absence, where environmental justice *introduces* an ecological dimension to citizenship where none was present before. This reading would be consistent with the dominant perspectives in environmental citizenship, which generally seek to bring nature into citizenship theory and practice. Instead, it is perhaps more fruitful to read environmental justice as a way in which *existing* socioecological dimensions of citizenship are contested, and the power relations that serve to consolidate them are brought into the light of public scrutiny. I have previously referred to a deep-set dualism between society and nature in mainstream North American environmentalism. Rather than perceiving this dualism as an *absence* of nature in citizenship, it is more accurate to view it as one of the key socioecological frames for a politics of nature, and hence, for a particular understanding of citizenly identity, virtue and responsibility vis-à-vis nature. Other related frames include that of nature as a resource for society, where citizenship entails political engagement with notions of wise use or sustainable management; and that of nature as an object of possessive acquisition, deriving from Locke's philosophies of labour and property, where citizenship includes an important bundle of rights to protect each individual's private holdings of 'improved' nature. Less dichotomous versions of the nature–society relationship in regimes of citizenship might include a naturalistic nationalism, something like the 'blood and soil' discourse of Nazi Germany, and nature as commodity, where ecology is integrated with the social institutions of market relations and the citizen identity of consumer. Of course, a range of such framings of a society–nature relationship inhabits any existing regime of citizenship, but the point is that citizenship is (and in some sense has been since at least Aristotle) thoroughly imbued with *socio-ecological* qualities. What then, is so special about environmental justice?

Existing regimes of citizenship mostly have the effect of narrowing the space for democratic exchange with regard to nature. To the extent that nature is public in such regimes, it is the object of narrowly defined, universalizing political discourses, such as those of technocratic resource management, national security, and market value. In liberal citizenship, for instance, it is only in the private sphere (where the right to freedom of conscience is located) that more diverse specific understandings of nature (and the identities related to them) may be pursued. As such, alternate ways of embodying or performing the socioecological dimensions of collective existence are effectively rendered *'Other'* to citizenship. Environmental justice mobilizations, however, involve the performance of *both* specificity *and* publicity, such that nature is drawn into the domain of citizenship as the object of democratic exchange. To put it another way, environmental justice has provided a language for actively linking recognition (specificity) and participation (publicity) towards the cause of substantive and redistributive justice. In doing so, it has contributed to an important shift away from the individual rights of social citizenship towards the collective rights claims of ethnic or racial groups and communities. Moreover, the discourses and practices of environmental justice have tied identity to place, with quite astounding implications for the shape of the social. Even as a broader global movement, Schlosberg (2004) identifies the strengths of environmental justice in its network logic, which conserves the diversity of locally based organizations and cultural affinities. Along similar lines, Douglas Torgerson (2006) argues that environmental justice points towards 'the possibility of multiple points of intersection – hybrid spaces of both commonality and tension – between and among different cultural and political standpoints in a local-global nexus' (726). In this context, the social, while connected to a universalizing discourse of justice or human rights, is nevertheless importantly open to local realities at the same time.

Given this open-ended character, a democratic citizenship of the social entails/requires an inclusive engagement across diverse identities and landscapes. The social, as an expression of human collectives consisting of homogeneous political subjects located in abstract political space, is, in this sense, no longer tenable. Needless to say, the concept of bounded, uniform, national citizenships is likewise complicated. Furthermore, if the social remains in important part a question of redistribution or recognition, it is more importantly linked to the various ways that these two dimensions come together in ecological space, as citizen-subjects constitute themselves as simultaneously ecological beings. In this way, the social and the ecological become coeval dimensions of subjectivity and collectivity, enfolded into the material and symbolic relations located in a diverse set of struggles for livelihood, dignity, self-determination, and environmental sustainability.

Notes

1 Some examples include the Canadian Biotechnology Action Network (http://www.cban.ca/About/Environmental-Justice, accessed Nov. 2007), the Conservation Council of New Brunswick (http://conservationcouncil.ca/archives/2005/ejc-e.pdf, accessed Nov. 2007), and the Vancouver, B.C., Bus Riders' Union – the language of environmental justice is particularly present in their "Women in Transit" project (http://bru.vcn.bc.ca/women, accessed Nov. 2007).

2 Among the members are some of the most influential environmental NGOs in the U.K., such as Friends of the Earth, RSPB, Greenpeace, and the Environmental Law Foundation.

3 The 2007 publication of a landmark report entitled *Making the Case for Environmental Justice in Central and Eastern Europe* was realized through

collaboration between the Brussels-based Health and Environment Alliance, and the Centre for Environmental Policy and Law, located at the Central European University, in Budapest. The report is available at http://www.env-health.org/IMG/pdf/Making_the_case_for_environmental_justice.pdf (accessed Nov. 2007).

4 http://www.foei.org/index.php (accessed Oct. 2006). See also Doherty (2006) for a discussion of Friends of the Earth's commitment to issues of social justice.

5 http://viacampesina.org/main_en/index.php (accessed Oct. 2006).

6 http://www.earthrights.org/ (accessed Oct. 2006).

7 http://www.botany.uwc.ac.za/inforeep/EJNF.htm (accessed Oct. 2006).

8 http://www.olca.cl/oca/index.htm (accessed Oct. 2006).

9 Such is largely the case, e.g., with the discourses and practices of environmental impact assessment, where public consultations are highly conditioned by the scientific and technical languages that are mobilized in accordance with the end of depoliticizing decisions on environmental matters.

10 This assertion of place-based knowledge is most clearly applicable in the case of indigenous peoples, but the politics of knowledge has also been documented in other sectors of the movement (e.g., Di Chiro 2004, Novotny 1998).

11 The City as the Site of the Social

ENGIN F. ISIN

Admittedly, the city is difficult to define, and there are three reasons for this: historical, geographical, and theoretical. Each interpreter is embedded in an historical period that provides the perspective from which the city is seen. An Athenian in 594 BCE would likely have seen the city from the dominant perspective of that time – and thus would surely have been quite concerned about the struggle between aristocrats and peasants. As soon as there are epochal changes, however, the grounds shift and perspectives change. That same Athenian would have seen the city quite differently in 322 BCE and been for less certain about the meaning of being Athenian when the ancient Greek city began losing its identity. Imagine the city as seen during the thirteenth and fourteenth centuries in Europe. A 'European' would certainly expect some form of corporate existence, as symbolized by a charter and guildhall, and perhaps a territorial jurisdiction, symbolized most typically by an encircling wall. By the eighteenth century, however, that European would have been astonished to observe that most cities had lost their charters and their walls had crumbled away. Meanwhile, our trusty Athenian, who would most likely have been searching for some form of citizenship to define the city, would have been astounded by the city of seventeenth-century Europe by its lack of citizenship. Seeing all this from our own epoch, what qualities or properties would we say define the city as such? Historical variations create difficulties in defining the city.

The variations, however, are not only attributable to historical epochs, for there are significant differences across geographies within any given epoch. Returning to our Athenian, in 594 BCE she or he certainly would have recognized Sparta as a city, but as a different *kind* of city from Athens. The European in the thirteenth and fourteenth centuries would have understood the profound differences between Lübeck and Padua. Expanding the scope towards ancient Mayan cities, if indeed the inhabitants of Tikal knew about Teotihuacán, they would have considered Tikal to be a very different city from Teotihuacán. Similarly, there is no reason to imagine that someone of Nara, in eighth-century Japan, would have seen Bianzhou, in China, as similar (Southall 1998).

While describing the difficulties of defining the city and some historical and geographical problem in doing so, we are nonetheless at the same referring to an entity that is called 'the city.' While arguing difficulties of definition, we seem to hold an understanding of the city as such. How is this possible? That brings us to the theoretical reasons for the difficulty of defining the city. The assumption so far has been that in each epoch or region there was a unified understanding of the city and that the variations were across these epochs and regions. That assumption must now be called into question. In any given historical and geographical moment of the city, identified as ancient Athens during the reign of Cleisthenes, say, or Bianzhou during the T'ang Dynasty, the city actually remained indefinable because of the contesting and contestable perspectives from which to define it. The Athens of Cleisthenes is difficult to define because Athens itself was an object of struggle among oligarchs, warriors, tyrants, and peasants (Lévêque and Vidal-Naquet 1964). Each and any combination thereof would produce a particular viewpoint on the events and forces defining the city at that moment. The accounts that we have inherited bear all the marks of these struggles. According to such accounts, Bianzhou during the T'ang Dynasty was an object of struggle at least between aristocrats and bureaucrats (Heng 1999). It is not possible to inherit an account that will have somehow jumped outside history, and it is impossible to jump outside our own history. This double articulation – investment of accounts that we have inherited and our own investment in those accounts – constitutes a theoretical perspective from which we see the city and that theoretical perspective is impossibly partial and invariably fragmented.

Yet, just because the city is difficult to define for these historical, geographical, and theoretical reasons does not mean that we have not attempted to understand the city as such. Indeed, the city as such has been defined as 'war machine,' 'space of citizenship,' 'cradle of democracy,' 'dense and heterogeneous settlement,' 'space of accumulation,' 'text,' 'sign' and so on. These 'as such' conceptions represent both the need to impose an order on cities and also a unified understanding of what is impossibly partial and invariably fragmented – the city. That our understandings are partial and fragmented does not mean that they are without value. It does, however, mean that often the failure to recognize their impartiality, either by the producers or users of these concepts, results in misunderstanding their limits. Yet, the question remains: despite these difficulties, how do we understand the city as such? Three modern scholars of the city, Fustel de Coulanges, Max Weber, and Lewis Mumford, each in his own way, struggled to hold an understanding of the city as such. What unites them is the struggle itself and the distinction they made between the city as *civitas* (virtual) and as *urbs* (actual).

Civitas and Urbs

Fustel was the first modern scholar to make a distinction between civitas and urbs. It is not that he believed he was the first. His argument was that this distinction was inherent in Greek and Roman thought. Fustel identified *civitas* as the religious and political association of families and tribes (1864: 126ff), while *urbs* was the actual place of assembly, the dwelling place and, above all, the sanctuary. For Fustel the ancients were deliberate and consistent in making this distinction, and they never reduced civitas to urbs. What is the importance of this distinction? The ancients maintained their belief in the existence of the city as an association, even if it did not have a corresponding spatial form to it. But the city's existence as association was much more than symbolic or 'ideal.' Because of this fundamental difference, Fustel believed that we could not infer the city as such from its spatial characteristics like concentration, arrangements, and elements of its buildings, bridges, and walls. Fustel investigated the city as *both* civitas and urbs.

Fustel considered the essence of the city to be 'religious.' When various tribes agreed to 'unite' and have the same worship, they founded the city as a sanctuary for this common worship. We may well disagree with Fustel, but his distinction between civitas and urbs points to the recognition of the difficulty of defining the city if we reduce various properties of the city to its definition or deduce its definition from those various properties. This distinction recognizes that the city cannot be defined by the properties of various cities but that the city as such can be grasped. But then what do we do when we disagree with an interpretation of the city and yet agree that it cannot be revealed merely by properties of various cities? On what basis can we have a dialogue on the city as such?

Max Weber (1909, 1921) tackled this problem with his analytical tool, the 'ideal type,' which recognizes that concepts are heuristic devices to order various empirical materials. Weber (1909: 385) argued that 'a genuinely analytic study comparing the stages of development of the ancient polis with those of the medieval city would be welcome and productive ... Of course ... such a comparative study would not aim at finding "analogies" and "parallels," as is done by those engrossed in the currently fashionable enterprise of constructing general schemes of development. The aim should, rather, be precisely the opposite: to identify and define the individuality of each development, the characteristics which made the one conclude in a manner so different from that of the other. This done, one can then determine the causes which led to these differences.' Here Weber was clearly opposed to the collection of comparative empirical data to fill a universal and developmental scheme. More emphatically, Weber (1921) insisted that specific qualities such as the presence of the wall or the autonomous administration of autonomous lawmaking couldn't be taken as qualities that define the city as such. It is evident that Weber saw the question of defining the city to be different from the question of developing ideal types. While developing various typologies of the city such as 'consumer city,' 'producer city,' Weber still insisted that these do not define the city but provided heuristic concepts with which to develop interpretations. If these types did not define the city as such, how did Weber define the city?

Weber used the distinction that Fustel emphasized between civitas and urbs and argued that the city was not only an association but it had developed a collective identity represented and embodied by citizenship (Weber 1921: 1245). The city was the city only insofar as it developed, cultivated, and made possible a legal and political status of belonging, that is, citizenship. It is in that sense that Weber argued that only the occidental city could be called the city since the oriental city lacked a corporate identity embodied in citizenship. For Weber the occidental city as such was citizenship. Although Weber can be questioned about this distinction between the occidental and oriental city (Isin 2002b), his theoretical insistence is unmistakable: while it is difficult to define the city by comparing empirical properties, it is still possible, if not worthwhile, to understand the city as such.

In *City in History*, Lewis Mumford (1961) maintained a Weberian understanding of the essence of the city as citizenship. He also used the distinction made by Fustel between civitas and urbs. Moreover, Mumford also implicitly endorsed the Weberian distinction between the occidental and oriental city, associating the latter with oriental despotism. (We don't need to deal with sociological orientalism here.) Thus, Mumford argued, the modern occidental city had resuscitated the despotic and oriental city by reducing citizens to subjects. His portrayal of the metropolis and megalopolis in *City in History* maintained his basic typology in *The Culture of Cities* (1938). Mumford was able to see the emerging outlines of the megalopolis because of his insistence on the essence of the city as civitas rather than a focus on urbs. Mumford (1961) was critical of Louis Wirth (1938), who in his view, attempted to deduce civitas from urbs.

What Fustel, Weber, and Mumford demonstrate is not the difficulty of defining the city but the significance of focusing on its essence in a *longue durée* history. If indeed the essence of the city is citizenship, as Weber argued, then the question remains whether the occidental city is the only city that can claim to have invented citizenship, as Weber also argued, or that the oriental city can also make an alternative claim. The answer to that question will unfold only through civilizational longue durée histories.

What I draw from Fustel, Weber, and Mumford is the distinction they made between civitas and urbs. When we speak about 'the city' often what we invoke is civitas. When we speak about cities we often invoke their specific characteristics. While civitas and urbs are irreducible to each other, they are also co-dependent: we cannot understand one without the other. I am convinced that the problem of civitas and urbs that Fustel, Weber, and Mumford articulated is akin to the philosophical problem of ontological difference as developed by Heidegger and taken up by Deleuze as the difference between the virtual and the actual (see Isin 2007). When we speak about 'cities' we refer to actual places. Clearly, 'the city' incorporates what we know about specific cities but it is somehow not reducible to them. Put another way, the city is more than the sum of its parts (cities).

This chapter argues for theorizing the city as such as the site of the social. If we are recasting the social in citizenship, the city cannot be a background or foreground of our investigations but it must be the ground on which citizenship is recast. We now need to discuss some basic ideas about conceptualizing the city as such as the site of the social. We then need a brief history (or more accurately historical ontology) of the city to illustrate two essential rights: *rights of the city* and *rights to the city*. Then we can draw some practical conclusions for policy and politics and juxtapose the idea of 'local' citizenship (rights of the city) against 'translocal' citizenship (rights to the city).

The City as the Site of the Social

Understanding the city as such is always under the shadow of Aristotle. (*Politics* is about the city as the site of the social despite the ideological translation of *polis* as 'the state' in modern languages.) Aristotle arrives at the essence of 'man' as being political by interpreting the 'constitutions' of various cities. His focus is on the city as a site that makes things possible rather than as a space in which things happen. The city is the site of the social insofar as it enables the social formation of citizens as rights-claimants (capable of being governed and to govern). Yet, as Arendt (1951) argued, the social and political mean radically different things for ancients and moderns. How does the *modern* city enable the social formation of rights-claimants capable of articulating rights? How does the modern city, for example, enable the formation of a subject who demands access to public places for people with disabilities? How does the city cultivate a subject who demands the right to be in public when wearing a veil or turban or carrying a ceremonial dagger? These may be modern questions but both ancient and modern questions presuppose and produce citizens as rights-claimants, and this is what I want to draw attention to with the city as such.

The city as the site of the social is key to understanding the formation of the kind of political subject that is a citizen who is the nucleus of political life. The city is the site through which the lives of people are organized, assembled together, and rendered meaningful. The city is the site through which socialization into various identities occurs, and it is the site through which individuals develop both their individuality and their sociality. I am using the term *through which* rather than *where* to indicate that the conception of the city as the site of the social does not only refer to its actual form with a spatially enclosed structure (urbs) but also includes its virtual form as relations, symbols, imaginaries, representations, categories, ideas, and ideals (civitas). The city is not a container in which social relations happen. I am concerned about the city as a site through which social relations are produced, reproduced, and transformed. This is akin to 'the city as a difference machine,' which I developed elsewhere (Isin 2002b). I have aimed to historically demonstrate how the city has been a battleground for various social groups that come into existence through it, and I call that battleground 'the site of the social' (cf. Isin 2005, 2007; Schatzki 2002).

It is impossible to develop the idea of citizens as rights-claimants without considering a history of the ancient Greek city and its subsequent Roman, medieval, and early modern variations. In much of that history, citizenship was articulated as belonging to the city and the social and political rights that derived from that belonging. In other words, rights of citizens who belonged to the city were derived from the *rights of the city* itself. The exact nature and extent of the rights of the city were matters of struggle throughout history up to and including the nineteenth and twentieth centuries. While the *rights of the city* continued to be contested matters in the twentieth century, various social, economic, and political transformations engendered new kinds of rights where claiming *rights to the city* became dominant modes of inclusion, belonging, and democratic engagement. The difference between rights of the city (involving attributes of loyalty, virtue, civism, discipline, and subsidiarity) and rights to the city (involving attributes of autonomy, appropriation, difference, security) is key to understanding the city as the site that enables the social formation of citizens as rights-claimants (Isin 2000a, 2002b, 2006).

The City and Citizenship

Although it is quite well known, it is worthwhile to visit briefly the historical relationship between citizenship and the city. There are different ways of visiting this relationship, but in my view the scholar who understood this relationship best and moved it to the centre of his thought was Max Weber (1921). By investigating the history of the city ranging from Mesopotamian and Egyptian cities to Chinese and Indian cities, Weber concluded that the associational character of the city was the foundation of citizenship. It was through the city that humans developed their associational dispositions of solidarity and the government that enabled them to develop the city itself as an association. But whereas in Greece and Rome this associational character evolved into the city as a legal corporation, other civilizations such as Indian, Chinese, and Islamic did not manage to transform the city into a legal entity. (The sociological orientalism of this thesis is not our concern here.) Thus, Weber concluded, and it has been the received view ever since, that it was in Greek and Roman cities that the special status of being *of* the city emerged: citizenship. In other words, those who have this special status acquire it only by belonging to the city. Other features that are necessary but not sufficient conditions of being citizens such as being male, eighteen years of age, and a warrior would mean nothing if one did not belong to the city. Belonging to the city, and belonging to the city alone, was the necessary condition of being a citizen. Certain virtues of belonging to the city came to be valued more than others such as sacrificing oneself for the city, working for the city, and participating in governing the city. How these virtues were articulated and how they evolved were, of course, different in both Greek and Roman cities, but the essential element of the relationship between the city and citizenship was such that the latter as status was intimately linked to the former.

With the decline of Greek cities and later of Roman cities the status that derived from being of the city also declined. In European history, therefore, the period in which various Germanic tribes ruled is considered a 'regress' or 'recess' of the city in history. As Weber (1921), Henri Pirenne (1925), and Lewis Mumford (1938) have told us, it was only when the city revived in the tenth and eleventh centuries that the special status of citizenship became possible. The importance of this argument is that the origins of citizenship do not only go back to ancient Greeks and Romans but also to medieval European cities. This is often overlooked since medieval citizenship never reached the lofty images of Greek and Roman citizenship. Yet, as Weber was the first to emphasize, modern European citizenship may well owe more to modest and mundane citizenship practices in medieval cities, guilds, universities, and corporations than anything else. But this was not without a struggle between the city and the nascent state, and it has been told and retold ever since as the struggle for a special form of citizenship, of the city versus the state. Fernand Braudel (1988) and Charles Tilly (1992, 1994) have told these struggles with specific inflections of their own. Braudel saw the struggle as a specific version of a universal battle between the city and the state, while Tilly focused more on the relationship with European capitalism and militarism. Anyway, it is impossible to agree on a singular interpretation of the struggle between the city and the state in European history between the eleventh and sixteenth centuries. It was during that period that many southern European but also some northern European cities developed certain rights and privileges that were wrested from the state such as taxation, minting coins, trade, and even maintaining armed forces. The specific combination of these rights varied from region to region and city to city, if not from state to state, but gradually the state became the triumphant political form that usurped all of these various rights and combined them within a territorial sovereign system by the seventeenth century (Poggi 1978, 1990).

The story of the seventeenth and eighteenth centuries as the age of absolutist states always features how the privileges of cities and by extension the privileges of those who resided in them were curtailed. All the various forms of association that had emerged in cities such as guilds, universities, companies, and cities themselves were brought under the government of the state as a sovereign entity. But the corporation as the expressive form of city privileges also made an ineluctable entry into history, which was eventually revived. Otto Gierke (1934), Fredric Maitland (2003), Anthony Black (1984), and Gerald Frug (1980) have provided eminent histories of these corporations. The upshot of those histories is that legal thought invented the corporation and literally incorporated the city into the state. Obviously, the rights and privileges of the city were formulated in legal practice as de facto rights of the city through which its residents – citizens – gained special status and thus rights. It was these rights that were usurped by the state through incorporation.

When in the nineteenth century various legal reforms came into being in both northern and southern European states, these by and large focused on realigning the privileges of the city and its relations with the state. There was no turning back to the arrangement where there were virtual if not actual sovereign rights and privileges of the city expressed in its corporate forms, but there was also no turning back to the era of the absolutist state, as it proved impossible to govern the growing complexities of the city. Thus, the city was reconceived increasingly in governmental terms within the state, and the struggles shifted their focus from rights and privileges to powers of the city as a corporation within the state. Still, in essence, those who resided in the city were deeply intertwined with its powers in such a way that the city prescribed, to an extent, their citizenship. However, that citizenship as a status of rights and privileges was no longer lodged in the city as their locus but in the sovereign state. Once the city was invented as a legal corporation combining its virtual and actual properties, the rights of the city became determinant elements of the rights of its inhabitants. Therefore, struggling for the rights of inhabitants automatically meant struggling for the rights of the city.

Since the nineteenth century the situation and the legal alignment between the city and the state have remained stable. While the struggles continued and the powers of the city were always at the forefront of these struggles, the alignment and the relationship remained the same in many legal systems and achieved a rather universal status. This does not mean that the distribution and allocation of powers between the state and the city are the same everywhere, but it does mean that despite differences, some arrangement between the city and the state exists to allocate differentiated powers (Loughlin 1986, 1996a, 1996b).

Rights of the City

It is this relationship that I would like to describe as the *rights of the city.* The city defined as association acquires its legal and political existence and status and it is from this that the status of those who belong to and reside in it is derived. The rights of the city as a sovereign and autarkic entity confer upon those who belong to it rights that otherwise would not accrue. This principle of the rights of the city continued to be invented and reinvented in modern legal history. When we investigate the struggles between states and cities in medieval societies, for example, we observe that the principles of sovereignty and autarky were objects of the most intense contestations in legal and political if not military fields. As mentioned earlier, these struggles were particularly intense between the seventeenth and eighteenth centuries, when the ascendancy of the European state was prominent. These struggles are well documented and constitute some of the liveliest debates among prominent nineteenth- and twentieth-century historians such as Fustel de Coulanges (1864), Lewis Mumford (1961), Charles Tilly (1992, 1994), Fernand Braudel (1988), and others (Spruyt 1994). These struggles between the city and the state about the rights of the city and the status of those who belong to it continued through modernity and the ascendancy of the modern state. Throughout the twentieth century loyalty, virtue, civism, discipline, and subsidiarity emerged as fundamental principles of the rights of the city within states (Isin 2000a). The city then emerged as that space where loyalty, virtue, civism, and the discipline of citizens were cultivated with the appropriate measure of its rights (subsidiarity). Many struggles we are familiar with ranging from traditional struggles such as governmental powers of cities to more recent struggles over amalgamations of various municipalities by senior levels of government can be considered examples of such struggles over the rights of the city. Citizenship in this mode was (and is) very much understood as the rights that the citizen derived from belonging to the city as a legal association. Even in its modern form, where belonging to the city does not confer any formal rights or status to the citizen (as belonging to the state does), belonging to the city confers substantive rights by virtue of being a space with a special government and legal jurisdiction. In fact, much of the debate over the decline of civic engagement in the twentieth century concerns the rights of the city. The assumption is that the decline in interest in city government is a reflection of the decline of the rights of the city as a municipal corporation and thus its ability to cultivate loyalty, virtue, civism, and discipline.

Rights to the City

While struggles over the rights of the city continued to evolve and were various, the *rights to the city* can be said to have existed from the very beginning but have received much less attention especially in the way I have formulated it. I have studied many cases of cities in history where various social groups while being outside the city still waged and won struggles for rights to the city – by maintaining property and other rights. In medieval cities, for example, itinerant merchants or scholars held special rights not of any specific city but rights to the city as such no matter where the city happened to exist. Similarly, in Greek and Roman cities there were practices through which citizens held certain rights to the city rather than any specific city such as Athens or Sparta. Admittedly, these rights not only received scant attention but also were themselves scant. Nonetheless, we can argue that the movement of rights to the city is not a contemporary issue alone. Yet, I believe that with those processes that came to be called, with all their attendant difficulties, postmodernization, globalization, and neoliberalization, we are witnessing the transformation of various social struggles into struggles over rights to the city.

These struggles can be seen through four distinct but interrelated themes: *autonomy, appropriation, difference,* and *security* (Isin 2006). The theme of autonomy that runs through the nineteenth and early twentieth centuries becomes not only a perspective from which to see the city at present but also to interpret the city in history. While the theme of autonomy highlights the independence of the city from the state in making certain decisions, it also comes to mean some form of determination by those who claim rights to the city. It often takes the form of creating 'temporary autonomous zones' in and through which certain rights-claims are made whose source of legal authority is neither the state nor the municipality. Take, for example, the two major issues of city declarations against the nuclear arms race and the proliferation or provision of sanctuary rights for refugees such as cities of refuge (Nyers 2006a). Anne McNevin, for example, argues that the struggles of *Sans-Papiers* (those without papers) involved the articulation of such rights (to the city) that did not exist before (2006a). As McNevin says, 'the strategies of the Sans-Papiers reflect the reconfigured spatial practices in and through which their identities as immanent outsiders have been constructed. In this respect their struggle is in, of and for the city. The dimensions of this city are cast in the context of a global political economy and the transnational practices of a colonial and neoliberal state' (147). Similarly, the appropriation of different forms of capital in and through the city or, rather, the city as a space of appropriation is also a strong theme of modern social and political thought on the city (Varsanyi 2006). Such appropriation again involved more than struggling for rights of the city but of rights of social groups appropriating spaces of the city. The movements about squatting rights and No One Is Illegal are examples of such rights to the city (Nyers 2003). Moreover, that the city, especially the modern city, was the gathering together of different social groups and the successful, that is, democratic, negotiation of their differences is among the most enduring but also recent examples of rights to the city (Isin and Siemiatycki 2002). Finally, the security of groups in the city also involved more than rights of the city but featured rights to the city in the sense of its security and freedom from arbitrary and precarious domination. Likewise, the securitization of states is by and large played and worked out through the city (Isin and Rygiel 2007).

I suggest that autonomy, appropriation, difference, and security remain essential attributes of the rights to the city. Yet, these attributes are not necessarily harmonious attributes. They engender tensions and conflicts. The autonomy that certain social groups seek threatens the appropriations of already formed social groups. (Consider struggles over 'gentrification' and 'gated communities.') The valorization of difference and diversity results in increased tensions around security. (Consider struggles over the building of mosques and their increasing entanglement with 'securitization.') It is through these tensions that the city becomes a site of struggles whose aims become articulating rights to the city. To understand the city at any given moment involves an attempt to grasp the seemingly infinite multiplicity of fractures opened by these tensions inherent in the city as a site of the social.

What is the essence of the difference between rights of the city (loyalty, virtue, civism, discipline, and subsidiarity) and rights to the city (autonomy, appropriation, difference, and security)? The articulation and claiming of rights of the city and rights to the city demand different practices. While rights of the city essentially revolve around legal rights and changes in law, rights to the city involve social rights and changes in norms. The city is the site of the social in this precise sense of *both* enabling the formation of social groups as claimants of rights that are not necessarily restricted to the rights of the city and of making use of rights that originate from the city. The city as the site of the social combines two distinct but related set of rights that I am describing as rights of the city and rights to the city. This is a fundamental difference that enables us to see how the struggles for redistribution and recognition (which are the foundations of citizenship as claims to justice) are essentially intertwined with struggles for the rights of and to the city as the site of the social. To understand the city as the site of the social *is* to investigate the concrete ways in which struggles for redistribution and recognition take shape through the articulations of these rights.

Struggles beyond Redistribution and Recognition

We have already suggested in this book that perhaps it is time to reverse the Marshallian sequence of rights as civil, political, and social and argue that citizenship is social before it is civil and political. Citizenship is social in the deep sense of that term as involving a way of coexisting that is inextricably co-dependent. If the city is the site of the social, as I suggest, then the city and citizenship are related and this is more than a historical contingency. I have already suggested that the city as a site of the social works insofar as it enables the social formation of rights-claimants capable of articulating entitlements and demands. The themes rights of the city and rights to the city then are essential elements of the city as the site of the social. It is through the city that individuals become social (understanding the self as a co-dependent entity coexistent with others), and becoming social is the ground on which civil and political rights become possible. In turn, it is a civil and political existence that presents justice as questions. Since coexistence both presupposes and engenders solidarity as well as conflict and competition, questions of justice are inherent in social existence.

It is against this background that we need to revisit the widely recognized argument that civic and political engagement has declined. Often three reasons dominate the argument that the loyalty to and identification of citizens with the city has declined: (1) there are other sources of identification such as professional occupation and consumption that are not territorially contained and are extensively organized stretching across delimited borders; (2) the city has both morphologically and governmentally become fragmented and is more difficult to identify with; (3) the increased spatial mobility of certain segments of the citizen body has reduced loyalty and identification to any one city. As a result of these three, it is argued that the citizen is able to conduct herself in various sites such as the professions, the workplace, and the Internet that have become more dominating spheres of virtue than the city. The citizen learns to create herself in a multiply situated manner rather than in a singular place or mode through mobility, cyberspace, and differentiated media. Moreover, many services that the city used to deliver according to the subsidiarity principle have either been privatized or shifted to other levels and types of government. As well, the institutions of the discipline of strangers and outsiders have either been shifted elsewhere or transformed into new modes of control and surveillance. As a result, the city may have become an empty shell whose territory marks out what were once the meaningful boundaries of the political. I shall argue that rather than becoming an empty shell, the city has become a medium through which rights to the city are still negotiated. That is why a distinction between rights of the city and right to the city is crucial. It enables us to differentiate the city as a legal entity with fixed territorial boundaries and as a non-legal *site* for the condensation of social relations. If the former gets tangled in issues of the rights of the city (e.g., taxation, voting, participation, service delivery), the latter redefines civic and political engagement across a wide variety of issues and boundaries (e.g., gentrification, building mosques, surveillance).

We have stated in chapter 1 that 'when people mobilize for legalizing same-sex marriage, rally for social housing, protest welfare rate cuts, debate employment insurance, advocate for the decriminalization of marijuana, wear attire such as turbans or headscarves in public spaces, seek affirmative action programs, or demand better health care access and services, they do not imagine themselves as struggling for the maintenance or expansion of social, cultural, or sexual citizenship rights. Instead, they invest in whatever issues seem most related and closest to their social lives, and dedicate their time and energy accordingly.' We drew two conclusions from this. First, these were irreducibly social struggles and warned against economism and culturalism. Second, such social struggles enable people to enact themselves as citizens as well as engage in questions of justice. Now, I can add a third conclusion by stating that these struggles are impossible to wage without the city as the site of the social.

We can give examples from struggles over same-sex marriage to the rights of patients that are not simply struggles over redistribution or recognition but struggles over rights to the city and are organized, enacted, performed, and articulated through the city. Some of those examples are already in this book especially exemplified in chapters by Cowen, Bilge, Latta, and Rygiel. I would argue that many social struggles are now significantly struggles over rights to the city (Bell and Binnie 2004, Fenster 2005, Mitchell 2003, Ruppert 2006, Secor 2003). Rather than struggles over rights that derive from belonging to the city, many social groups have struggled over rights to the city by, what I would call, staging or enacting themselves through the city. For groups to enact themselves through the city means to organize, assemble, appropriate, stage, symbolize, and imagine themselves, in short, constitute themselves as social groups, by claiming rights to and through the city and using various technologies that bridge the gap between their actual and virtual presences. (The dichotomies such as city against countryside, city against nature, and urban against rural, are not sensible or helpful. Social struggles involving the countryside, the rural, or nature are organized and enacted through the city and are mediated by it.)

The effect of these struggles is that they are not only about loyalty, virtue, civism, discipline and subsidiarity (rights of the city) but more about autonomy, appropriation, difference, and security (rights to the city). This has implications for recasting the social in citizenship.

Translocal Citizenship

The city as such is the site of the social. The city produces citizens as rights-claimants. These rights are of two kinds: rights of the city and rights to the city. The rights of the city are articulated through five distinct but interrelated themes of loyalty, virtue, civism, discipline, and subsidiarity. These rights define local citizenship, which is bounded by, contained in, and expressed through a territorial jurisdiction. By contrast, the rights to the city are expressed through four, also distinct and interrelated themes of autonomy, appropriation, difference, and security. These rights define translocal citizenship, which is unbounded, unbundled, and extraterritorial. These themes of the *rights of the city* and *rights to the city* are neither mutually exclusive nor complementary but often-conflictual 'goods' of the city that make it the social site par excellence. Today, those involved in the politics of and policy towards the city practically and intuitively understand these goods and work through them. The task of social and political thought is to express and describe that practical and intuitive understanding. What are the implications of such an understanding of the city and recasting the social in citizenship?

Throughout this book the chapter authors articulate different ways of tackling the conflict between redistribution and recognition and stress the difficulty of maintaining such a distinct analytical difference in social struggles concerning rights and citizenship. By considering the city as the site of the social, I have aimed to demonstrate that the city is fundamental in recasting the social in citizenship. Now I wish to turn to a few concrete examples.

Consider housing as a policy site. Such a policy site rarely, if at all, is considered to be an aspect of social citizenship, let alone citizenship. Various activist groups have argued in the past that housing should be considered a social right but that has always faced stiff resistance. What if we expand the notion of housing from being merely a shelter into a right that defines not only a right to housing (politics) but also a right to housing that is, let's say, environmentally sustainable (ethics), *and* even socially pleasurable (aesthetics)? Here we see social, environmental, and cultural rights colliding through politics, aesthetics, and ethics and various scales of policy that are currently kept discrete and contiguous. Similarly, when immigration policy is defined as a state policy, the housing of immigrants is then left to 'lower' scales of government. Yet, if the right to housing, and more importantly, the right to environmentally sustainable *and* socially pleasurable housing is considered to be a class of rights, which that I have described as rights to the city, then we begin to see that compartmental policy and politics, which consider immigration as a state-level policy and housing as local-level, are deeply inadequate and inhibiting. Why should immigrants not have the right to housing that eliminates automobile dependency, reduces energy consumption, curbs greenhouse emissions, and facilitates access to social amenities and everyday pleasures by virtue of its *actual* design? That these policy sites are kept separate results in desocialization: the demands that citizens (in this case 'immigrants') make about housing, commuting, and consumption are considered private and separate claims *to* markets. Moreover, policies act as containers: they contain issues and subjects within territorial, cultural, ethnic, and other boundaries. If indeed the city is the site through which human lives hang together, the coexistence and co-dependence that this implies belies such demands being private and market-based claims. They are indeed social demands, arising from social situations of citizens and producing social consequences. These situations and consequences are inherently translocal and overflow the boundaries that are set up to contain them (Ma 2002).

Similarly, consider the controversy over wearing certain symbolically charged attire in public places. To split such acts into redistribution or recognition and interpret them as demands for tolerance, accommodation, or recognition belies the fact that these acts may well have originated from social inequalities such as lack of access to social services and the attendant consequences of alienation, disfranchisement, and misrecognition. Not investigating the social foundation and social consequences of social acts and interpreting them as 'religious,' 'cultural,' or 'ethnic' acts not only desocializes but also essentializes them. Thus, translocal and multiply situated identities are contained within boundaries. This often results in irresolvable political (and policy) debates over where to 'draw the line' concerning such acts, which displaces social and political questions onto other disconnected, hopelessly reductionist, and essentialist debates. When such acts make claims on the city as the site of the social, they ought to be interpreted as rights to the city in the forms of appropriation, autonomy, difference, and security. What that means is that such acts and the way in which they have been interpreted have to be understood within the context of the practices that constitute the city as the site of the social. Such investigations would not always begin with already accepted terms and categories that contain acts. Rather, they would focus on why such terms and categories have come to acquire strategic values of containment for specific groups involved in the struggle and how these values are produced through *actual* spaces.

Clearly, the current organizational structure of policy and politics does not correspond with the complexities of the intersections between the social and the political and the properties of the city as the site of the social and its translocal relationships. Recasting the social in citizenship at a minimum means to investigate not only traditional rights *of* the city in constituting citizens but also their rights *to* the city as a constitutive element of citizenship.

If indeed existing structures and institutions are inadequate to conceive the city as the site of the social and to differentiate between rights of the city and rights to the city, how can we imagine institutions and structures that are more appropriate? I will end this chapter with a proposal on translocal citizenship and the formation of translocal authorities. I have mentioned that often the debates over the rights of the city get displaced into the sharing and distribution of powers between central and local (or municipal) authorities. Since the sovereignty of the state is organized as an exclusive and hierarchical territory, the rights of the city are always constituted within that framework as a territorial container. The language of central versus local authorities and centralization versus decentralization dominates such debates. While local authorities constituted as territorial containers may serve to deliver certain services that are inherently local such as infrastructure, many other services are translocal in character. This is, of course, the well-known subsidiarity principle: the service is delivered at the most appropriate scale. This principle assumes a hierarchical and exclusive relationship between various 'scales' of government (Isin 2007). Since the rights to such services also inherit a translocal character, they often take the form of rights to the city as such rather than to a specific city or locality. For such rights it might be more appropriate to create 'translocal authorities.' Such authorities would come into being when a social group constitutes itself by appropriating the city as the site of the social and whose claims involve translocal rights: rights that cannot be granted by the existing territorial jurisdictions (Isin and Turner 2007). Marisol García (2006: 753), for example, argues that for this reason we cannot place too much emphasis on 'urban citizenship.' As long as we understand urban citizenship as being solely about rights of the city she is certainly right. But if we differentiate rights of the city from rights to the city, then urban citizenship can surely include translocal rights that cannot be obtained through or contained by the rights of the city (i.e., the rights that the city can confer within its jurisdiction). If we conceive translocal citizenship as those rights that are articulated as rights to the city, then new avenues begin to open up. Those social groups that can constitute themselves as translocal, can claim both representation and taxation powers. In modern states all deliberative assemblies are structured on the basis of territorial containers. The representation and taxation of translocal authorities would, however, radically alter the constitution of deliberative politics. Translocal authorities do not need to be contained within states either. As such organizations as Doctors Without Borders or Reporters Without Borders illustrate, translocal forms of citizenship organized through the city as the site of the social transcend state boundaries. But currently such organizations remain as 'charity' organizations, and there are no formal ways of recognizing them with taxation and representation. Similarly, one can argue that homelessness is a translocal phenomenon. If there is a social group that constitutes itself as a translocal authority then it can use resources that come from various scales to address the issue of homelessness. Those activists who spend considerable energies and investment in various scales of government find themselves being shifted from scale to scale. Instead, they can focus those energies and investments on the translocal authority constituted to deal with it. Of course, how certain groups should be recognized and legally constituted as translocal authorities, what powers of representation and taxation they should have, and their longevity are immensely complex issues and should be properly the objects of political negotiation and deliberation.

Are there historical examples of translocal authorities? We might think of guilds, universities, chapters, associations, and unions as examples of translocal authorities, but the legal framework in which they are created and the traditions that they follow make it impossible for them to act as translocal authorities. Thus, while it is important that the legal tradition, which has been traced by Frug (1980), has to be recognized and understood, to create such authorities we also need to invent a new legal form that goes beyond the theory of corporations that dominated political thought since at least the fourteenth century. It would also go beyond conceiving associational life *only* through intermediate institutions between the individual and the state – as a tradition of social and political thought ranging from Alexis de Tocqueville to Emile Durkheim has understood since the nineteenth century. Many will object that the formation of such translocal authorities is unwieldy and likely to generate more bureaucracy and confusion. But such deliberation and negotiation and the formation of new authorities may well invigorate citizenship politics much more than the incessant repetition about the decline of active citizenship. In fact, rather than a decline of citizenship there has been a considerable proliferation and multiplication of citizenship politics that does not find expression in the arcane sovereign structures of the state that are built on territorial appropriations and its machinations.

Acknowledgments

I am grateful to Alex Latta, Deborah Cowen, Xiaobei Chen, and Danielle Juteau for their insightful comments on an earlier draft.

12 Conclusion: The Socius of Citizenship

ENGIN F. ISIN

We have emphasized throughout this book that governing democratic states and societies is undergoing significant transformations and that these transformations are well rehearsed in debates over securitization, globalization, neoliberalization, and postmodernization in the social sciences and humanities in the past twenty years or so (Harvey 1989, Hirst and Thompson 1999, Huysmans 2006, Nyers 2006a). Whatever the disagreements among scholars about these transformations, their causes, consequences, and genealogies, as well as their naming, it is reasonable to assume a convergence on the idea that governing states and societies today is not confined to contiguous and contained territories. The world in which we govern ourselves today is a world of intense and mediated communications; movements of people, goods, and money; and social movements across and through boundaries, frontiers, and borders which themselves are rapidly shifting, changing, and mutating (Amin 2002). Each chapter in this book attests to one or another aspect of these transformations and investigates their attendant impacts on the ways in which social relations develop and unfold. It has also long been recognized that governing democratic states increasingly requires incorporating (through loyalty, belonging, attachment, allegiance, investment, fidelity) subjects into their own governance (Foucault 1982, Rose 1996b). But, given the recent transformations, the incorporation of the subject into her or his state is increasingly envous – mostly because of these transformations (Mann 1987, Turner 1990). The state-citizen and nation-citizen couplets do not operate in straightforward ways, if they ever did (Clarke et al. 2007). If creating citizens is the condition of making states, governing is a project of managing across emerging and mutating subjects (both citizens and non-citizens), scales, and sites of citizenship.

This way of describing citizenship reveals that perhaps citizenship is social before it is civil or political. That state authorities must invest in subjects, citizens and non-citizens, is hardly a new insight. But that state authorities increasingly find themselves implicated in governing citizens and non-citizens through a growing number of sites makes social governance or governing the social a significant object of governing the state. The habitus of the citizen and non-citizen as the object of government brings into being various sites of government all of the following: eating, smoking, housing, commuting, romancing, reproducing, consuming, speaking habits, entertaining, learning, travelling, and leisure, sexual, and clothing habits and actions. These various sites of the social become objects of government insofar as they also are sites of contestation, resistance, differentiation, and identification. Conversely, they become sites of struggle insofar as they become objects of government. The argument that perhaps citizenship is social before it is civil or political reverses the well-known Marshallian conception (1950) of citizenship as being civil and political before it is social. Marshall made his assumption in two ways. First, by historically considering civil and political rights as precursors of social rights, he presumed that civil and political rights were prior. Second, by substantively considering civil and political rights as necessary but not sufficient conditions of citizenship that are made possible only by social rights, Marshall accorded primacy to civil and political rights.

Janine Brodie demonstrates that this points to at least two conceptions of the social. The first concerns the dense fabric of relations that constitute humans as social beings who coexist with their fellow beings in and through conflict *and* cooperation that undergird norms, laws, and customs. She notes that this sense of the social derives from Latin *socius*, fellowship. Here socius as fellowship is understood not *only* as the locus of sociability but also of conflict, tension, and strife (Derrida 1997) – Socius is also the name we have given to the research program that we have established. The second conception of the social concerns entitlements that guarantee a modicum of security in a given state. Here the social essentially means social rights, and Marshall's main focus was this conception of the social. *The two conceptions (socius and rights) are related but must remain distinct. That is the binding thread that runs through the chapters of this volume.* The idea that citizenship is social before it is civil or political rests on the idea that social produces subjects who have the right to have rights, as Hannah Arendt (1958) may have put it.

If civil and political rights enable social rights, in the second sense of the social, then we are arguing that the first sense of the social enables civil and political rights. The consequences of this argument are so significant, as we have attempted to illustrate with both theoretical and empirical investigations, that we describe our project: 'recasting the social in citizenship.'

Danielle Juteau points out that the immediate consequence of our argument is to call into question any ostensible opposition between struggles over redistribution of resources (e.g., income security, welfare) and struggles over recognition (e.g., same-sex marriage, wearing the veil in public spaces). To assume that these two forms of struggle are either sequential or exclusive is to collapse two meanings of the social into one, which Juteau rightly identifies as reductionism. By focusing on the debate over Islamic arbitration tribunals in Ontario, she teases out the perils of interpreting the demands for private arbitration as merely multicultural demands: Multiculturalism is a contested *social site* that combines paradoxical but strategic alignments among various social groups to enhance their cultural, economic, and political interests. Sirma Bilge demonstrates another aspect of multiculturalism as a contested social site, with her focus on the retreat from multiculturalism on grounds of gender justice. More is at stake than gender justice. Bilge shows that casting gender justice as the rights of minorities within minorities has the effect of making gender justice a safe ground on which to maintain the interests of established majorities. This can be clearly seen in debates over wearing the veil in public spaces, where the fantasy of colonial rescue furthers the interests of majorities as they incorporate subaltern sisters and refuse to interpret veil-wearing as a social act of communication but insist on interpreting it as a symbol of oppression. Juteau and Bilge both show how in debates over multiculturalism social acts are displaced onto 'merely cultural' symbols and how these displacements themselves serve as social strategies of domination, and are not merely 'errors' of interpretation.

A second consequence of our argument is that if citizenship is social before it is civil and political, when social relations stretch across boundaries – as they do in intense ways in our age – they respatialize the content and the extent of social rights. Daiva Stasiulis examines how transnational mobilities are rapidly reconfiguring national social policies. The formation of transnational households is engendering the formation of new subjects who constitute themselves entitled to social rights across state boundaries. This complex respatializing of social rights cannot be captured by terms such as *postnational*, *global*, or *cosmopolitan* forms of citizenship because this respatialization is creating hybrid allegiances and loyalties rather than territorially contained and hierarchical identifications. The migrant-citizen is a very complex subject position. Kim Rygiel shows another effect of this respatialization when she considers states to be active and engaging actors in the transnationalization of citizenship rather than passive recipients of a developing international or cosmopolitan regime somehow 'beyond' them. Despite our understanding of citizenship as a nation-state regime of governing, it has also become a global regime of governing population movement through practices of securitization. In developing this argument, Rygiel investigates various global social practices through which people are sorted into citizens and non-citizens – practices that include detention camps, border controls, security zones, traveller registries, and the tagging of individual bodies. Taken together, Rygied calls this immense assemblage of movement control a global citizenship regime, one with its own distinct rationalies and directives.

A third consequence of recasting the social in citizenship is the articulation of new sites of citizenship. Alex Latta and Engin Isin focus on two different yet intersecting sites. Latta examines the emergence of a new domain that can be called environmental justice. Even more recent is that environmental justice and social justice are seen to be connected. Here 'environmental care,' to draw a parallel with 'social care,' joins the question of justice and all that it implies for redistribution and recognition. Latta shows that this enjoinment is fraught with difficulties and that the environment is a paradoxical site of citizenship. If we follow the dominant discourse on environmental justice, for example, we get trapped in the image of a 'caring green citizen' who is unable, unwilling, or even incapable of asking critical questions about the relationship of environment and injustice. Yet, this enjoinment is where the environment becomes a site of struggle over the social. As we investigate ecological citizenship as a site of *social* struggle, we become able to see the new *political* spaces of engagement that open up: We see environmental citizenship as *a* site that intensifies the social. Isin insists that the city is *the* site of the social. Obviously, by the city he does not mean a territorially contained and delimited space, but as such, something almost like a gravitational field around and through which social groups form or, to continue the physics metaphor, orbit. Conceived in this way, it becomes impossible to envisage citizenship as an expression of a territorial container, and Isin develops a provocative conception of citizenship that is translocal rather than contained.

A fourth consequence of our argument is that there are new and emerging practices that interpolate subjects into ways of acting that render them rights-bearing or responsibility-owing citizens. Xiaobei Chen demonstrates how the child has emerged as a rights-bearing citizen and how this citizen has become articulated into the biopolitics of regulating migration by constituting the image of a normal child whose biological capital (neurological state and young age) secures the health of the state. State racism becomes here a strategy for sorting people into categories according to their biological capital. Paul Kershaw examines social care and points to the emergence of a new responsibility-owing citizen. The retrenchment from social services in the past two decades was accompanied by a discourse on workfare through which new actors other than the state were responsibilized without problematizing male irresponsibility for social care. Kershaw recasts this discourse by observing the need to 'oblige men to care.' This argument would be familiar in governmentality studies. Kershaw's analysis shows how the discourse on social care has produced unintended consequences by enabling women to turn what had been their private responsibilities into labour market reforms, where certain types of work that had been previously considered voluntary are now considered paid work. Moreover, Kershaw's and Stasiulis's analyses taken together reveal a complex paradox of the labour market in social care: where women transform their private responsibility into public service, while women from elsewhere are imported – as migrant workers – to be employed in private care, which in turn, has the effect of absolving male members of households from responsibilities of household work. This is a demonstration of how the social in citizenship produces new subjects (citizens and non-citizens) that shift scales from the ostensibly private sphere of *oikos* (*domestic* work) to cosmos (*transnational* labour migration) to create pressures on *national* social policy.

If citizenship is social before it is civil or political, a fifth consequence that follows is that often a reversal occurs in citizenship between rights and responsibilities. Cowen shows that military service has involved such reversals. Once considered a definitive citizenship obligation, military service has increasingly become optional across the advanced capitalist Anglo-American world and now some European states as well. Military service is no longer considered to be a citizenship duty, let alone a definitive one. Increasingly, military service has become enriched with social services to make it attractive to generations that have lost interest in (or the zeal for) dying for their nation. As Cowen makes clear social services for soldiers are not new. States have always had to provide services for their soldier-citizens to ensure loyalty. But what is new is the extent to which services such as income security, housing, and pensions are now being provided to soldiers. Moreover, the bitter irony of the rediscovery of social services for soldier-citizens is the coincidence with the neoliberal curtailing of such services to civilian-citizens. As pointed out in this volume numerous times, at a time when neoliberal rationales of government urge self-reliance and stigmatize social insurance or social security as 'dependence,' militaries have increasingly been making their soldier-citizens dependent on their social assistance. Cowen captures this irony by noting that a Canadian prime minister declared universalism to be a vice for civilian-citizens (before he took the office) and a virtue for soldier-citizens (after he took the office). The soldier-citizen lives for his or her nation rather than dying for it. Being a soldier-citizen becomes a right rather than a duty through recasting the social in citizenship, and the soldier-citizen is now seen worthy of entitlements for which the civilian-citizen is not eligible.

We have shown that recasting the social in citizenship involves investigating new subjects (citizens and non-citizens), scales, reversals, and sites of citizenship, as they challenge each other and create a web of rights and responsibilities that stretches across already defined domains whether these are territorialized or deterritorialized. We offer these chapters as articulations of an interdisciplinary research program. Each one is subject to further refinement and development. Nevertheless, if we take the consequences that we have outlined as guiding principles, these investigations are evidence that citizenship is social before civil or political, a distinction between struggles over redistribution and recognition is analytical rather than actual, social relations stretch across scales, producing new sites and subjects of contestation – and all of this in various reversals is destabilizing the relationships between rights and responsibilities.

Acknowledgments

I am immensely grateful for the useful insights and critical comments provided by Janine Brodie, Danielle Juteau, and Paul Kershaw on an earlier draft of this chapter, as well as those of three anonymous referees.

Bibliography

Abramovitz, M. 1996. *Regulating the Lives of Women: Social Welfare Policy from Colonial Times to the Present*. Boston: South End Press.

Abu-Laban, Y., and C. Gabriel. 2002. *Selling Diversity: Immigration, Multiculturalism, Employment Equity, and Globalization*. Peterborough: Broadview Press.

– 2003. Security, immigration and post-September 11 Canada. In *Reinventing Canada: Politics of the 21st Century*, eds. J. Brodie and L. Trimble. 290–306. Toronto: Prentice-Hall.

Abu-Lughod, L. 2002. Do Muslim women really need saving? Anthropological reflections on cultural relativism and its others. *American Anthropologist* 104(3): 783–90.

ACLU (American Civil Liberties Union). Surveillance under the USA Patriot Act. http://www.aclu.org/SafeandFree/SafeandFree.cfm?ID=12263&c=206

– 2002. 'ACLU Calls Immigrant Registration Program Pretext for Mass Detentions.' 19 Dec. Retrieved 15 Jan. 2003 from http://www.aclu.org/SafeandFree/SafeandFree.cfm?ID=11503&c=206

– 2003. The Five Problems with CAPPS II: Why the Airline Passenger Profiling Proposal Should Be Abandoned. 25 Aug., 1–4. http://www.aclu.org/news/NewsPrint.cfm?ID=13356&c=206

Adoption Council of Canada. Retrieved 3 Jan. 2007 from www.adoption.ca/news.

AFFORD (African Foundation for Development) 2000. Globalisation and development: A diaspora dimension. Submission to the Department for International Development's White Paper on Globalisation and Development, May.

Afshar, H., R. Aitken, and M. Franks. 2005. Feminisms, Islamophobia and identities. *Political Studies* 53(2): 262–83.

Agamben, G. 1995. *Homo Sacer: Sovereign Power and Bare Life.* Stanford: Stanford University Press.

Agnew, J. 1994. The territorial trap: The geographical assumptions of international relations theory. *Review of International Political Economy* 1(1): 53–80.

– 1996. *Resisting Discrimination: Women from Asia, Africa, and the Caribbean and the Women's Movement in Canada*. Toronto: University of Toronto Press.

Aguiar, L.L.M. 2006. The new 'in-between' peoples: Southern-European transnationalism. In *Transnational Identities and Practices in Canada*, eds. V. Satewich and L. Wong. 202–15. Vancouver: UBC Press.

Agyeman, J. 2005. *Sustainable Communities and the Challenges of Environmental Justice*. New York: New York University Press.

Agyeman, J., R.D. Bullard, and B. Evans, eds. 2003. *Just Sustainabilities: Development in an Unequal World*. Cambridge, MA: MIT Press.

Ahmed, L. 1992. *Women and Gender in Islam: Historical Roots of a Modern Discourse*. New Haven: Yale University Press.

AI (Amnesty International). 2002. Australia-Pacific: Offending human dignity – the 'Pacific Solution.' 26 Aug. http://www.amnesty.org/en/library/info/asalz/org/2002

– 2003. Strengthening Fortress Europe in Times of War: Amnesty International Commentary on U.K. Proposals for External Processing and Responsibility Sharing Arrangements with Third Countries Presented at En Council of ministers (JHA Council) Justice and human affairs, Veria, 28–9 March. Brussels: Amnesty International EU.

Aleinikoff, T.A., and D.B. Klusmeyer, eds. 2001. *Citizenship Today: Global Perspectives and Practices*. Washington, DC: Carnegie Endowment for International Peace.

Al-Hibri, A. 1999. Is Western Patriarchal Feminism Good for Third World / Minority Women? In *Is Multiculturalism Bad for Women?*, ed. J. Cohen, M. Howard, and M.C. Nussbaum. 41–6. Princeton, NJ: Princeton University Press.

Althusser, L. 1976. Idéologie et appareils idéologiques d'État. In *Positions*. 77–125. Paris: Editions socials.

Amin, A. 2002. Spatialities of globalisation. *Environment and Planning A* 34: 385–99.

Amos, V., and P. Parmar. 2001 [1984]. Challenging imperial feminism. In *Feminism and Race*, ed. K. Bhavnani. 17–32. Oxford: Oxford University Press.

Anderson, B. 2000. *Doing the Dirty Work? The Global Politics of Domestic Labour*. London: Zed Books.

Andreas, P. 1998. The escalation of U.S. immigration control in the post-NAFTA era. *Political Science Quarterly* 13(4): 591–615.

Andreas, P., and T. Snyder. 2000. *The Wall around* the West: *State Borders and Immigration Controls in North America and Europe*. Lanham: Rowman and Littlefield.

Appadurai A. 1996. *Modernity at Large: Cultural Dimensions of Globalization*. Minneapolis: University of Minnesota Press.

Arat-Koc, S. 1989. In the privacy of our own home: Foreign domestic workers as solution to the crisis in the domestic sphere in Canada. *Studies in Political Economy* 28: 33–58.

– 2002. Hot Potato: Imperial wars or benevolent interventions? Reflections on 'global feminism' post September 11th. *Atlantis* 26(2): 433–44.

– 2006. Whose transnationalism? Canada, 'clash of civilizations' discourse, and Arab and Muslim Canadians. In *Transnational Identities and Practices in Canada*, ed. V. Satzewich and L. Wong. 216–40. Vancouver: UBC Press.

Arendt, H. 1951. *The Origins of Totalitarianism*. Harvest Book. New York: Harcourt Brace Jovanovich.

– 1958. *The Human Condition*. Chicago: University of Chicago Press.

– 1968 [1958]. The decline of the nation-state and the end of the rights of men. In *The Origins of Totalitarianism*. 266–302. San Diego, New York, and London: Harcourt Brace Jovanovich.

– 1970. *On Violence*. New York: Harcourt Brace.

Bacher, J. 1988. Too good to last: The social service innovations of wartime housing. *Women and Environments* 10: 10–13.

Back, L., M. Keith, A. Khan, K. Shukra, and J. Solomos. 2002. New labour's white heart: Politics, multiculturalism and the return of assimilation. *Political Quarterly* 72(2): 445–54.

Bader, V. 1995. Citizenship and exclusion: Radical democracy, community, and justice, or, what is wrong with communitarianism? *Political Theory* 23(2): 211–46.

– 2005. Associative democracy and minorities within minorities. In *Minorities within Minorities*, ed. A. Eisenberg and J. Spinner-Halev. 319–39. Cambridge: Cambridge University Press.

Baier, A.C. 1987. The need for more than justice. *Canadian Journal of Philosophy* Suppl 13: 41–56.

Bakan, A.B., and D. Stasiulis. 1995. Making the match: Domestic placement agencies and the racialization of women's household work. *Signs: Journal of Women in Culture and Society* 20(2): 303–35.

– 1996. Structural adjustment, citizenship, and foreign domestic labour: The Canadian case. In *Rethinking Restructuring: Gender and Change in Canada*, ed. I. Bakker. Toronto: University of Toronto Press.

– eds. 1997. *Not One of the Family: Foreign Domestic Workers in Canada*. Toronto: University of Toronto Press.

Bakker, I., and S. Gill, eds. 2003. *Power, Production, and Social Reproduction*. London: Palgrave.

Balasubramanyam, V.N., and Y. Wei. n.d. The Diaspora and Development. http://www.nottingham.ac.uk/economics/leverhulme/seminars/pdf/yingqi_wei.pdf

Barbalet, J.M. 1988. *Citizenship: Rights, Struggle and Class Inequality.* Minneapolis: University of Minnesota Press.

Barry, B. 2001. *Culture and Equality: An Egalitarian Critique of Multiculturalism.* Cambridge, MA: Harvard University Press.

Barry, J. 1999. *Rethinking Green Politics: Nature, Virtue and Progress.* London: Sage.

Barry, K. 2006. Home and Away: The Construction of Citizenship in an Emigration Context. New York University School of Law, New York University Public Law and Legal Theory Working Papers, Paper #23. http://lsr.nellco.org/nyu/plltwp/papers/23

Barth, F. 1969. *Ethnic Group and Boundaries. The Social Organization of Culture Difference.* Boston: Little, Brown.

Bartlett, L. 2008. Australia ends controversial immigration policy. Agence France Presse. http://news.yahoo.com/s/afp/20080208/wl_afp/australianauruimmigration:_ylt=Asz4GIVOEHZ4arSsLGX3jf2ROrqF

Basch, L., N.G. Schiller, and C.S. Blanc. 1994. *Nations Unbound: Transnational Projects, Postcolonial Predicaments, and Deterritorialized Nation-States.* Amsterdam: Gordon and Beach.

Bashevkin, S. 2005. Training a spotlight on urban citizenship: The case of women in London and Toronto. *International Journal of Urban and Regional Research* 29: 9–25.

Bauböck, R. 1994. Changing the boundaries of citizenship: The inclusion of immigrants in democratic polities. In *From Aliens to Citizens*, ed. R. Bauböck. 199–232. Aldershot: Avebury.

Bauder, H. 2005. Small centres will benefit from immigrant influx. *Toronto Star.* 29 Sept.

Baudrillard, J. 1983. In the *Shadow of Silent Majorities ... or the End of the Social.* New York: Semiotext(e).

Bauman, Z. 2000. *Liquid Modernity.* London: Polity.

BBC News. 2001. Australia's offshore camps are 'hellish.' *BBC News.* 6 Dec. http://news.bbc.co.uk/1/hi/world/asia-pacific/1695930.stm

Beck, U., and E. Beck-Gernsheim. 2002. *Individualization: Institutionalized Individualism and Its Social and Political Consequences.* London: Sage.

Bell, D., and J. Binnie. 2004. Authenticating queer space: Citizenship, urbanism and governance. *Urban Studies* 41(9): 1807–20.

Benhabib, S. 2002. *The Claims of Culture: Equality and Diversity in the Global Era.* Princeton, NJ: Princeton University Press.

– 2004. *The Rights of Others: Aliens, Residents and Citizens*. Cambridge: Cambridge University Press.

Bentham, J. 1843. Pauper management improved. In *Jeremy Bentham's Works*, vol. 8, ed. John Bowring. Edinburgh: William Tait.

Bennett, C.J. 2005. What happens when you book an airline ticket? The collection and processing of passenger data post-9/11. In *Global Surveillance and Policing: Borders, Security and Identity*, ed. E. Zuriek and M.B. Salter. 113–138. Portland: Willan.

Berghahn, S., and P. Rostock. 2006. Cultural diversity, gender equality: The German case. Paper presented at the Gender Equality and Cultural Diversity: European Comparisons and Lessons Conference, Vrije Universiteit, Amsterdam, 8–9 June.

Berkowitz, B. 2003. Latinos on the front lines: U.S. military targets Latinos for Iraq and future twenty-first century wars. Working for Change. Retrieved from 5 May 2006. http://www.workingforchange.com/article. cfm?ItemID=15792

Berlant, L. 1997. *The Queen of America Goes to Washington City: Essays on Sex and Citizenship*. Durham and London: Duke University Press.

Best, J. 1990. *Threatened Children: Rhetoric and Concern about Child-Victims*. Chicago and London: University of Chicago Press.

Beveridge, W. 1942. *Social Insurance and Allied Services*. Presented to Parliament by Command of His Majesty. London: HMSO, CMND 6404.

Bezanson, K., and Meg Luxton, eds. 2006. *Social Reproduction: Feminist Political Economy Challenges Neo-Liberalism*. Montreal and Kingston: McGill-Queen's University Press.

Bhalla, N. 2007. India child malnourishment rates worse than Africa. 21 Feb. Reuters AlertNet. http://www.alertnet.org/thenews/newsdesk/DEL334973.htm

Bhushan, R. 2006. India Calls. Will You Come for Pravasi Bharatiya Divas? *India eNews*. Nov. http://www.indiaenews.com/nri/20061126/30054.html

Bigo, D. 1998. Sécurité et immigration: vers une gouvernementalité par l'inquiétude? *Cultures & Conflits* 31/32: 11–34.

– 2002. Security and immigration: Towards a critique of the governmentality of unease. *Alternatives* 27: Special issue, 63–92.

Bilge, S. 2005. Between a rock and a hard place: Minority women's citizenship in Canada, its intersecting, inequalities, and what an intersectional theorizing can offer? In *Proceedings of the CCMW Symposium Muslim Women's Equality Rights in the Justice System: Gender, Religion and Pluralism*. 71–6. Toronto: Canadian Council of Muslim Women.

– 2006a. Le dilemme genre/culture ou comment penser la citoyenneté des femmes minoritaires au-delà de la *doxa* féminisme/multiculturalisme? In

Diversité de foi, égalité de droit, Actes du Colloque, ed. Conseil du Statut de la femme, 89–98. Québec: Gouvernement du Québec. http://www.csf.gouv.qc.ca/telechargement_publication/index.php?id=348
– 2006b. Penser l'agentivité des femmes musulmanes: quels enjeux épistémologiques et politiques? Paper presented at the Colloquium Relations ethniques, rapports de genre et diversité religieuse, CEETUM, Montreal, 30 March.
Black, A. 1984. *Guilds and Civil Society in European Political Thought from the Twelfth Century to the Present*. Ithaca, NY: Cornell University Press.
Blank, D. 1999. A veil of controversy. *Interventions: International Journal of Postcolonial Studies* 1(4): 536–54.
Bommes, M., and A. Geddes, eds. 2000. *Immigration and Welfare: Challenging the Borders of the Welfare State*. London: Routledge.
Bond, P. 2000. Environmental justice: Economic growth, ecological modernization or environmental justice? Conflicting discourses in post-apartheid South Africa. *Capital, Nature, Society* 11(1): 33–61.
Bourdieu, P. 1961. *The Algerians*. Boston: Beacon Press.
– 1977. *Outline of a Theory of Practice*. Cambridge: Cambridge University Press.
– 1979. *La distinction. Critique sociale du jugement*. Paris: Les éditions de minuit.
– 1980. *The Logic of Practice*. Stanford: Stanford University Press.
– 1986. The forms of capital. In *Handbook for Theory and Research for the Sociology of Education*, ed. J. Richardson. Westport, CT: Greenwood.
– 1994. *Practical Reason: On the Theory of Action*. Stanford: Stanford University Press.
Bouzar, D., 2004. Françaises et musulmanes, entre réappropriation et remise en question des normes. In *Le foulard islamique en questions*, ed. C. Nordmann. 54–64. Paris: Editions Amsterdam.
Bouzar, D., and S. Kada. 2003. *L'une voilée, l'autre pas*. Paris: Albin Michel.
Bowles, S., and Gintis, M. 1986. *Democracy and Capitalism*. London: Routledge and Kegan Paul.
Bradshaw, J., and E. Mayhew. 2003. Are welfare states financing their growing elderly populations at the expense of their children? *Family Matters* 66: 20–5.
Braudel, F. 1988. *The Structures of Everyday Life*, vol. 1, *Civilization and Capitalism 15th – 18th Century*. New York: Harper and Row.
Bredal, A. 2005. Tackling forced marriages in the Nordic countries: Between women's rights and immigration control. In *'Honour': Crimes, Paradigms, and Violence against Women*, ed. L. Welchman and S. Hossain. 332–53. London and New-York: Zed Books.
Breton, R. 1984. The production and allocation of symbolic resources: An analysis of the linguistic and ethnocultural fields in Canada. *Canadian Review of Sociology and Anthropology* 21: 125–44.

Brodie, J. 1996. *Women and Canadian Public Policy.* Toronto: Harcourt Brace.

– 1997. Restructuring and the new citizenship. In *Women and the Canadian Welfare state: Challenges and Change,* ed. Patricia Evans and Gerda Wekerle. 126–40. Toronto: University of Toronto Press.

– 2002a. Three stories of Canadian citizenship. In *Contesting Canadian Citizenship: Historical Readings,* ed. R. Adamoski, D. Chunn, and R. Menzies. Peterborough: Broadview.

– 2002b. Citizenship and solidarity: Reflections on the Canadian way. *Citizenship Studies* 6(4): 377–94.

– 2003. Globalization, In/security and the paradoxes of the social. In *Power, Production, and Social Reproduction,* eds. I. Bakkar and S. Gill. 47–65. London: Palgrave.

– 2004. Introduction: Globalization and citizenship beyond the national state. *Citizenship Studies* 8(4): 323–32.

– 2008. The new social 'isms': Individualization and social policy re-form in Canada. In *Contested Individualization: Debates about Contemporary Personhood,* ed. C. Howard. London: Routledge.

Brooks-Gunn, J., G.J. Duncan, and J.L. Aber, eds. 1997a. *Neighborhood Poverty: Context and Consequences for Children,* vol. 1. New York: Russell Sage Foundation.

– eds. 1997b. *Neighborhood Poverty: Policy Implications in Studying Neighbourhoods,* vol. 2. New York: Russell Sage Foundation.

Brown, D.L., and D. Priest. 2003. Deported terror suspect details torture in Syria. *Washington Post.* 5 Nov., A01.

Brown, W. 2005. *Edgework: Critical Essays on Knowledge and Politics.* Princeton, NJ: Princeton University Press.

– 2006. *Regulating Aversion: Tolerance in the Age of Identity and Empire.* Princeton, NJ: Princeton University Press.

Brubaker, R. 2001. The return of assimilation? Changing perspectives on immigration and its sequels in France, Germany, and the United States. *Ethnic and Racial Studies* 24(1): 531–48.

Brunn, E., and J. Crosby. 1999. *Our Nation's Archive: The History of the United States in Documents.* New York: Black Dog and Leventhal.

Brysk, A., and G. Shafir. 2004. Introduction: Globalization and the citizenship gap. In *People Out of Place: Globalization, Human Rights and the Citizenship Gap,* ed. A. Brysck and G. Shafir. 3–9. New York: Routledge.

Buck-Morss, S. 2000. *Dreamworld and Catastrophe: The Passing of Mass Utopia in East and West.* Cambridge, MA: MIT Press.

Bulbeck, C.1998. *Re-orienting Western Feminisms.* Cambridge: Cambridge University Press.

Bullard, R.D., ed. 1994. *Unequal Protection: Environmental Justice and Communities of Color.* San Francisco: Sierra Club.

Bullard, R.D. 2005a. Introduction. In *The Quest for Environmental Justice: Human Rights and the Politics of Pollution*. 1–18. San Francisco: Sierra Club.

Bullard, R.D., ed. 2005b. *The Quest for Environmental Justice: Human Rights and the Politics of Pollution*. San Francisco: Sierra Club.

Bullard, R.D., and D. Smith. 2005. Women warriors of color on the front line. In *The Quest for Environmental Justice: Human Rights and the Politics of Pollution*, ed. R.D. Bullard. 62–84. San Francisco: Sierra Club.

Bullard, R.D., S.G. Johnson, and A.O. Torres. 2005. Addressing global poverty, pollution, and human rights. In *The Quest for Environmental Justice: Human Rights and the Politics of Pollution*, ed. R.D. Bullard. 279–97. San Francisco: Sierra Club.

Butler, J. 1998. Merely cultural. *New Left Review* no. 227: 33–44.

– 2004. *Precarious Life*. London and New York: Verso.

Burton, A. 1992. White women's burden. In *Western Women and Imperialism: Complicity and Resistance*, ed. N. Chaudhuri and M. Strobel. 137–57. Bloomington: Indiana University Press.

Buzan, B., O. Waever, and J. de Wilds. 1998. *Security: A New Framework for Analysis*. Boulder: Lynne Rienner.

Byrne, J., L. Glover, and C. Martinez, eds. 2002. *Environmental Justice: Discourses in International Political Economy*. New Brunswick, NJ: Transaction.

Cairns, A.C., J.C. Courtney, P. MacKinnon, H.J. Michelmann, and D.E. Smith, eds. 1999. *Citizenship, Diversity, and Pluralism: Canadian and Comparative Perspectives*. Montreal and Kingston: McGill-Queen's University Press.

Calliste, A. 1991. Canada's immigration policy and domestics from the Caribbean: The second domestic scheme. In *Race, Class, Gender: Bonds and Barriers*, ed. J. Vorst et al. Toronto: Garamond Press.

Camacho, D.E., ed. 1998. *Environmental Injustices, Political Struggles: Race, Class, and the Environment*. Durham, NC: Duke University Press.

Cameron, B. 2006. Social reproduction and Canadian federalism. In *Social Reproduction: Feminist Political Economy Challenges Neoliberalism*, ed. K. Bezanson and M. Luxton. Montreal and Kingston: McGill-Queen's Press.

Campbell, D. 1994. The deterritorialization of responsibility: Levinas, Derrida, and ethics after the end of philosophy. *Alternatives* 19: 455–84.

– 1998. *Writing Security*. Minneapolis: University of Minnesota Press.

Campion-Smith, B. 2005. Immigrants' 'heavy burden' on taxpayers. *Toronto Star*. 5 Oct.

Canada, Canadian Forces Applied Research Unit (CFPARU). 1974. *Unskilled Male Recruits for the Canadian Forces: Trends and Projections to 1985*. C.A.U. Cotton, Captain. Report 74–5. Oct.

– CFPARU. 1975. *An Overview of Findings from the CFPARU Applicant Survey, Summer 1975.* C.A.U. Cotton, Captain, and F.C. Pinch, Captain. Working Paper 75–8. Dec.
– 1918. House of Commons, *Debates*, 13th Parliament, 2559.
– 1935. Speech from Throne, 17 Jan. http://www.collectionscanada.ca/primeministers/index-e.html
– Royal Commission on Aboriginal People. 1996. *Looking Forward, Looking Back*, (vol.1) and *Gathering Strength* (vol. 3).
Canaday, M. 2003. Building a straight state: Sexuality and social citizenship under the 1944 G.I. Bill. *Journal of American History* 90: 935–57.
Canadian Bar Association. 2005. Immigration and Refugee Protections Act – Family Reunification Issues.
Canadian Council of Muslim Women (CCMW). 2004. Submission to Ms Marion Boyd: Review of the Ontario Arbitration Act and Arbitration Processes, Specifically in Matters of Family Law. http://www.ccmw.com
Carter, A. 1998. Liberalism and the obligation to military service. *Political Studies* 46: 68–81.
Castells, M. 1977. *The Urban Question: A Marxist Approach*. Translated by A. Sheridan. London: Edward Arnold.
Castles, S., and A. Davidson. 2000. *Citizenship and Migration: Globalization and the Politics of Belonging*. New York: Routledge.
CBC News Online. 2004. Medical tourism: Need surgery, will travel. 18 June. http://www.cbc.ca/news/background/healthcare/medicaltourism.html
CBC Publication. 1938. *The Canadian Constitution*. Toronto: Nelson.
CBP (U.S. Customs and Border Protection). 2008. NEXUS Program Description. http://www.cbp.gov/xp/cgov/travel/trusted_traveler/nexus_prog/nexus.xml (accessed 10 Jan. 2008)
CBSA (Canada Border Services Agency). 2005. Fact Sheet. Advanced Passenger Information/Passenger Name Records. http://www.cbsa-asfc.gc.ca/media/facts-faits/004-eng.html
– 2007a. CANPASS: Streamlines Customs Clearance for Frequent Travellers. http://www.cbsa-asfc.gc.ca/prog/canpass/menu-eng.html (accessed 2007)
– 2007b. CANPASS: Air. http://www.cbsa-asfc.gc.ca/prog/canpass/canpassair-eng.html (accessed 3 July 2007)
– 2007c. NEXUS. http://www.cbsa-asfc.gc.ca/prog/nexus/menu-eng.html
– 2008. The Free and Secure Trade Program. http://www.cbsa-asfc.gc.ca/prog/fast-expres/menu-eng.html (accessed 2 Feb.)
CCR (Center for Constitutional Right). FAQs: The Military Commissions Act. http://www.ccr-ny.org/learn-more/faqs%3A-military-commisions-act

Ceyhan, A., and A. Tsoukala. 2002. The securitization of migration in Western societies: Ambivalent discourses and policies. *Alternatives* 27: 21–39.

Chakravarti, U. 1990. Whatever happened to the *Vedic Dasi*? Orientalism, nationalism and a script for the past. In *Recasting Women: Essays in Indian Colonial History*, ed. K. Sangari and S. Vaid. 27–87. New Brunswick, NJ: Rutgers University Press.

Chaliland, G., and J.-P. Rageau. 1995. *The Penguin Atlas of Diasporas*. New York: Viking Penguin.

Chaudhuri, N., and M. Strobel, eds. 1992. *Western Women and Imperialism: Complicity and Resistance*. Bloomington: Indiana University Press.

Chen, X. 2001. Tending the Gardens of Citizenship: Child Protection in Toronto, 1880s–1920s. Doctoral dissertation, Faculty of Social Work, University of Toronto.

– 2003a. The birth of the child-victim citizen. In *Re-Inventing Canada: Politics of the 21st Century*, ed. J. Brodie and L. Trimble. 189–202. Toronto: Pearson Education.

– 2003b. Constituting 'dangerous parents' through the spectre of child death: A critique of child protection restructuring in Ontario. In *Making Normal: Social Regulation in Canada*, ed. Deborah Brock. 209–34. Scarborough, ON: Thomson Nelson.

– 2003c. 'Parents go global:' A report on an intercountry adoption research project. *Variegations: New Research Directions in Human and Social Development* 1: 10–14.

– 2005. *Tending the Gardens of Citizenship: Child Saving in Toronto, 1880s–1920s*. Toronto: University of Toronto Press.

Christie, N. 2000. *Engendering the state: Family, Work and Welfare in Canada*. Toronto: University of Toronto Press.

Christoff, P. 1996. Ecological citizens and ecologically guided democracy. In *Democracy and Green Political Thought*, ed. B. Doherty and M. de Geus. 151–69. London and New York: Routledge.

Citizenship and Immigration Canada (CIC). 2004. Form letter sent to people who submitted the Application to Sponsor a Member of the Family Class. Ottawa: CIC.

– 2005a. An Immigration System for the 21st Century. News Release 2005–09. Ottawa: CIC.

– 2005b. Citizenship and Immigration Minister Joe Volpe Announced Tripling of the Number of Parents and Grandparents Immigrating to Canada in 2005. News Release 2005–11. Ottawa: CIC.

– 2006. Annual Report to Parliament on Immigration, 2006. Retrieved 12 Jan. 2007 from http://www.cic.gc.ca/english/pub.annual-report2006

– 2007. International Adoption and the Immigration Process. Retrieved 2 Jan. 2007 from http://www.cic.gc.ca/english/sponsor/adopt-4

Clancy-Smith, J. 1998. Islam, gender and identities in the making of French Algeria, 1830–1962. In *Domesticating the Empire: Race, Gender and Family Life in French and Dutch Colonialism*, ed. J. Clancy-Smith and F. Gouda. 154–74. Charlottesville: University Press of Virginia.

Clark, C. 2005. Ottawa set to announce immigration overhaul. *Globe and Mail*. 25 Sept.

Clarke, J. 2004. *Changing Welfare, Changing States: New Directions in Social Policy*. London: Sage.

– 2008. Subordinating the Social? Neo-liberalism and the remaking of welfare capitalism. *Cultural Studies*.

Clarke, J., J.E. Newman, N. Smith, E. Vidler, and L. Westmarland. 2007. *Creating Citizen-Consumers: Changing Publics and Changing Public Services*. London: Sage.

Clausewitz, C. von. 1918. *On War*, 3 vols. Translated by Col. J.J. Graham, notes by Col. F.N. Maude. London: K. Paul, Trench, Trubner.

– 1976. *On War*. Princeton: Princeton University Press.

Cleveland, G., and M. Krashinsky. 1998. *The Benefits and Costs of Good Child Care: The Economic Rationale for Public Investment in Young Children*. Toronto: Childcare Resource and Research Unit (CRRU), Centre for Urban and Community Studies, University of Toronto.

Cohen, E.A. 1985. *Citizens and soldiers: The Dilemmas of Military Service*. Ithaca, NY: Cornell University Press.

Cohen, J., M. Howard, and M. Nussbaum, eds. 1999. *Is Multiculturalism Bad for Women?* Princeton, NJ: Princeton University Press.

Cohen, L. 2003. Where it hurts: Indian material for an ethics of organ transplantation. *Zygon®* 38(3): 663–88.

Cohen, R. 1995. Rethinking Babylon: Iconoclastic conceptions of the diasporic experience. *New Community* 21(1): 5–18.

Cole. D. 2002. Enemy aliens. *Stanford Law Review* 54(953): 953–1004.

Coleman, D.L. 1996. Individualizing justice through multiculturalism: The liberals' dilemma. *Columbia Law Review* 96(5): 1093–1167.

Coleman, M. 2005. U.S. statecraft and the U.S.–Mexico border as security/economy nexus. *Political Geography* 24: 185–209.

Collacott, M. 2002. *Canada's Immigration Policy: The Need for Major Reform*. Vancouver: Fraser Institute.

– 2005. Immigration reform, done badly. *National Post*. 21 April.

Collins, P.H. 1991. *Black Feminist Thought: Knowledge, Consciousness, and the Politics of Empowerment*. New York and London: Routledge.

– 1994. Shifting the center: Race, class, and feminist theorizing about motherhood. In *Mothering: Ideology, Experience, and Agency*, ed. E.N. Glenn, G. Chang, and L.R. Forcey. New York: Routledge.

Comfort, S. 2002. Struggle in Ogoniland: Ken Saro-Wiwa and the cultural politics of environmental justice. In *The Environmental Justice Reader: Politics, Poetics and Pedagogy*, ed. J. Adamson, M.M. Evans, and R. Stein. 229–46. Tucson: Arizona University Press.

Conservation Council of New Brunswick. 2006. *The New Brunswick Charter for Environmental Justice*. Retrieved 26 Nov. 2007 from http://conservationcouncil.ca/archives/2005/ejc-e.pdf

Côté, A., M. Kérisit, and M.-L. Côté. 2001. *Sponsoring… for Better or for Worse: The Impact of Sponsorship on the Equality Rights of Immigrant Woman*. Ottawa: Status of Women Canada.

Courchene, T.J. 1997. ACCESS: A Convention on the Canadian Economic and Social Systems. In *Assessing ACCESS: Towards a New Social Union*. Kingston, ON: Institute of Intergovernmental Relations, Queen's University.

Cowen, D. 2005a. Welfare warriors: Towards a genealogy of the soldier citizen in Canada. *Antipode* 37: 654–78.

– 2005b. Suburban citizenship? The rise of targeting and the eclipse of social rights in Toronto. *Social and Cultural Geography* 6: 335–57.

– 2006. Fighting for 'freedom': The end of conscription and the neoliberal project of citizenship in the United States. *Citizenship Studies* 10: 167–83.

– 2008. *Military Workfare: The Soldier and Social Citizenship in Canada*. Toronto: University of Toronto Press.

Cowen, D., and E. Gilbert. 2007. Securing the homeland: War and familial citizenship. In *War, Citizenship and Territory*, ed. D. Cowen and E. Gilbert. 261–80. New York: Routledge.

Craig, L., J.W. Wilson, and R.L. Clark. 2002. *A History of Public Sector Pensions in the United States*. Philadelphia: University of Pennsylvania Press.

Crenshaw, K. 1991. Mapping the margins: Intersectionality, identity politics, and violence against women of color. *Stanford Law Review* 43(6): 1241–99.

Crichlow, W. 2002. Western colonization as disease: Native adoption and cultural genocide. *Critical Social Work* 2(2): 104–27.

CTV News. 2006. Harper unveils veteran's charter, thanks soldiers. 6 April, online edition. Retrieved 4 July 2006 from http://www.ctv.ca/servlet/ArticleNews/story/CTVNews/20060406/harper_veterans_060406

Curry, M.R. 2004. The profiler's question and the treacherous traveler: Narratives of belonging in commercial aviation. *Surveillance and Society* 1(4): 475–99.

Curtin, D. 1999. *Chinnagounder's Challenge: The Question of Ecological Citizenship*. Bloomington and Indianapolis: Indiana University Press.

Curtis, K. 1999. *Our Sense of the Real: Aesthetic Experience and Arendtian Politics.* Ithaca and London: Cornell University Press.

Dalby, S. 1991. Critical geopolitics: Difference, discourse and dissent. *Environment and Planning D: Society and Space* 9: 261–83.

Daly, M., and J. Lewis. 2000. The concept of social care and the analysis of contemporary welfare states. *British Journal of Sociology* 51(2): 281–98.

Davies, C. 1992. Native children and the child welfare system in Canada. *Alberta Law Review* 30: 1200–15.

Davis, D.–A. 2006. *Battered Black Women and Welfare Reform: Between a Rock and a Hard Place.* Albany: State University of New York Press.

Davis, M. 2005. Gentrifying disaster: In New Orleans ethnic cleansing, GOP-Style. *Mother Jones*, online edition. 25 Oct.

De Chiro, G. 1998. Environmental justice from the grassroots: Reflections on history, gender, and expertise. In *The Struggle for Ecological Democracy: Environmental Justice Movements in the United States*, ed. D. Faber. 104–36. New York: Guilford Press.

Dean, H. 1996. *Welfare, Law and Citizenship*. London: Prentice-Hall.

Dean, H., and M. Melrose. 1999. *Poverty, Riches and Social Citizenship*. Basingstoke: Macmillan.

Dean, M. 1999. *Governmentality: Power and Rule in Modern Society.* London: Sage.

Debbané, A.–M., and R. Keil. 2004. Multiple disconnections: Environmental justice and urban water in Canada and South Africa. *Space and Polity* 8(2): 209–25.

Deleuze, G. 1979. Fore word: The rise of the social. In *The Policing of Families*, J. Donzelot. New York: Pantheon.

– 1992. Postscript on the societies of control. *October* 59 (Winter): 3–7.

– 1994. *Difference and Repetition*. Translated by P. Patton. New York: Columbia University Press.

Deleuze, G., and F. Guattari. 1994. *What Is Philosophy?* New York: Columbia University Press.

Delphy, C. 2002. Une guerre pour les femmes afghanes? *Nouvelles Questions Féministes* 21(1): 98–109.

– 2006. Antisexisme ou antiracisme? Un faux dilemme. *Nouvelles Questions Féministes* 25(1): 59–83.

Democratic Leadership Council (DLC). 1988. Citizenship and National Service: A Blueprint for Civic Enterprise. Retrieved 4 June 2006 from http://www.dlc.org/ndol_ci.cfm?kaid=115&subid=145&contentid=250408

Derrida, J. 1997. *Politics of Friendship*. London: Verso.

DHS, U.S. Department of Homeland Security. 2004. *Report to the Public on Events Surrounding jetBlue Data Transfer: Findings and Recommendations,* 1–10. 20 Feb. Washington, DC: Privacy Office, DHS.

Di Chiro, G. 2004. Producing roundup ready communities? Human genome research and environmental justice policy. In *New Perspectives on Environmental Justice: Gender, Sexuality, and Activism*, ed. R. Stein. 139–60. New Brunswick, NJ: Rutgers University Press.

Dijkink, G. 2005. Soldiers and nationalism: The glory and transience of a hard-won territorial identity. In *The Geography of War and Peace: From Death Camps to Diplomats*, ed. C. Flint. 113–22. Oxford: Oxford University Press.

Dobson, A. 2003a. *Citizenship and the Environment*. Oxford: Oxford University Press.

– 2003b. Social justice and environmental sustainability: Ne'er the twain shall meet? In *Just Sustainabilities: Development in an Unequal World*, ed. J. Agyeman, R.D. Bullard, and B. Evans. 83–95. London: Earthscan.

Dobson, A., and D. Bell, eds. 2006. *Environmental Citizenship*. Cambridge, MA: MIT Press.

Dobson, A., and A. Valencia Sáis. 2005. *Citizenship, Environment, Economy*. London: Routledge.

Docquier, F., and A. Marfouk. 2004. *Measuring the International Mobility of Skilled Workers (1990–2000)*. World Bank Working Paper 3381. Washington, DC: World Bank.

Doherty, B. 2006. Friends of the earth international: Negotiating a transnational identity. *Environmental Politics* 15(5): 860–80.

Doherty, B., and M. de Geus, eds. 1996. *Democracy and Green Political Thought: Sustainability, Rights and Citizenship*. London: Routledge.

Donzelot, J. 1984. *L'invention du Social: Essai sur le declin des passion politiques*. Paris: Fayard.

– 1988. The promotion of the social. *Economy and Society* 17(3): 395–427.

Doorn, J. van. 1975. *The Soldier and Social Change: Comparative Studies in the History and Sociology of the Military*. Beverley Hills: Sage.

Draper, D., and B. Mitchell. 2001. Environmental justice considerations in Canada. *Canadian Geographer* 45(1): 93–8.

Dua, E. 1999. Beyond diversity: Exploring the ways in which the discourse of race has shaped the institution of the nuclear family. *Scratching the Surface: Canadian Anti-racist Feminist Thought*, ed. E. Dua and A. Robertson. 237–60. Toronto: Women's Press.

Dustin, M. 2007. *Gender Equality and Cultural Diversity: European Comparisons and Lessons: Research Report*. London: Nuffield Foundation and the LSE Gender Institute.

Dustin, M., and A. Phillips. 2007. Gender equality, cultural diversity: The British experience. Paper prepared for workshop on Gender Equality, Cultural Diversity: European Comparisons. Amsterdam, 8–9 June.

Dutton, P.V. 2002. *Origins of the French Welfare State: Struggle for Social Reform in France, 1914–1947*. Cambridge: Cambridge University Press.

Duxbury, L., and C. Higgins. 2003. *Where to Work in Canada? An Examination of Regional Differences in Work-Life Practices*. Vancouver: B.C. Council of the Families.

Dwyer, C. 1999. Veiled meanings: Young British Muslim women and the negotiation of difference. *Gender, Place and Culture* 6(1): 5–26

Dyer, R. 1997. *White*. London: Routledge.

Editorial. 2005. *Globe and Mail*. 31 Aug.

Edwards, V. 2002. Don't Mention It! The Oka Crisis and the Recruitment of Aboriginal Peoples. Canada, Department of National Defence. Retrieved 8 Nov. 2003 from http://www.cda-cdai. ca/symposia/2002/edwards.htm

Ehrkamp, P., and H. Leitner. 2003. Beyond national citizenship: Turkish immigrants and the (re)construction of citizenship in Germany. *Urban Geography* 24: 127–46.

– 2006. Guest editorial. Rethinking immigration and citizenship: New spaces of migrant transnationalism and belonging. *Environment and Planning A* 38(9): 1591–7.

Eisenberg, A. 2005. Identity, multiculturalism and religious arbitration: The debate over Shari'a law in Canada (draft).

El Guindi, F. 1999. *Veil: Modesty, Privacy and Resistance*. New York: Berg.

Elden, S. 2001. *Mapping the Present: Heidegger, Foucault and the Project of a Spatial History*. London: Athlone.

Emond, E.P. 1994. An Environmental Bill of Rights – Ontario Style. *Government Information in Canada/Information Gouvernementale au Canada* 1(23). http://library2.usask.ca/gic/v1n2/emond/emond.html

Enloe, C. 1989. *Bananas, Beaches and Bases: Making Feminist Sense of International Politics*. Berkeley: University of California Press.

Entzinger, H. 1994. Y a-t-il un avenir pour le modèle néerlandais des minorités ethniques? *Revue européenne des migrations internationales* 10(1): 73–92.

– 2003. The Rise and Fall of Multiculturalism: The Case of the Netherlands. In *Toward Assimilation and Citizenship*, ed. C. Joppke and E. Morawaska. 59–86. New York: Palgrave-Macmillan.

EPIC (Electronic Privacy Information Awareness Center). Secure Flight. http://www.epic.org/privacy/airtravel/secureflight.html

Esping-Andersen, G. 1990. *The Three Worlds of Welfare Capitalism*. Princeton, NJ: Princeton University Press.

– 2002. *Why We Need a New Welfare State*. Oxford: Oxford University Press.

Esping-Andersen, G., and S. Sarasa. 2002. The generational conflict reconsidered. *Journal of European Social Policy* 12(1): 5–21.

Faber, D. 1998a. The struggle for ecological democracy and environmental justice. In *The Struggle for Ecological Democracy: Environmental Justice Movements in the United States*, ed. D. Faber. 1–26. New York: Guilford Press.

– ed. 1998b. *The Struggle for Ecological Democracy: Environmental Justice Movements in the United States*. New York: Guilford Press.

Faist, T. 2000. *The Volume and Dynamics of International Migration and Transnational Social Spaces*. Oxford: Oxford University Press.

– 2007. The fixed and porous boundaries of dual citizenship. In *Dual Citizenship in Europe: From Nationhood to Societal Integration*. Hampshire: Ashgate.

Fanon, F. 1965. Algeria unveiled. In *A Dying Colonialism*. 35–67. New York: Grove.

Faulks, K. 1998. *Citizenship in Modern Britain*. Edinburgh: Edinburgh University Press.

– 2000. *Citizenship*. London: Routledge.

Fekete, L. 2004. Anti-Muslim racism and the European security state. *Race and Class* 46(1): 3–29.

– 2006. Enlightened fundamentalism? Immigration, feminism and the right. *Race and Class* 48(2): 1–22.

Fenster, T. 2005. The right to the gendered city: Different formations of belonging in everyday life. *Journal of Gender Studies* 14(3): 217–31.

Finkel, A. 1977. Origins of the welfare State in Canada. In *The Canadian state: Political Economy and Political Power*, ed. L. Panitch. 344–70. Toronto: University of Toronto Press.

– 2006. *Social Policy and Practice in Canada: A History*. Waterloo, ON: Wilfrid Laurier University Press.

Finkelhor, 1995. The victimization of children: A developmental perspective. *American Journal of Orthopsychiatry* 65(2): 177–93.

Finn, J. 2005. Potential threats and potential criminals: Data collection in the national security entry-exit registration system. In *Global Surveillance and Policing: Borders, Security and Identity*, ed. E. Zuriek and M.B. Salter. 139–56. Portland: Willan.

Flax, J. 1995. Race/gender and the ethics of difference: A reply to Okin's 'Gender inequality and cultural differences.' *Political Theory* 23(3): 500–10.

Foucault, M. 1969. *The Archaeology of Knowledge and the Discourse on Language*. Translated by A.M.S. Smith. New York: Pantheon.

– 1982. Afterword: The Subject and Power. In *Michel Foucault: Beyond Structuralism and Hermeneutics*, ed. H.L. Dreyfus and P. Rabinow. Chicago: University of Chicago Press.

– 1989. *Foucault Live: Collected Interviews*, 1961–1984. New York: Semiotexte.

– 1997. *Society Must Be Defended: Lectures at the College de France*. New York: Picador.

– 2003. *Society Must Be Defended.*

– Fraser, N. 1994. After the family wage: Gender equity and the welfare state. *Political Theory* 22(4): 591–618.

– 1995. From redistribution to recognition? Dilemmas of justice in a 'post-socialist age.' *New Left Review* 212 Special issue, Equality and deconstruction: 68–93.

– 1997. A rejoinder to Iris Young. *New Left Review* 223: 126–9.

– 1998. Heterosexism, misrecognition and capitalism: A response to Judith Butler. *New Left Review* 228: 140–9.

– 2000. Rethinking recognition. *New Left Review* no. 3: 107–20.

Fraser, N., and L. Gordon. 1992. Contract versus charity: Why is there no social citizenship in the United States? *Socialist Review* 22: 45–68.

Fraser, N., and A. Honneth. 2003a. The Point of Recognition: A Rejoinder to the Rejoinder. In *Redistribution or Recognition? A Political-Philosophical Exchange.* 237–67. New York: Verso.

– 2003b. Redistribution as Recognition: A Response to Nancy Fraser. In *Redistribution or Recognition? A Political-Philosophical Exchange.* 110–97. New York: Verso.

– 2003c. *Redistribution or Recognition?: A Political-Philosophical Exchange.* London: Verso.

Frost, J. 2004. Social citizenship and the city. *Journal of Urban History* 30(2): 289–98.

Frug, G.E. 1980. The city as a legal concept. *Harvard Law Review* 93(6): 1057–1154.

Fustel de Coulanges, N.D. 1978 [1864]. *The Ancient City: A Study on the Religion, Laws, and Institutions of Greece and Rome.* Translated by W. Small. New York: Doubleday.

Gaard, G. 2004. Toward a queer ecofeminism. In *New Perspectives on Environmental Justice: Gender, Sexuality, and Activism*, ed. R. Stein. 21–44. New Brunswick, NJ: Rutgers University Press.

Gangolli, L.V., R. Duggal, and A. Shukla, eds. 2005. *Review of Healthcare in India.* Mumbai: Centre for Enquiry into Health and Allied Themes.

García, M. 2006. Citizenship practices and urban governance in European cities. *Urban Studies* 43(4): 745–65.

Gaspard, F., and F. Khosrokhavar. 1995. *Le foulard et la République.* Paris: La Découverte.

Gierke, O. 1934. *Natural Law and the Theory of Society, 1500–1800.* Cambridge: Cambridge University Press.

Gilbert, L., and C. Phillips. 2003. Practices of urban environmental citizenships: Rights to the city and rights to nature in Toronto. *Citizenship Studies* 7(3): 313–30.

Gilroy, P. 2004. Against race. *Imagining Political Culture beyond the Color Line.* Cambridge, MA: Harvard University Press.
– 2005. *Postcolonial Melancholia.* New York: Columbia University Press.
Girdner, E.J., and Smith, J. 2002. *Killing Me Softly: Toxic Waste, Corporate Profit, and the Struggle for Environmental Justice.* New York: Monthly Review Press.
Glazer, N. 1997. *We Are All Multiculturalists Now.* Cambridge, MA: Harvard University Press.
Glick Schiller, N., L. Basch, and C. Szanton Blanc. 1992. *Towards a Transnational Perspective on Migration: Race, Class, Ethnicity, and Nationalism Reconsidered.* New York: Annals of the New York Academy of Sciences.
Goar, C. 2004. Safety net for the 21st century. *Toronto Star.* 9 Aug.
Goldring, L. 1998. The power of status in transnational social fields. In *Transnationalism from Below,* ed. M.P. Smith and L.E. Guarnizo. New Brunswick, NJ: Transaction.
Gordon, L. 1994. *Pitied But Not Entitled: Single Mothers and the History of Welfare, 1890–1935.* New York: Free Press.
Government of British Columbia. 2006. *What Choices Would You Make? Budget 2007 Consultation Paper.* Victoria: B.C. Ministry of Finance.
Graham, J.R, and L.M. Querido. 2001. Canadian social welfare in the twenty-first century. *Journal of Canadian Studies* 35: 297–304.
Gramsci, A. 1997 [Posthume, 1975]. *Selections from the Prison Notebooks.* Translated and edited by Q. Hoare and G. Nowell Smith. New York: International Publishers.
Green, L. 1994. Internal minorities and their rights. In *Group Rights,* ed. J. Baker. 101–17. Toronto: University of Toronto Press.
Gregory, D. 1994. *Geographical Imaginations.* London: Blackwell.
Grewal, I. 1996. *Home and Harem.* Durham, NC: Duke University Press.
Grubel, H. 2005. *Immigration and the Welfare State in Canada: Growing Conflicts, Constructive Solutions.* Vancouver: Fraser Institute.
Guest, D. 1985. *The Emergence of Social Security in Canada.* Vancouver: University of British Columbia Press.
– 1987. World War II and the welfare state in Canada. In *The 'Benevolent' State: The Growth of Welfare in Canada,* ed. A. Moscovitch and J. Albert. Ottawa: Carleton University Press.
Guillaumin, C. 1977. Race et nature: système des marques. Idées de groupe naturel et rapports sociaux. *Pluriel* 11: 40–56.
– 1978. Pratique du pouvoir et idée de nature (1): L'appropriation des femmes. *Questions féministes* (2): 5–30. Trans. in C. Guillaumin (1995), *Racism, Sexism, Power, and Ideology* (New York: Routledge).
– 2002 [1972]. *L'idéologie raciste. Genèse et langage actuel.* Paris: Gallimard folio.

Gutmann, A. 2001. Introduction. In *Human rights as Politics and Idolatry*, ed. M. Ignatieff et al. vii–xxviii. Princeton NJ: Princeton University Press.
– ed. 1994. *Multiculturalism: Examining the Politics of Recognition*. Princeton, NJ: Princeton University Press.
Habermas, J. 1990. *The New Conservatism*. Cambridge, MA: MIT Press.
– 1994 [1992]. Struggles for recognition in the democratic constitutional state. In *Multiculturalism: Examining the Politics of Recognition*, ed. A. Gutmann. 107–48. Princeton, NJ: Princeton University Press.
Haggerty, K.D., and R.V. Ericson. 2000. The surveillant assemblage. *British Journal of Sociology* 51(4): 605–22.
Hall, R. 2006. Multiculturalism Meets Feminism. *The Knoll* no. 1 (Jan.) Retrieved 16 Dec. 2006 from http://www.theknoll.ca/php/display.php?article_id=2
Hall, S. 1985. Signification, representation, ideology: Althusser and the post-structuralist debates. *Critical Studies in Mass Communication* 2(2): 91–113.
– 1986. Gramsci's relevance for the study of race and ethnicity. *Journal of Communication Inquiry* 10(2): 5–27.
– 1999. From Scarman to Stephen Lawrence. *History Workshop Journal* 48: 187–97.
Hamilton, K. 2003. Migration and development: Blind faith and hard-to-find facts. *Migration Information Source.* Washington, DC: Migration Policy Institute.
Hamilton, W. 2006. New urbanism: It's in the army now. *New York Times*. 8 June, D1.
Hansen, T.B., and F. Stepputat. 2005. Introduction. In *Sovereign Bodies: Citizens, Migrants, and States in the Postcolonial World*, ed. T.B. Hansen and F. Stepputat. 1–36. Princeton, NJ: Princeton University Press.
Hardin, B. 1999. Race, poverty and the militarized welfare state. Poverty and Race Research Action Council. Jan./Feb.
Hardt, M., and A. Negri. 2000. *Empire.* Cambridge, MA: Harvard University Press.
– 2004. *Multitude: War and Democracy in the Age of Empire.* New York: Penguin.
Harper, S. 1994. Speech to the Colin Brown Memorial Dinner, National Citizens Coalition. Retrieved 10 May 2006 from http://www.intheirownwords.ca/harper.html
– 2006. Address by the Prime Minister to the Graduates of a Basic Infantry Soldier Course at Canadian Forces Base, Wainwright, 13 April. Text retrieved 10 May 2006 from http://www.pm.gc.ca
Harvey, D. 1973. *Social Justice and the City.* London: Edward Arnold.
– 1989. *The Condition of Postmodernity: An Enquiry into the Origins of Cultural Change*. Cambridge: Blackwell.
– 1996. *Justice, Nature and the Geography of Difference*. Oxford: Blackwell.
– 2005. *A Brief History of Neoliberalism*. Oxford: Oxford University Press.

Harzig, C., and D. Hoerder. 2006. Transnationalism and the age of mass migration, 1880–1920. In *Negotiating Borders and Belonging: Transnational Identities and Practices in Canada*, ed. V. Satzewich and L. Wong. Vancouver: UBC Press.

HAT (Humanist Association of Toronto). Elka Enola. Comments about the Boyd Report. http://humanist.toronto.on.ca/sharialetters.html

Hayden, D. 1980. What would a non-sexist city be like? In *Women and the American City*, ed. C Stimpson. 170–87. Chicago: University of Chicago Press.

Hayek, F. 1944. *The Road to Serfdom*. New York: Routledge.

Hayter, T. 2001. Open borders: The case against immigration controls. *Capital and Class* 75: 149–56.

Heckman, J., and L. Lochner. 2000. *Rethinking Education and Training Policy. Securing the Future: Investing in Children from Birth to College*, 47–83. New York: Russell Sage Foundation.

Heidegger, M. 1927. *Being and Time*. Trans. by J. Stambaugh, *SUNY Series in Contemporary Continental Philosophy*. Albany: State University of New York Press.

Hélie-Lucas, M.-A. 1999. Women, nationalism, and religion in the Algerian liberation struggle. In *Rethinking Fanon*, ed. N. Gibson. 271–82. Amherst, NY: Humanity Books.

Heng, Chye Kiang. 1999. *Cities of Aristocrats and Bureaucrats: The Development of Medieval Chinese Cities*. Honolulu: University of Hawaii Press.

Himmelfarb, G. 1984. *The Idea of Poverty: England in the Industrial Age*. New York: Alfred A. Knopf.

Hindess, B. 1993. Liberalism, socialism, and democracy: Variations on a governmental theme. *Economy and Society* 26(2): 257–72.

– 2000. Citizenship in the international management of populations. *American Behavioural Scientist* 43(9): 1486–97.

– 2002. Neo-liberal citizenship. *Citizenship Studies* 6(2): 127–43.

– 2003. Responsibility for others in the modern system of states. *Australian Sociological Association* 39(1): 23–30.

Hirst, P.Q., and G. Thompson. 1999. *Globalization in Question: The International Economy and the Possibilities of Governance*, 2nd ed. Cambridge: Polity Press.

Hobsbawm, E. 1990. *Nations and Nationalism since 1780: Programme, Myth, Reality*. Cambridge: Cambridge University Press.

– 1994. *The Age of Extremes: A History of the World, 1914–1991*. New York: Vintage.

Hobson, B., ed. 2002. *Making Men into Fathers: Men, Masculinites and the Social Politics of Fatherhood*. Cambridge, Cambridge University Press.

Hobsons. 2006. *Graduate and Employment Training 2006: Guide for Ethnic Minorities*. London: United Kingdom. http://www.get.hobsons.co.uk/advice/equality-ethnicity

Hofrichter, R., ed. 2002. *Toxic Struggles: The Theory and Practice of Environmental Justice.* Salt Lake City: University of Utah Press.

Hollifield, J.F. 2004. The emerging migration state. *International Migration Review* 38(3): 885–912.

Holston, J. 1998. Spaces of insurgent citizenship. In *Making the Invisible Visible: A Multicultural Planning History,* ed. L. Sandercock. 37–56. Berkeley and Los Angeles: University of California Press.

– 1999. *Cities and Citizenship.* Durham, NC: Duke University Press.

Honneth, A. 1996a. *The Fragmented World of the Social: Essays in Social and Political Philosophy.* Edited by K. Baynes. Albany: State University of New York Press.

– 1996b. *The Struggle for Recognition: The Moral Grammar of Social Conflicts.* Translated by J. Anderson. Cambridge, MA: MIT Press.

– 2001. Recognition or redistribution? Changing perspectives on the moral order of society. *Theory, Culture and Society* 18(2–3): 43–55.

Hoodfar, H. 2003. More than clothing: Veiling as an adaptive strategy. In *The Muslim Veil in North America,* ed. S. Alvi, H. Hoodfar, and S. McDonough. 3–40. Toronto: Women's Press.

Hooks, B. 1990. *Yearning: Race, Gender and Cultural Politics.* Boston: South End Press.

HRW (Human Rights Watch). 2002a. *'By Invitation Only': Australian Asylum Policy.* 1–94. New York: HRW.

– 2002b. *Not for Export: Why the International Community Should Reject Australia's Refugee Policies: A Human Rights Watch Briefing Paper.* New York: HRW.

Huysmans, J. 1995. Migrants as a security problem: Dangers from securitizing societal Issues. In *Migration and European Integration: The Dynamics of Inclusion and Exclusion,* ed. R. Miles and D. Thrätnhardt. 53–72. London: Pinter.

– 2006. *The Politics of Insecurity: Fear, Migration, and Asylum in the EU.* London: Routledge.

ICAO (International Civil Aviation Organization). 2004a. ICAO Facilitation (FAL) Division – Twelfth Session Cairo, Egypt, 22 March to 2 April. FAL/12–WP/4 (5/11/03).

– 2004b. ICAO News Release. PIO 04/04.

India, Ministry of Home Affairs. n.d. Dual Citizenship: Overseas Citizenship of India (OCI). http://mha.nic.in/oci-main.htm

Indo-Asian News Service. 2006. Redefine India Poverty Benchmark, Says Study. *India Resource Center.* http://www.indiaresource.org/news/2006/1024.html

Inglehart, R., and P. Norris. 2003. *Rising Tide: Gender Equality and Cultural Change around the World.* Cambridge: Cambridge University Press.

International Organization of Migration (IOM). 2006. Global Estimates and Trends. http://www.iom.int/jahia/Jahia/cache/offonce/pid/254

Ionescu, D. 2006. Engaging Diasporas as Development Partners for Home and Destination Countries: Challenges for Policymakers. Paper prepared for IOM, Geneva.

Isin, E.F. 1997. Who is the new citizen? Toward a genealogy. *Citizenship Studies* 1(1): 115–32.

– 2000a. Introduction: Democracy, citizenship and the city. In *Democracy, Citizenship and the Global City*, ed. E.F. Isin. 1–21. London: Routledge.

– 2000b. *Democracy, citizenship and the Global City*. New York: Routledge.

– 2002a. City, Democracy and citizenship: Historical images, contemporary practices. In *Handbook of Citizenship Studies*, ed. E.F. Isin and B.S. Turner. 305–16. London: Sage.

– 2002b. *Being Political: Genealogies of Citizenship*. Minneapolis: University of Minnesota Press.

– 2004. The neurotic citizen. *Citizenship Studies* 8: 217–35.

– 2005. Engaging, being, political. *Political Geography* 24: 373–87.

– 2006. Theorizing the European city. In *Handbook of Contemporary European Social Theory*, ed. G. Delanty. 323–32. London: Routledge.

– 2007. City state: Critique of scalar thought. *Citizenship Studies* 11(2): 211–28.

Isin, E.F., and G.M. Nielsen, eds. 2008. *Acts of Citizenship*. London: Zed Books.

Isin, E.F., and M. Siemiatycki. 2002. Making space for mosques: Claiming urban citizenship. In *Race, Space and the Law: The Making of a White Settler Society*, ed. S. Razack. 185–209. Toronto: Between the Lines.

Isin, E.F., and B.S. Turner, eds. 2002. *Handbook of Citizenship Studies*. London: Sage.

Isin, E.F., and B.S. Turner. 2007. Investigating citizenship: An agenda for citizenship studies. *Citizenship Studies* 11(1): 5–17.

Isin, E.F., and K. Rygiel. 2007. Abject spaces: Frontiers, zones, camps. In *Logics of Biopower and the War on Terror*, ed. E. Dauphinee and C. Masters. 181–203. Houndmills: Palgrave.

Isin, E.F., and P.K. Wood. 1999. *Citizenship and Identity*. London: Sage.

Itzigsohn, J. 2000. Immigration and the boundaries of citizenship: The institutions of immigrants' political transnationalism. *Immigration Migration Review* 34(4): 1125–54.

Ivy, M. 1993. Have you seen me? Recovering the inner child in late twentieth-century America. *Social Text* 37: 227–52.

Jacobson, D. 1996. *Rights across Borders: Immigration and the Decline of Citizenship*. Baltimore: Johns Hopkins University Press.

James, M. 2006. *Misrecognized Materialists: Social Movements in Canadian Constitution Politics*. Vancouver: UBC Press.

Jayawardena, K. 1995. *The White Woman's Other Burden: Western Women and South Asia during British Rule*. London: Routledge.

Jelin, E. 2000. Towards a global environmental citizenship. *Citizenship Studies* 4(1): 47–62.

Jenkins, R. 1997. *Rethinking Ethnicity: Arguments and Explorations*. London: Sage.

Jenkins, S. 1945. Australia plans full employment. *Far Eastern Survey* 17: 240–2.

Jenson, J. 2001. Canada's shifting citizenship regime: Investing in children. In *The Dynamics of Decentralization: Canadian Federalism and British Devolution*, ed. T.C. Salmon and M. Keating. 107–24. Montreal and Kingston: McGill-Queen's University Press.

Jenson, J., and S.D. Phillips. 2002. Redesigning the Canadian citizenship regime: Remaking the institutions of representation. In *Citizenship, Markets and the State*, ed. C. Crouch, K. Eder, and D. Tambini. Oxford: Oxford University Press.

Jerrett, M., R.T. Burnett, P. Kanaroglou, and J.R. Brook. 2001. A GIS-environmental justice analysis of particulate air pollution in Hamilton, Canada. *Environment and Planning A* 33: 955–73.

Jiménez, M. 2005. Is the current model of immigration the best one for Canada? *Globe and Mail*. 12 Dec.

– 2006. Immigrants' families shortchanged, suit says. *Globe and Mail*. 31 May.

– 2007. How Canadian are you? *Globe and Mail*. 12 Jan.: A1, A5.

Jones-Correa, M. 2002. Under two flags: Dual nationality in Latin America and its consequences for the United States. *International Migration Review* 3(84): 34–67.

Joppke, C. 2004. The retreat from multiculturalism in the liberal state: Theory and policy. *British Journal of Sociology* 55(2): 237–57.

Joppke, C., and Morawska, E., eds. 2003. *Toward Assimilation and Citizenship: Immigrants in Liberal Nation-States*. Houndmills: Palgrave-Macmillan.

Joyce, P., ed. 2002. *The Social in Question: New Bearings in History and the Social Sciences*. London: Routledge.

Juteau, D. 1997. Beyond multiculturalist citizenship: The challenge of pluralism in Canada. In *Citizenship and Exclusion*, ed. V. Bader. 96–112. London: Macmillan.

– 1999. *L'ethnicité et ses frontières*. Montreal: PUM.

– 2000. Patterns of social differentiation in Canada: Understanding their dynamics and bridging the gaps. *Canadian Public Policy* 26: S95-S107.

– 2002. The citizen makes an entrée: Redefining the national community in Quebec. *Citizenship Studies* 6(4): 441–58.

– 2006. Forbidding ethnicities in French sociological thought: The difficult circulation of knowledge and ideas. *Mobilities* 1(3): 391–408.

– 2002. *Social Differentiation. Patterns and Process*. Toronto: University of Toronto Press.

Juteau, D., and N. Laurin. 1989. From nuns to surrogate mothers: Evolution of the forms of the appropriation of women. *Feminist Issues* (1): 13–41.

Juteau-Lee, D., with L. Laforge. 1979, *Frontières ethniques en devenir / Emerging Ethnic Boundaries.* Ottawa: Editions de l'Université d'Ottawa.

Kaplan, A. 2005. Where is Guantánamo? *American Quarterly* 57(3): 831–58.

Kaplan, W., ed. 1993. *Belonging: The Meaning and Future of Canadian Citizenship.* Montreal and Kingston: McGill-Queen's University Press.

Katznelson, I. 2005. *When Affirmative Action Was White: An Untold History of Racial Inequality in Twentieth-Century America.* New York: W.W. Norton.

Keating, D.P., and C. Hertzman, eds. 1999. *Developmental Health and the Wealth of Nations: Social, Biological, and Educational Dynamics.* New York: Guilford Press.

Keaton, T.D. 2006. *Muslim Girls and the Other France: Race, Idenity Politics and Social Exclusion.* Bloomington: Indiana University Press.

Kebede, A. 2005. Grassroots environmental organizations in the United States: A Gramscian analysis. *Sociological Inquiry* 75(1): 81–108.

Kelly, M. 2004. Racism, nationalism and biopolitics: Foucault's *Society Must Be Defended*, 2003. *Contretemps* 4: 58–70.

Kelly, P., ed. 2002. *Multiculturalism Reconsidered.* Cambridge: Polity Press.

Kelly, P. and T. Lusis. 2006. Migration and the transnational habitus: Evidence from Canada and the Philippines. *Environment and Planning A* 38(5): 831–47.

Kent, T. 2004. 'In the national interest': A social policy agenda for a new century – restore cooperative federalism, modernize medicare, put children first. *Policy Options / Options Politiques* (Aug.): 24–9.

Kershaw, P. 2002. Beyond the spousal tax credit: Rethinking the tax treatment of caregiving and dependency (again!) in the light of the Law Commission Report. *Canadian Tax Journal* 50(6): 1949–78.

– 2005. *Carefair: Rethinking the Responsibilities and Rights of Citizenship.* Vancouver: UBC Press.

– 2006. Carefair: Choice, duty and the distribution of care. *Social Politics* 13(3): 341–71.

– 2007. Measuring Up: Family benefits in B.C. and Alberta in international perspective. *IRPP Choices* 13(2): 1–42.

Kershaw, P., B. Forer, L.G. Irwin, C. Hertzman, and V. Lapointe. 2007. Toward a social care program of research: A study of neighborhood effects on child development. *Early Education and Development* 18(3): 535–60.

Kershaw, P., J. Pulkingham, and S. Fuller. Forthcoming. Expanding the subject: Violence, care and (in) active male citizenship. *Social Politics*.

Kershen, N. 1995. L'influence du Rapport Beveridge sur le plan français de sécurité sociale de 1945. *Revue française de science politique* 45: 570–95.

Kher, U. 2006. Outsourcing your heart. *Time*. 21 May. http://www.time.com/time/magazine/article/0,9171,1196429-1,00.html

Khosrokhavar, F. 1996. L'universel abstrait, le politique et la construction de l'islamisme comme forme d'altérité. In *Une Société Fragmentée?*, ed. M. Wieviorka. 133–70. Paris: Editions La Découverte.

King, D., and M. Wickham-Jones. 1999. From Clinton to Blair: The Democratic (Party) origins of welfare to work. *Political Quarterly* 70: 62–74.

Kingfisher, C., ed. 2002. *Western Welfare in Decline: Globalization and Women's Poverty*. Philadelphia: University of Pennsylvania Press.

Kirwin, W. 1996. The future of the welfare state during the decline of the nation state. In *Ideology, Development and Social Welfare: Canadian Perspectives*, ed. W. Kirwin, 205–14. Toronto: Canadian Scholars' Press.

Klausen, J. 1999. *War and Welfare: Europe and the United States, 1945 to the Present*. New York: St Martin's Press.

Kline, M. 1992. Child welfare law – best interests of the child – ideology and First Nations. *Osgoode Hall Law Journal* 30: 375–425.

– 1995. Complicating the ideology of motherhood: Child welfare law and First Nation women. In *Mothers in Law: Feminist Theory and the Legal Regulation of Motherhood*, ed. M.A. Fineman and I. Karpin. 118–41. New York: Columbia University Press.

Knijn, T., and M. Kremer. 1997. Gender and the caring dimension of welfare states: Toward inclusive citizenship. *Social Politics* 4(3): 328–61.

Kofman, E. 2002. Contemporary European migrations, civic stratification and citizenship. *Political Geography* 21: 1035–54.

Kohen, D., C. Hertzman, and D. Willms. 2002. The importance of quality child care. In *Vulnerable Children*, ed. D. Willms. 261–76. Edmonton: University of Alberta Press.

Koopmans, R., P. Statham, M. Giugni, and F. Passy. 2005. *Contested Citizenship: Immigration and Cultural Diversity in Europe*. Minneapolis: University of Minnesota Press.

Korteweg, A.C. 2006. The murder of Theo Van Gogh: Gender, religion, and the struggle over immigrant integration in the Netherlands. In *Migration, Citizenship, Ethnos*, ed. M. Bodemann and G. Yurdakul. 147–65. New York: Palgrave-Macmillan.

Krauss, C. 2002. Blue-collared women and toxic-waste protests: The process of politicization. In *Toxic Struggles: The Theory and Practice of Environmental Justice*, ed. R. Hofrichter. 107–17. Salt Lake City: University of Utah Press.

Kukathas, C. 2001. Is feminism bad for multiculturalism? *Public Affairs Quarterly* 15: 83–97.

Kuptsch, C., and P. Martin. 2004. Migration and Development: Remittances and Cooperation with the Diaspora. April. http:// www.ilo.org/public/ english/ bureau/inst/research/migration.htm

Kurtz, H. 2005. Alternative visions for citizenship practice in an environmental justice dispute. *Space and Polity* 9(1): 77–91.

Kymlicka, W. 1995. *Multicultural Citizenship: A Liberal Theory of Minority Rights.* Oxford: Clarendon Press.

– 1999. Comments on Shachar and Spinner-Halev: An update from the multiculturalism wars. *Multicultural Questions* 1: 112–31.

– 2005. Testing the bounds of liberal multiculturalism. *Muslim Women's Equality Rights in the Justice System: Gender, Religion and Pluralism. Proceedings.* 53–68. Toronto: Canadian Council of Muslim Women.

Kymlicka, W., and W. Norman. 1994. Return of the citizen: A survey of recent work on citizenship theory. *Ethics* 104: 352–81.

– 2000. Citizenship in culturally diverse societies: Issues, contexts, concepts. In *Citizenship in Diverse Societies,* ed. W. Kymlicka and W. Norman. 1–43. Oxford and New York: Oxford University Press.

Kymlicka, W., and K.G. Banting, eds. 2006. *Multiculturalism and the Welfare State: Recognition and Redistribution in Contemporary Democracies.* Oxford: Oxford University Press.

Laclau, E., and C. Mouffe. 1985. *Hegemony and Socialist Strategy: Towards a Radical Democratic Politics.* London: Verso.

Lahav, G. 1998. Immigration and the state: The devolution and privatisation of immigration control in the EU. *Journal of Ethnic and Migration Studies* 24(4): 675–94.

Lamont, M., and V. Molnar. 2002. The study of boundaries in the social sciences. *Annual Review of Sociology* 28: 167–95.

Lamoureux, D. 1992. La citoyenneté: de l'exclusion à l'inclusion. In *Citoyenneté et Nationalité: Perspective en France et au Québec,* eds. D. Colas, C. Emeri, and J. Zylberberg. 53–67. Paris: Presses Universitaires de France.

Larner, W. 2000. Post-welfare state governance: Towards a code of social and family responsibility. *Social Politics* 7(2): 244–65.

Larner, W., and Craig. D. 2005. After neoliberalism? Community activism and local partnerships in Aotearoa New Zealand. *Antipode* 37(3): 402–24.

Latour, B. 2005. *Reassembling the Social: An Introduction to Actor-Network-Theory.* Oxford: Oxford University Press.

Latta, P.A. 2007. Locating democratic politics in ecological citizenship. *Environmental Politics* 16(3): 377–93.

Law Commission of Canada. 2006. Crossing Borders: Law in a Globalized World. Discussion Paper. March. http://www.lcc.gc.ca

Lazreg, M. 1988. Feminism and difference: The perils of writing as a woman on women in Algeria. *Feminist Studies* 14(1): 81–107.

– 1990. Gender and politics in Algeria: Unrevealing the religious paradigm. *Signs* 15(4): 755–80.

– 1994. *The Eloquence of Silence: Algerian Women in Question*. London: Routledge.

Leckie, R. (Air Marshal). 1954. Canada's Air Force ... A new look. *Canadian Geographical Journal* (Sept.): 100–13.

Lefebvre, H. 1991. *The Production of Space*. Oxford: Blackwell.

Lefort, C. 1982. *The Political Forms of Modern Society*. Cambridge, MA: MIT Press.

Lévêque, P., and P. Vidal-Naquet. 1996 [1964]. Cleisthenes the Athenian: An *Essay on the Representation of Space and Time in Greek Political Thought from the End of the Sixth Century to the Death of Plato*. Translated by D.A. Curtis. Atlantic Highlands, NJ: Humanities Press.

Levitt, P. n.d. Social Remittances – Culture as a Development Tool. http://www.un-instraw.org/en/images/stories/remmitances/documents/Forum/peggy_levitt.pdf

Levitt, P., and N. Nyberg-Sörenson. 2004. The transnational turn in migration studies. *Global Migration Perspectives*, no. 6. Switzerland: Global Commission on International Migration.

Lewis, R., and S. Mills. 2003. Introduction. In *Feminist Postcolonial Theory*. 1–21. New York: Routledge.

Ley, D. 2003. Seeking Homo Economicus: The Canadian state and the strange story of the business immigration program. *Annals of the Association of American Geographers* 93(2): 426–41.

Li, P. 1998. *The Chinese in Canada*. New York: Oxford University Press.

– 2003. *Destination Canada: Immigration Debates and Issues*. Toronto: Oxford University Press.

– 2004. The place of immigrants: Politics of difference in territorial and social space. *Canadian Diversity* 3(2): 23–8.

Lister, R. 1997. *Citizenship: Feminist Perspectives*. New York: New York University Press.

Little, M. 1998. *No Car, No Radio, No Liquor Permit: The Moral Regulation of Single Mothers in Ontario, 1920–1997*. New York: Oxford University Press.

Lizin, A.-M. 2004. *Au delà du voile: Laïcité, féminisme et mondialisation*. Brussels: Editions Luc Pire.

López, A. 2005. *Postcolonial Whiteness: A Critical Reader on Race and Empire*. Albany: State University of New York Press.

Loughlin, M. 1986. *Local Government in the Modern State*. London: Sweet and Maxwell.
– 1996a. *Legality and Locality: The Role of Law in Central-Local Government Relations*. Oxford: Clarendon Press.
– 1996b. The constitutional status of local government. In *Local Democracy and Local Government*, ed. L. Pratchett and D. Wilson. 38–61. Basingstoke: Macmillan.
Low, A.M. 1943. *Benefits of War*. London: Gifford.
Lubbers, R. 2002. Opening Statement by Mr Rudd Lubbers UNHCR, Geneva, 30 sept. UNHCR Report of the Executive Committee of the Programme of the UNHCR. Fifty-third session (30 sept. – 4 oct. 2002) General Assembly Official Records. Fifty-seventh Session. Supplement No. 12A (A/57/12/Add.1) United Nations, New York. http://www.un.org/issues/docs/documents/a5712add1.pdf
Luzi, J. 2004. http://www.athletes.org
Ma, E.K.-W. 2002. Translocal spatiality. *International Journal of Cultural Studies* 5(2): 131–52.
MacGregor, S. 2006. *Beyond Mothering Earth: Ecological Citizenship and the Politics of Care*. Vancouver: UBC Press.
Mackay, B. 2006. Outsourcing your CT scan. *Ottawa Citizen*. 22 Oct.: A5.
Mackenzie, S. 1989. Restructuring relations of work and life: Women as environmental actors, feminism and geographical analysis. In *Remaking Human Geography*, ed. A. Kobayashi and S. Mackenzie. 40–61. London: Unwin Hyman.
Mahler, S.J. 1998. Theoretical and empirical contributions: Towards a research agenda for transnationalism. In *Transnationalism from Below*, eds. M.P. Smith and L.E. Guarnizo. New Brunswick, NJ: Transaction.
Mahmood, S. 2005. *The Politics of Piety. The Islamic Revival and the Feminist Subject*. Princeton: Princeton University Press.
Maitland, F.W. 2003. *State, Trust, and Corporation*. Cambridge: Cambridge University Press.
Mann, M. 1987. Ruling class strategies and citizenship. *Sociology* 21(3): 339–54.
– 1988. *States, War and Capitalism: Studies in Political Sociology*. Oxford: Blackwell.
Marcelo, R. 2003. India fosters growing 'medical tourism' sector. *Financial Times*. 2 July.
Marsh, L. 1943. *Report on Social Security for Canada*.
Marsh, M. 1990. *Suburban Lives*. New Brunswick, NJ: Rutgers University Press.
Marshall, T.H. 1950. *Citizenship and Social Class*. Cambridge: Cambridge University Press.
– 1965 [1949]. *Class, Citizenship, and Social Development*. New York: Doubleday.
Martinez-Alier, J. 2003. Mining conflicts, environmental justice and valuation.

In *Just Sustainabilities: Development in an Unequal World*, ed. J. Agyeman, R.D. Bullard, and B. Evans. 201–28. Cambridge, MA: MIT Press.

Marx, K. 1963. *The 18th Brumaire of Louis Bonaparte*. New York: International Publishers.

Massey, D. 1977. A global sense of place. In *Reading Human Geography: The Poetics and Politics of Inquiry*, ed. T. Barnes and D. Gregory. 315–23. London and New York: Arnold.

– 1994. *Space, Place and Gender*. Minneapolis: University of Minnesota Press.

May, S., T. Modood, and J. Squires. 2004. Ethnicity, nationalism, and minority rights: Charting the disciplinary debates. In *Ethnicity, Nationalism, and Minority Rights*, ed. S. May, T. Modood, and J. Squires. 1–26. Cambridge: Cambridge University Press.

McClintock, A. 1995. *Imperial Leather: Race, Gender and Sexuality in Colonial Context*. New York: Routledge.

McDonald, D.A. 2005. Environmental racism and neoliberal disorder in South Africa. In *The Quest for Environmental Justice: Human Rights and the Politics of Pollution*, ed. R.D. Bullard. 255–78. San Francisco: Sierra Club.

McDowell, L. 1983. Towards an understanding of the gender division of urban space. *Environment and Planning D* 1: 59–72.

– 1999. *Gender, Identity and Place: Understanding Feminist Geographies*. Minneapolis: University of Minnesota Press.

McInnis, P. 2002. *Harnessing Labour Confrontation: Shaping the Postwar Settlement in Canada, 1943–1950*. Toronto: University of Toronto Press.

McIntosh, T. 2000. Is the social union too 'healthy'? Re-thinking labour market policy. *Policy Options* (April): 48–9.

McLaren, A.T., and T.L. Black. 2005. *Family Class and Immigration in Canada: Implications for Sponsored Elderly Women*. Research on Immigration and Integration in the Metropolis (RIIM). Working Paper Series, No. 05-26. Vancouver: Vancouver Centre of Excellence.

McNevin, A. 2006. Political belonging in a neoliberal era: The struggle of the san-papiers. *Citizenship Studies* 10(2): 135–51.

– 2007. Irregular migrants, neoliberal geographies and spatial frontiers of 'the political.' *Review of International Studies* 33: 655–74.

Med Journeys. n.d. The Med Journey's Difference. Retrieved 26 Feb. 2006 from http://www.medjourneys.com/

METRAC (Metropolitan Action Committee on Violence against Women and Children; Pamela Cross). 2005. An Analysis of Marion Boyd's Review 'Dispute Resolution in Family Law: Protecting Choice, Promoting Inclusion.' http://www.metrac.org

Miles, R. 1988. *Racism*. London: Routledge.

Miller, P., and N. Rose. 1990. Governing economic life. *Economy and Society* 19(1): 1–31.

Mills, S. 1998. Post-colonial feminist theory. In *Contemporary Feminist Theories*, eds. S. Jackson and J. Jones. 98–112. Edinburgh: Edinburgh University Press.

Mink, G. 2002. *Welfare's End*, rev. ed. Ithaca and London: Cornell University Press.

Minow, M. 1986. Rights for the next generation: A feminist approach to children's rights. *Harvard Women's Law Journal* 9(1): 1–24.

Mitchell, D. 2003. *The Right to the City: Social Justice and the Fight for Public Space*. New York: Guilford Press.

Mitchell, T. 2002. *Rule of Experts: Egypt, Techno-Politics, Modernity*. Berkeley: University of California Press.

– 2005. Economists and the economy in the twentieth century. In *The Politics of Method in the Human Sciences: Positivism and Its Epistemological Others*, ed. G. Steinmetz. 126–41. Durham, NC: Duke University Press.

Modood, T. 1997. Introduction. In *The Politics of Multiculturalism in the New Europe: Racism, Identity and Community*, ed. T. Modood and P. Werbner. 1–25. London: Zed Books.

– 2007. *Multiculturalism*. London: Polity.

Moghissi, H. 1999. *Feminism and Islamic Fundamentalism. The Limits of Postmodern Analysis*. London: Zed Books.

Mohanty, C.T. 1988. Under Western eyes: Feminist scholarship and colonial discourses. *Feminist Review* 30: 60–88.

Mol, A. P.J. 2000. The environmental movement in an era of ecological modernization. *Geoforum* 31: 45–56.

Mongia, R.V. 2003. Race, nationality, mobility: A history project. In *After the Imperial Turn: Thinking with and through the Nation*, ed. A. Burton. 196–213. Durham, NC: Duke University Press.

Monture, P. 1989. A vicious circle: Child welfare and the First Nations. *Canadian Journal of Women and the Law* 3: 1–17.

Moodley, K. 1984. The predicament of racial affirmative action: A critical review of equality now. *Queen's Quarterly* 91: 795–806.

Mookherjee, M. 2005. Affective citizenship: Feminism, postcolonialism and the politics of recognition. *Critical Review of International Social and Political Philosophy* 8(1): 31–50.

Moors, A. 2004. Islam and fashion on the streets of San'a, Yemen. *Etnofoor* 16(2): 41–56.

– 2005. Submission. *ISIM Review* 15 (Spring): 8–9. http://www.isim.nl/files/review15/review15–8.pdf

Moreno, L., and N. McEwan. 2003. The Welfare State and Territorial Politics: An Under-Explored Relationship. ECPR Joint Sessions, Workshop 10.

University of Edinburgh. http://essex.ac.uk/ECPR/events/jointsessions/paperarchive/edinburgh/ws10/MorenoMcEwen.pdf

Morissette, R., J. Myles, and G. Picot. 1995. Earnings polarization in Canada, 1969–1991. In *Labour Market Polarization and Social Policy Reform*, ed. K.G. Banting and C.M. Beach. 23–50. Kingston, ON: Queen's University School of Policy Studies.

Morton, D. 1990. *A Military History of Canada*. Edmonton: Hurtig.

Moskos, C. 2005. Towards a New Conception of the Citizen Soldier. Foreign Policy Research Institute. 7 April. Retrieved 15 March 2005 from www.fpri.org/enotes/20050407.military.moskos.newconceptioncitizensoldier.html

Muller, B. 2004. (Dis)qualified bodies: Securitization, citizenship and 'identity management.' *Citizenship Studies* 8(3): 279–94.

Mumford, L. 1938. *The Culture of Cities*. New York: Harcourt, Brace and World.

– 1961. *The City in History: Its Origins, Its Transformations, and Its Prospects*. London: Harcourt Brace Jovanovich.

Murphy, L. 2003. America, Land of the Watched: CAPPS II and the Dangers of Unchecked Surveillance. Remarks by Laura Murphy, Director, ACLU Washington Legislative Office at the National Press Club, 25 Aug., Washington, DC. http://www.aclu.org/SafeandFree/SafeandFree.cfm?ID=13355&c=206

Murphy, M., and S. Harty. 2003. Post-sovereign citizenship. *Citizenship Studies* 7(2): 181–97.

Mutimer, D. 2007. Sovereign contradictions: Maher Arar and the indefinite future. In *The Logics of Biopower and the War on Terror: Living, Dying, Surviving*, ed. E. Dauphinee and C. Masters. 160–79. Houndmills: Palgrave-Macmillan.

Nadesan, M.H. 2002. Engineering the entrepreneurial infant: Brain science, infant development toys, and governmentality. *Cultural Studies* 16(3): 401–32.

Narayan, K. 1997. How native is a 'native' anthropologist? In *Situated Lives: Gender and Culture in Everyday Life*, ed. L. Lamphere, H. Ragone, and P. Zavella. 23–41. New York: Routledge.

National Council of Welfare Report. 2004. *Poverty Profile 2001: Number 122*. Ottawa: Ministry of Public Works and Government Services.

Neubeck, K.J., and N.A. Cazenave. 2001. *Welfare Racism: Playing the Race Card against America's Poor*. New York: Routledge.

New York Times. 2006. New urbanism: It's in the army now. 8 June. http://www.nytimes.com/2006/06/08/garden/08military.html?_r=1&oref-slogin

Newby, H. 1996. Citizenship in a green world: Global commons and human stewardship. In *Citizenship Today: The Contemporary Relevance of T.H. Marshall*, ed. M. Bulmer and A.M. Rees. 209–21. London: UCL Press.

Newman, B. 1976. British Army and Social Change: Military Organizations and Social Change with Particular Reference to the British Army, 1962–1975. Doctoral dissertation, NE London Polytechnic.

No Border Network. 2002. Campaign to Combat Global Migration Management. *IOM Counter-Bulletin*. http://www.noborder,org/about/index.html

No One Is Illegal U.K. 2003. No One Is Illegal Manifesto. 6 Sept. http://www.noii.org.uk

Novotny, P. 1998. Popular epistemology and the struggle for community health in the environmental justice movement. In *The Struggle for Ecological Democracy: Environmental Justice Movements in the United States*, ed. D. Faber. 137–58. New York: Guilford Press.

Nussbaum, M. 1999. *Sex and Social Justice*. New York: Oxford University Press.

Nyers, P. 2003. Abject cosmopolitanism: The politics of protection in the anti-deportation movement. *Third World Quarterly* 24(6): 1069–93.

– 2006a. The accidental citizen: Acts of sovereignty and (un)making citizenship. *Economy and Society* 35(1): 22–41.

– 2006b. *Rethinking Refugees: Beyond States of Emergency.* New York: Routledge.

Ó Tuathail, G. 1996. *Critical Geopolitics: The Political of Writing Global Political Space*. London: Routledge.

O'Neill, J. 1994. *The Missing Child in Liberal Theory: Towards a Covenant Theory of Family, Community, Welfare and the Civic State*. Toronto: University of Toronto Press.

O'Neill, K. 2003. Using Remittances and Circular Migration to Drive Development. *Migration Information Source*. 1 June. Retrieved 26 Feb. 2007 from http://www.migrationinformation.org/USfocus/display.cfm?ID=133

O'Neill, O. 1992. Children's rights and children's lives. *International Journal of Law, Policy and the Family* 6(1): 24–42.

OECD. 2006. *Starting Strong II: Early Childhood Education and Care*. Paris: OECD.

Offe, C. 1984. *Contradictions of the Welfare State*. Cambridge, MA: MIT Press.

Okin, S. 1994. Gender inequalities and cultural differences. *Political Theory* 22(1): 5–21.

– 1999. Is multiculturalism bad for women? and Response. In *Is Multiculturalism Bad for Women?*, ed. J. Cohen, M. Howard, and M.C. Nussbaum. 9–24. Princeton, NJ: Princeton University Press.

Omi, M., and H. Winant. 1986. *Racial Formation in the United States. From the 1960s to the 1980s*. New York: Routledge and Kegan Paul.

Ong, A. 1996. Cultural citizenship as subject making: Immigrants negotiate racial and cultural boundaries in the United States. *Current Anthropology* 37(5): 737–62.

– 1999. *Flexible Citizenship: The Cultural Logics of Transnationality.* Durham and London: Duke University Press.

– 2003. *Buddha Is Hiding: Refugees, Citizenship in the New America*. Berkeley: University of California Press.
– 2005. Splintering cosmopolitanism: Asian immigrants and zones of autonomy in the American West. In *Sovereign Bodies: Citizens, Migrants, and States in the Postcolonial World*, ed. T.B. Hanesha and F. Stepputat. Princeton, NJ: Princeton University Press.
– 2006. *Neoliberalism as Exception: Mutations in Citizenship and Sovereignty*. Durham, NC: Duke University Press.
Ong, A., and S.J. Collier, eds. 2005. *Global Assemblages: Technology, Politics and Ethics as Anthropological Problems*. New York: Blackwell.
Oppenheimer, M. 2005. Voluntary action and welfare in post-1945 Australia: Preliminary perspectives. *History Australia* 2: 16–18.
Orozco, M. 2003. *The Impact of Migration in the Caribbean and Central American Region*. Focal Policy Paper FPP-03-03, Ottawa: Canadian Foundation for the Americas.
Papastergiadis, N. 2000. *The Turbulence of Migration: Globalization, Deterritorialization and Hybridity*. Oxford: Polity Press.
Parekh, B. 2000. *The Future of Multi-Ethnic Britain*. London: Runnymede Trust.
– 2004. Recognition or redistribution? A misguided debate. In *Ethnicity, Nationalism, and Minority Rights*, ed. S. May, T. Modood, and J. Squires. 199–213. Cambridge: Cambridge University Press.
Parreñas, R.S. 2001. *Servants of Globalization: Women, Migration, and Domestic Work*. Stanford: Stanford University Press.
Patel, D. 2006. The maple-neem Nexus: Transnational links of South Asian Canadians. In *Transnational Identities and Practices in Canada*, ed. V. Satzewich and L. Wong. Vancouver: UBC Press.
Pecoud, A., and de Guchteneire, P. 2004. *Migration, Human Rights and the United Nations: An Investigation into the Low Ratification Record of the U.N. Migrant Workers Convention*. Global Migration Perspectives, no. 3. Geneva: GCIM.
Pellerin, H. 2005. Borders, migration and economic integration: Towards a new political economy of borders. In *Global Surveillance and Policing: Borders, Security and Identity*, ed. E. Zuriek and M.B. Salter. 51–65. Portland: Willan.
Peña, D.G. 2002. Endangered landscapes and disappearing peoples? Identity, place, and community in ecological politics. In *The Environmental Justice Reader: Politics, Poetics and Pedagogy*, ed. J. Adamson, M.M. Evans, and R. Stein. 58–81. Tucson: University of Arizona Press.
– 2003. Identity, place and communities of resistance. In *Just Sustainabilities: Development in an Unequal World*, ed. J. Agyeman, R.D. Bullard, and B. Evans. 146–67. London: Earthscan.

– 2005. *Mexican Americans and the Environment: Tierra y Vida.* Tucson: University of Arizona Press.

Phillips, A. 1997. From inequality to difference: A severe case of displacement? *New Left Review,* no. 224: 124–53.

– 2007. *Multiculturalism without Culture.* Princeton, NJ: Princeton University Press.

Pirenne, H. 1925. *Medieval Cities: Their Origins and the Revival of Trade.* Princeton, NJ: Princeton University Press.

PMU. 2005. Progressive Muslims Oppose Introduction of Shari'a Law in Canada. Official Response by PMU on the Marion Boyd Report. http://www.pmuna.org/archives/2005/01/progressivemus2

Poggi, G. 1978. *The Development of the Modern State: A Sociological Introduction.* Stanford: Stanford University Press.

– 1990. *The State: Its Nature, Development, and Prospects.* Cambridge: Polity Press.

Polanyi, K. 1957 [1944]. *The Great Transformation: The Political and Economic Origins of Our Time.* Boston: Beacon Press.

Porter, J. 1975. Ethnic pluralism in Canadian perspective. In *Ethnicity: Theory and Experience,* ed. N. Glazer and D. Moynihan. 267–304. Cambridge, MA: Harvard University Press.

Powell, M. 2002. The hidden history of social citizenship. *Citizenship Studies* 6(3): 229–44.

Preston, R. 1972. Military influences on the development of Canada. In *The Canadian Military: A Profile,* ed. H. Massey. 49–85. Toronto: Copp Clark.

Prins, B. 2002. The nerve to break taboos: New realism in the Dutch discourse on multiculturalism. *Journal of International Migration and Integration* 3(3/4): 363–80.

Prins, B., and S. Saharso. 2006. Cultural diversity, gender equality: The Dutch case. Paper presented at the Gender Equality and Cultural Diversity: European Comparisons and Lessons Conference, Vrije Universiteit, Amsterdam, 8–9 June.

Privacy International. 2004. An Open Letter to the ICAO: A Second Report on 'Towards an International Infrastructure for Surveillance of Movement.' 30 March. http://www.privacyinternational.org/issues/terrorism/rpt/icaobackground.html

Province, The. 2004. Our outdated immigration policies need youth. 12 Aug.

Pulido, L. 1996. *Environmentalism and Economic Justice: Two Chicano Struggles in the Southwest.* Tucson: University of Arizona Press.

– 1998. Ecological legitimacy and cultural essentialism: Hispano grazing in the southwest. In *The Struggle for Ecological Democracy: Environmental Justice*

Movements in the United States, ed. D. Faber. 293–311. New York: Guilford Press.

Pushchak, R. 2002. Environmental justice and the EIS: Low-level military flights in Canada. *International Journal of Public Administration* 25(23): 169–91.

Quadagno, J.S. 1994. *The Color of Welfare: How Racism Undermined the War on Poverty.* New York: Oxford University Press.

Rabinow, P., and N. Rose. 2003. Thoughts on the Concept of Biopower Today. Unpublished paper. Retrieved 1 May 2006 from http://www.molsci.org/files/Rose_Rabinow_Biopower_Today

Rajan, S.R. 1993. *Real and Imagined Women: Gender, Culture and Postcolonialism.* London: Routledge.

Ramesh, R. 2005. This U.K. patient avoided the NGS list and flew to India for a heart bypass. Is health tourism the future? *Guardian*. 1 Feb.

Ramusack, B. 1990. Cultural missionaries, maternal imperialists, and feminist allies: British women activists in India, 1865–1945. *Women's Studies International Forum* 13(4): 309–22.

Rayment, S. 2006. Say hello to sailors at gay march. *Daily Telegraph,* online ed. Retrieved 25 June 2006 from http://www.telegraph.co.uk/news/main.jhtml?xml=/news/2006/06/25/ngay25.xml&sSheet=/news/2006/06/25/ixuknews.html

Razack, S. 2000. Your place or mine? Transnational feminist collaboration. In *Anti-Racist Feminism*, ed. A. Calliste and G. Dei. 39–53. Halifax: Fernwood Press.

– 2004. Imperiled Muslim women, dangerous Muslim men and civilized Europeans: Legal and social responses to forced marriages. *Feminist Legal Studies* 12(2): 129–74.

Resnick, S.A., and R.D. Wolff. 1996. Markets, private property, socialism, and capitalism. In *Marxism Today: Essays on Capitalism, Socialism and Strategies for Social Change*, ed. C. Polychroniou and H.R. Targ. 119–42. Westport, CT: Praeger.

Rex, J., and G. Singh. 2003. Multiculturalism and political integration in modern nation-states – thematic introduction. *International Journal on Multicultural Societies* 5(1): 3–19.

Rich, A. 1979. Disloyal to civilization: Feminism, racism, gynephobia. In *On lies, Secrets, and Silence: Selected Prose, 1966–1978*. 275–310. New York: W.W. Norton.

Richards, J. 1997. *Retooling the Welfare State: What's Right, What's Wrong, What's to Be Done.* Ottawa: C.D. Howe Institute/Renouf Publishing.

Rygiel, K. 2006. Protecting and proving identity: The Biopolitics of waging war through citizenship in the post 9/11 era: In *(En)Gendering the War on Terror:*

War Stories and Camouflage Politics, ed. K. Hunt and K. Rygiel. 140–62. Burlington, VT: Ashgate Press.

Roche, M. 1992. *Rethinking Citizenship: Welfare, Ideology and Change in Modern Society.* Cambridge: Polity Press.

Rodrik, D. 1998. The global fix. *New Republic* 219(18): 17–21.

Romero, M. 1992. *Maid in the USA.* New York: Routledge.

Rorty, R. 2000. Is 'cultural recognition' a useful notion for leftist politics? *Critical Horizons* 1(1): 7–20.

Rose, N. 1996a. Governing 'advanced' liberal democracies. In *Foucault and Political Reason*, ed. A. Barry, T. Osborne and N. Rose. Chicago: University of Chicago Press.

– 1996b. The death of the social? Re-figuring the territory of government. *Economy and Society* 25(3): 327–56.

– 1999a. *Powers of Freedom: Reframing Political Thought.* Cambridge: Cambridge University Press.

– 1999b. *Governing the Soul: The Shaping of the Private Self.* London: Free Association of Books.

Rose, N., and P. Miller. 1992. Political power beyond the state: Problematics of government. *British Journal of Sociology* 43: 173–205.

Ruddick, S. 1992. Das gesellscahftliche konstruiren: Armut, Geslechtverhältnisse und Familie im goldenen Zeitalter. In *Hegemonie und Staat*, ed. A. Demirovic, H.-P. Krebs, and T. Sablowski. 290–303. Munster: Westfalisches Dampfboot Verlag.

Rudolph, C. 2003. Security and the political economy of international migration. *American Political Science Review* 97(4): 603–20.

Ruggie, J.G. 1993. Territoriality and beyond: Problematizing modernity and international relations. *International Organization* 47(1): 139–74.

Ruppert, E.S. 2006. Rights to public space: Regulatory reconfigurations of liberty. *Urban Geography* 27(3): 271–92.

Russell, S.S. 2003. Migration and Development: Reframing the International Policy Agenda. *Migration Information Source.* June. http://www.migrationinformation.org/Feature/display.cfm?ID=126

Saïd. E. 1978. *Orientalism.* London: Penguin.

– 2003. Préface (2003). In *L'Orientalisme. L'Orient créé par l'Occident.* Paris: Seuil.

Saíz, A.V. 2005. Globalization, cosmopolitanism and ecological citizenship. *Environmental Politics* 14(2): 163–78.

Sales, R. 2002. The deserving and the undeserving? Refugees, asylum seekers and welfare in Britain. *Critical Social Policy* 22: 456–78

Salter, M. 2004. Passports, mobility, and security: How smart can the border be? *International Studies Perspectives* 5(1): 71–91.

Sandikci, O., and G. Ger. 2005. Aesthetics, ethics and the politics of the Turkish headscarf. In *Clothing as Material Culture*, ed. S. Kuechler and D. Miller. 61–82. Oxford: Berg.

Sandilands, C. 2004. Sexual politics and environmental justice: Lesbian separatists in rural Oregon. In *New Perspectives on Environmental Justice: Gender, Sexuality, and Activism*, ed. R. Stein. 109–26. New Brunswick, NJ: Rutgers University Press.

Sands, P. 2005. *Lawless World: Making and Breaking Global Rules*. London and New York: Penguin.

Sassen, S. 2006. *Territory, Authority, Rights: From Medieval to Global Assemblages*. Princeton, NJ: Princeton University Press.

Satzewich, V., and L. Wong, eds. 2006a. *Transnational Identities and Practices in Canada*. Vancouver: UBC Press.

– 2006b. Introduction: The meaning and significance of transnationalism. In *Transnational Identities and Practices in Canada*, ed. V. Satzewich and L. Wong. 1–17. Vancouver: UBC Press.

Saunders, D. 2006. What Canada needs now: A million poor Africans. *Globe and Mail*. 17 June.

Saunders, P. 1986. *Social Theory and the Urban Question*, 2nd ed. London: Hutchinson Education.

Schatzki, T.R. 2002. *The Site of the Social: A Philosophical Account of the Constitution of Social Life and Change*. University Park: Pennsylvania State University Press.

Schermerhorn, R.A. 1970. *Comparative Ethnic Relations: A Framework for Theory and Research*. New York: Random House.

Schild, V. 2000. Neo-liberalism's new gendered market citizens: The 'civilizing' dimension of social programmes in Chile. *Citizenship Studies* 4(3): 275–305.

Schlosberg, D. 1999. *Environmental Justice and the New Pluralism*. Oxford: Oxford University Press.

– 2004. Reconceiving environmental justice: Global movements and political theories. *Environmental Politics* 13(3): 517–40.

Schwartz, H. 1997. On the origin of the phrase 'social problems.' *Social Problems* 44(2): 276–96.

Scobey, D. 2001. The spectre of citizenship. *Citizenship Studies* 5(1): 11–26.

Scott, D., and C. Oelofse. 2005. Social and environmental justice in South African cities: Including 'invisible stakeholders' in environmental assessment procedures. *Journal of Environmental Planning and Management* 48(3): 445–67.

Secor, A.J. 2003. Citizenship in the city: Identity, community, and rights among women migrants to Istanbul. *Urban Geography* 24(2): 147–68.

Segal, D. 1989. *Recruiting for Uncle Sam: Citizenship and Military Manpower Policy*. Lawrence: University Press of Kansas.

Shachar, A. 2000. The puzzle of interlocking power hierarchies: Sharing the pieces of jurisdictional authority. *Harvard Civil Rights – Civil Liberties Review.* 35: 385–426.

– 2001. *Multicultural Jurisdictions: Cultural Differences and Women's Rights*. Cambridge: Cambridge University Press.

– 2007. The worth of citizenship in an unequal world. *Theoretical Inquiries in Law* 8(2): 367–88.

Shafir, G. 2004. Citizenship and human rights in an era of globalization. In *People Out of Place: Globalization, Human Rights and the Citizenship Gap*, ed. A. Brysk and G. Shafir. 11–25. New York: Routledge.

Sharma, N. 2002. Open The Borders! Interview by Cynthia Wright. *New Socialist Magazine* 37. http://www.newsocialist.org/magazine/37/article02.html

– 2006. White nationalism, illegality and imperialism: Border controls as ideology. In *(En)Gendering the War on Terror: War Stories and Camouflage Politics*, ed. K. Hunt and K. Rygiel, 117–39. Burlington, VT: Ashgate.

Shaver, S. 2002. Australian welfare reform: From citizenship to supervision. *Social Policy and Administration* 36(4): 331–45.

Shewell, H. 2004. *'Enough to Keep Them Alive': Indian Welfare in Canada, 1873–1965*. Toronto: University of Toronto Press.

Siltanen, J. 2002. The fate of social citizenship in Canada. *Citizenship Studies* 6(4): 395–414.

Silver, C. 2000. Being there: The time dual-earner couples spend with their children. *Canadian Social Trends* (Summer): 26–9.

Simmel, G. 1971 [1903]. Metropolis and mental life. In *On Individuality and Social Forms*, ed. D.N. Levine, 324–39. Chicago: University of Chicago Press.

Simon, P.-J. 1983. Le sociologue et les minorités: connaissance et idéologie. *Sociologie et Sociétés* 15(2): 9–21.

Singel, R. 2004. Secure Flight Gets Wary Welcome. *Wired News*. 8 Aug. http://www.wired.com/news/privacy/1,64748-0.html

Singer, B. 2006. Thinking the 'Social' with Claude Lefort. *Thesis Eleven* 87: 83–95.

Skocpol, T. 1992. *Protecting soldiers and mothers: The political origins of social policy in the United States*. Cambridge, MA: Belknap Press.

Smith, A.M. 2001. Missing poststructuralism, missing Foucault: Butler and Fraser on capitalism and the regulation of sexuality. *Social Text* 19(2): 103–225.

Smith, G. 2005. Green citizenship and the social economy. *Environmental Politics* 14(2): 273–89.

Smith, M. 2005. Ecological citizenship and ethical responsibility: Arendt, Benjamin and political activism. *Environments* 33(3): 51–63.

Smith, N. 1984. *Uneven Development: Nature, Capital and the Production of Space.* London: Blackwell.

Soja, E. 1989. *Postmodern Geographies: The Reassertion of Space in Critical Social Theory.* London and New York: Verso.

Solberg, M. 2006. Reports on Plans and Priorities 2006–2007. Citizenship and Immigration Canada. Retrieved 12 Jan 2007 from http://www.tbs-sct.gc.ca/rpp/0607/CI-CI

Solomos, J. 1988. Varieties of Marxist conceptions of 'race,' class and state: A critical analysis. In *Theories of Race and Ethnic Relations,* ed. J. Rex and D. Mason. 84 –109. New York: Cambridge University Press.

Southall, A.W. 1998. *The City in Time and Space.* Cambridge: Cambridge University Press.

Soysal, Y. 1994. *Limits of Citizenship: Migrants and Postnational Membership in Europe.* Chicago: University of Chicago Press.

Spelman, E. 1988. *Inessential Woman.* Boston: Beacon Press.

Spivak, G.C. 1988. Can the subaltern speak? In *Marxism and the Interpretation of Culture,* ed. C. Nelson and L. Grossberg. 271–313. Urbana: University of Illinois Press.

Sponsor Your Parents (SYP). 2007. http://www.sponsoryourparents. ca

Spruyt, H. 1994. *The Sovereign State and Its Competitors: An Analysis of Systems Change.* Princeton Studies in International History and Politics. Princeton, NJ: Princeton University Press.

SSHRC. 2004a. *From Granting Council to Knowledge Council: Renewing the Social Sciences and Humanities in Canada,* vol. 1, *Consultation Framework on SSHRC'S Transformation.* Ottawa: Social Sciences and Humanities Research Council (SSHRC).

SSHRC. 2004b. *From Granting Council to Knowledge Council: Renewing the Social Sciences and Humanities in Canada,* vol. 2, *Background Facts for the Consultation on SSHRC's Transformation.* Ottawa: SSHRC.

SSHRC. 2005. *From Granting Council to Knowledge Council: Renewing the Social Sciences and Humanities in Canada.* Vol. 3, *Report on the Consultations.* Ottawa: SSHRC.

Stalker, P. 2000. *Workers without Frontiers: The Impact of Globalization On International Migration.* Boulder, CO: Lynne Rienner Publishers; Geneva: International Labour Office.

Stanley, J., and B. Steinhardt. 2003. *Bigger Monster, Weaker Chains: The Growth of an American Surveillance Society.* New York: American Civil Liberties Union.

Star-Phoenix. 2005. Regional focus to immigration can be effective. 27 Sept.

Stasiulis, D. 2002a. Introduction: Reconfiguring Canadian citizenship. *Citizenship Studies* 6(4): 365–75.

– 2002b. The active child citizen: Lessons from Canadian policy and the children's movement. *Citizenship Studies* 6(4): 507–38.

Stasiulis, D.K., and A.B. Bakan. 2003. Negotiating citizenship: Migrant women in Canada and the global system. London: Palgrave-Macmillan.

Stasiulis, D.K., and D. Ross. 2006. Security, flexible sovereignty, and the perils of multiple citizenship. *Citizenship Studies* 10(3): 329–48.

Statewatch 2003. EU: Commission 'Compromises' and Agrees on Handing Over Passenger Data to USA. *Statewatch News*, online. http://www.statewatch.org/news/2003/dec/11euuspassengerdeal.htm

Statham, P. 2003. New conflicts about integration and cultural diversity in Britain: The Muslim challenge to race relations. In *The Challenge of Diversity: European Social Democracy Facing Migration, Integration, and Multiculturalism*, ed. R. Cuperus, K. Duffek, and J. Kandel. 126–49. Munich: Studien-Verlag.

Statistics Canada. 2006. *Women in Canada*. Ottawa: Ministry of Industry.

Stein, J.G., ed. 2007. *Uneasy Partners: Multiculturalism and Rights in Canada*. Waterloo: Wilfrid Laurier University Press.

Stein, R., ed. 2004. *New Perspectives on Environmental Justice: Gender, Sexuality, and Activism*. New Brunswick, NJ: Rutgers University Press.

Stenson, K., and P. Watt. 1999. Governmentality and the 'death of the social'? A discourse analysis of local government texts in south-east England. *Urban Studies* 36: 189–201.

Stolcke, V. 1995. Talking culture: New boundaries, new rhetorics of exclusion in Europe. *Current Anthropology* 36(1): 1–24.

Stopler, G. 2003. Countenancing the oppression of women: How liberals tolerate religious and cultural practices that discriminate against women. *Columbia Journal of Gender and Law* 12: 154–221.

Struthers, J. 1998. Family allowances, old age security, and the construction of entitlement in the Canadian welfare state, 1943–1951. In *The Veterans Charter and Post-World War II Canada*, ed. P. Neary and J. Granatstein. 179–204. Montreal and Kingston: McGill-Queen's University Press.

Swank, D. 2002. *Global Capitalism, Political Institutions and Policy Change in Developed Welfare States*. Cambridge: Cambridge University Press.

Swanson, J. 2005. Recognition and redistribution: Rethinking culture and the economic. *Theory, Culture and Society* 224: 87–118.

Taylor, C. 1994 [1992]. The politics of recognition. In *Multiculturalism: Examining the Politics of Recognition*, ed. A. Gutmann. 25–74. Princeton, NJ: Princeton University Press.

Taylor, P.J. 1994. The state as container: Territoriality in the modern world system. *Progress in Human Geography* 18(2): 151–62.

Tazreiter, C. 2003. Asylum-Seekers as Pariahs in the Australian State Security Against the Few. U.N. University World Institute for Development Economics Research (WIDER) Discussion Paper no. 2003/19, Feb. http://www.unu.edu/hq/library/Collection/PDF_files/WIDER/WIDERdp2003.19.pdf

Teelucksingh, C. 2002. Spatiality and environmental justice in Parkdale (Toronto). *Ethnologies* 24(1): 119–41.

Ten, C.L. 1993. Liberalism and multiculturalism. In *Multiculturalism, Difference and Postmodernism*, ed. G.L. Clark, D. Forbes, and R. Francis. 54–67. Melbourne: Longman Cheshire.

Teo, P. 2000. Racism in the news: A critical discourse analysis of news reporting in two Australian newspapers. *Discourse and Society* 11(1): 7–49.

Tersigni, S. 2005. La pratique du hijab en France. In *La politisation du voile en France, en Europe et dans le monde arabe*, ed. F. Lorcerie. 37–52. Paris: L'Harmattan.

Third World Network, Environment Liaison Centre International, and Danish 92 Group. 2002. Prepcom IV: Dialogue Paper by Non-governmental Organisations. Retrived 17 Aug. 2006 from http://www.twnside.org.sg/title/prepcom4.htm

Tillotson, S. 2000. *The Public at Play: Gender and the Politics of Recreation in Post-War Ontario*. Toronto: University of Toronto Press.

Tilly, C. 1992. *Coercion, Capital, and European States, AD, 990–1992*. Cambridge, MA: Blackwell.

– 1994. Entanglements of European cities and states. In *Cities and the Rise of States in Europe, AD 1000 to 1800*, ed. C. Tilly and W.P. Blockmans. 1–27. Boulder, CO: Westview.

Titmuss, R. 1958. *Essays on 'the Welfare State'*. London: George Allen and Unwin.

Torgerson, D. 1999. *The Promise of Green Politics: Environmentalism and the Green Public Sphere*. Durham, NC: Duke University Press.

– 2006. Expanding the green public sphere: Post-colonial connections. *Environmental Politics* 15(5): 713–30.

Toronto Star. 2005a. Editorial: Population report urgent wake-up call. 30 Sept.

– 2005b. Ottawa plans 40% rise in immigration. 25 Sept.

Torpey, J. 1998. Coming and going: On the state monopolization of the legitimate Means of movement. *Sociological Theory* 16(3): 239–59.

Triantafillou, P., and A. Moreita. 2002. Rehearsing citizenship: The governing of juvenile delinquency in colonial Malaya. *Citizenship Studies* 6(3): 325–40.

TSA (Transport Security Administration). Secure Flight Program. http://www.tsa.gov/what_we_do/layers/secureflight/index.shtm

Tully, J. 2000. Struggles over recognition and distribution. *Constellations* 74: 469–82.

– 2002. The illiberal Liberal: Brian Berry's polemical attack on multiculturalism. In *Multiculturalism Reconsidered*, ed. P. Kelly. 102–114. Cambridge: Polity Press.

– 2005. Two meanings of global citizenship: Modern and diverse. Paper presented at the Meanings of Global Citizenship Conference, Liu Centre and Trudeau Foundation, University of British Columbia, Vancouver, 9–10 Sept.

Turner, B.S. 1990. Outline of a theory of citizenship. *Sociology* 24(2): 189–217.

– 1997. From governmentality to risk: Some reflections on Foucault's contribution to medical sociology. In *Foucault, Health and Medicine*, ed. A. Petersen and R. Bunton. London and New York: Routledge.

U.K. Government. 2003. A New Vision for Refugees. March 7. 1–31. http://www.proasyl.info/texte/europe/union/2003/UK_NewVision.pdf

U.K. Government. 2004. Asylum and Immigration (Treatment of Claimants, etc.) Act. Office of Public Sector Information. http://www.opsi.gov.uk/acts/acts2004/ukpga_20040019_en_1

U.K. Government. 2005. Prevention of Terrorism Act. Office of Public Sector Information http://www.opsi.gov.uk/acts/acts2005/ukpga_20050002_en_1

Unger, N.C. 2004. Women, sexuality, and environmental justice in American history. In *New Perspectives on Environmental Justice: Gender, Sexuality, and Activism*, ed. R. Stein. 45–77. New Brunswick, NJ: Rutgers University Press.

United Nations, Economic Commission for Europe. Aarhus Convention. Retrieved 27 Aug. 2006 from http://www.unece.org/env/pp/welcome.html

– General Assembly. 1948. Universal Declaration of Human Rights. Retrieved 2 Jan. 2008 from http://www.multiculturalaustralia.edu.au/doc/unhrights_ 1.pdf

U.S. White House. 2002. U.S.-Canada Smart Border/ 30 Point Action Plan Update. 6 Dec. Office of the Press Secretary. http://www.whitehouse.gov/news/releases/2002/12/20021206-1.html

Valdivielso, J. 2005. Social citizenship and the environment. *Environmental Politics* 14(2): 239–54.

Valencia Sáis, A. 2005. Globalisation, cosmopolitanism and ecological citizenship. *Environmental Politics* 14(2): 163–78.

Valverde, M. 2005. Michel Foucault, *Society Must Be Defended: Lectures at the College de France, 1976–77. Law, Culture and the Humanities* 1: 119–31.

Van der Veer, P. 2005. Virtual India: Indian IT labor and the nation-state. In *Sovereign Bodies: Citizens, Migrants, and States in the Postcolonial World*, ed. T.B. Hansen and F. Stepputat. 169–91. Princeton, NJ: Princeton University Press.

Van Hear, N. 1998. New diasporas: The mass exodus, dispersal and regrouping of migrant communities. Seattle: University of Washington Press.

Vanstone, A. (Senator and Minister for Immigration and Multicultural and Indigenous Affairs). 2003. *Border Protection: Unauthorised Arrivals and Detention – Information Paper.* Government of Australia. http://www.minister.immi.gov.au/media_releases/ruddock_media01/r01131_bgpaper.htm

Varsanyi, M. 2006. Interrogating 'urban citizenship' vis-à-vis undocumented migration. *Citizenship Studies* 10: 229–49.

Venel, N. 1999. *Musulmanes françaises. Des pratiquantes voilées à l'université.* Paris: L'Harmattan.

Venter, J.C. 2005. India emerging as biotech outsourcing destination. *biopeer: the global life sciences research community blog*. 20 May. http://www.biopeer.com/biopeer/2005/05/strongindia_eme.htm

Vertovec, S. 1999. Conceiving and researching transnationalism. *Ethnic and Racial Studies* 22(2): 447–62.

Volpp, L. 2005. Feminism versus multiculturalism. In *Domestic Violence at the Margins: Readings in Race, Class, Gender and Culture,* ed. N.J. Sokoloff and C. Pratt, 39–49. Piscataway, NJ: Rutgers University Press.

Vosko, L. 2003. Gender differentiation and the standard/non-standard employment distinction in Canada: A Genealogy of Policy Interventions in Canada. In *Social Differentiation: Patterns and Processes,* ed. D. Juteau. 25. Toronto and Montreal: University of Toronto Press.

Waever, O. 1995. Securitization and desecuritization. In *On Security,* ed. R. Lipschutz. 46–86. New York: Columbia University Press.

Walby, S. 1986. *Patriarchy at Work.* Cambridge: Polity Press.

Walker, R.B.J. 1993. *Inside/Outside: International Relations as Political Theory.* Cambridge Studies in International Relations. Newcastle: Cambridge University Press.

Wallace, E. 1950. The origin of the social welfare state in Canada, 1867–1900. *Canadian Journal of Economics and Political Science* 16(3): 383–93.

Walters, W. 2002. Deportation, expulsion and the international policing of aliens. *Citizenship Studies* 6(3): 265–92.

Walzer, M. 1984. Liberalism and the art of separation. *Political Theory* 12(3): 315–30.

Wang, H.-L. 2004. Regulating transnational flows of people: An institutional analysis of passports and visas as a regime of mobility. *Identities* 11(3): 351–76.

Ware, V. 1992. *Beyond the Pale: White Women, Racism and History.* London: Verso.

Weber, M. 1958 [1921]. *The City.* New York: Free Press.

– 1976 [1909]. *The Agrarian Sociology of Ancient Civilizations*. Translated by R.I. Frank. London: New Left Books.

– 1978 [1968; 1921–22]. *Economy and Society,* vol. 1. Edited by E. Fischoff et al.; translated from *Wirtschaft und Gesellschaft, Grundriss der verstehenden Soziologie*. Berkeley and Los Angeles: University of California Press.

– 1981 [1923]. *General Economic History.* New Brunswick, NJ: Transaction.

Weiner, T. 2005. A new call to arms: Military health care. *New York Times*. 14 April.

Westra, L. 1999. Environmental racism and the First Nations of Canada: Terrorism at Oka. *Journal of Social Philosophy* 30(1): 103–24.

White, M., and A. Hunt. 2000. Citizenship: Care of the self, character and personality. *Citizenship Studies* 4(2): 93–116.

Wiegers, W. 2002. *The Framing of Poverty as 'Child Poverty' and Its Implications for Women*. Ottawa: Status of Women Canada.

Wilensky, H. 1975. *The Welfare State and Equality: Structural and Ideological Roots of Public Expenditure*. Berkeley: University of California Press.

Williams, F. 1987. Racism and the discipline of social policy: A critique of welfare theory. *Critical Social Policy* 7: 4–29 .

Wilson, R. 1942. Facilitation of naturalization through military service. *American Journal of International Law* 36: 454–60.

Wilson. T.J. 1996. Feminism and the institutionalized racism. *Feminist Review* 52: 1–26.

Wirth, L. 1938. Urbanism as a way of life. *American Journal of Sociology* 44(1): 1–24.

Withol de Wenden, C. 2003. Multiculturalism in France. *International Journal on Multicultural Studies* 5(1): 77–87.

WLUML (Women Living Under Muslim Law). 2005. Support Canadian Women's Struggle against Shari'a Courts. http://www.wluml.org

Wolf, S. 1994 [1992]. Comment. In *Multiculturalism: Examining the Politics of Recognition*, ed. A. Gutmann. 75–86. Princeton, NJ: Princeton University Press.

World Bank. 2006. *Global Economic Prospects 2006: Economic Implications of Remittances and Migration.* Washington, DC: International Bank for Reconstruction and Development/World Bank.

Wright, C. 2003. Moments of emergence: Organizing by and with undocumented and non-citizen people in Canada after September 11. *Refuge* 21(3): 5–15.

Young, I. M. 1989. Polity and group difference: Critique of the ideal of universal citizenship. *Ethics* 99: 250–74.

– 1990. *Justice and the Politics of Difference*. Princeton, NJ: Princeton University Press.

– 1997. Unruly categories: A critique of Nancy Fraser's dual systems theory. *New Left Review* no. 222: 147–60.

– 2000. Social difference as a political resource. In *Inclusion and Democracy*, 81–120. New York: Oxford University Press.

Yuval-Davis, N. 1992. Fundamentalism, multiculturalism and women. In *Race, Culture and Difference*, ed. J. Donald and A. Rattansi, 278–93. London: Sage and Open University.

Zimmerman, J. 2001. The 'nature' of urbanism on the new urbanist frontier: Sustainable development, or defense of the suburban dream. *Urban Geography* 22: 249–67.

Zuriek, E., and M.B. Salter, eds. 2005. *Global Surveillance and Policing: Borders, Security and Identity*. Portland: Willan.

www.ingramcontent.com/pod-product-compliance
Lightning Source LLC
LaVergne TN
LVHW040757070826
844660LV00025B/1170

* 9 7 8 0 8 0 2 0 9 6 3 7 1 *